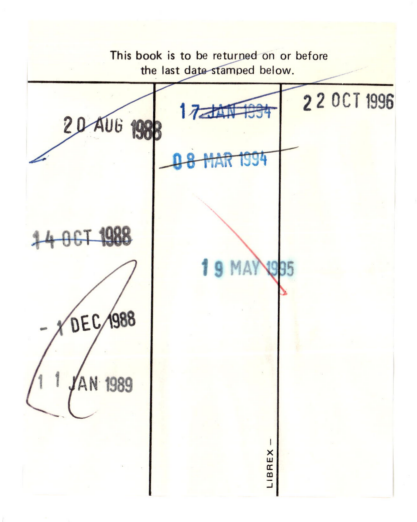

This book is to be returned on or before
the last date stamped below.

20 AUG 1988

17 JAN 1994

22 OCT 1996

08 MAR 1994

14 OCT 1988

19 MAY 1995

- 1 DEC 1988

1 1 JAN 1989

LIBREX —

Energy in
Food
Processing

Energy in World Agriculture

Editor-in-Chief
B.A. Stout
Agricultural Engineering Department
Texas A & M University
College Station, TX 77843, U.S.A.

Energy in World Agriculture, 1

Energy in Food Processing

Edited by

R. PAUL SINGH

Department of Agricultural Engineering,
University of California, Davis, CA 95616, U.S.A.

ELSEVIER
Amsterdam – Oxford – New York – Tokyo 1986

ELSEVIER SCIENCE PUBLISHERS B.V.
Sara Burgerhartstraat 25
P.O. Box 211, 1000 AE Amsterdam, The Netherlands

Distributors for the United States and Canada:

ELSEVIER SCIENCE PUBLISHING COMPANY INC.
52, Vanderbilt Avenue
New York, NY 10017

ISBN 0-444-42446-6 (Vol. 1)
ISBN 0-444-42445-8 (Series)

Printed in The Netherlands

General Preface

Agriculture is essentially an energy-conversion process – the transformation of solar energy, fossil fuel products and electricity into food and fiber for human beings. Primitive agriculture involved little more than scattering seeds on the land and accepting meager yields. Modern agriculture, however, combining petroleum-based fuels to power tractors and self-propelled machines with energy-intensive fertilizers and pesticides, results in greatly increased yields. Various parts of the world are at different stages of agricultural development; therefore, energy-use practices vary widely.

Energy Crises of the 1970's

In 1973, the Organization of Petroleum Exporting Countries (OPEC) placed an embargo on the shipment of petroleum to certain industrialized countries. As a result, world crude oil prices quickly rose from around US$3 to over US$11 a barrel.

In 1978 and 1979, the situation in Iran disrupted the normal flow of oil, causing its price to double yet again.

Energy in 1980's and 90's

After peaking at over US$38 a barrel in 1981, oil prices receded, and interest in energy in general to some extent dissipated in the industrialized countries. Although energy consumption is increasing, research on conservation and alternative sources has become reduced or even eliminated. In other parts of the world, in the less developed countries and countries with limited domestic supplies of oil or gas, however, a high level of interest in and concern about energy supplies and costs continues.

For example, in the Punjab State of India, diesel fuel supplies are inadequate during peak seasons and long lines of tractors form at fuel supply stations. Also in the Punjab, electricity supplies are inadequate to meet all needs, so farmers are supplied with power during the day for their irrigation pumps and other users are cut off. At night, the supplies are reversed. Not surprisingly, there is great concern about energy for agriculture in the Punjab and other similar regions of the world. Developing countries, in general, recognize that to feed their growing populations, more energy will be needed in the agricultural sector.

Why an Agricultural Energy Reference Book Series?

A reliable supply of energy, in the right form, at the right time and at affordable prices, is an essential prerequisite for high agricultural productivity. During the decade from the mid-70's to the mid-80's, hundreds of research projects were conducted around the world with the general goals of (1) improving the efficiency of energy utilization, or (2) developing alternatives to petroleum or natural gas for use in agriculture and the food industry.

The purpose of this international energy reference book series is to bring together in a concise form the basic principles and the most relevant data concerning both the efficient use of energy in agriculture and the food industry and alternative energy sources for agriculture. Social and economic implications, world-wide, are discussed along with each technology.

An initial series of six volumes is planned, though other volumes may be added to the series. The subjects covered will include Energy in food processing, Energy in plant nutrition and pest control, Use of electrical energy in agriculture, Analysis of agricultural energy systems, Energy in farm production, and Renewable energy for agriculture.

B.A. STOUT
College Station, TX, 1986

Preface to Vol. 1

Energy derived from fossil fuels has played a key role in the development of the modern food industry. Mechanization of food handling and conveyance, thermal processing to assure safety of food and conversion processes that create new forms of food are examples of activities in which the food industry has relied on energy to carry out the desired operations and obtain high processing efficiencies. In many regions of the world where energy is in short supply and available only at high cost, facilities for food processing and preservation are minimal and as a consequence, the food losses in these areas are generally high.

Prior to the 1973 Arab oil embargo on certain Western nations, the low cost of energy and its ready availability permitted manufacturers to design a variety of food-processing equipment, with a great emphasis on high production efficiencies and reliability. However, an appropriate emphasis on energy efficiency was then generally disregarded. Such processing equipment became the target of investigation during the last decade as the price of oil increased and questions as to the long-term availability of affordable energy became more serious. Energy conservation programs were instituted to develop improvements in the use of energy in conducting various unit operations.

This book is a compilation of research data and results from studies undertaken during the last decade on four different continents. There are five major sections that provide a comprehensive treatment of such topics as methods used in energy accounting, measurement of energy, and exergy analysis. Quantitative data are presented on energy consumption in a variety of food industries such as blanching, freezing, canning, irradiation, evaporation, membrane processing, and dairy and catering establishments. Energy generation and heat recovery in the food industry is discussed along with an economic analysis of energy use in food processing. Twenty-one chapters are contributed by authors who have headed major studies on energy use in food processing in their respective countries. Many of the data reported and analyzed in this book are presented in an international perspective. It is intended that this information will be useful to practising engineers and future researchers on energy use in food processing around the world.

During the time during which the chapters for this book were being written and edited, there has been a sharp drop in oil prices. If one examines the changes brought about by the price of oil during the last decade, it is noteworthy that the oil prices have had a varied influence on energy consumption. The quadrupling of oil prices in 1973–74 did not immediately reduce energy consumption in the United States, mainly due to price controls and increased importation of oil. However, the tripling of oil prices in 1978–79 resulted in an increased emphasis on energy conservation and the design of energy-efficient equipment. Oil exploration in more difficult areas became more cost-competitive. During the last decade, the total world oil consumption dropped from 65.1 million barrels per day in 1974 to 59.2 million barrels per day in 1985. The worldwide recession in the early 1980's and the overproduction of oil contributed to a sharp drop in oil prices in 1986.

The measures taken during the last decade for energy conservation cannot be reversed quickly and they are expected to maintain the lid on excessive increases in energy demand for oil-based sources in the near future. If oil prices continue to remain low for the next several years, then the situation can change considerably. The odds of finding more oil are declining at the moment because tumbling prices have forced oil companies to slash their exploration and drilling budgets. Many experts believe that the 1986 oil-price collapse, though substantially benefiting the economies of many nations, may have triggered an irreversible set of forces that will renew the dependence on insecure sources of petroleum. While the falling oil prices are resulting in a picking up of the world economy, they are also at the same time making it unstable. Developing countries, from Mexico to Indonesia, which had built their dreams on the revenues from oil, are now watching in anguish as their hopes of prosperity evaporate. With the widening gap between oil production and consumption, one can expect the major industrial nations to increase their reliance on imported oil, and this is bound to cause a resurgence of artificial increases in oil prices.

It is vital that the food industry should maintain a visionary approach, with a continued vigorous program on energy conservation. Economics will generally dictate which energy-conserving technologies will be adopted; however, the design of new equipment must involve better and creative engineering approaches to minimizing energy wastage. The information given in this book is intended to help design energy-conserving technologies for the food industry as it prepares itself for the 21st century.

R. PAUL SINGH
Davis, CA, 1986

Contents

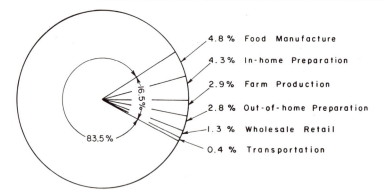

Fig. 1.1. Energy use in the U.S. food system as a percentage of total U.S. energy consumption.

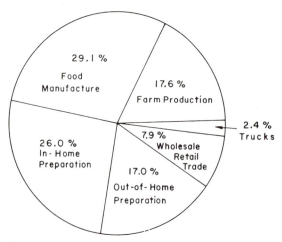

Fig. 1.2. Energy use in various components of the U.S. food system (Singh, 1978).

A report by FEA (1976) indicated that of total U.S. energy consumption, 2.9% is used for farm production, 4.8% for food manufacture (processing), 4.3% for in-home food preparation, 2.8% for out-of-home food preparation, 0.5% for wholesale food trade, and 0.8% for retail trade. These data, shown in Fig. 1.1, included direct and indirect energy consumption and transportation costs within individual components.

In Fig. 1.2, the energy costs of individual components are shown as a percentage of the energy consumed by the U.S. food system. It is evident that while farm production consumes only 18% of the energy expended by the food system, the remaining 82% is spent on processing, marketing and preparation. The food processing and the in-home preparation components of the food system are the leading energy consumers. These data emphasize the importance of various components in terms of the energy consumption and the opportunities for energy conservation in all components of the food system.

3. FOOD INDUSTRY'S SHARE OF COMMERCIAL ENERGY

The energy consumption by the food industry is tabulated annually by the U.S. Department of Commerce. This tabulation is done by using the Standard Industrial Classification (SIC). The food industry is designated SIC 20. Food Processing is divided into nine groups at the 3-digit level and 47 at the 4-digit designation of SIC.

TABLE 1.1

Energy consumption, employment, value added and value of shipments of six leading energy consuming industries in United States

Industry groups	Gross energy (10^{12} Btu)	Employment ($\times 1000$)	Value added (million $)	Value of shipments (million $)
Primary metal	2 276.8	1 062	49 550.6	141 942.1
Chemical and Allied	2 716.7	892	80 032.3	180 459.2
Petroleum and Coal	1 177.9	152	26 740.3	224 131.4
Stone, clay and glass	1 122.3	589	24 853.9	48 000.4
Paper and allied	1 278.4	635	32 366.7	80 233.8
Food and kindred	948.0	1 511	80 794.7	272 139.6
All industries	11 873.8	20 264	837 605.5	2 017 542.5

Data based on Census of Manufactures, U.S. Department of Commerce (1981).
10^{12} Btu $\approx 1.055 \times 10^{15}$ J $= 1.055$ PJ.

The nine groups at the 3-digit level are:
201, Meat products (4 sectors)
202, Dairy products (5 sectors)
203, Preserved fruits and vegetables (6 sectors)
204, Grain mill products (7 sectors)
205, Bakery products (2 sectors)
206, Sugar, confectionary products (6 sectors)
207, Fats and oils (5 sectors)
208, Beverages (6 sectors)
209, Miscellaneous foods, kindred products (6 sectors).
Examples of the 4-digit sectors are:
2023, Condensed and evaporated milk
2037, Canned fruits and vegetables
2062, Cane sugar refining.

The energy consumption data are compiled by the U.S. Department of Commerce based on above classification and published in the *Annual survey of manufactures* (USDC, 1980).

According to the U.S. Department of Commerce, Bureau of the Census, the food industry (other than agricultural production) consumed 948 trillion Btu or about 1 EJ with a total expenditure of almost $4000 million for energy in 1980. In aggregate, the food and kindred products industry in the United States is the sixth largest energy consuming industry (Table 1.1). The food industry consumed about 8% of the total energy used by all manufacturing industries.

According to the data from USDC (1981), if one considers employment, value added and value of shipment, the food industry ranks number one within the group of six leading energy-consuming industries as shown in Fig. 1.3.

The energy consumption within the food industry has experienced a continuous growth in the past. The short-term decline in 1973 during the Middle East oil embargo has been more than recovered (Fig. 1.4). For the next two decades, the rate of energy consumption is expected to grow continuously. According to Adolfson (1982), for some of the food industries such as wine, seafood, coffee and ice, the annual rate of growth of energy consumption will be greater than 3%.

Chapter 1 references, p. 9.

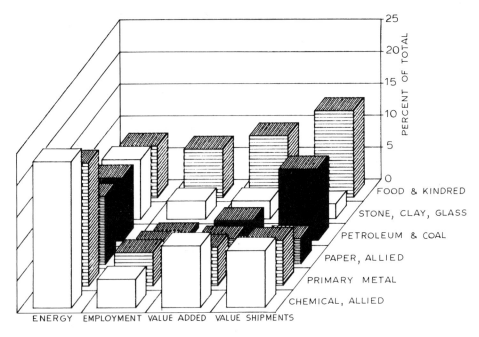

Fig. 1.3. Leading energy-consuming industries in the U.S.A. (USDC, 1980).

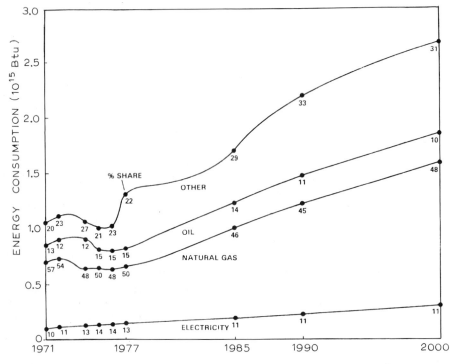

Fig. 1.4. Types of energy use in the U.S. food industry (Adolfson, 1982). Number at data points represent percent share.
10^{15} Btu $\approx 1.055 \times 10^{18}$ J $= 1.055$ EJ.

4. LEADING ENERGY-CONSUMING FOOD INDUSTRIES

The energy consumption by food industries can be examined either in terms of the total energy consumption or the energy intensity. In Fig. 1.5, ten food industries are ranked in terms of their total energy consumption. These ten

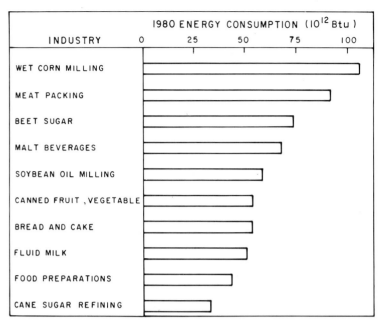

Fig. 1.5 Ten leading energy-consuming food industries (USDC, 1980).
10^{12} Btu $\approx 1.055 \times 10^{15}$ J $= 1.055$ PJ.

food industries consume over half of the total energy consumed by all industries within the food and kindred products industrial group. The wet corn milling industry is the biggest energy-consuming food industry in the United States. According to Adolfson (1982), the share of these industries, as large energy consumers, is continuously increasing. Among this industrial group, one finds both energy-intensive as well as energy-extensive industries. The wet corn milling and beet sugar processing are also leading energy-intensive industries: they require two to three times more energy per dollar value when compared with other leading energy-intensive industries.

The ranking of food industry in terms of energy intensities is shown in Fig. 1.6. Both beet sugar processing and wet corn milling require high energy levels per unit of output.

The food industry in the United States is highly diversified with processing plants ranging from small plants to large industrial units. It has been estimated that there are over 28 000 manufacturing establishments concerned with processing of foods (USDC, 1981). This large diversification offers ample opportunities in developing energy conserving measures. In the case of small plants, these measures must require low capital expenditure. However, in the case of large plants, higher investments on energy-conserving equipment may be justified as long as the payback on such equipment is attractive.

5. TYPES OF ENERGY SOURCES USED IN THE FOOD INDUSTRY

The food industry requires energy for a variety of equipment, such as gas-fired ovens, dryers, steam boilers, electrical motors, refrigeration equipment, and heating, ventilation and air-conditioning systems.

Natural gas is the dominant source of energy use by the U.S. food industry. Almost 50% of the gross energy used in food processing is obtained from natural gas (Fig. 1.4). This role of natural gas as a major source of energy for the food industry has remained unchanged in the last few decades.

Chapter 1 references, p. 9.

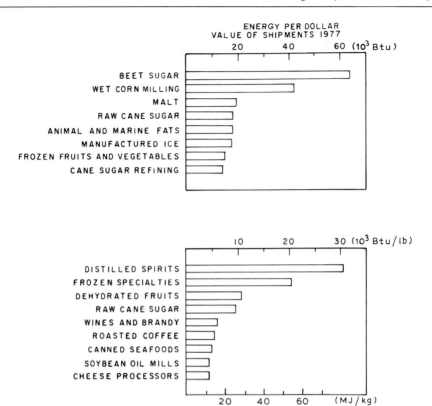

Fig. 1.6. Leading energy-intensive food industries (USDC, 1980).
10^3 Btu $\approx 1.055 \times 10^6$ J $= 1.055$ MJ.

Fifteen percent of the energy consumption is in the form of fuel oil including both middle distillates and residual oil.

Purchased electricity accounts for about 13% of the gross energy consumption. As shown in Fig. 1.4, industries associated with fluid milk processing, frozen fruits and vegetables, and manufactured ice depend mostly on electricity.

About 22% of the gross energy is obtained from propane, butane, and other petroleum products, coke, coal and some renewable energy resources. In the case of beet sugar processing and wet corn milling where large size plants have high demands for process steam, coal is often used.

6. COST OF ENERGY

Between 1973 and 1986, the cost of energy has escalated dramatically. Based on the data of the U.S. Department of Commerce, the manufacturers' index of the average cost of selected fuels and purchased electrical energy is shown in Fig. 1.7. Considering 1971 as the base year, the price of natural gas rose sharply, six or seven times, whereas electrical energy has increased about three times (Fig. 1.8). In 1980, electrical energy was most expensive at $9.70 compared to natural gas at $2.60 per million Btu. This dramatic increase in costs of energy was halted during 1982–1983 due to worldwide recession.

Along with the increased cost of energy, the equipment costs have also increased during the last decade as shown in Fig. 1.9. However, the increase in equipment costs has not been as dramatic as that in energy costs. This trend promoted the installation of heat recovery equipment to conserve energy.

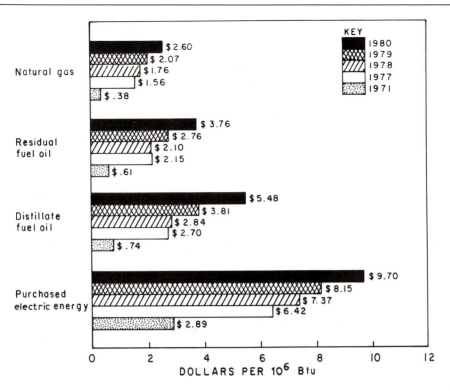

Fig. 1.7. Energy cost per million Btu of selected fuels and electricity consumed by all manufacturing industries (USDC, 1980).
10^6 Btu $\approx 1.055 \times 10^9$ J $= 1.055$ GJ.

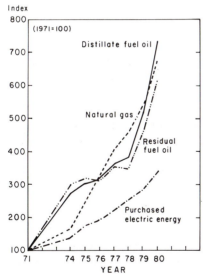

Fig. 1.8. Manufacturer's index of the average energy cost of selected fuels and purchased electricity (Singh, 1984).

Within the food industry, the principal types of energy use include direct fuel use, steam and electricity. Nearly one-half of energy use is in the form of direct fuel use. As shown in Fig. 1.10, two-thirds of electric consumption is used in generating mechanical power to operate conveyors, pumps, compressors and other machinery. Refrigeration equipment is the next most important consumer of electricity.

Chapter 1 references, p. 9.

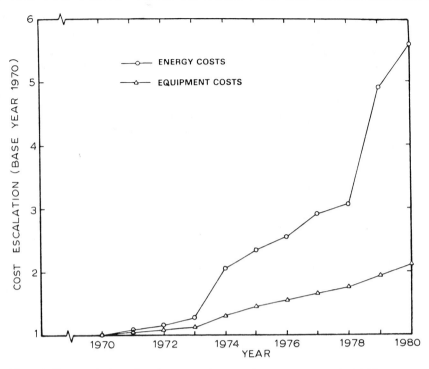

Fig. 1.9. Cost escalation of equipment and energy in a 10-year period (Adolfson, 1982).

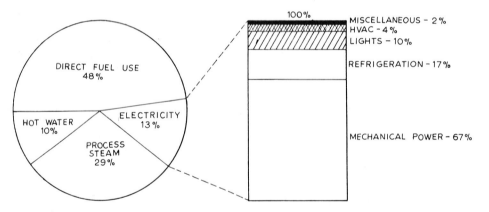

Fig. 1.10. Electricity and fuel use in the food and kindred products industry (Adolfson, 1982). HVAC, heating, ventilation and air-conditioning.

7. TIMELINESS OF ENERGY AVAILABILITY

The U.S. food system is critically dependent on adequate supplies of energy. Since food is a perishable commodity, timely availability of energy is necessary to carry out the various processing operations. For example, many vegetable and fruit canning plants operate for only a few weeks of the year, and a critical shortage of fuel during the processing season would have a major impact on this industry. Since many of the processing plants are located close to or in urban areas, large stockpiling of fuel oil or coal at plant location is often difficult.

The role of transportation in food handling cannot be over-emphasized. The transportation industry depends mostly on petroleum products. The key link provided by transportation between the producer and the consumer would be very seriously impacted in the case of shortages or possible rationing of petroleum. At present nearly half of the trucks on major highways carry agricultural and food products.

In summary, the food processing industry in the United States is heavily dependent on energy derived from non-renewable resources. It is imperative that the major emphasis should continue towards energy conservation. The timely availability of energy to this industry should not be overlooked. In the following chapters, several food industries will be examined individually in terms of their energy use.

8. REFERENCES

Adolfson, W.F., 1982. Photovoltaic off-farm agricultural applications, Vol. II. Tech. Rep. SAND 81-7175/II, prepared for Sandia National Laboratories, Albuquerque, NM, 106 pp.

DPRA, 1974. Industrial energy studies of selected food industries. Report prepared for the Federal Energy Office, U.S. Department of Commerce. Development Planning and Research Associates, Manhatten, KS.

FEA, 1976. Energy use in the food system. Office of Industrial Programs, Federal Energy Administration, U.S. Government Printing Office, Washington, DC.

Fritsch, A.J., Dujack, L.W. and Jimerson, D.R., 1975. Energy used in production, processing, delivery and marketing of selected food items. CSPI Energy Ser. VI, Center for Science in the Public Interest, Washington, DC.

Hirst, E., 1973. Energy use for food in the U.S. ORNL-NSF-EP-57, U.S. Atomic Energy Commission, Oak Ridge National Laboratory, Oak Ridge, TN.

MRI, 1974. The energy requirements of meal preparation: a comparison of restaurant vs home. MRS Proj. 3889-D (R) for National Restaurant Association. Midwest Research Institute.

Singh, R.P., 1978. Energy accounting in food process operations. Food Technol., 32 (4): 40–46.

Singh, R.P., 1984. Energy management in the food industry. In: B. McKenna (Editor), Engineering and Food, Vol. 2. Elsevier Applied Science Publishers, London, pp. 901–915.

SRI, 1972. Patterns of energy consumption in the United States. Prepared for the Executive Office of the President, Office of Science and Technology by Stanford Research Institute. U.S. Government Printing Office, Washington, DC.

Steinhart, J.S. and Steinhart, C.W., 1974. Energy use in the food system. Science, 184: 307.

USDA, 1974. The U.S. food and fiber section: energy use and outlook. Economic Research Service, U.S. Department of Agriculture. U.S. Government Printing Office, Washington, DC.

USDC, 1973. 1972 Census of manufactures. Fuels and electric energy consumed. MC 72 (SR-6), Special Report Series, Bureau of Census, U.S. Department of Commerce, Washington, DC.

USDC, 1980. Annual survey of manufactures, fuels and electric energy consumed, industry groups and industries. M80 (AS)-4.1, Bureau of Census, U.S. Department of Commerce, Washington, DC.

USDC, 1981. Annual survey of manufactures, statistics for industry groups and industries. M81 (AS)-1, Bureau of Census, U.S. Department of Commerce, Washington, DC.

Part I

Methods of Energy Accounting

Chapter 2

Regression Analysis for Assessing and Forecasting Energy Requirements

M.A. RAO

1. INTRODUCTION

In most food processing plants, several products are produced in each plant. More often than not, an energy source, such as a fuel or electricity, is used for functions shared by many products. Knowledge of energy consumption for each food product is useful for several purposes such as budgeting, comparing year to year consumption for a given product, forecasting energy requirements in a plant, and for planning plant expansion. In general, instrumentation needed to measure the energy consumption for a specific product or process is expensive. In addition, installation of the metering equipment can interfere with the operation of the plant and trained personnel will be needed to operate the equipment properly. Further, the data on energy consumption and the quantity of a product processed can be obtained only over relatively short time periods, and one needs to average the recorded quantities in order to obtain meaningful results.

Regression analysis can be used to estimate the energy consumption of each product from data on the total consumption of each energy source and the production of the food products (Vergara et al., 1978; Cleland et al., 1981; Jacobs, 1981). The analysis can be performed, if desired, for a specific energy source such as electricity or a fuel for thermal energy. The results of the analysis can be used for forecasting energy requirements in food processing plants. Because the analysis can be performed utilizing statistical programs on computers and programmable calculators, it will cost much less than studies based on metering consumption of fuels and electricity for specific unit operations.

The major disadvantage of the method is that one cannot obtain information on the energy consumption for individual unit operations. Also it would be desirable to have a large number of data points available for accurate analysis and reliable coefficients of the regression equations. This requires that special efforts be made to obtain reliable data on energy consumption and production.

2. REGRESSION ANALYSIS FOR ONE-PRODUCT PLANTS

It can be assumed that the energy source (fuel or electricity) consumed in a plant during a specific time period is due to all the activities for which the energy source was employed. The activities can be classified into those that are related to the processing of the food products and those which are not related to food processing, such as space heating or air conditioning.

Chapter 2 references, p. 17.

For simplicity, let us first consider a food processing plant (or a unit of it) producing only one product and one in which the consumption of energy sources for production-related activities is known. This situation can be encountered either in plants which, due to their geographical location, do not require energy use for space heating and air conditioning or in plants where energy consumption for the said activities is metered separately. The energy consumed in the plant per unit time (day, week or month), y, and production during the same time period, x (kg or t), can be related by a linear relationship:

$$y = a_0 + a_1 x \tag{1}$$

where a_0 is the base load or the overhead energy expenditure during the time interval under consideration due to consumption during start up of equipment, for cleaning, and other support operations. The coefficient a_1 is the energy consumed for producing unit mass of the product per unit time.

Equation (1) was applied to the direct energy (DE) consumption in a spray-dried coffee plant by Okada et al. (1980). DE was the sum of the fuels for thermal energy and electricity consumed in the plant. The consumption of DE and the production of spray-dried coffee during a 2-year period were subjected to linear regression analysis and were found to be related by the equation:

$$DE \text{ (MJ/month)} = 4.19 \times 10^6 + 38.9x \text{ (kg of coffee per month)} \tag{2}$$

The correlation coefficient, R, for the data was 0.978. The magnitude of a_0 (4.19×10^6) represents the average non-production related energy consumption or the base load (MJ) per month for the 2-year period during which the data were gathered. One can apportion the base load energy consumption per kg of coffee by dividing it by the average monthly production. It must be noted that the base load will be different for different time periods employed in the regression analysis. The coefficient a_1 (38.9) indicates the direct energy consumed (MJ) for producing 1 kg of instant coffee in the studied plant.

Another example of the use of regression analysis for plants or units producing single products is the study of Gasparino Filho et al. (1984) in a plant which produced frozen concentrated orange juice (FCOJ) and animal feed from the orange residues. In this plant it was possible to determine the consumption of fuel oil and electricity for the FCOJ and the animal feed units. The magnitudes of the coefficients a_0, a_1, and the correlation coefficient, R, for FCOJ and animal feed for 3 years are given in Table 2.1.

TABLE 2.1

Energy coefficients for 65°B-concentrated orange juice and citrus animal feed (Gasparino Filho et al. 1984)

	1978	1979	1980
Concentrated orange juice			
Coefficient a_0 (TJ/month)	11.46	4.19	4.51
Coefficient a_1 (GJ/t)	4.27	4.65	4.35
Correlation coefficient, R	0.96	0.99	0.97
Citrus animal feed			
Coefficient a_0 (TJ/month)	7.04	4.29	2.27
Coefficient a_1 (GJ/t)	5.36	5.65	6.28
Correlation coefficient, R	0.97	0.98	0.99

°B, degree Brix = % sucrose (w/w).

In Table 2.1 it can be seen that the base load or the overhead energy consumption both in the FCOJ and the citrus animal feed units was high in 1978 in comparison to that in the other years. In particular, the base load for the concentrated orange juice unit was very high, probably due to poor co-ordination between harvesting operations and operation of the processing plant. The lower base loads for both the units during 1979 and 1980 indicate improvement in the operating efficiency of the two units.

It must be emphasized that the accuracy of the method in predicting energy consumption depends on the availability of a large number of data points. In the examples cited, data were available for intervals of one month. One can obtain data over shorter time periods, such as a week or a day, in order to have more data points at hand. When the time period is a day or a week, for reliable results it is necessary that the energy recordings are made at the same time of day. Likewise, the data on the production of foods must correspond to the time period selected.

3. REGRESSION ANALYSIS FOR MULTI-PRODUCT PLANTS

First, food processing plants producing more than one product and in which the energy consumption for space heating and air conditioning is either not significant or can be corrected for will be considered. Analysis of plants in which the energy for space heating and air conditioning is aggregated with the total energy consumption will be discussed in the next section.

3.1. Analysis of plant data without seasonal effects

In the case of a plant with multiple products, the relationship between energy consumed and products produced can be written as:

$$y = a_0 + \sum a_i x_i \tag{3}$$

where y is the energy consumed (J) over a given time period, x_i is the quantity of each product produced during the time period, a_0 is the base or the overhead load, and a_i is the energy coefficient per unit mass of each product for the time period being considered. The coefficients a_0 and a_i can be determined by means of multiple linear regression analysis.

In the following, several guidelines are presented in order that reliable results may be obtained from multiple linear regression analysis of energy consumption and production data of processing plants (Vergara et al., 1978; Cleland et al., 1981).

(1) The size of the data for analysis must be at least five times the number of products, but it should not be so large that handling the data becomes a difficult task.

(2) One may combine a product with a small production volume with another product, particularly if they have similar energy paths. For example, if a product is produced during a few days, its volume is likely to be very small and the production data can be combined with that of another product.

(3) Products which require very small amounts of energy may be omitted from the analysis. For example, when a product is being only packaged without a reasonable amount of processing and the others are subjected to extensive processing it may be omitted from the analysis; this is tantamount to assigning a negligible or a zero energy consumption for it.

(4) In the event the production rates of two products are well correlated, such as the rate of one being an exact multiple of the other, spurious results will be obtained. In this situation, the data of the product with the lower

Chapter 2 references, p. 17.

TABLE 2.2

Direct energy[a] consumption (MJ/kg) for the processing of selected foods (Cleland et al., 1981)

Type of product	Direct energy (MJ/kg)
Frozen vegetables	2.51[b]
Canned fruit and vegetables	2.92
Dehydrated vegetables	41.4
Processed fish products	3.9[b]
Ice cream	0.62[b,c]

[a] Direct energy is the sum of fuels for thermal energy and electricity; it does not include base load energy consumption.
[b] Does not include energy consumption for refrigerated storage at the plant.
[c] Energy consumption in MJ/l.

production rates can be combined with another product having a similar energy path. However, in some situations this may not be possible and the method cannot be used. For example, in the case of the orange juice and citrus animal feed units (Section 2) the production rates of the two products were highly correlated, but there were no other products in the plant for combining the production data. Therefore, multiple linear regression analysis would not have been a suitable method for determining the coefficients of the two products from the data of the orange juice plant as a whole.

It is best to analyze production and energy consumption data first in the form they are available, and examine the results. This analysis can be followed by either combining or omitting some of the products in subsequent analysis, i.e., a trial and error procedure must be followed. The best model is that with as few coefficients as possible and in which each coefficient is statistically significant (Cleland et al., 1981). The latter can be ascertained by examining statistical parameters, such as Student's t value, which are provided as output by statistical packages available on computers along with the magnitudes of the energy coefficients.

Cleland et al. (1981) applied multiple regression analysis to food processing plants in New Zealand and the direct energy consumption for several products from their study are given in Table 2.2. It is interesting to note that, as expected, dehydrated vegetables required more energy per kg than the canned or the frozen forms. Also, the value of 2.92 MJ/kg of canned fruit and vegetables is nearly equal to the lower range of values reported by Vergara et al. (1978) for a cannery in western New York.

3.2. Analysis of plant data with seasonal effects

When a substantial portion of the energy consumption in a processing plant is for space heating and air conditioning, one will observe a cyclical pattern in the energy consumption data. In general, thermal energy from fuels is used for space heating and electricity is used for air conditioning. In the analysis of chemical plants, Jacobs (1981) employed the model:

$$E_s = A \cos (2\pi t/12) + B \sin (2\pi t/12) \tag{4}$$

where E_s is the seasonal energy requirement (J), A and B are coefficients to be determined by regression analysis, and t is the time period for which the prediction is being made and it is the number of the month in the study period. Equation (4) is applicable for a 12-month cycle, but it can be rewritten for other convenient time periods.

3.2.1. Modeling energy conservation efforts

Energy conservation efforts reduce the energy consumption in a plant. It appears that in most plants the obvious energy conservation efforts with big gains have been implemented first and these have been followed by measures that were less effective than the preceding measures. In general, each successive increment of reduction in energy consumption became more difficult. Jacobs (1981) suggested that a declining exponential function can be used to model the effects of energy conservation measures:

$$E_c = C(1 - e^{-Dt}) \qquad (5)$$

where E_c is the reduction in energy consumption due to conservation effort, C and D are constants to be determined, and t is the time period for which the forecast is being made.

Equations 3–5 can be combined and the coefficients a_0, a_i, A, B, C, and D can be determined by non-linear regression analysis of data from a plant. In the event, the consumption of thermal energy and electricity need to be modeled separately, two sets of the combined equation must be solved.

It is obvious that one must have at hand a large data base for reliable analysis. Jacobs (1981) employed energy consumption and production data of a plant during the period 1972–1979 in order to determine the magnitudes of the coefficients of the combined model. The same coefficients were employed to predict the energy consumption in 1980 with good accuracy. It must be noted that the predicted energy consumption is as good as the production forecast, so that one must obtain the most accurate forecast possible. It appears that the type of model proposed by Jacobs (1981) can be employed for forecasting the energy requirements in food processing plants, particularly those located in the cooler regions of the world which have significant energy consumption for space heating.

4. SUMMARY

Regression analysis can be a useful tool for estimating the energy consumption for specific food products and for forecasting the energy requirements at a future date. One drawback of the method is that information on individual unit operations cannot be obtained. Because the analysis can be performed using programmable calculators and computers, it is not as expensive as installing metering equipment for measuring the consumption of energy by each process equipment. Once the analysis has been performed in a given plant, it can be updated periodically in order to obtain better insight into the operation of the plant as a function of time.

5. REFERENCES

Cleland, A.C., Earle, M.D. and Boag, I.F., 1981. Application of multiple linear regression to analysis of data from factory energy surveys. J. Food Technol., 16: 481–492.

Gasparino Filho, J., Vitali, A.A., Viegas, F.C.P. and Rao, M.A., 1984. Energy consumption in a concentrated orange juice plant. J. Food Proc. Eng., 7: 77–89.

Jacobs, W.P., 1981. Forecasting energy requirements. Chem. Eng., 88(5): 97–99.

Okada, M., Rao, M.A., Lima, J.E. and Torloni, M., 1980. Energy consumption and the potential for conservation in a spray-dried coffee plant. J. Food Sci., 45: 685–688.

Vergara, W., Rao, M.A. and Jordan, W.K., 1978. Analysis of direct energy usage in vegetable canneries. Trans. ASAE, 21: 1246–1249.

Chapter 3

Energy Accounting of Food Processing Operations

R. PAUL SINGH

1. INTRODUCTION

A method to account for energy use in a food processing plant was presented by Singh (1978). This method differs from the traditional energy audit procedures, as the objective of energy accounting is to determine the quantity of energy consumed at various locations within a processing plant. This information is necessary before sound energy conservation approaches may be attempted to reduce energy consumption in the plant.

2. ENERGY ACCOUNTING METHOD

The energy accounting method involves seven procedural steps: determination of the objective, selection of a system boundary, charting a process flow diagram, identification of all mass and energy inputs, measurements of all mass and energy inputs, identification of all mass and energy outputs, and measurement or estimation of all mass and energy outputs. The objective of the energy accounting study allows determining how many of the following procedural steps may be involved. A brief description of the energy accounting steps follows:

(1) *Determination of the objective.* An energy accounting study is often designed with a particular objective in mind. An example of such an objective may be to seek information needed to develop energy use profiles for a given food processing plant. Another accounting objective may be to focus on specific processing equipment to investigate the feasibility of energy conservation modifications.

(2) *Selection of a system boundary.* Selection of an objective for energy accounting should assist in a clear definition of the system to be considered. A system boundary allows a choice of the items that will be considered or neglected in the accounting study. The importance of this step lies in the correct interpretation of the results by the users. The system boundary also assists in determining the total cost of the accounting study.

(3) *Process flow diagram.* The flow diagram assists in identification of various units to be included in the energy accounting study. The diagram is useful when presenting results of energy accounting study. Symbols useful in drawing energy accounting flow diagram (Fig. 3.1) were given by Singh (1978).

Chapter 3 references, p. 67.

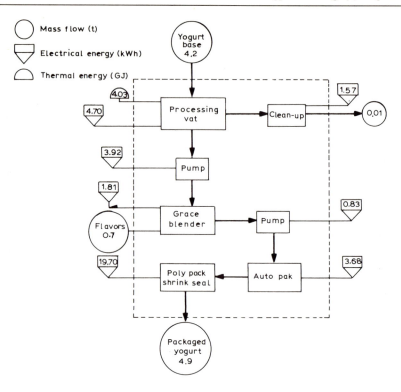

Fig. 3.2. Energy accounting diagram of yogurt manufacturing (Brusewitz and Singh, 1981). Basis: 4.16-m^3 batch of yogurt.

t, (metric) tonne = 10^3 kg ≈ 1102 short ton.

TABLE 3.1

Electrical equipment (for full vat) used in yogurt manufacturing (Brusewitz and Singh, 1981)

Equipment name	Name plate[a] (hp)	Operating current (A)	Operating time (h)	Energy per mass of product		Energy conservation (%)
				(Wh/kg)	(kJ/kg)[b]	
Agitator in processing vat	2 1	4.0 3.8	3.5 @Hi 0.5 @Lo	0.96	10.14	13
Product pump from vat to blender	5	12.2	1.08	0.80	8.49	11
Grace blender	1	3.1	1.96	0.37	3.93	5
Pump from blender to packager's surge tank	1 1/2	3.9	0.72	0.17	1.79	2.3
Filling cartons auto-pak	Multiple motors	4.6	2.30	0.75	7.95	10.2
Shrink-wrap plastic-wrap cartons together	10 kW heater and motors	7.5/19.5	2.30	4.02	42.38	54
Product pump for clean-up	5	14.8	0.36	0.32	3.40	4.5
Total				7.39	78	100

[a] All motors are 220 V, three-phase; hp, (British) horsepower ≈ 745.7 W.
[b] Assuming 1 Wh ≜ 10.5506 kJ (fossil fuel equivalence).

TABLE 3.2

Energy used in the manufacture of yogurt[a] (Brusewitz and Singh, 1981)

	Run number			Average
	1	2	3	
Packaging date in March 1979	20	27	30	
Volume of base yogurt (m^3)	4.16	4.16	4.16	
Mass product packaged (kg)	5058	4808	4853	
Initial yogurt temperature (°C)	18.3	8.3	9.4	
Max. yogurt temperature (°C)	92	88	88	
Average steam condensate temperature (°C)	75	80	74	
Time steam on (min)	90	79	78	
Well water (m^3)	9.39	8.10	6.96	
Chilled water (m^3)	78.73	49.21	49.96	
Thermal energy from steam (GJ)	3.78	3.87	3.82	
Chilled water energy (GJ)[b]	0.37	0.12	0.12	
Energy (FFE) for heating and cooling (GJ)[c]	6.27	5.34	5.28	
Energy (FFE) heating and cooling (kJ/kg product)	1240	1110	1088	1146
Energy (FFE) for packaging (kJ/kg product)	78	78	78	78
Energy heating, cooling and packaging (kJ/kg product)	1318	1188	1166	1224
Heating (% of total)	71	85	85	80
Cooling (% of total)	23	9	9	14
Packing (% of total)	6	6	6	6

[a] Assume boiler efficiency = 80%.
[b] Assuming the overall process to obtain chilled water from fossil fuel is 24% efficient.
[c] FFE, fossil fuel equivalence.

The steam and cooling water flow rates are shown in Table 3.2. The thermal energy requirements were computed to be 1146 kJ/kg, the range was from 1088 to 1240 kJ/kg for three runs. Combining the electrical and thermal energy indicated that 80% of the total energy consumption was for heating of the yogurt base from 10°C to 87.8°C. The electrical consuming equipment used only 6%.

In developing energy conservation opportunities, it was found that the steam to the processing vat was turned on and off manually. If the operator does not turn the steam off at the appropriate time there is energy wastage. For each 1°C over-heating an additional 2.7% energy loss occurred. In the packing operation the shrink-wrap machine is a major electric consumer. Alternative packaging schemes that will allow this unit to be turned off during no-use period can significantly reduce the energy wastage. The condensate, currently dumped in the drain, can be used as a boiler feed water. Every 6.1°C rise in boiler feed water temperature reduces the boiler fuel requirements by 1%. These are some of the recommendations that resulted from this accounting study.

4. RESULTS FROM ENERGY ACCOUNTING OF U.S. FOOD INDUSTRIES

During the last decade, several researchers have attempted to collate data on energy use by individual unit operations for various food industries. In a project conducted to determine the feasability of voltaic applications in the agricultural and food industries, Adolfson (1982) has compiled most of the published data on energy consumption by various food industries. Flow

Chapter 3 references, p. 67.

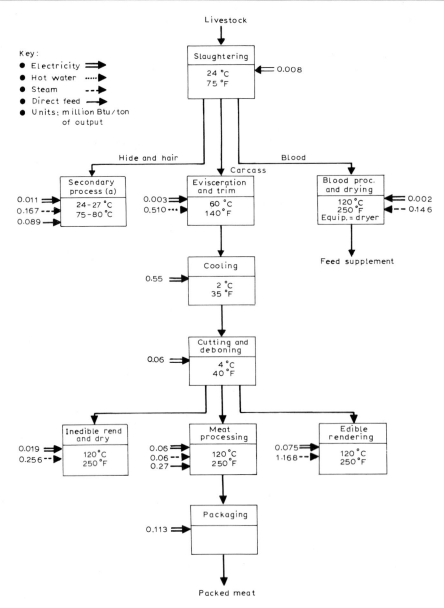

Fig. 3.3. Process energy flow diagram of meat packing. SIC: 2011.
(a) Includes scalding and dehairing, singeing, polishing, hide removal and processing.
Source: Hamel (1979).
10^6 Btu/ton $\approx 1.16 \times 10^{12}$ J/kg $= 1.16$ TJ/kg.

diagrams indicating mass and energy inputs at the various processing steps for food industries are shown in Figs. 3.3 to 3.48. It should be noted that the data in these figures are obtained from a variety of sources, thus considerable variability is expected. However, these data should provide useful bench-mark values for comparisons. It is hoped that future studies on these topics will assist in further refinement of these data.

5. ACKNOWLEDGEMENT

The assistance of Mr. William F. Adolfson, Advanced Technology, Inc., Arlington, VA, in preparing the process energy diagrams is gratefully acknowledged.

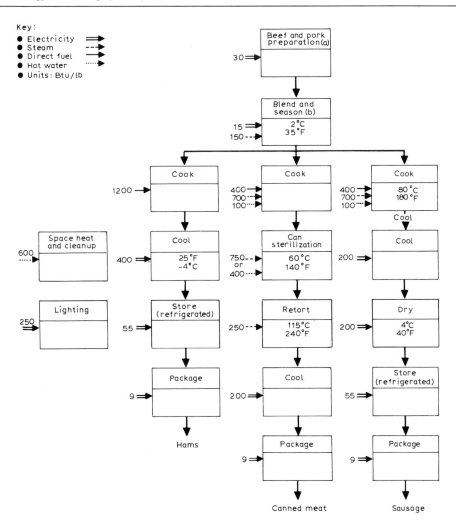

Fig. 3.4. Process energy flow diagram of sausage and prepared meat manufacturing.
(a) Cutting, trimming, boning, flaking, rough grinding, tempering. SIC: 2013.
(b) Spice, pickle, cure, grind, mix, stuff.
Sources: DPRA (1974), Battelle Columbus Laboratories (1977), USDC (1981); estimate by Hagler, Bailley & Co.
Btu/ton $\approx$ 1.16 $\times$ 10^6 J/kg = 1.16 MJ/kg.

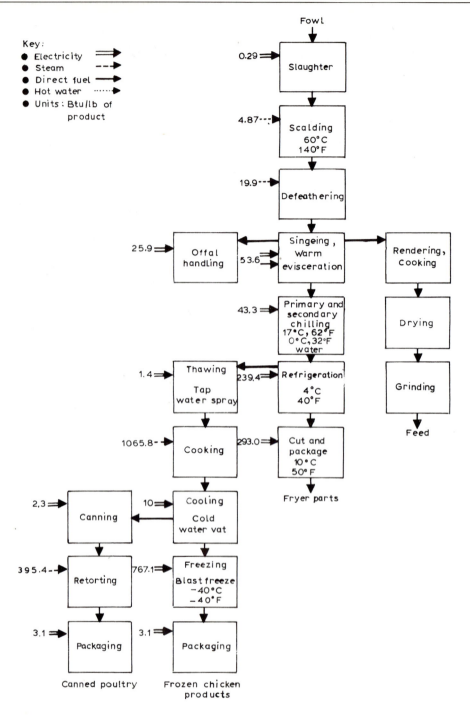

Fig. 3.5. Process energy flow diagram of poultry processing. Energy use is per carcass weight through the primary and secondary chilling step; thereafter, it is per weight of chicken product. SIC: 2016/2017.
Btu/lb = 2.326 kJ/kg.

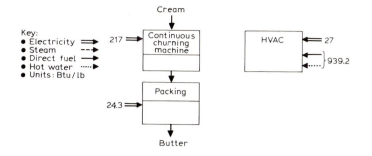

ENERGY BALANCE

	(Btu/lb)	(kJ/kg)
Electrical energy		
Process	241.3	561.3
HVAC	27.0	62.0
Total	268.3	624.3
Thermal energy		
Hot water (5%)	1383.4	3217.8
HVAC (35%)	939.2	2184.6
Losses (15%)	402.5	936.2
Total	2725.1	6338.6

Fig. 3.6. Process energy flow diagram of creamery butter manufacturing. SIC: 2021.
Btu/lb = 2.326 kJ/kg.

Chapter 3 references, p. 67.

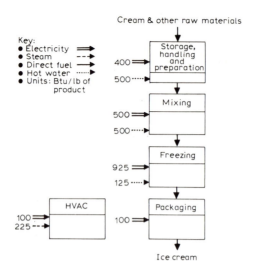

ENERGY BALANCE

	(Btu/lb)	(kJ/kg)
Electrical energy		
Process	1925	4477
HVAC	100	233
Total	2025	4710
Thermal energy*		
Process hot water	1125	2617
HVAC	225	523
Total	1350	3140

*Losses included.

Fig. 3.9. Process energy flow diagram of ice cream and frozen desserts manufacturing. SIC: 2024.
Source: Hagler, Bailley & Co.
Btu/lb = 2.326 kJ/kg.

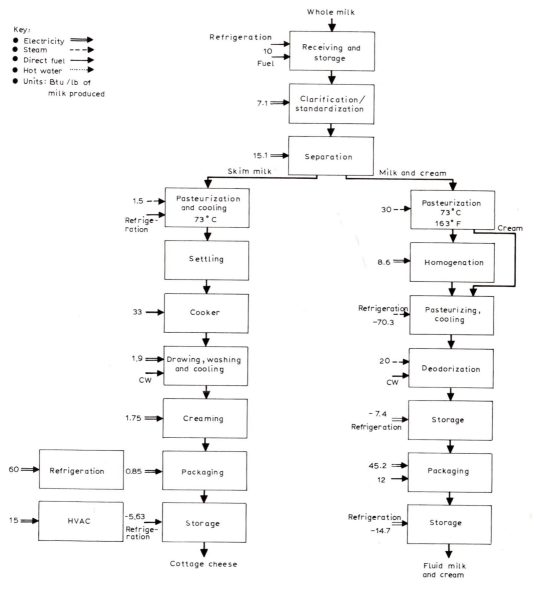

ENERGY BALANCE

	(Btu/lb)	(kJ/kg)
Electrical energy		
Process	140.5	326.8
HVAC	15.0	34.9
Lighting	12.0	27.9
Auxiliary	37.5	87.2
Total	205.0	476.8
Thermal energy		
Steam	84.5	196.5
Hot water	138.8	322.8
HVAC	28.7	66.8
Losses	166.5	387.3
Total	418.5	973.4

Fig. 3.10. Process energy flow diagram of fluid milk and cottage cheese manufacturing. SIC: 2026. Source: Hamel (1979).
Btu/lb = 2.326 kJ/kg.

Chapter 3 references, p. 67.

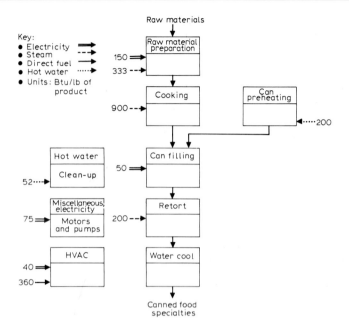

ENERGY BALANCE

	(Btu/lb)	(kJ/kg)
Electrical energy		
Process	275	640
Lighting and HVAC	40	93
Total	315	732
Thermal energy		
Steam	1433	3333
Hot water	720	1675
Direct	170	395
HVAC	360	837
Losses	1080	2512
Total	3763	8752

Fig. 3.11. Process energy flow diagram of canned food specialities. SIC: 2032.
Btu/lb = 2.326 kJ/kg.

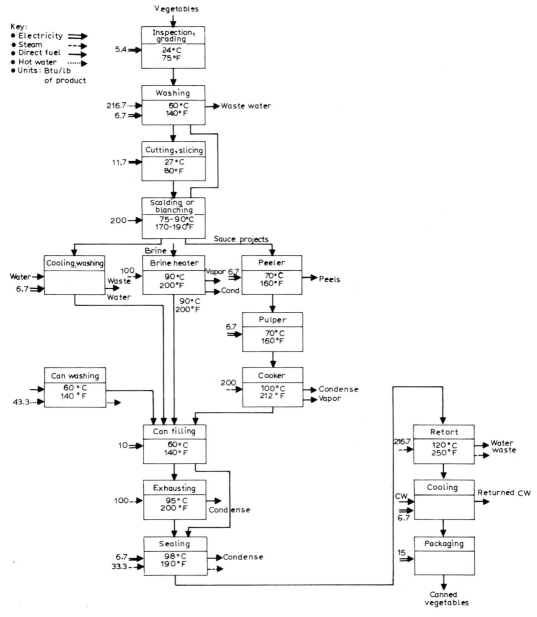

ENERGY BALANCE

	(Btu/lb)	(kJ/kg)
Electrical energy		
Process	82.1	191
Lighting	4	9
Total	86.1	200
Thermal energy		
Steam	850	1977
Hot water	260	605
Clean up	333	775
HVAC	280	651
Losses	507	1179
Total	2230	5187

Fig. 3.12. Process energy flow diagram of manufacturing canned fruits and vegetables. SIC: 2033. Btu/lb = 2.326 kJ/kg.

Chapter 3 references, p. 67.

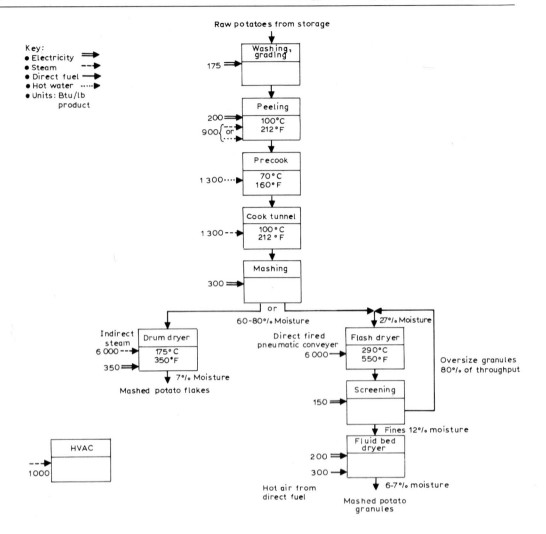

ENERGY BALANCE

	(Btu/lb)	(kJ/kg)
Electrical energy		
Process	1023	2380
Lighting	50	116
Total	1073	2496
Thermal energy		
Steam	2200	5117
Hot water	1300	3025
Direct	6300	14654
HVAC	1000	2326
Losses	1700	3954
Total	12500	29075

Fig. 3.13. Process energy flow diagram of mashed potato granules and flakes manufacturing in the dehydrated fruits, vegetables and soups industry. SIC: 2034.
Btu/lb = 2.326 kJ/kg.

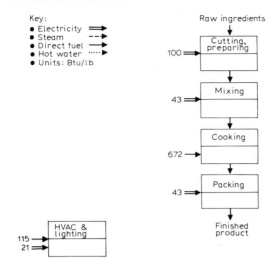

ENERGY BALANCE

	(Btu/lb)	(kJ/kg)
Electrical energy		
Process	186	433
Lighting and HVAC	21	49
Total	207	482
Thermal energy		
Clean-up hot water	250	581
Direct fuel*	672	1563
Losses	100	233
HVAC	115	268
Total	1137	2645

*Can be also steam.

Fig. 3.14. Process energy flow diagram of manufacturing pickles, sauces and salad dressings. SIC: 2035.
Sources: telephone interviews by Adolfson (1982); estimates by Hagler, Bailley & Co.
Btu/lb = 2.326 kJ/kg.

Chapter 3 references, p. 67.

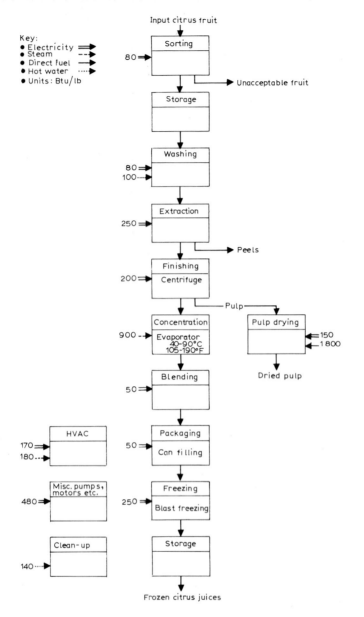

Key:
● Electricity
● Steam
● Direct fuel
● Hot water
● Units : Btu/lb

Input citrus fruit

Sorting
80

Unacceptable fruit

Storage

Washing
80
100

Extraction
250

Peels

Finishing
Centrifuge
200

Pulp

Concentration
Evaporator
40–90°C
105–190°F
900

Pulp drying
150
1800

Dried pulp

Blending
50

HVAC
170
180

Packaging
Can filling
50

Misc. pumps,
motors etc.
480

Freezing
Blast freezing
250

Clean-up
140

Storage

Frozen citrus juices

ENERGY BALANCE

	(Btu/lb)	(kJ/kg)
Electrical energy		
Process	1570	3652
HVAC	170	395
Total	1740	4047
Thermal energy		
Process steam	900	2093
Hot water	240	558
Direct	1800	4187
Losses	420	977
HVAC	180	419
Total	3540	8234

Fig. 3.15. Process energy flow diagram of frozen citrus juice manufacturing in the frozen fruits and vegetables industry. SIC: 2037.
Sources: DPRA (1974), ITC (1977).
Btu/lb = 2.326 kJ/kg.

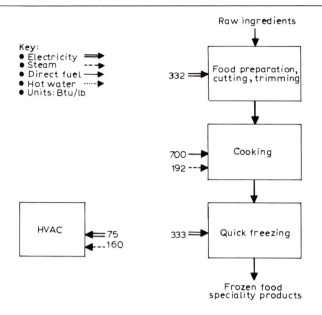

ENERGY BALANCE

	(Btu/lb)	(kJ/kg)
Electrical energy		
Process	665	1547
HVAC	75	175
Lighting	38	88
Total	778	1810
Thermal energy		
Steam	192	447
Hot water	65	151
Direct	700	1628
HVAC	160	372
Losses	478	1112
Total	1595	3710

Fig. 3.16. Process energy flow diagram of frozen food speciality products. SIC: 2038. Btu/lb = 2.326 kJ/kg.

Chapter 3 references, p. 67.

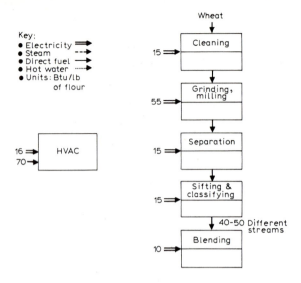

ENERGY BALANCE

	(Btu/lb)	(kJ/kg)
Electrical energy		
Process	110	256
HVAC	16	37
Total	126	293
Thermal energy		
Process	10	23
HVAC	70	163
Losses	30	70
Total	110	256

Fig. 3.17. Process energy flow diagram of wheat flour manufacturing in the flour and other grain mill products industry. SIC: 2041.
Source: Farrall (1976).
Btu/lb = 2.326 kJ/kg.

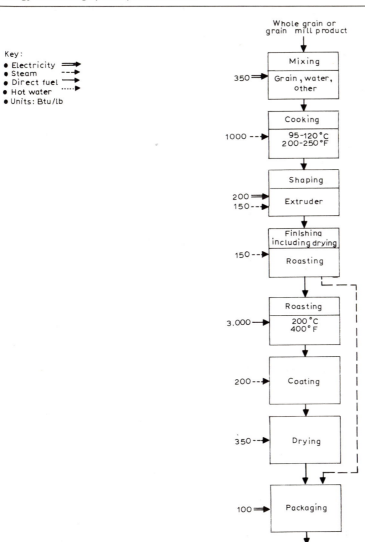

Key:
- Electricity ⟹
- Steam ---►
- Direct fuel ─►
- Hot water ·····►
- Units: Btu/lb

Whole grain or
grain mill product

350 ⟹ Mixing / Grain, water, other

1000 --► Cooking / 95–120 °C / 200–250 °F

200 ⟹ / 150 --► Shaping / Extruder

150 --► Finishing including drying / Roasting

3,000 ─► Roasting / 200 °C / 400 °F

200 --► Coating

350 --► Drying

100 ⟹ Packaging

Cereal breakfast food

ENERGY BALANCE

	(Btu/lb)	(kJ/kg)
Electrical energy		
Process	650	1512
Other	59	137
Total	709	1649

Thermal energy

Process heat	without toasting		with toasting	
	(Btu/lb)	(kJ/kg)	(Btu/lb)	(kJ/kg)
Process steam	1850	4303	3000	6978
Other*	506	1177	506	1177
Losses	550	1279	550	1279
Total	2906	6759	4056	9434

*Including HVAC and clean-up.

Fig. 3.18. Process energy flow diagram of manufacturing cereal breakfast foods. SIC: 2043.
Btu/lb = 2.326 kJ/kg.

Chapter 3 references, p. 67.

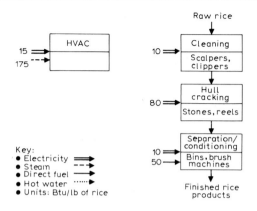

ENERGY BALANCE

	(Btu/lb)	(kJ/kg)
Electrical energy		
Process	100	233
HVAC	15	35
Total	115	268
Thermal energy		
Process	50	116
HVAC	175	407
Losses	57	133
Total	282	656

Fig. 3.19. Process energy flow diagram of rice milling. SIC: 2044.
Source: Farral (1976).
Btu/lb = 2.326 kJ/kg.

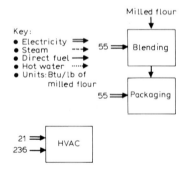

ENERGY BALANCE

	(Btu/lb)	(kJ/kg)
Electrical energy		
Process	110	256
Lighting	21	49
Total	131	305
Thermal energy		
HVAC	236	549
Clean-up hot water	12	28
Total	248	577

Fig. 3.20. Process energy flow diagram of blended and prepared flour manufacturing. SIC: 2045.
Btu/lb = 2.326 kJ/kg.

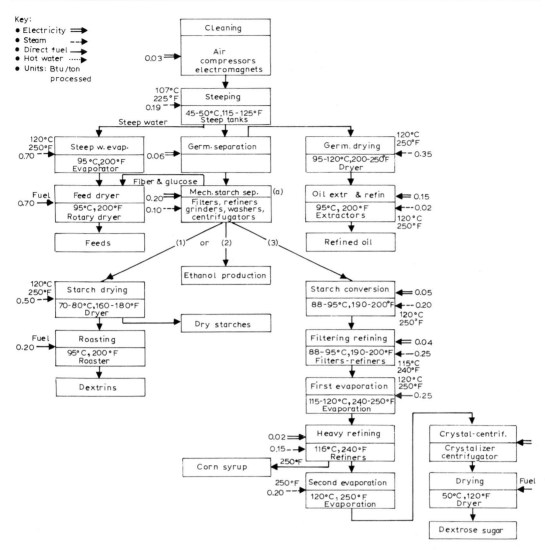

Fig. 3.21. Process energy flow diagram of wet corn milling. Large plant processing about 2700 t/day (100 000 bushels per day). SIC: 2046.

(a) Includes filtration, separation, refining, grinding, washing, centrifugation and rewashing.

Sources: DPRA (1974), Hamel (1979).

10^6 Btu/ton $\approx 1.16 \times 10^{12}$ J/kg $= 1.16$ TJ/kg; bushel $= 27.2155$ kg.

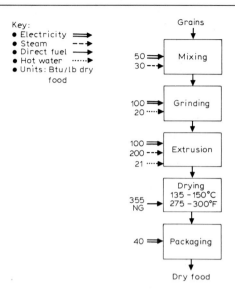

ENERGY BALANCE

	(Btu/lb)	(kJ/kg)
Electrical energy		
Process & Lighting	290	675
Thermal energy		
Direct	355	826
Steam	230	535
Clean-up	41	95
Loss	84	195
Total	710	1651

Fig. 3.22. Process energy flow diagram of manufacturing dry dog, cat and other pet food. SIC: 2047.
Plant size: about 50 000 t/year (1000 million lb per year).
Source: industry interviews by Adolfson (1982).
Btu/lb = 2.326 kJ/kg.

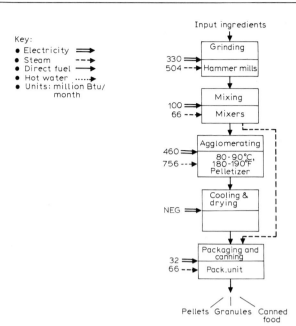

ENERGY BALANCE

	(Btu/lb)	(kJ/kg)
Electrical energy		
Process	43.5	101
Other	4.7	11
Total	48.2	112
Thermal energy		
Process steam	69.6	162
Other	9.6	22
Total	79.2	184

Fig. 3.23. Process energy flow diagram of formula feed manufacturing in the prepared feed industry. SIC: 2048. Plant size: about 10 000 t/month.
Source: AFMA (1977).
10^6 Btu/month $\approx 1.055 \times 10^9$ J/month $= 1.055$ GJ/month.

Chapter 3 references, p. 67.

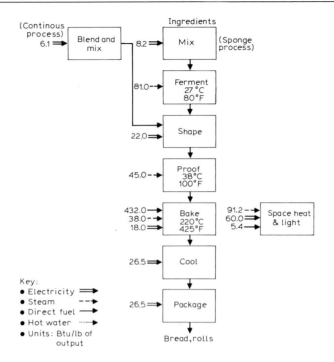

Fig. 3.24. Process energy flow diagram of bread rolls manufacturing. SIC: 2051.
Btu/lb = 2.326 kJ/kg.

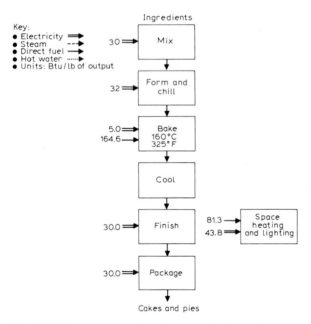

Fig. 3.25. Process energy flow diagram of cakes and pies manufacturing. SIC: 2051.
Btu/lb = 2.326 kJ/kg.

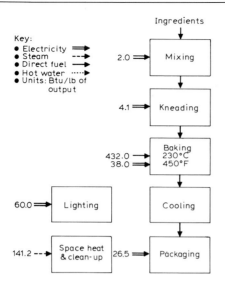

Fig. 3.26. Process energy flow diagram of cookies and crackers manufacturing. SIC: 2052. Btu/lb = 2.326 kJ/kg.

Chapter 3 references, p. 67.

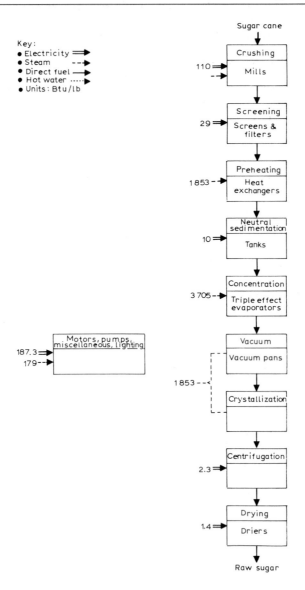

ENERGY BALANCE

	(Btu/lb)	(kJ/kg)
Electrical energy		
Process	191	444
Lighting	10	23
Total	201	467
Thermal energy		
Process steam	7411	17238
Steam drive	389	905
Losses	1259	2928
Total	9059	21071

Fig. 3.27. Process energy flow diagram of raw cane sugar manufacturing. SIC: 2061. 1 t of sugar canes gives 65–70 kg of raw sugar.
Source: Hagler, Bailly & Co., based on industry interviews by Adolfson (1982).
Btu/lb = 2.326 kJ/kg.

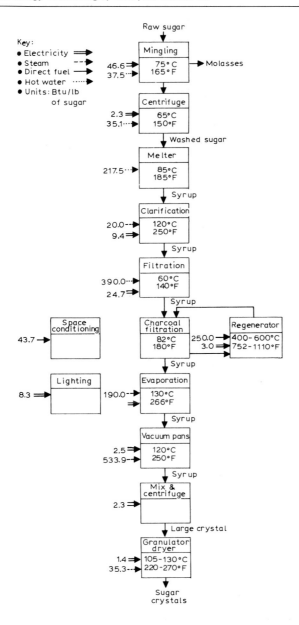

Fig. 3.28. Process energy flow diagram of cane sugar refining. SIC: 2062.
Btu/lb = 2.326 kJ/kg.

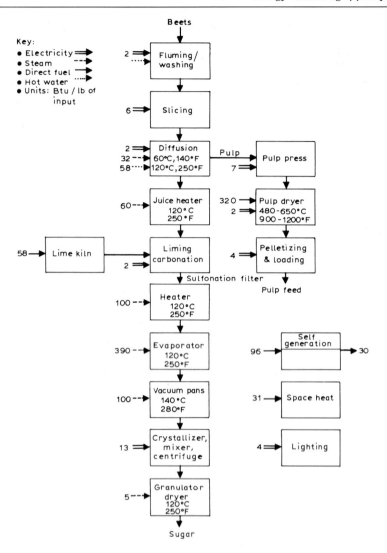

Fig. 3.29. Process energy flow of beet sugar manufacturing. SIC: 2063.
Btu/lb = 2.326 kJ/kg.

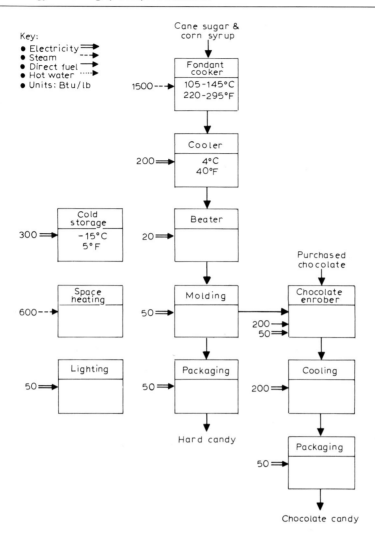

Fig. 3.30. Process energy flow diagram of manufacturing confectionary products. SIC: 2065.
Source: USDC (1981); estimates by Hagler, Bailly & Co.
Btu/lb = 2.326 kJ/kg.

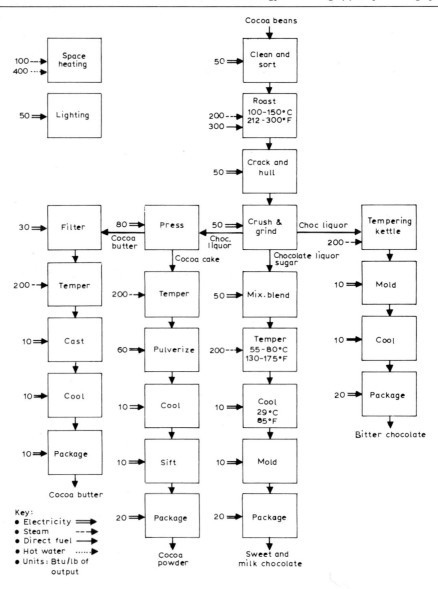

Fig. 3.31. Process energy flow diagram of manufacturing chocolate and cocoa products. SIC 2066.
Sources: USDC (1981); estimates by Hagler, Bailly & Co.
Btu/lb = 2.326 kJ/kg.

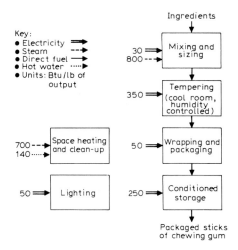

Fig. 3.32. Process of energy flow diagram of manufacturing chewing gum. SIC: 2067. Btu/lb = 2.326 kJ/kg.

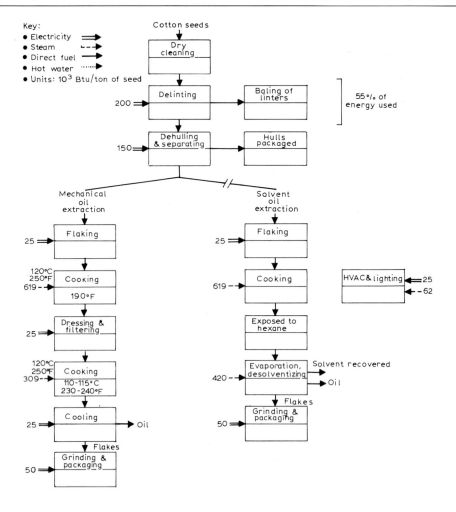

ENERGY BALANCE

	(Btu/lb)	(kJ/kg)
Electrical energy		
Process	238	553
HVAC & Lighting	12	28
Total	250	581
Thermal energy		
Steam	464	1080
HVAC	31	72
Losses	124	288
Total	619	1440

Fig. 3.33. Process energy flow diagram of cotton seed oil milling. SIC: 2074.
Sources: National Cottonseed Products Association (1978); industry interviews.
10^3 Btu/ton $\approx 1.16 \times 10^9$ J/kg = 1.16 GJ/kg.

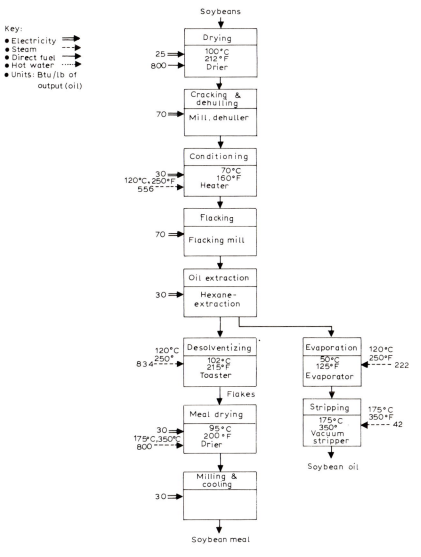

ENERGY BALANCE

	(Btu/lb)	(kJ/kg)
Electrical energy		
Process	285	663
Other*	130	302
Total	415	965
Thermal energy		
Process steam	2454	5708
Cleanup water	290	675
Space heat	276	642
Direct heat	800	1860
Total	3820	8885
Losses	546	1270
Total	4366	10155

*Cooling tower, miscellaneous.

Fig. 3.34. Process energy flow diagram of manufacturing soybean oil. SIC: 2075.
Source: Hamel (1979); industry interviews by Adolfson (1982).
Btu/lb = 2.326 kJ/kg.

Chapter 3 references, p. 67.

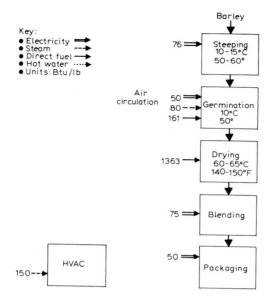

ENERGY BALANCE

	(Btu/lb)	(kJ/kg)
Electrical energy		
Total	251	584
Thermal energy		
Process	1604	3731
HVAC & losses	150	349
Total	1754	4080

Fig. 3.39. Process energy flow diagram of malt manufacturing. SIC: 2083.
Btu/lb = 2.326 kJ/kg.

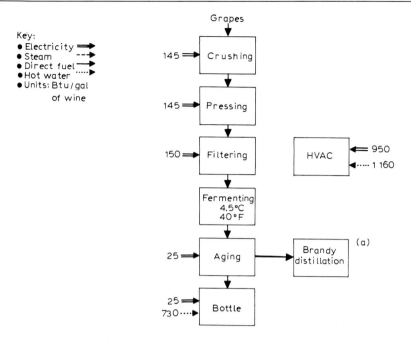

Key:
● Electricity ➡
● Steam ---➤
● Direct fuel ➤
● Hot water ·····➤
● Units: Btu/gal
of wine

Grapes

145 ⟹ Crushing

145 ⟹ Pressing

150 ⟹ Filtering   HVAC   ⟸ 950
                                ◀···· 1 160

Fermenting
4.5°C
40°F

25 ⟹ Aging ⟶ Brandy distillation   (a)

25 ⟹
730 ····▶ Bottle

ENERGY BALANCE

	(Btu/gal)	(kJ/l)
Electrical energy		
Process	490	137
HVAC & Lighting	950	265
Total	1440	402
Thermal energy		
Hot water	730	204
HVAC	1160	323
Losses	810	226
Total	2700	753

Fig. 3.40. Process energy flow diagram of wine making. SIC: 2084.
(a) Process similar to SIC 2085 (Fig. 3.41).
Source: industry interviews by Adolfson (1982).
Btu/gal ≈ 280 J/l.

Chapter 3 references, p. 67.

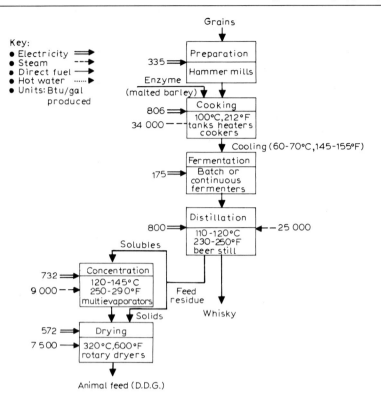

ENERGY BALANCE

	(Btu/gal)	(kJ/l)
Electrical energy		
Process	3420	958
HVAC & Lighting	180	50
Total	3600	1008
Thermal energy*		
Steam	68000	19040
Direct	7500	2100
Total	75500	21140

*Hot water recovered; HVAC negative; losses included.

Fig. 3.41. Process energy flow diagram of manufacturing distilled, rectified and blended liquors.
SIC: 2085.
Source: ITC (1977).
Btu/gal ≈ 280 J/l.

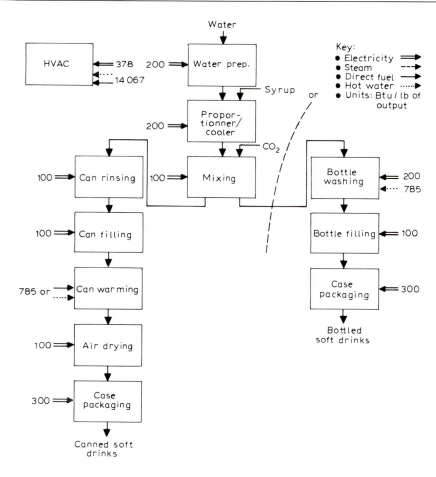

ENERGY BALANCE

	(Btu/lb)	(kJ/kg)
Electrical energy		
Process	1100	2559
HVAC	378	879
Total	1478	3438
Thermal energy		
Direct heat	400	930
HVAC	4067	9460
Hot water*	575	1337
Losses	500	1163
Total	5542	12890

*Including clean-up (190 Btu/lb ≈ 440 kJ/kg).

Fig. 3.42. Process energy flow diagram of manufacturing bottled and canned soft drinks. SIC: 2086. Source: Hagler, Bailly & Co., industry interviews by Adolfson (1982). Btu/lb = 2.326 kJ/kg.

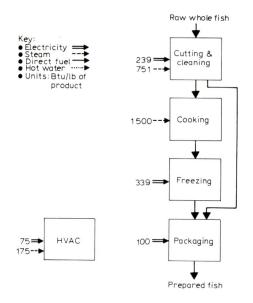

ENERGY BALANCE

	(Btu/lb)	(kJ/kg)
Electrical energy		
Process	678	1577
HVAC & Lighting	75	174
Total	753	1751
Thermal energy		
Steam*	2251	5236
Hot water	175	407
Losses	1114	2590
HVAC	175	407
Total	3715	8640

*Can be also direct fuel.

Fig. 3.45. Process energy flow diagram of preparing fresh or frozen packaged fish. SIC: 2092.
Sources: Havighorst (1976); estimates by Hagler, Bailly & Co.
Btu/lb = 2.326 kJ/kg.

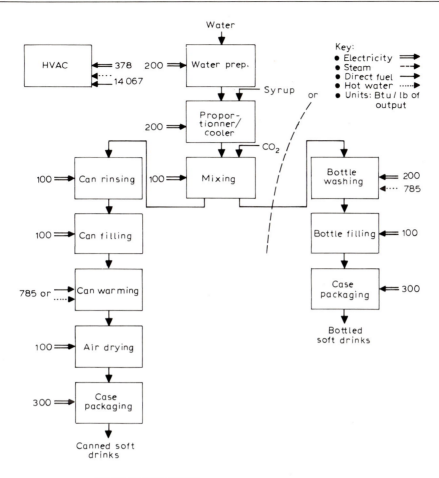

ENERGY BALANCE

	(Btu/lb)	(kJ/kg)
Electrical energy		
Process	1100	2559
HVAC	378	879
Total	1478	3438
Thermal energy		
Direct heat	400	930
HVAC	4067	9460
Hot water*	575	1337
Losses	500	1163
Total	5542	12890

*Including clean-up (190 Btu/lb ≈ 440 kJ/kg).

Fig. 3.42. Process energy flow diagram of manufacturing bottled and canned soft drinks. SIC: 2086. Source: Hagler, Bailly & Co., industry interviews by Adolfson (1982). Btu/lb = 2.326 kJ/kg.

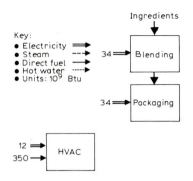

ENERGY BALANCE

	(10⁹ Btu)	(TJ)
Electricity	80	84
Natural gas	350	370

Fig. 3.43. Process energy flow diagram of flavoring extracts manufacturing in a medium-sized plant. SIC: 2087.
10^9 Btu $\approx 1.055 \times 10^{12}$ J $= 1.055$ TJ.

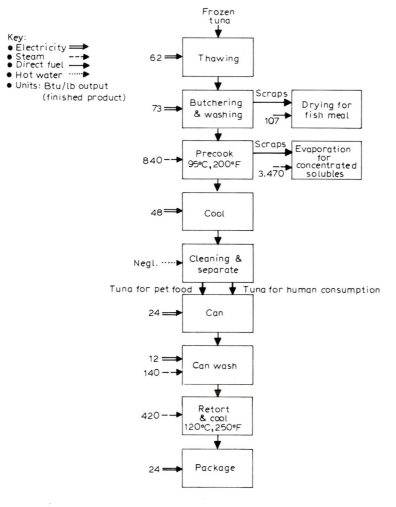

ENERGY BALANCE

	(Btu/lb)	(kJ/kg)
Electrical energy		
Process	243	565
Lighting	13	30
Total	256	595
Thermal energy		
Steam	4870	11327
Direct	107	249
Losses	2087	4854
Total	7064	16430

Fig. 3.44. Process energy flow diagram of canned and dried seafood manufacturing. SIC: 2091. Source: EPA (1974).
Btu/lb = 2.326 kJ/kg.

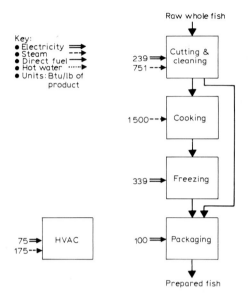

ENERGY BALANCE

	(Btu/lb)	(kJ/kg)
Electrical energy		
Process	678	1577
HVAC & Lighting	75	174
Total	753	1751
Thermal energy		
Steam*	2251	5236
Hot water	175	407
Losses	1114	2590
HVAC	175	407
Total	3715	8640

*Can be also direct fuel.

Fig. 3.45. Process energy flow diagram of preparing fresh or frozen packaged fish. SIC: 2092.
Sources: Havighorst (1976); estimates by Hagler, Bailly & Co.
Btu/lb = 2.326 kJ/kg.

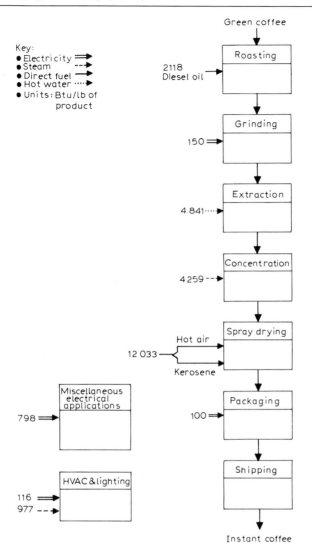

ENERGY BALANCE

	(Btu/lb)	(kJ/kg)
Electrical energy		
Process	1048	2438
HVAC & Lighting	116	270
Total	1164	2708
Thermal energy*		
Steam	4259	9906
Hot water	4841	11260
Direct	12033	27990
HVAC	977	2272
Total	22110	51428

*Losses included.

Fig. 3.46. Process energy flow diagram of roasted coffee manufacturing. SIC: 2095.
Sources: Okada et al. (1980); estimates by Hagler, Bailly & Co.
Btu/lb = 2.326 kJ/kg.

Chapter 3 references, p. 67.

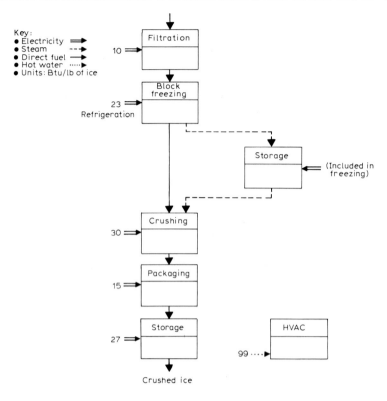

ENERGY BALANCE

	(Btu/lb)	(kJ/kg)
Electrical energy		
Process	313	728
Lighting	16	37
Total	329	765
Thermal energy		
HVAC	91	212

Fig. 3.47. Process energy flow diagram of manufactured ice. SIC: 2097.
Btu/lb = 2.326 kJ/kg.

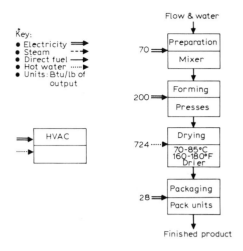

ENERGY BALANCE

	(Btu/lb)	(kJ/kg)
Electrical energy		
Process	298	693
HVAC	15	35
Total	313	728
Thermal energy		
Hot water	724	1684
HVAC	80	186
Total	804	1870

Fig. 3.48. Process energy flow diagram of macaroni and spaghetti manufacturing. SIC: 2098.
Source: industry interviews by Adolfson (1982).
Btu/lb = 2.326 kJ/kg.

6. REFERENCES

Adolfson, W.F., 1982. Photovoltaic off-farm agricultural applications, Vol. III. Tech. Rep. SAND 81-7175/III. Prepared for Sandia National Laboratories, Albuquerque, NM, 645 pp.

AFMA, 1977. Energy management for the feed industry. American Feed Manufacturers Association, Arlington, VA. Cited in Adolfson (1982).

Batelle Columbus Laboratories, 1977. Survey of the applications of solar thermal energy systems to industrial process heat. Columbus, OH. Cited in Adolfson (1982).

Brusewitz, G.H. and Singh, R.P., 1981. Energy accounting and conservation in the manufacture of yogurt and sour cream. Trans. ASAE, 24: 533–536.

Carroad, R., Singh, R.P., Chhinnan, M.S., Jacob, N.L. and Rose, W.W., 1980. Energy use quantification in the canning of clingstone peaches. Presented at 39th Annual Meeting of Institute of Food Techologists, 10–13 June 1979, St. Louis, MO. J. Food Sci., 45(3): 723–735.

Chhinnan, M.S. and Singh, R.P., 1981. Energy conservation in a continuous atmospheric retort. Lebensm. Wiss. Technol., 14: 122–126.

Chhinnan, M.S., Singh, R.P., Pederson, L.D., Carroad, P.A., Rose, W.W. and Jacob, N.L., 1980. Analysis of energy utilization in spinach processing. Trans. ASAE, 23: 503–507.

DPRA, 1974. Industrial energy study of selected food industries. NTIS PB-237-316, Development, Planning and Research Associates, Inc., Manhattan, KS. Cited in Adolfson (1982).

Farral, A. W., 1976. Food Engineering Systems, Vols. 1, 2. AVI, Westport, CT. Cited in Adolfson (1982).

Hagler, Bailly & Co., Lowry, Jr., Washington, DC, personal communication, 1982. Cited in Adolfson (1982).

Hamel, B.B., 1979. Energy analysis of 108 industrial processes. Department of Mechanical Engineering, Drexel University, Philadelphia, PA. Cited in Adolfson (1982).

Havighorst, C.M., 1976. Perky produces pies by the millions. Food Eng., June: 38–39. Cited in Adolfson (1982).

ITC, 1977. Analysis of the economic potential of solar thermal energy to provide industrial process heat. NTIS COO/2029, InterTechnology Corporation. Cited in Adolfson (1982).

National Cotton Seed Products Association, 1978. Cottonseed and its products. Memphis, TN. Cited in Adolfson (1982).

Okada, M., Rao, M.A., Lima, J.E. and Torloni, M., 1980. Energy consumption and the potential for conservation in a spray-dried coffee plant. J. Food Sci., 45: 865–688. Cited in Adolfson (1982).

Singh, R.P., 1978. Energy accounting in food process operations. Food Technol., 32(4): 40–46.

Singh, R.P., Carroad, P.A., Chhinnan, M.S., Rose, W.W. and Jacob, N.L., 1980. Energy accounting in canning tomato products. J. Food Sci., 45(3): 735–739.

USDC, 1981. 1977 Census of Manufactures. MC 77-I, Industrial Series, Bureau of Census, U.S. Department of Commerce, Washington, DC.

USEPA, 1974. Development document for effluent limitations, guidelines and standards of performance of the catfish, crab, shrimp, and tuna segments of the canned and preserved sea food processing industry point source category. NTIS PB-238-614. Cited in Adolfson (1982).

Chapter 4

Exergy Analysis: A Diagnostic and Heat Integration Tool

ENRIQUE ROTSTEIN

1. INTRODUCTION

The idea of exergy has been the object of renewed interest as energy has become more and more a critical factor in industrial economics. Nevertheless, it is not new. Exergy, also called thermodynamic availability was already known in the past century. The first explicit mention of the term available energy was apparently made by Maxwell (1871). Gouy (1889) was probably the first to write an extended analysis of its definitions and practical use, starting from ideas put forward by Lord Kelvin, Tait and Maxwell. Gibbs (1931) considered in 1873 the available energy of system and medium, when analyzing the thermodynamic properties of substances by means of surfaces in the energy–volume–entropy space. Keenan (1949) defined and discussed the engineering applications of the property to closed system and steady flow processes. Haywood (1974) made a critical historical review of the theorems of thermodynamic availability as they apply to physical processes. Sophos et al. (1980a) reviewed applications of exergy analysis to energy conservation, heat integration and process synthesis, including processes where there are chemical changes. Rotstein and Stephanopoulos (1979), Sophos et al. (1980a, b) and Rotstein et al. (1980) used the ideas of exergy and the creation of entropy in the selection of technologies. Two books containing additional background information and discussion of applications are: Ahern (1980) and Gaggioli (1980). Rotstein (1983) presented a computer package which performs exergy balance and showed several examples of industrial utilization.

Little application of these principles has been made to the food industries. One such application (Trägårdh, 1981) shows data on exergy calculations in sweet whey powder production, production of starch derivatives and baked soft cakes, with no reference to the production of entropy. Rotstein (1983) discussed the use of the exergy balance as a diagnostic tool for energy optimization in food processes.

In this chapter the foundations of exergy analysis are presented, starting from the contributing energy and entropy balances. It is shown that, when a food industry is considered, the exergy balance presents valuable information with respect to energy utilization: optimum theoretical energy performance, departure from the optimum and consumption of utilities. Since heat integration is a classical method of saving energy, the pinch point procedure to accomplish this task is discussed and the resulting heat integration is evaluated in terms of the production of entropy, as well as in economic terms. A specific example, a tomato paste plant, illustrates that energy savings correlate with decreasing productions of entropy. On the other hand, from a return on

---

Chapter 4 references, p. 85.

original investment standpoint, there is piece-wise correlation up to an optimum economical configuration.

2. ENERGY BALANCE AND ENTROPY BALANCE

Consider an open system and its surroundings. The surroundings are large enough, as compared with the system, to remain unaffected by exchanges with it; they are uniform, time-invariant and do not experience local changes at the exchange surfaces. These are necessary requirements to warrant that heat exchanges with the surroundings be reversible from the surroundings side. Notice that in general terms the atmospheric air meets these requirements.

Energy, mass, entropy and, as it will be demonstrated, exergy, are extensive properties; this means that their value is proportional to the amount of matter involved. As a result they are subject to accounting and it is useful to obtain the corresponding balance expressions. They will all be of the type:

$$\text{Accumulation} = \begin{bmatrix} \text{Input–Output} \\ \text{without mass} \\ \text{exchange} \end{bmatrix} + \begin{bmatrix} \text{Input–Output} \\ \text{with mass} \\ \text{exchange} \end{bmatrix} + \begin{bmatrix} \text{Internal} \\ \text{production of} \\ \text{the property} \end{bmatrix} \quad (1)$$

When the property being considered is energy, interactions without mass exchange include heat and useful work exchange. Interactions with mass exchange are given by energy carried by streams entering and leaving the system; in usual food processing situations this is represented by the stream enthalpy, kinetic and potential energy changes being negligible. Because energy is conserved, there is no production of energy. Thus, the energy balance equation corresponding to equation (1) can be written:

$$\frac{\mathrm{d}U}{\mathrm{d}t} = \sum_{q_{\text{in}}} w_q \hat{H}_q - \sum_{q_{\text{out}}} w_q \hat{H}_q + \sum_{l_{\text{in}}} \dot{Q}_l - \sum_{l_{\text{out}}} \dot{Q}_l + \dot{W}_{\text{u}} + \dot{W}_{\text{exp}} \quad (2)$$

where q_{in} are input process streams, q_{out} output process streams, l_{in} is the input heat exchange surface, l_{out} the output heat exchange surface, U the system internal energy, w_q are mass flow rates, $\hat{H}_q$ specific stream enthalpies, $\dot{Q}_l$ heat fluxes per unit time, and $\dot{W}_{\text{u}}$ and $\dot{W}_{\text{exp}}$ useful and expansion work per unit time.

If the property under consideration is entropy (S), interactions without mass exchange correspond to entropy fluxes only, i.e., to the heat fluxes involved; interactions with mass exchange result from the stream entropies $\hat{S}_q$ as they are carried by each stream and production of entropy may or may not occur. Equation (1) can be written as:

$$\frac{\mathrm{d}S}{\mathrm{d}t} = \sum_{q_{\text{in}}} w_q \hat{S}_q - \sum_{q_{\text{out}}} w_q \hat{S}_q + \sum_{l_{\text{in}}} \frac{\dot{Q}_l}{T_l} - \sum_{l_{\text{out}}} \frac{Q_l}{T_l} + \dot{R}_s \quad (3)$$

where T_l is the heat exchange surface temperature. The production of entropy value is:

$$\dot{R}_s \geqslant 0 \quad (4)$$

depending on whether the process is reversible ($\dot{R}_s = 0$) or irreversible ($\dot{R}_s > 0$).

3. EXERGY BALANCE

The expansion work against p_0, the pressure of the surroundings, can be written:

$$\dot{W}_{\text{exp}} = -p_0 \frac{\mathrm{d}V}{\mathrm{d}t} \quad (5)$$

For symbols see Appendix: Nomenclature, p. 87.

If the heat transfer at each heat exchange surface takes place from surroundings at T_0, then:

$$\frac{\dot{Q}_l}{T_l} = \frac{\dot{Q}_l}{T_0} \tag{6}$$

Using equation (5) in (2), and (6) in (3), multiplying the latter by T_0, subtracting from equation (2) and rearranging the resulting expression:

$$\frac{\mathrm{d}(U + p_0 V - T_0 S)}{\mathrm{d}t} = \sum_{q_{\mathrm{in}}} w_q(\hat{H}_q - T_0 \hat{S}_q) - \sum_{q_{\mathrm{out}}} w_q(\hat{H}_q - T_0 \hat{S}_q) + \dot{W}_{\mathrm{u}} - T_0 \dot{R}_s \tag{7}$$

Equation (7) is a combined expression of the energy and entropy balance; as such it represents both the first and second principle. Exergy is defined on the basis of this equation; a distinction is made between system exergy:

$$B_{\mathrm{sys}} = U + p_0 V - T_0 S \tag{8}$$

and stream exergy:

$$\hat{B}_q = \hat{H}_q - T_0 \hat{S}_q \tag{9}$$

Using the definitions in equation (7), the exergy balance for an unsteady state system becomes:

$$\frac{\mathrm{d}B_{\mathrm{sys}}}{\mathrm{d}t} = \sum_{q_{\mathrm{in}}} w_q \hat{B}_q - \sum_{q_{\mathrm{out}}} w_q \hat{B}_q + \dot{W}_{\mathrm{u}} - T_0 \dot{R}_s \tag{10}$$

From a practical industrial standpoint unsteady state analysis is rare. The usual case corresponds to steady state where:

$$\frac{\mathrm{d}B_{\mathrm{sys}}}{\mathrm{d}t} = 0 \tag{11}$$

and as a result, it follows from equation (10) that:

$$\sum_{q_{\mathrm{out}}} w_q \hat{B}_q - \sum_{q_{\mathrm{in}}} w_q \hat{B}_q = \dot{W}_{\mathrm{u}} - T_0 \dot{R}_s \tag{12}$$

Designing the exergy change between outgoing and incoming streams:

$$\Delta B = \sum_{q_{\mathrm{out}}} w_q \hat{B}_q - \sum_{q_{\mathrm{in}}} w_q \hat{B}_q \tag{13}$$

Equation (12) may be written more compactly:

$$\Delta B = \dot{W}_{\mathrm{u}} - T_0 \dot{R}_s \tag{14}$$

The physical meaning of an exergy change follows from equations (14) and (4). For a reversible process, $\dot{R}_s = 0$, and:

$$\Delta B = W_{\mathrm{u,r}} \tag{15}$$

Thus, the exergy change of a reversible process equals the useful work associated with that process. If the sign convention implicit in (1) is used (work outputs are negative, work inputs are positive), then the exergy change is the minimum work in the algebraic sense. In absolute values, equation (15) means that the exergy change is the most useful work that can be obtained from a work-producing process or the least useful work required by a work-consuming process. Figure 4.1 shows a work-producing process, Fig. 4.2 a work-consuming one.

From the above it follows that exergy change and creation of entropy are the energy bounds of any process or set of processes (Rotstein, 1983). Exergy

Chapter 4 references, p. 85.

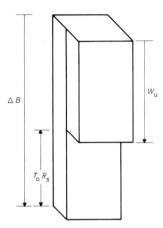

Fig. 4.1. A work-producing process. If it were reversible, it would provide $\Delta B = -50$ kWh; as it is, it provides $W_u = -27$ kWh. Thus, $T_0 R_s = 23$ kWh.

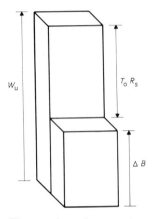

Fig. 4.2. A work-consuming process. Ideally it would consume $\Delta B = 20$ kWh, in practice it requires $W_u = 45$ kWh. $T_0 R_s = 25$ kWh.

change is the best possible performance that could be hoped for; because it implies reversible processes, it is approachable but unattainable. Creation of entropy represents the actual performance, as such it is evolutionary in nature, it can be improved by optimization to approach zero, thus driving the useful work term closer to the invariant exergy bound. It should be clear that equation (12) is in a sense a balance of useful work and the entropy production term can be regarded as work lost because of irreversibilities. Entropy production, work lost by irreversibility or lost work are terms which can be used indiscriminately, but the physical meaning of entropy production, in which by necessity $T_0 \dot{R}_s > 0$, must always be taken into account. In fact, since ΔB can be calculated and work consumption can be measured, obtaining a negative value for entropy production is a sure indication that something is wrong with either the data or the calculations.

4. ROLE OF UTILITIES

In a typical food processing plant, there are process streams which consist of raw materials, products, wastes and intermediate materials which are produced as the raw materials undergo the corresponding transformations. This is represented by box P and the streams shown in Fig. 4.3; all intermediate streams are inside P. The intermediate streams are usually subject to, or the

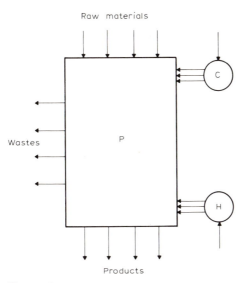

Fig. 4.3. Straightforward heating and cooling. Each requirement is met with utilities expenditure. P, food process; C, cooling utilities; H, heating utilities.

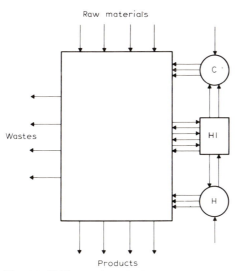

Fig. 4.4. Utility savings by heat integration. C, cooling utilities; H, heating utilities; HI, heat integration.

result of, operations which consume or release energy: blanching, cooking, retorting, drying, stripping, etc. All energy requirements result in the usage of primary utilities such as fuel, cooling water, steam, hot air and electricity. The maximum usage of utilities corresponds to the use of one utility per cooling or heating requirement, as shown in Fig. 4.3. On the other hand, it is often possible to take advantage of the energy level of a stream instead of consuming additional utilities. A typical example is when a product stream which needs to be cooled is sent through a heat exchanger to heat a process stream which requires heating; this results in savings in both heating and cooling utilities. This task is called heat integration (Umeda et al., 1979) and it is illustrated in Fig. 4.4. Utilities are a crucial part of the energy analysis and utility saving is mandatory in energy conservation. For that reason it is convenient to isolate heating and cooling utility streams from process streams in equation (12). (Electrical utilities are included in the $\dot{W}_u$ term.) To do this the q ports in (12) are classified as those which belong to process streams and those which belong

Chapter 4 references, p. 85.

TABLE 4.3

Pinch point algorithm

---

(1) Make a list of entrance and exit temperatures for all streams, in the order of increasing temperatures. These are the k points.

(2) Identify those hot temperatures for which:

$$\left(\frac{dQ_h}{dT}\right)_{k-} > \left(\frac{dQ_h}{dT}\right)_{k+}$$

where $k-$ and $k+$ are understood to occur immediately before and after T_k, respectively. The temperatures identified as T_k^*, are the likely pinch candidates, together with the upper and lower-most temperatures of the list. Do the same for cold streams using the inverse test equation:

$$\left(\frac{dQ_c}{dT}\right)_{k-} < \left(\frac{dQ_c}{dT}\right)_{k+}$$

(3) For all likely pinch candidates, T_k^* belonging to a hot stream, one can calculate:

$$\Delta Q_k = Q_h(T_k^*) - Q_c(T_k^* - \Delta T_{min})$$

for those belonging to a cold stream:

$$\Delta Q_k = Q_h(T_k^* + \Delta T_{min}) - Q_c(T_k^*)$$

(4) The pinch point corresponds to the temperature resulting in the largest $\Delta Q_k = \Delta Q_{max}$. Also:

$$Q_R = \Delta Q_{max}$$

$$Q_H = Q_R + Q_{c\,tot} - Q_{h\,tot}$$

---

pinch point is reached, the minimum production of entropy corresponding to ΔT_{min} has been reached. The algebraic summation over process streams quantifies the process energy exchange in terms of ideal work. Analogous information is given for the utilities by the algebraic summation over utility streams. Thus, heat integration for minimum utilities consumption has a clear meaning in terms of the exergy balance: it corresponds to minimum production of entropy, as well as to minimum ideal work give-away by the process and utility streams.

The pinch point may be located using the numerical algorithm shown in Table 4.3 (Urbicain and Rotstein, 1984). Other procedures suggested in the past are a problem table (Linnhoff and Flower, 1978) and a graphical method (Umeda et al., 1979). Cerdá et al. (1983) presented a linear programming method and Urbicain and Rotstein (1984) an analytical approach which applies to variable or constant specific heats. After locating the pinch point, heat integration may be materialized by using design rules established by Linnhoff and Hindmarsh (1983). Alternatively, a debottlenecking procedure may be followed (Umeda et al., 1979): the identified pinch is removed by changing operating conditions and/or equipment, until a satisfactory utilities consumption is reached; then, the design rules are used for the final structure.

7. HEAT INTEGRATION, EXERGY BALANCE AND ECONOMICS: THE CASE OF THE TOMATO PASTE PLANT

Forciniti et al. (1985) have carried out the heat integration of the tomato paste plant described earlier (Fig. 4.5). This was done by integration after pinch location for different $\Delta T'_{min}$ values without structural changes and by debottlenecking, introducing vapor recompression which in turn resulted in different pinch locations. Three options for vapor recompression were studied:

TABLE 4.4

Heat integration: economic and thermodynamic results

Network	Fixed cost (10³ $/year)	Total cost (10³ $/year)	Savings (10³ $/year)	Preliminary profit estimate (10³ $/year)	$T_0 R_s$ (MJ/h)	Return on original investment (%)
(1) Original case	—	455.8	—	—	16 927.9	—
(2) (ΔT_{min} = 40°C)	5.8	441.4	20.2	14.4	16 219.8	246.6
(3) (ΔT_{min} = 30°C)	11.9	424.5	43.2	31.3	15 278.4	263.18
(4) (ΔT_{min} = 25°C)	13.8	419.9	49.6	35.8	15 016.7	260.35
(5) (ΔT_{min} = 20°C)	16.4	417.3	54.9	38.5	14 831.6	234.70
(6) (ΔT_{min} = 15°C)	20.1	414.5	61.3	41.3	14 535.7	206.38
(7) (ΔT_{min} = 10°C)	25.7	414.9	66.6	40.9	14 309.6	158.84
(8) (ΔT_{min} = 5°C)	38.3	421.1	73.0	34.7	14 041.8	90.63
(9) 2nd effect VR:[a] ΔT_{min} = 10°C	82	377.8	160	78	9545.0	95.09
(10) 1st and 2nd effect VR: ΔT_{min} = 10°C	72.2	286.5	241.4	169.2	7160.4	234.45
(11) 1st and 2nd effect VR: ΔT_{min} = 5 and 10°C	67.5	270.2	253.1	185.6	6690.6	275.06

[a] VR, vapor recompression.

Notes: The original case differs in $T_0 R_s$ from the value in Table 4.2 because of minor differences in system definition. Cases 1–8 correspond to the original pinch structure. Cases 9–11, to modified pinch structure.

Chapter 4 references, p. 85.

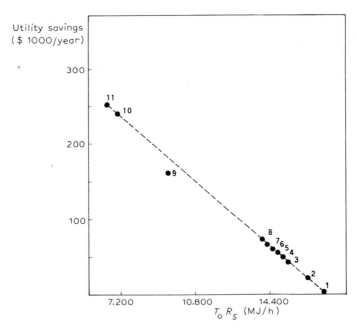

Fig. 4.9. Savings in utilities as a function of entropy production for all cases studied. Numbers on data points refer to cases described in Table 4.4.

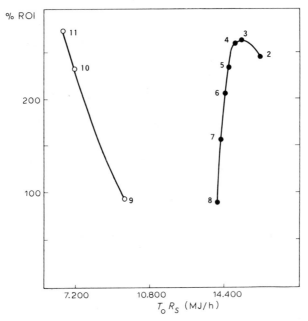

Fig. 4.10. Percentage return on investment (ROI) as a function of production of entropy.

compressing the second effect vapor and the first and second effects vapor, with $\Delta T_{\min} = 10°C$, and the latter with $\Delta T_{\min} = 5°C$ in the evaporator. Table 4.4 shows the results. In this table fixed cost refers to the depreciated cost of heat exchangers and other equipment; total cost is fixed cost plus utilities cost; savings refer to utilities which are not used because of heat integration and preliminary profit estimate is the difference between savings and fixed cost. Return on original investment (ROI) is used to measure profitability. It is the percentage relationship of profit over fixed cost.

Figure 4.9 illustrates results from the thermodynamic analysis. It can be seen that, from a thermodynamic standpoint there is a strong correlation between decreasing production of entropy and savings in utilities. In other words, the closer the process approach to reversibility, the smaller will be the exergy change and the larger will be the utility saving. From an economic standpoint, savings are obtained through investment in heat exchange area and, in the cases of pinch modification, investment in compressors. There is no reason why these investments should be linear in their dependence with respect to production of entropy. In fact Fig. 4.10 shows an optimum ROI for the original pinch cases, corresponding to $\Delta T_{min} = 30°C$; for lower ΔT_{min} values savings have a lower impact in compensating the investment. All cases being considered the best heat integrated structure in terms of profitability is that with vapor recompression in both evaporator effects and $\Delta T_{min} = 5°C$.

8. CONCLUSIONS

The exergy balance is both a powerful diagnostic tool for energy conservation and a way to carry out this conservation.

As a diagnostic tool, all terms of the balance are meaningful. The balance itself is a balance of useful work. The left hand side of (16) provides a measure of the ideal work that can be obtained from, or provided to, process streams. On the right hand side of (16), the first term is power input or output; the next two terms represent ideal work that could be secured from, or produced by, utilities. Last but not least, the production of entropy represents lost work, i.e., the difference between ideal reversible performance and actual energy consumption.

The diagnostic is a basis upon which to assess a situation. To move on from a process configuration to a new less energy consuming one, heat integration is recommended. The pinch procedure provides a systematic way to do that. It has been shown that searching for the pinch is equivalent to searching for the lowest feasible production of entropy or exergy change. There is an almost linear correlation between decreasing production of entropy and savings in utilities. On the other hand, from an economic standpoint, there is an optimum which cannot be predicted a priori.

The main lines for exergy analysis are by now well-defined. Some of the lines that require future work are instrumental. Lack of good data on transport properties results in correspondingly poor predictions. Equipment and process design should take into account the contrasting information from thermodynamics and economics, bearing in mind that the latter is subject to change as relative prices change. Another avenue of research which deserves exploration is to carry the macroscopic ideas of exergy balance to the level of equipment design.

9. REFERENCES

Ahern, J.E., 1980. The Exergy Method of Energy Systems Analysis. Wiley, New York, NY, 295 pp.

Cerdá, J., Westerberg, A.W., Mason, D. and Linnhoff, B., 1983. Minimum utility usage in heat exchanger network synthesis – a transportation problem. Chem. Eng. Sci., 38: 373–387.

Chang, H.D. and Tao, L.C., 1981. Correlations of enthalpies of food systems. J. Food Sci., 46: 1493–1497.

Charm, S.E., 1963. Fundamentals of Food Engineering. AVI, Westport, CT, 592 pp.

Denbigh, K.G., 1956. The second law efficiency of chemical processes. Chem. Eng. Sci., 6: 1–9.

De Nevers, N. and Seader, J.D., 1979. Mechanical lost work, thermodynamic lost work and thermodynamic efficiencies of processes. 68th AIChE Meeting, 1 April 1979, Houston, TX, 57 pp.

Fitzmorris, R.E. and Mah, R.S.H., 1980. Improving distillations column design using thermodynamic availability analysis. AIChE J., 26: 265.

Forciniti, D., Rotstein, E. and Urbicain, M.J., 1985. Heat recovery and exergy balance in a tomato paste plant. J. Food Sci., 50: 934–939.

Chapter 5

Exergy Analysis for Energy Conservation in the Food Processing Industry

CHRISTIAN TRÄGÅRDH

1. INTRODUCTION

The First Law of Thermodynamics requires that for a given system the energy is conserved so that all changes in the total energy content of the system are zero. Thus energy is non-destructible, it is only used to perform a desired operation in this connection.

However, experience shows that it is not possible to use all the energy. This relationship is formalized in the Second Law of Thermodynamics.

It is possible to define available energy and non-available energy. By available energy we mean energy that is capable of accomplishing a certain duty or by using the original concepts of thermodynamics, energy that is totally transformable into any other kind of energy by the participation of the actual surroundings. There is a maximal availability of any energy source and that fraction of the energy is denoted *exergy*. The rest of the energy is denoted *anergy*. We can thus conclude that energy consists of exergy and anergy either of which may be zero:

$$\text{energy} \; = \; \text{exergy} \; + \; \text{anergy} \tag{1}$$

Examples of energy sources that consist only of exergy are: electrical energy, potential energy and kinetic energy. An example of an energy source consisting of both exergy and anergy is heat, where the temperature differs from the surroundings. An example of an energy source consisting only of anergy is heat with the same temperature as the surroundings.

Thence, in terms of exergy and anergy the First Law of Thermodynamics can be formulated:

> In all operations and processes the sum of energy and anergy remain constant.

The Second Law of Thermodynamics may correspondingly be formulated as:
> – all irreversible processes transform exergy to anergy
> – only for reversible processes does exergy remain constant
> – it is impossible to transform anergy into exergy.

In all technical and natural processes entropy is generated as a consequence of irreversibilities. Examples are given in Table 5.1 (London, 1982). One example of a process where no irreversibilities occur is in the idealized heat engine represented by the Carnot cycle. Energy, in the form of heat, is transferred from a hot to a cold reservoir, producing a limited, but maximal amount of work corresponding to the exergy content of the energy from the hot reservoir.

The irreversibilities causing a transformation of exergy into anergy implies that the energy within the system loses some of its power to produce 'work'

Chapter 5 references, p. 100.

TABLE 5.1

Examples of irreversible processes in energy transfer operation

- fluid viscous dissipation (pressure drop in pipes, valves, etc.)
- solid to solid friction
- free expansion
- mixing of dissimilar fluid
- mixing of similar fluids at different temperatures
- electrical resistance heating
- chemical reaction such as combustion
- heat transfer across a finite temperature difference
- non-equilibrium phase change
- solution of a solid in a solvent

when leaving it thus reducing its 'quality'. If it was possible to perform technical processes without exergy losses a perpetuum mobile would be a reality. However, it is the aim of exergy analysis of technical processes, in this case the energy flows in food processing industries, to combat irreversibilities in the energy transformations (Grassmann, 1979). A deeper theoretical presentation of these thermodynamic relationships are discussed, for example, in Baehr (1981) and Baloh (1982).

Reducing irreversibilities and the corresponding maintenance of exergy have economic consequences, apart from conservation. Very often it is combined with economic efforts in the form of more expensive equipment to lower some of the irreversibilities listed in Table 5.1 (some of them are unavoidable in practical cases). On the other hand the work produced in the proper cascading of the energy flow increases where it is often possible to put a price on it. An optimization in money terms based on a thermodynamic approach seems reasonable. Examples are presented by London (1982) and Baloh (1982).

Of course it is hard to see any great advantage in making exergy balances of those systems which are presented here; besides, the actual measurements were not planned for exergy calculations. They will, however, demonstrate how irreversibilities are created, their origin, their magnitude and how they could be lowered. They will not tell how the remaining exergy could be utilized to make the efforts worthwhile. To make this possible and thereby show the real benefits, whole systems must be considered. The real benefit of exergy analyses lies in the possibility of cascading the energy flows if the exergy is to a sufficiently large extent conserved.

2. METHODS

Exergy balances according to the methodologies presented in Chapter 4 for some unit operations are often used in the food processing industries. The data for this chapter are based on measurements from some small or medium-sized Swedish food industries and some overall results have already been published: Trägårdh et al. (1980) and Trägårdh (1981). Apart from the measurements, data for the physical properties of those streams entering and leaving the system boundaries were needed. These data were obtained from tables, diagrams and formulae found in Mörtstedt (1963), Tschubik and Maslow (1973), Baloh (1982) and Grigull (1982). As seen in the definitions given, energy in the form of potential and kinetic energy is not included in the calculations and for the convenience of the readers the exergy formulae actually used are represented.

NOMENCLATURE

A Heat transfer area (m^2)
c_p Specific heat capacity (J kg^{-1}°C^{-1})
e_w Specific exergy (J kg^{-1})
e Specific energy (J kg^{-1})
h Specific enthalpy (J kg^{-1})
k Total heat transfer coefficient (J s^{-1} m^{-2})
p Partial pressure (Pa)
R Gas constant (J mol^{-1} K^{-1})
s Specific entropy (J kg^{-1} K^{-1})
T Temperature (K)
v Temperature (°C)
$\dot{Q}$ Heat transfer rate (J s^{-1})

Subscripts
a air
l liquid
v vapor

2.1. Calculations of exergy content

The definition of specific exergy is expressed here as (see Nomenclature):

$$e_w = h - h_0 - T_0(s - s_0) \tag{2}$$

where qualities with subscript 0 represents the state of the surroundings.

For an isobar or incompressible case, equation (2) is:

$$e_w = c_p(T - T_0 - T_0 \ln T/T_0) \tag{3}$$

if no change of phase occurs. Equation (3) is used for all liquids and solids where no solidification, melting, evaporation or condensation take place.

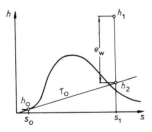

Fig. 5.1. Exergy content estimation of pure steam from an enthalpy–entropy diagram using the surrounding line.

In the case of pure steam, a Mollier enthalpy–entropy diagram for water and steam as illustrated in Fig. 5.1 was used. The specific exergy content becomes:

$$e_w = h_i - h_2$$

For humid air, the air itself, and the water the calculations are done separately. Thus the air exergy is calculated using equation (4) which is derived from equation (2). The water exergy is then:

$$e_{w,a} = c_p(T - T_0) - T_0(R \ln p_0/p + c_p \ln T/T_0) \tag{4}$$

divided into two fractions:
(1) Water above the saturation level at the state of the surroundings:

$$e_{w,l} = i - i_0 - T_0(s - s_0) \tag{5}$$

Here the i and s represent superheated vapour and i_0 and s_0 liquid water at T_0.

Chapter 5 references, p. 100.

(2) For the non-condensed water the exergy content is calculated as:

$$e_{w,v} = c_p(T - T_0) - T_0(R \ln p_0/p + c_p \ln T/T_0) \qquad (6)$$

The total exergy content of the humid air is then:

$$e_w = e_{w,a} + x_l e_{w,l} + x_v e_{w,v}$$

and expressed as J per kg of dry air.

For fuels, the effective heat of combustion multiplied by 0.95 is used.
The surrounding reference conditions were 15°C and 760 mmHg.

2.2. Calculation of energy content

As the potential and kinetic energy contents were not taken into account, the corresponding enthalpies were used as energy contents.

For liquids and solids with no phase change:

$$e = c_p v$$

For steam and water the steam tables are used.
For humid air:

$$e = c_{p,a} v + x_v h_v$$

For fuels the effective heat of combustion is used as their energy content.

2.3. Calculation of heat content

The heat content of an energy source is calculated as the amount of heat that would be released to the surroundings (15°C and 750 mmHg) in order to obtain equilibrium.

3. RESULTS

The concept of exergy and the methods for its calculation have been applied to some food processing factories which have interesting energy intensive unit operations (Trägårdh, 1981). The factories analyzed here are: a sweet whey powder plant containing the energy-intensity unit operations, evaporation and spray drying; a starch derivate powder plant containing three different driers, pneumatic flash drier, fluid-bed drier and roller drier; and a bakery where the interesting unit is a tunnel oven.

3.1. Sweet whey powder production

A factory in southern Sweden produced 900 t of demineralized powder per year, with an energy input of 2.4 MJ electricity plus 21.1 MJ oil per kg powder. The whey was first concentrated from a dry matter (DM) content (wet basis) of 6.7 to 20% in a three-stage falling-film evaporator, equipped with thermal steam recompression. The concentrate was demineralized through electrodialysis. A second concentration was made in the same evaporator, to raise the dry matter content to 55% before drying to 97% DM. The overall energy usages, based on measurements, are given in Table 5.2.

The evaporation and spray drying were the operations with the highest energy demand, and so a closer analysis of these systems was done. In Tables 5.3 and 5.4 the streams of energy and exergy are given for the evaporator and the spray drier, respectively.

TABLE 5.2

Energy demand for the production of sweet whey powder

	Energy input (MJ/kg DM)	
	Electricity	Steam[a]
First evaporation	0.30	6.3
Electrodialysis	0.99	
Second evaporation	0.10	2.1
Spray drying	1.05	5.6
Total	2.44	14.7

[a] Heat of vaporization only.

TABLE 5.3

Streams of mass, enthalpy and exergy for a 3-stage evaporator with thermal vapour recompression. Evaporating capacity 3563 kg water per h and an extrapolation to 3578 kg/h

	Mass (kg/h)	Enthalpy (MJ/h)	Exergy (kJ/h)	Heat (MJ/h)
Streams to evaporator				
Steam, saturated at 1 MPa,	920	2554	815	2497
Sweet whey 8°C, 6.7% DM	5358	166	2	
		2720	817	
Streams from evaporator				
Saturated vapour 43°C (33°C)	723	1864 (1859)	157 (101)	1819
Condensate 60°C (57°C)	1470	369 (355)	20 (17)	277
Condensate 2 + 3, 49°C (45°C)	2290	469 (435)	18 (14)	325
Concentrate 43°C, 20% DM (33°C)	1795 (1780)	284 (218)	9 (4)	184
		2986	204 (136)	

TABLE 5.4

Streams of mass, enthalpy and exergy for a spray drier with an evaporating capacity of 230 kg water per h and an extrapolation to 262 kg water per h

	Mass (kg/h)	Enthalpy (MJ/h)	Exergy (MJ/h)	Heat (MJ/h)
Streams to drier				
Air, 178°C, $X = 0.004$	11 000	2080	375	1802
Sweet whey 8°C, 55% DM	530 (673)	12 (15)	≈ 0	
		2092 (2095)	375	
Streams from drier				
Air, 94°C, $X = 0.0211$	11 000	1653 (1578)	126 (112)	1195
Powder 90°C, 97% DM	300 (412)	45 (61)	4.2 (4.9)	
80°C, 90% DM		1698 (1639)	130 (117)	

For the evaporator we have a good thermal efficiency, since the energy is re-used. It could be improved further if more stages were added. The exergy figures show, however, that the reversibility of the process is rather low, mainly due to the temperature differences in the different stages. Thermal diffusion across a finite temperature difference is one process which causes the irreversibilities mentioned in Table 5.1. In this case we also have phase change

Chapter 5 references, p. 100.

(condensation) not in equilibrium. Thus if there was the possibilities of using the exergy in the streams leaving the evaporator, it would be worth considering an increase in temperature at the last stage. This would also, however, mean an increased heat transfer area in the evaporator. Notice the difference in exergy content between the steam and the vapor, as compared to the heat content. This means that the loss of exergy accomplishes the work of efficient evaporation; efficient in the meaning of high heat flux. (A high specific exergy content means that the energy sources are easy to use.) The figures in parentheses are approximate calculations of what would happen if the boiling temperature of the third stage of an evaporator, with a diminished heat transfer area, was decreased by 10°C. Two things are demonstrated:

(a) an improved energy utilization is obtained;

(b) the exergy efficiency is lowered because of the increased driving force (temperature difference) (Table 5.5).

Convective air drying normally requires a high energy input, and this is demonstrated in the case of the spray drier. The thermal efficiency is not very good for the spray drier, which was observed by Trägårdh (1981) when

TABLE 5.5

Thermal and exergetic efficiency for investigated operations

Operation	Thermal efficiency[a]	Exergetic efficiency[b]	Energy demand	Exergy consumption
			(MJ/kg evaporated water)	
Steam-air heat exchanger A	0.75	0.43		
Steam-air heat exchanger B	0.79	0.32		
Evaporator[c]	3.35 (3.36)	0.25 (0.17)	0.717 (0.714)	0.172 (0.190)
Spray drier	0.29 (0.34)	0.34 (0.30)	9.04 (7.94)	1.08 (1.00)
Flash drier	0.45	0.11	6.52	0.76
Fluid-bed drier	0.28	0.55	12.8	0.35
Roller drier	0.51	0.09	4.5	1.25
Tunnel oven	0.07	0.18	33.6	26.2

[a] Based on the ratio between obtained work (for heat exchangers $= \Delta H_{air}$, for water removal $= R$) and supplied heat.
[b] Based on the ratio between usable exergy in the streams from the operation and the supplied used exergy.
[c] Figures in parentheses represent modified operations.

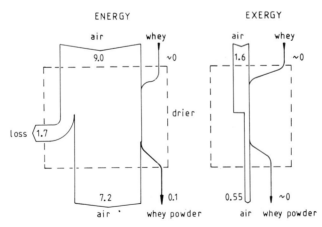

Fig. 5.2. Energy and exergy flowsheets for the spray drier. (Figures represent MJ/kg evaporated water.)

examing the operating lines. This can also be seen in the energy balance of Tables 5.4 and 5.5. Exergy loss due to irreversibilities is shown in Fig. 5.2. The irreversibilities in this case are effects of the temperature difference between the air and the product, and probably because the evaporation does not take place in equilibrium. Table 5.4 shows a rough calculation, in which the air temperature was changed to 80°C instead of the measured 94°C, thus giving a more moist product. As expected, it improves the energy utilization, but also the exergy utilization. This does not mean that the process became less irreversible; on the contrary. The decrease in exergy content of the exhaust air was not so big as the increase in capacity because of the increasing humidity of the air.

3.2. Production of starch derivates

The overall energy input and usage for the factory investigated is given in Table 5.6. Special attention was paid to the different driers, since they are big energy users. Mainly two types of modified starch products were produced, cold-swelling and warm-swelling, with different drying characteristics. Thus different types of driers were also used; a pneumatic flash drier, a fluid-bed drier, and a roller drier. In the two first mentioned, air is the heat and mass transfer medium (convective), while in the case of the roller drier the heat is supplied conductively through a steel roll, and the water removed directly through evaporation (boiling). The temperatures and temperature differences also varied in the different driers.

Steam-heated heat exchangers were used to heat the air in both the flash and fluid-bed driers. Their energy and exergy balances are presented in Table 5.7 and Figs. 5.3 and 5.4. The major reasons for the exergy loss (conversion of exergy to anergy) are in these cases due to the temperature difference between the steam and the heated air (the logarithmic mean temperatures were 85 and 87 K, respectively, if considering only air and steam temperatures). The figures imply that the larger mean temperature difference for heat exchanger 2 resulted in a larger exergy loss. Naturally other differences, such as design and other operating conditions also influence the magnitude of the irreversibilities as demonstrated by Bejan (1977), but are not known for these exchangers. For an ideal heat transfer operation with no exergy losses, the required heat transfer area would be infinitely larger requiring that the temperature difference

TABLE 5.6

Energy input to a starch finishing factory

	Energy input (MJ/kg product)	
	Electricity	Oil
Warm-swelling starch		
Heating of starch	0.23	0.12
Flash drying	0.13	1.87
Fluid bed drying	0.62	1.40
Cold-swelling starch		
heating of starch	0.31	0.12
roller drying	0.53	5.48
other processing machinery	0.15	–
compressed air	0.05	–
lighting	0.03	–
heating, warm water, ventilation	0.08	0.21
others	–	0.63
Total average	0.88	4.3

Chapter 5 references, p. 100.

TABLE 5.9

Streams of mass, enthalpy and exergy for a fluid-bed drier with a capacity of 56 kg water per h

	Mass (kg/h)	Enthalpy (MJ/h)	Exergy (MJ/kg)	Heat (MJ/h)
Streams to drier				
Air, 87°C, $X = 0.009$	6465	717	51	473
Starch, 16°C, 79% DM	455	16	~0	
		733	~51	
Streams from drier				
Air, 66°C, $X = 0.018$	6465	725	28	355
Starch, 66°C, 92% DM	399	47	3	
		772	31	

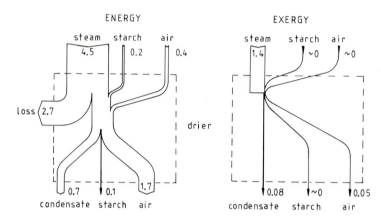

Fig. 5.5. Energy and exergy flowsheets for the roller drier. (Figures represent MJ/kg evaporated water.)

the opposite situation: the high temperature in the flash drying process gives a difference causing high exergy losses. Figures 5.3 and 5.4 demonstrate these differences where considering both heat transfer operations the exergy efficiencies are 5 and 18%, respectively.

For the cold-swelling starch line, where the starch is roller dried, an exergy efficiency in between was measured. However a large portion of the evaporated water was not captured by the ventilation system resulting in a large energy loss but also exergy loss to the surrounding atmosphere as is seen in Table 5.10. There are thus three kinds of irreversibilities taking place during the roller drying, finite temperature heat diffusion, non-equilibrium phase change, heat convection to the surroundings from surfaces not covered with product or dried product. Their relative magnitude is illustrated in Fig. 5.5.

3.3. Production of baked soft cakes

The investigated factory produced 570 000 kg of different soft cakes a year in a gas-fired tunnel oven. The total energy input was 279 GJ electricity, 1073 GJ gasol-propane and 814 GJ oil.

Measurements were carried out for one type of production (round sponge cakes in moulds). The figures given in Table 5.11 are calculated from the following data: the oven capacity, the water loss of the product, the gasol consumption and the temperature of the exhaust air. Energy, mass and water

TABLE 5.10

Streams of mass, enthalpy and exergy for a roller drier with a capacity of 630 kg water per h

	Mass (kg/h)	Enthalpy (MJ/h)	Exergy (MJ/h)	Heat (MJ/h)
Streams to drier				
Steam, 0.76 MPa (168°C)	1035	2861	875	2799
Starch, 43°C, 40% DM	1080	147	4	
Air, 20°C, $X = 0.0099$	6500	277	~ 0	
		3285	879	
Streams from drier				
Starch, 102°C, 965% DM	450	78	8	
Air, 40°C, $X = 0.0485$	6500	1072	30	795
Condensate, 102°C	1035	445	48	378
		1595	86	

TABLE 5.11

Streams of mass, enthalpy and exergy for a gas-fired tunnel oven with a capacity of 84 kg of sponge cakes or 11 kg of evaporated water per h

	Mass (kg/h)	Enthalpy (MJ/kg)	Exergy (MJ/kg)	Heat (MJ/kg)
Streams to oven				
Gasol propane	8	370	352	370
Air, 25°C, $X = 0.0092$	1341	65	~ 0	
Sponge cakes, 25°C	95	7	~ 0	
		442	352	
Streams from oven				
Sponge cakes, 95°C	84	24	2	
Air, 200°C, $X = 0.0272$	1336	371	62	355
Transmission, measured		47	0	
		442	64	

balances were used in the calculations. The transmission loss was calculated from measurements of area, insulation and temperature difference.

The energy demand and especially the exergy consumption was high, see also Table 5.5. In this case, the exergy losses seem to be extremely high, as compared to the driers. It is caused by the high exergy content of the heat source used (gasol-propane). (If the exergy input to the driers had been calculated from the oil used in the boilers, the figures would have looked different.) A reduction would be achieved if the water content in the exhaust air could be raised, which would also result in a decrease of the air flow. In this temperature range the relative humidity of air would be almost unaffected. The limiting factors are the oxygen demand of the burner and amount of heat and water produced at combustion. Another heating method ought to be evaluated.

4. CONCLUSIONS

In the preceding text it is shown how exergy balances and flow sheets are used to detect irreversibilities both regarding their origin and magnitude. However, in the cases evaluated here only two types, were detectable: heat transfer across a finite temperature difference, and non-equilibrium phase

Chapter 5 references, p. 100.

change. Others, such as friction, expansion, chemical reaction, mixing, etc. also existed, of course, but the measurements were not performed and planned accordingly.

In every unit operation investigated, the exergy losses increased with the thermal efficiency of the processes. This is governed by the change of entropy and thus natural, very often a high temperature difference yielding a high energy loss, means a high utilization of supplied energy and a high thermal efficiency. In systems used today, this is of no disadvantage as it reduces the capital costs of the equipment as well as the energy costs. For an efficient re-circulation or cascading of energy, it is, however, of value to improve the reversibility of the process. This could be seen as an optimization between efficient exergy use and capital costs.

6. REFERENCES

Baehr, H.D., 1981. Thermodynamik: Eine Einführung in die Grundlagen und ihre technischen Anwendung. Springer-Verlag, Berlin, 440 pp.

Baloh, T., 1982. Exergie. Technische Universität Berlin, Berlin, 239 pp.

Bejan, A., 1977. The concept of irreversibility in heat exchanger design. J. Heat Transfer, 99: 374–380.

Grassman, P., 1979. Energie und Exergy. Aufspüren der Verluste durch Exergibilanzen. Verfahrenstechnik, 13: 28–31.

Grigull, V. (Editor), 1982. Properties of water and steam in SI-units. Springer-Verlag, Berlin, 192 pp.

London, A.L., 1982. Economics and the second law: an engineering view and methodology. Int. J. Heat Mass Transfer, 25: 743–751.

Mörstedt, S.-E., 1963. Data och diagram. Svenska Bokförlaget, Stockholm, 79 pp.

Trägårdh, C., 1981. Energy and exergy analysis in some food processing industries, Lebensm. Wiss. Technol., 14: 213–217.

Trägårdh, C., Solman, A. and Malmström, T., 1980. In: P. Linko, Y. Mälkkö, J. Olkku and J. Larinkari (Editors), Energy Relations in Some Swedish Food Industries. Food Process Engineering. Vol. 1. Applied Science Publishers, London, pp. 199–206.

Tschubik, I.A. and Maslow, A.M., 1973. Wärmephysikalische Konstanten von Lebensmitteln und Halbfabrikaten. VEB, Fachbuchverlag, Leipzig, 176 pp.

Part II

Measurements of Energy

Chapter 6

Selection of Electric Motors and Electrical Measurements on Motors for Maximum Efficiency

GERALD D. KNUTSON

1. INTRODUCTION

Electric motors use 64% of the electrical energy generated in the U.S.A., according to the Federal Energy Administration. In the past 10 to 20 years, electric motors were primarily chosen on the basis of price, bearing type and frame, and, as a result, cheaper, but less energy-efficient motors were sold. The average standard commercial motor (10 hp and less) built in 1975 has an efficiency rating significantly lower than the average standard motor of Arthur D. Little, Inc. (ADL, 1976). With the increased price of electrical energy it is important to consider energy efficiency along with price, bearing type and frame when buying electrical motors. The following text is intended to help with the selection and proper use of electric motors in order to achieve the lowest possible total cost.

2. EFFICIENCY

Motor efficiency (in percent) is the shaft horsepower divided by the electrical input horsepower multiplied by 100. Efficiency indicates what percentage of energy is being converted into useful work and, therefore, directly affects energy usage. Consider a 5-hp electrical motor with an efficiency of 77% and a 40 000-h life expectancy. At \$0.08 per kW h that motor will use over \$14 000 worth of electricity; a 3% improvement in efficiency to 80% will save \$580 over the life of the motor. Most 5-hp motors can be purchased for much less than \$580 (Knutson, 1981).

2.1. Potential savings through improved efficiency

A simple way of calculating the dollar savings from reduced energy usage due to a higher-efficiency motor is as follows (cf. NEMA, 1977b).

$$S = 0.746 \, P \, CN(100/E_B - 100/E_A)$$

where S are savings (\$); P is the power rating of the specified load expressed in British horsepower (hp); C energy cost (\$ per kW h); N running time (h); E_A efficiency (%) of motor A at specified load (higher-efficiency motor), E_B efficiency (%) of motor B at specified load (lower-efficiency motor).

---

hp, (British) horsepower = 550 lbf ft s^{-2} ≈ 745.7 W.

Chapter 6 references, p. 120.

2.2. Choosing a high-efficiency motor

Manufacturers today are doing their best to improve upon the efficiency of their electric motors. There are several manufacturing techniques which result in improved motor efficiency: first, reduce the air gap between the rotor and the stator by using higher tolerance bearings and more rigid shafts; second, reduce 'copper losses' by increasing the conductivity of the wiring in the motor; third, reduce 'core losses' by selecting better core material, and, finally, reduce 'windage losses' by careful design of the motor's cooling fan. These techniques result in higher manufacturing cost, but can result in reduced energy and total costs.

Choosing a motor that will meet the loading requirements and operate at high efficiency used to be a difficult task; rarely was efficiency listed on a motor's nameplate. In 1978, National Electrical Manufacturers Association (NEMA) adopted a standard nameplate designation called the Efficiency Index for polyphase squirrel-cage integral-horsepower motors with continuous ratings. On the nameplate was the caption Efficiency Index or Eff. Index, followed by a letter which relates to the motor's full-load efficiency (Table 6.1). In 1982, NEMA required listing of the nominal efficiency directly on the nameplate (Fig. 6.1). Other items displayed on a motor's nameplate are listed in Table 6.2.

TABLE 6.1

Efficiency index of polyphase squirrel-cage integral horsepower motors with continuous ratings (ANSI/NEMA, 1978, MG1–12.536)

Efficiency index letter	Nominal efficiency	Minimum efficiency
A	–	95.0
B	95.0	94.1
C	94.1	93.0
D	93.0	91.7
E	91.7	90.2
F	90.2	88.5
G	88.5	86.5
H	86.5	84.0
K	84.0	81.5
L	81.5	78.5
M	78.5	75.5
N	75.5	72.0
P	72.0	68.0
R	68.0	64.0
S	64.0	59.5
T	59.5	55.0
U	55.0	50.5
V	50.5	46.0
W	–	46.0

Minimum efficiency refers to the minimum full-load efficiency that would be expected of a motor with a given index letter; nominal efficiency is the average full-load efficiency of a large population of motors having the same index letter.

Unfortunately, there is a discrepancy between standard techniques on how to measure motor efficiency. The International, British and Japanese standards all yield efficiencies which are higher than the NEMA technique (Garcia and Tuttle, 1983). Care must be taken when comparing motors of different manufacturers to make sure they are using the same standard technique for measuring efficiency.

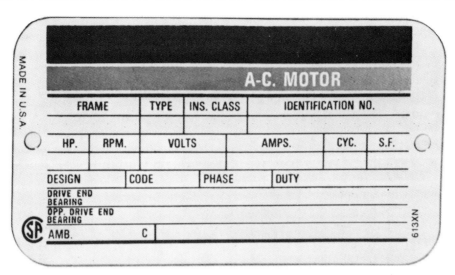

Fig. 6.1. The motor name plate gives motor characteristics. Code designation, service factor, time rating and temperature rise are important considerations in selecting a motor.

TABLE 6.2

Nameplate information (USDA, 1974)

Frame and type. The NEMA designation for frame designation and type.

Horsepower. Horsepower rating of the motor.

Motor code. Designated by a letter indicating the starting current required. The higher the locked-rotor kilovolt-ampere (kVA), the higher the starting current surge.

Cycles, or Hertz. The electrical line voltage frequency at which the motor is designed to be operated in cycles per second (Hz).

Phase. The number of phases on which the motor operates.

Revolutions per minute (RPM). The speed of the motor at full load.

Voltage. The voltage or voltages of operation.

Thermal protection. An indication of thermal protection provided for the motor, if it is provided.

Amps. The rated current in amperes at full load.

Time or duty. Time rating of the motor showing the duty rating as continuous or as a specific period of time the motor can be operated.

Ambient temperature, or temperature rise. The maximum rise of the motor above the ambient air at rated load.

Service factor. The amount of overload that the motor can tolerate on a continuous basis at rated voltage and frequency.

Insulation class. A designation of the insulation system used, primarily for convenience in rewinding.

NEMA design. A letter designation for integral horsepower motors specifying the motor characteristics.

Efficiency index. A letter designation for polyphase squirrel-cage integral horsepower motors which specifies the motor's full load efficiency (see Table 6.1).

In addition, bearing designations are often given on the nameplate for both ends of the shaft for convenience in replacement.

Chapter 6 references, p. 120.

TABLE 6.3

Characteristics and applications of polyphase induction motors (after NEMA, 1977b)

Size	Classification[a]	Starting torque (% rated load torque)	Breakdown torque (% rated load torque)	Starting current (% rated load current)	Slip	Typical applications	Relative efficiency
Integral horsepower	Design B	70–275[b]	175–300[b]	600–700	1–5%	Fans, blowers, centrifugal pumps and compressors,	High
Large	Normal starting torque and normal starting current	60–100	175–200	600–650	0.5–2%	motor-generator sets, etc., where starting torque requirements are relatively low.	
Integral horsepower	Design C	200–250[a]	190–225[a]	600–700	5% Max.	Conveyors, crushers, stirring machines, agitators,	High
Large	High starting torque and normal starting current	150–200	190–200	600–650	0.5–2%	reciprocating pumps and compressors, etc., where starting under load is required.	
Integral horsepower	Design D	275	275	600–700 600–650	5–8% 8–13%	High peak loads with or without flywheels such as	Medium at 5–8% slip; low at 8–13% slip
Large	High starting torque and high slip	250–300	275–325 250–300	500–600 450–550	5–8% 8–13%	punch presses, shears, elevators, extractors, winches, hoists, oil-well pumping and wire-drawing machines.	
Integral horsepower and large	Wound rotor	Any torque up to the breakdown value	175–275[a]	Adjustable (depends on starting torque required)	Adjustable	Where high starting torque with low inrush, frequent starting, or limited speed control are required and where high inertias must be accelerated.	Medium at full speed; lower at reduced speeds

[a] Design A, motor-performance characteristics are similar to those for Design B motors, except that the starting current is higher than the values shown in the table.
[b] Higher values are for motors having lower horsepower ratings.

TABLE 6.4

Alternating-current single-phase fractional-horsepower motors rated 1/20 to 1 hp, 250 V or less (after NEMA, 1977c)

Application	Motor type	Horsepower	Speed (RPM)	Starting torque	Efficiency
Fans					
Direct drive	Permanent split capacitor	1/20–1	1625, 1075, 825	Low	High
	Shaded pole	1/20–1/4	1550, 1050, 800	Low	Low
	Split phase	1/20–1/2	1725, 1140, 850	Low	Medium
Belted	Split phase	1/20–1/2	1725, 1140, 850	Medium	Medium
	Capacitor start–induction run	1/8–3/4	1725, 1140, 850	Medium	Medium
	Capacitor start–capacitor run	1/8–3/4	1725, 1140, 850	Medium	High
Pumps					
Centrifugal	Split phase	1/8–1/2	3450	Low	Medium
	Capacitor start–induction run	1/8–1	3450	Medium	Medium
	Capacitor start–capacitor run	1/8–1	3450	Medium	High
Positive displacement	Capacitor start–induction run	1/8–1	3450, 1725	High	Medium
	Capacitor start–capacitor run	1/8–1	3450, 1725	High	High
Compressors					
Air	Split phase	1/8–1/2	3450, 1725	Low or Medium	Medium
	Capacitor start–induction run	1/8–1	3450, 1725	High	Medium
	Capacitor start–capacitor run	1/8–1	3450, 1725	High	High
Refrigeration	Split phase	1/8–1/2	3450, 1725	Low or Medium	Medium
	Permanent split capacitor	1/8–1	3250, 1625	Low	High
	Capacitor start–induction run	1/8–1	3450, 1725	High	Medium
	Capacitor start–capacitor run	1/8–1	3450, 1725	High	High
Industrial	Capacitor start–induction run	1/8–1	3450, 1725, 1140, 850	High	Medium
	Capacitor start–capacitor run	1/8–1	3450, 1725, 1140, 850	High	High
Farm	Capacitor start–induction run	1/8–3/4	1725	High	Medium
	Capacitor start–capacitor run	1/8–3/4	1725	High	High
Major appliances	Split phase	1/6–1/2	1725, 1140	Medium	Medium
	Capacitor start–induction run	1/6–3/4	1725, 1140	High	Medium
	Capacitor start–capacitor run	1/6–3/4	1725, 1140	High	High
Commercial appliances	Capacitor start–induction run	1/3–3/4	1725	High	Medium
	Capacitor start–capacitor run	1/3–3/4	1725	High	High
Business equipment	Permanent split capacitor	1/20–1/4	3450, 1725	Low	High
	Capacitor start–induction run	1/8–1	3450, 1725	High	Medium
	Capacitor start–capacitor run	1/8–1	3450, 1725	High	High

Chapter 6 references, p. 120.

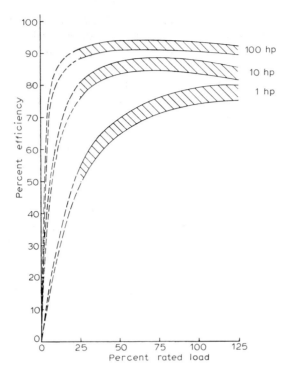

Fig. 6.2. Typical efficiency versus load curves for 1800-RPM three-phase 60-Hz design B squirrel-cage induction motors. The curves indicate a general relationship. Values will vary with individual motor type and manufacturer. After NEMA (1977b).

Tables 6.3 and 6.4 are intended to aid in choosing the motor type which will fit the application and give the highest possible efficiency. Of course, within each motor category there is a range of efficiencies depending on manufacturer and model. That is why knowing the motor's full-load efficiency is essential; if the full-load efficiency is not listed on the nameplate, contact the manufacturer for the information.

2.3. Effect of load on efficiency

To achieve high efficiency it is not enough to buy a motor rated with a high full-load efficiency – the motor must be correctly matched to the job. Figure 6.2 shows that a motor's efficiency is reduced if it is operating at 25% or less of its rated load; this is especially true for smaller horsepower motors. (Correct motor loading is even more critical with respect to power factor which will be discussed later.)

Not only is there increased energy consumption from having an oversized motor, there is the expense of buying more horsepower than is necessary. Remember, an attempt to save money by using a surplus motor which is either oversized or a low-efficiency motor may end up being a money losing proposition. As little as 3% improvement in efficiency can result in savings that will pay for a new motor.

2.4. Starting versus no-load energy consumption (energy consumption and load shedding) (NEMA, 1977b)

"For applications where motors run for an extended period of time at no load between loaded periods, energy may be saved by shutting down the motor and restarting it at the beginning of the next load period. The energy balance is affected by the motor speed, horsepower rating, and external inertia referred to the motor shaft. For a typical 4-pole 15 horsepower Design B induction motor driving a load with inertia equal to the motor inertia, one acceleration will use 7 kilowatt-seconds of energy. No-load losses for this application are 500 watts. The energy consumption for one start is, therefore, equal to the energy consumption for 14 seconds of running at no load. In this example, energy can be saved by shutting down between starts only if the rest period exceeds 14 seconds. When making the decision to shut down or run at no load, other factors must be considered; these include motor type and speed, starting frequency, restriction on inrush current, the extra winding stress imposed by repeated accelerations, and the need for motor cooling (heat dissipation may be greater when the motor is running at no-load than when it is de-energized). Smaller motors with external inertia equal to rotor inertia may be started as frequently as once per minute. With an increase in the motor size and/or connected load inertia, the number of starts must be reduced. For specific applications, the motor manufacturer should be consulted."

"For applications where motors run continuously, load shedding is sometimes used to conserve energy. In this case the apparatus is cycled off and on rather than being run continuously. Again, the energy balance and the motor's thermal capability will be affected by the previously mentioned factors."

2.5. Effect of motor horsepower and speed on efficiency

In general, high-horsepower motors have a potential for higher full-load efficiencies than smaller motors (Fig. 6.2). This results in a potential for energy saving by using a large motor (fully loaded) with power transmitted to several points instead of several smaller motors. However, losses in power transmission devices can quickly eat up those potential savings. Similarly, motors with high synchronous speeds usually have higher full-load efficiencies (Fig. 6.3). However, losses in speed-reducing devices such as pulleys and gears can reduce the potential energy saving to zero or worse.

3. POWER FACTOR

Equally important, in terms of energy usage, to motor efficiency is 'power factor', the fraction of the total current which is effective in producing power. Even though the rest of the current is not effective in producing power, it still must flow through the motor, producing added heat (energy loss). Electrical energy lost as heat per hour (W h/h) is equal to (total current)^2 × resistance ($A^2 \Omega = V A$). This 'ineffective current' either lags or leads the system voltage by 90° and, therefore, a power factor is described as either lagging or leading.

The power factor of a motor or other electrical device is determined almost entirely by the nature of the motor or device, and for the most part is not related to the characteristics of the power-supply system. Most AC motors (except synchronous motors) have a lagging power factor ranging from 0.5 to 0.9 (the ideal power factor is 1.0); synchronous motors can have a power factor ranging from 1.0 to a leading power factor of 0.6, depending on design (see Table 6.5).

3.1. Potential benefits from improving power factor

A normal watt-hour meter shows only the true power delivered to the system, irrespective of power factor; therefore, for those customers billed by a watt-hour meter, overall improvement of the power factor may not reduce the

TABLE 6.5

Power factor of typical AC loads (Electric Machinery Mfg, 1950)

Unity or near-unity power factor		Lagging power factor		Leading power factor	
Load	Approximate power factor	Load	Approximate power factor	Load	Approximate power factor
Incandescent lamps	1.0	Induction motors (at rated load) split-phase below 1 hp	0.55–0.75	Synchronous motors	0.9, 0.8, 0.7, 0.6, etc., leading power factor depending on rated leading power factor for which they are built
Fluorescent lamps (with built-in capacity)	0.95–0.97	split-phase, 1–10 hp capacitor-start,	0.75–0.85		
		capacitor-run motors	0.9–1.0		
Resistor heating apparatus	1.0				
		Polyphase, squirrel cage high speed, 1–10 hp	0.75–0.90		
Synchronous motors (also built for leading) power factor operation	1.0	high speed, 10 hp and larger	0.85–0.92	Synchronous condensers	Nearly zero leading power factor (output practically all leading reactive kVA).
		low speed	0.70–0.85		
Rotary converters	1.0	wound rotor	0.80–0.90		
		Groups of induction motors	0.50–0.85	Capacitors	Zero leading power factor (output practically all leading reactive kVA).
		Welders motor-generator type	0.50–0.60		
		transformer type	0.50–0.70		
		Arc furnaces	0.80–0.90		
		Induction furnaces	0.60–0.70		

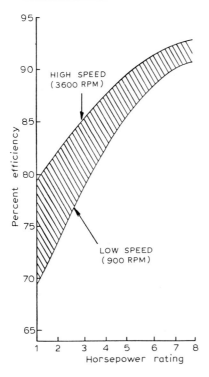

Fig. 6.3. Typical full-load efficiency versus power rating curves for three-phase 60-Hz design B squirrel-cage induction motors. The curves indicate a general relationship. Values will vary with individual motor type and manufacturer. After NEMA (1977b).

utility bill directly because the main losses due to low power factor occur in utility lines and transformers. However, for larger utility customers special rates are usually available for those customers who have a high power factor (a high power factor is usually considered to be near 1.0, with an average of near 0.85) – contact the utility company for details.

Even though direct benefit through lower utility bills may not be available to you, there are other benefits from improving the power factor:

(1) Using motors (or any equipment having a high power factor will cause all electrical equipment between the motor and the utility connection (including the motor, transformers, switches, and wiring) to carry less current, and therefore to run cooler – which could result in longer equipment life. It may also be possible to use equipment having less electrical capacity because of reduced current, thereby reducing capital costs.

(2) Any equipment having a high power factor will cause smaller voltage drops in transmission lines. This is especially important when the equipment is far from the utility connection. A high voltage drop can adversely affect a motor's efficiency, horsepower and life.

(3) Where standby electrical generators are used, a high overall power factor will reduce the necessary capacity of the generator; this reduces capital costs.

(4) High power factor equipment in an air-conditioned building reduces the air-conditioning load, which in turn reduces energy consumption.

(5) High power factor equipment reduces energy consumption and increases the effective generation capacity of the utility, thereby benefiting the utility company and its customers.

Chapter 6 references, p. 120.

3.2. Choosing a high-power factor motor

Since the power factor is usually not listed on the nameplate, contact the manufacturer or calculate by using the following nameplate information:
– single-phase:

$$F = 746\ P/VIE$$

– three-phase:

$$F = \frac{746}{\sqrt{3}}\ P/VIE = 431\ P/VIE$$

where F is the per unit power factor at full load (per unit $F = \%F/100$); P rated horsepower (hp); V rated voltage (V); I rated current (A); E per unit nominal full-load efficiency (per unit $E = \%E/100$). If this information is not available on the motor's nameplate, contact the manufacturer.

When selecting a new motor, purchase of a motor with a high power factor is desirable; however, for large electrical users, selection of a synchronous motor with a leading power factor which balances out other lagging power factor equipment may be desirable. Selection of the proper leading power factor motor should be done by a qualified electrical engineer.

3.3. Effect of load on power factor

Again, just as with efficiency, a motor's power factor is affected by loading. If a motor is operating below its rated capacity the power factor is reduced, which increases the motor's energy consumption (Fig. 6.4).

3.4. Effect of motor horsepower and speed on power factor

High horsepower, high-speed motors generally have higher peak power factors (Figs. 6.4 and 6.5). As pointed out in the discussion on efficiency, one high-horsepower motor used to transmit power to several locations may be less costly and use less energy than several smaller motors operating at lower efficiencies (if losses in transmission devices do not erase the advantage). The same goes for buying high-efficiency high-speed motors and reducing the speed with pulley and gears. The motor and power-transmission system must be analyzed carefully.

3.5. Improving power factor on existing equipment

Most electrical loads have a lagging power factor; this factor can be corrected by balancing with equipment having a leading power factor. Motors with lagging power factors can be corrected by adding capacitors (capacitors have a leading power factor) to each motor or at a central location; or correction can be made by replacing several lagging power factor motors with the proper leading power factor synchronous motors. Power factor correction by adding capacitors should be done only by a qualified electrician and is usually only advisable for large utility customers who can take advantage of a rate reduction for improving their power factor.

The National Electrical Manufacturers Association warns (ANSI/NEMA, 1978, MG 1-14.44): "In no case should power factor improvement capacitors be applied in ratings exceeding the maximum safe value specified by the motor manufacturer. Excessive improvement may cause over excitation resulting in high transient voltages, currents, and torques that can increase safety hazards

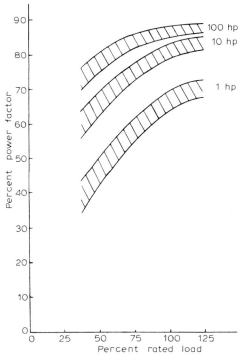

Fig. 6.4. Typical power factor versus load curves for 1800-RPM three-phase 60-Hz design B squirrel-cage induction motors. The curves indicate a general relationship. Values will vary with individual motor type and manufacturer. After NEMA (1977b).

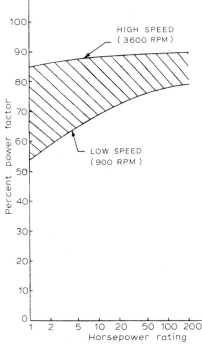

Fig. 6.5. Typical full-load power factor versus power rating curves for three-phase 60-Hz design B squirrel-cage induction motors. The curves indicate a general relationship. Values will vary with individual motor type and manufacturer. After NEMA (1977b).

to personnel and cause possible damage to the motor or to the driven equipment. For additional information on safety considerations in the application of power factor improvement capacitors, see NEMA Publication No. MG2, 'Safety standard for construction and guide for selection, installation and use

Chapter 6 references, p. 120.

of electric motors and generators' (NEMA, 1977a). Also see 'Power factor corrections – motor circuit' under article 460 of the National Electrical Code" (NFPA, 1975).

In equipment which is operating below its rated load or equipment with a variable load, there is a solid state device called a 'power factor controller' which when added to an induction motor improves the power factor to near the motor's full load power factor. This device developed by the National Aeronautics and Space Administration (NASA) senses "the phase lag between the voltage and current. This information is fed to the electronic controller. This circuit forces the motor to run at a constant predetermined optimum power factor, regardless of load or line voltage variations (within the limits of the motor)" (NASA, 1977).

Underloaded motor. The advantages and characteristics of a power factor controller, as described by NASA (1977), are:

The power factor controller applies to induction-type electric motors, the most commonly used type in all major home appliances and motors used by industry. It also applies to single-phase and three-phase motors.

Can be used with most existing motors without modification to the motor.

The device determines the load on the motor by sensing the phase relationship between voltage and current.

When the load is reduced, the controller reduces the applied voltage by means of a solid state switch. This minimizes wasted power.

As the load increases, the power factor controller increases the voltage to that required for optimum operation.

Each percent reduction in power wasted allows a utility to add a like percentage of customer load without increasing capital equipment.

The power factor controller causes the motor to run quieter and cooler. Cooler temperatures extend motor life.

The power factor controller saves on air-conditioning costs.

The power factor controller may reduce the energy costs that large users of motors pay for having a poor power factor.

Payback time for the device can be enhanced by double duty. With modification, it can be used as a means for:
(a) turning the motor on and off;
(b) limiting inrush current in large motors.

4. ELECTRICAL MEASUREMENTS ON ELECTRIC MOTORS

There are two basic measurements used to check electric motors to make sure that they are operating under the conditions for which they were designed: voltage and current. If one knows how voltage and current affect a motor's performance and how to make these measurements, then one has most of the information necessary to find out if a motor is operating at its maximum potential.

Utility companies provide a specified voltage plus and minus a given amount, for instance 115 ± 5 V. It is a good idea to ask the utility what voltage or voltages are supplied to your facility. Knowing the voltage provided is important because each electric motor has a specific voltage (in some cases two voltages) at which it was designed to operate, the voltage (or the two voltages) being listed on the motor's name plate. Operating a motor at voltages other than those for which the motor was designed, can cause the motor to operate inefficiently and damage to the motor is likely. Most motors can tolerate a small deviation from their designed operating voltage (usually $\pm 10\%$);

however, when the voltage is either above or below the desired range, action should be taken. If the supplied voltage is above the acceptable voltage range of the motor, then the motor should be replaced with one that was designed for the voltage provided by the utility company. Low voltage may be caused by an excessive voltage drop in the wiring leading from the utility connection to the motor. Low voltage causes electric motors to draw more current which increases energy consumption and results in excessive heating of the electrical system. An excessive voltage drop can occur when the diameter of the wire between the utility connection and the motor is too small. The diameter of your facility's wiring becomes more critical as the distance from the utility connection to the motor increases. To see if an excessive voltage drop is occurring, measure the voltage at the utility connection and again at the motor when the motor is operating; if the voltage is significantly lower at the motor, then it may be necessary to replace the wiring leading to the motor with wire which is larger in diameter.

Voltage can be measured quite easily with a volt meter or a volt-ohm meter (VOM meter). Several precautions must be followed, however, in order to prevent injury to one's self or to the volt meter. Since an exposed portion of the electrical conductor is necessary to measure voltage, there is a potential danger of electrocution. Do *not* touch any portion of the exposed wire with anything except the probes of the volt meter; even if you believe the voltage is turned off. Make sure that the volt meter is rated at a voltage equal to, or higher than, the voltage which you are measuring, and follow the instructions on the volt meter exactly. It is not necessary to disconnect any of the wiring of the motor. Usually the best place to find exposed electrical conductor is at the motor's switch or at the motor's overload protection device. Follow the instructions on the volt meter. Double check to make sure that the volt meter probes are connected to the proper jacks and that the correct scale for measuring voltage is enabled. Single-phase motors are usually connected to the utility service with three wires – hot (supplied voltage), common and ground; voltage is read by placing one probe on the hot and the other on the common terminal. Three-phase motors are usually connected to the utility service with four wires – three hot (supplied voltage) and one ground; voltages should be read across each of the three possible pairs of hot terminals. On a three-phase motor make sure that all three voltages are within 5% of each other.

Knowing the current (measured in ampere) flowing through a motor is extremely important because it indicates the load on the motor. The 'load' is the amount of horsepower which is being developed by the motor; a fully loaded motor is developing 100% of the horsepower for which it was designed. If the measured current moving through a motor is equal to the current listed on the name plate, then the motor is fully loaded; if it is drawing less current, it is underloaded.

The current drawn by a motor can be measured with a clamp-on ammeter (Fig. 6.6). The current passing through a wire is measured by clipping the ammeter around the wire. The ammeter's instruction manual should be consulted before any readings are attempted. Remember to make sure the scale on the ammeter is high enough to accommodate the expected current. Be careful not to touch any electrically live wires. Only one wire at a time should be measured; an incorrect reading will occur if more than one wire is passed through the clip at one time. It is unnecessary to disconnect any of the motor's wires to measure current with a clamp-on ammeter, and not necessary to have an electrically exposed portion of the wire. On a single-phase motor, current can be read in either the hot or the common wires. Each of the three current-carrying leads of a three-phase motor should be measured; they should each carry approximately the same amount of current.

Chapter 6 references, p. 120.

Fig. 6.6. Clamp-on ammeter.

Load can also be estimated by using an accurate RPM meter. A fully loaded induction motor will run at the RPM listed on its name plate, and a completely unloaded motor will run at synchronous speed. Actually a complete unloaded motor will not run quite at synchronous speed because of the internal load of the motor itself. The speed of a partially loaded motor will be proportional to the difference between the loaded RPM and the synchronous speed, RPM_{syn}. Synchronous speed can be calculated by dividing the number of pairs of poles per phase into the utility frequency in cycles per minute. The formula for calculating load is:

$$\text{percent load} = \frac{RPM_{syn} - RPM_{actual}}{RPM_{syn} - RPM_{full}} \times 100\%$$

where

$$RPM_{syn} = \frac{60 \text{ Hz}}{\text{number of pairs of poles per phase}}$$

RPM_{full}, fully-loaded RPM, is taken from the motor nameplate; and RPM_{actual}, the loaded RPM, is measured with an accurate RPM meter. An example of a percent load calculation is as follows: a single-phase induction motor operating under a 60-Hz utility, having a fully-loaded RPM of 1725 listed on the nameplate, four poles (i.e., two pairs of poles) and a measured RPM when in use of 1750 revolutions per minute will have a synchronous speed of 1800 revolutions per minute and a percent load of 67%.

In addition to voltage and current measuring devices there are other devices that can be useful for checking motor performance. A watt-hour meter can be used to check the energy consumption of an individual motor. Utility companies commonly use watt-hour meters to measure the energy consumption of its customers. A watt-hour meter can also be used to measure the power consumption of the device (or devices) connected to it. With a stop watch (or watch which reads accurate to seconds) measure the time required for the meter disc to make several revolutions. Kilowatts can be calculated using the following formula:

$$\text{kilowatts} = 3.6 \, MK \, \frac{\text{number of disc revolutions}}{\text{time (s) for the revolutions}}$$

TABLE 6.6

Common electric formulae (after ANSI/NEMA, 1978)

Quantity	Single-phase	Three-phase	
Volt-amperes (VA)	VI	$\sqrt{3}\, VI$	$1.73\, VI$
Kilovolt-amperes (kVA)	$\dfrac{VI}{1000}$	$\dfrac{\sqrt{3}\, VI}{1000}$	$\dfrac{1.73\, VI}{1000}$
Watts (W)	VIF	$\sqrt{3}\, VIF$	$1.73\, VIF$
Kilowatts (kW)	$\dfrac{VIF}{1000}$	$\dfrac{\sqrt{3}\, VIF}{1000}$	$\dfrac{1.73\, VIF}{1000}$
Reactive volt-amperes (VAR)	$VI\sqrt{1-(F)^2}$	$\sqrt{3}\, VI\sqrt{1-(F)^2}$	$1.73\, VI\sqrt{1-(F)^2}$
Reactive kilovolt-amperes (kVAR)	$\dfrac{VI\sqrt{1-(F)^2}}{1000}$	$\dfrac{\sqrt{3}\, VI\sqrt{1-(F)^2}}{1000}$	$\dfrac{1.73\, VI\sqrt{1-(F)^2}}{1000}$

where K is the disc constant, usually printed on the face of the meter; and M a multiplier, the ratio of current transformers used to rating of meter. This number is usually 1.0; check with the utility company to make sure.

With the kilowatts calculated from the watt-hour meter and an accurate voltage and current measurement, the power factor can be calculated using one of the following formulae:
– single-phase:

$$F = \frac{\text{kilowatts from watt-hour meter}}{VI}$$

– three-phase:

$$F = \frac{\text{kilowatts from watt-hour meter}}{\sqrt{3}\ VI} = \frac{\text{kilowatts from watt-hour meter}}{1.73\ VI}$$

Remember this is the power factor for the load present on the motor and not necessarily the full-load power factor (unless the motor is fully loaded). However, watts can be calculated from the voltage and current measurements if the power factor is known (see Table 6.6 which includes formulae for watts along with other formulae relating to electric motors).

Power factor meters are also available to measure a motor's power factor. In addition, they often measure voltage and current. There are current meters which record the current over time on a strip chart; these meters are useful when the load on a motor changes periodically (as with air compressors). There are also meters called either 'TOU meters' (time of use) or 'energy monitors' available which record the energy consumption and the maximum kilowatt demand for different periods of the day; these are useful for those who are billed under a utility rate in which a penalty is charged to those who use electrical energy during the peak energy consumption periods of the day.

5. OTHER IMPORTANT FACTORS

In addition to energy considerations there are many other specifications which must be satisfied. The load requirements of each job must fit the capabilities of the motor. For instance, each type of motor has its own starting and running torque characteristics and must be equal to the task required by it. Starting current characteristics also vary with motor type and are important in cases of loads with high starting torque requirements, particularly where

Chapter 6 references, p. 120.

TABLE 6.7

Definitions (after ANSI/NEMA, 1978)

Explosion-proof machine (MG 1-1.26). An explosion-proof machine is a totally-enclosed machine whose enclosure is designed and constructed to withstand an explosion of a specified gas or vapor which may occur within it to prevent the ignition of the specified gas or vapor surrounding the machine by sparks, flashes or explosions of the specified gas or vapor which may occur within the machine casing.

Dust-ignition-proof machine (MG 1-1.26). A dust-ignition-proof machine is a totally-enclosed machine whose enclosure is designed and constructed in a manner which will exclude ignitable amounts of dust or amounts which might affect performance or rating, and which will not permit arcs, sparks, or heat otherwise generated or liberated inside of the enclosure to cause ignition or exterior accumulations or atmospheric suspensions of a specific dust on or in the vicinity of the enclosure.

Water-proof machine (MG 1-1.26). A water-proof machine is a totally-enclosed machine so constructed that it will exclude water applied in the form of a stream from a hose, except that leakage may occur around the shaft provided it is prevented from entering the oil reservoir and provision is made for automatically draining the machine. The means for automatic draining may be a check valve or a tapped hole at the lowest part of the frame which will serve for application of a drain pipe.

Mg 1-1.41, Efficiency. The efficiency of a motor or generator is the ratio of its useful power output to its total power input and is usually expressed as a percentage.

MG 1-1.42, Power factor. The power factor of an alternating-current motor or generator is the ratio of the kilowatt input (or output) to the kVA input (or output) and is usually expressed as a percentage.

MG 1-1.43, Service factor–alternating-current motors. The service factor of an alternating-current motor is a multiplier which, when applied to the rated horsepower, indicates a permissible horsepower loading which may be carried under the conditions specified for the service factor (see MG 1-14.35.).

MG 1-1.46, Full-load torque. The full-load torque of a motor is the torque necessary to produce its rated horsepower at full-load speed. In pounds at a 1-foot radius, it is equal to the horsepower times 5252 divided by the full-load speed (in RPM).

MG 1-1.47, Locked-rotor torque (static torque). The locked-rotor torque of a motor is the minimum torque which it will develop at rest for all angular positions of the rotor, with rated voltage applied at rated frequency.

MG 1-1.48, Pull-up torque. The pull-up torque of an alternating-current motor is the minimum torque developed by the motor during the period of acceleration from rest to the speed at which breakdown torque occurs. For motors which do not have a definite breakdown torque, the pull-up torque is the minimum torque developed up to rated speed.

MG 1-1.49, Breakdown torque. The breakdown torque of a motor is the maximum torque which it will develop with rated voltage applied at rated frequency, without an abrupt drop in speed.

MG 1-1.50, Pull-out torque. The pull-out torque of a synchronous motor is the maximum sustained torque which the motor will develop at synchronous speed with rated voltage applied at rated frequency and with normal excitation.

MG 1-1.51, Pull-in torque. The pull-in torque of a synchronous motor is the maximum constant torque under which the motor will pull its connected inertia load into synchronism, at rated voltage and frequency, when its field excitation is applied.

MG 1-1.52, Locked-rotor current. The locked-rotor current of a motor is the steady-state current taken from the line with the rotor locked and with rated voltage (and rated frequency in the case of alternating-current motors) applied to the motor.

MG 1-1.54, Ambient temperature. Ambient temperature is the temperature of the surrounding cooling medium, such as the gas (including air) or the liquid, which comes into contact with the heated parts of the apparatus.

MG 1-1.56, Starting capacitance for a capacitor motor. The starting capacitance for a capacitor motor is the total effective capacitance in series with the starting winding under locked-rotor conditions.

current-carrying capacities of lines and/or transformers are limited. Before any motor is purchased ask your dealer to check if it is the correct type of motor for the job.

The environment in which the motor must operate may necessitate a special type of motor enclosure. If the motor is going to operate in a dusty location, the motor may be required to be dust-ignition proof, or if the motor is operating in a wet location it may be necessary to be water-proof. A hot environment may necessitate a motor built for extreme temperatures. There are many other considerations necessary when buying an electric motor; Table 6.7 provides some of the NEMA definitions used in motor specifications which are useful when considering the purchase of a motor.

Once a motor is in place, it is important to follow a simple maintenance routine in order to extend the motor's life and to keep the motor operating at its peak efficiency. Some of the important items to check are as follows:

Do not allow dust or debris to build up on any motor.

Lubricate all bearings in the drive train including motor bearings per manufacturer's specifications.

Keep all power transmitting belts in proper tension and alignment.

Make sure adequate voltage is being provided. This is especially necessary after new electrical equipment has been installed on the same electrical circuit.

Safety note. The nip points (also called 'pinch' or 'mesh' points) on all driven gears, belts, chains, sheaves, pully sprockets, idlers, and rollers should be totally guarded. This includes shafts which protrude more than half their diameter from bearings.

6. CONCLUSIONS

When purchasing a new motor, select for a high efficiency and high power factor.

Make sure the horsepower required is closely matched to the motor's horsepower. (Fully load the motor.)

Consider the combined efficiency of the drive train and the motor to make sure the best overall efficiency is attained.

Large electrical users should contact their utility company to find the financial benefits of power factor improvements.

Check all motor nameplates to find full load efficiency and full load power factor. Contact the motor manufacturer if the information is not available on the nameplate. A new higher efficiency motor could pay for itself.

Have motors checked to make sure they are fully loaded. An underloaded motor replaced with a smaller more fully loaded motor may save you money.

Make sure all electrical codes are followed.

7. ACKNOWLEDGEMENTS

I would like to acknowledge Professor Bill Chancellor, of the Agricultural Engineering Department, University of California, Davis, CA, and Robert G. Curley, P.E., Extension Agricultural Engineer, Cooperative Extension, University of California, Davis, CA, for their help and support and the National Electrical Manufacturers Association for the permission to quote material and to reproduce tables and figures of their Standards Publications © 1977, 1978 NEMA. Table 6.5 is reproduced by permission of Electric Machinery, Power Systems Group, McGraw-Edison Company.

Chapter 6 references, p. 120.

8. REFERENCES

ADL (Arthur D. Little, Inc.), 1976. Energy efficiency and electric motors. FEA/D-76/381, Washington, DC, 189 pp.

ANSI/NEMA, 1978. Motors and generators. Stand. Publ. MG 1-1978, National Electrical Manufacturers Association, Washington, DC.

Electric Machinery Mfg, 1950. The ABC of Power, E.M. Synchronizer, 200 SYN 50, Electric Machinery Mgf, Power Systems Group, Minneapolis, MN, 22pp.

Garcia, A. and Tuttle, W.E., 1983. Specifications and selection of electric motors. Pap. MCR-83-124, American Society of Agricultural Engineers, St. Joseph, MI, 15 pp.

Knutson, G., Curley, R. and Chancellor, B., 1981. Selecting electric motors for maximum efficiency. Leafl. 21240, Division of Agricultural Sciences, University of California, Davis, CA, 18 pp.

NASA, 1977. Power factor controller. Brief MFS-23280, Marshall Space Flight Center, National Aeronautics and Space Administration, AL, 28 pp.

NEMA, 1977a. Motors and generators. Stand. Publ. MG 2-1977, National Electrical Manufacturers Association, Washington, DC.

NEMA, 1977b. Energy management guide for selection and use of polyphase motors. Stand. Publ. MG 10-1977, National Electrical Manufacturers Association, Washington, DC.

NEMA, 1977c. Energy management guide for selection and use of single-phase motors. Stand. Publ. MG 11-1977, National Electrical Manufacturers Association, Washington, DC.

NFPA, 1975. National Electrical Code. Stand. Publ. NFPA 70-1975, National Fire Protection Association, Boston, MA.

USDA, 1974. Selecting and using electric motors. Farmers Bull. 21240, U.S. Department of Energy Washington, DC, 56 pp.

Chapter 7

Measurement of Steam Flow

R. PAUL SINGH

1. INTRODUCTION

Steam flow measurements are an important part of energy accounting studies. This chapter is intended to provide a method useful in measurement of steam flows using an orifice plate and pitot-tube type sensors. The description involves information on installation of orifice meters in steam pipes. In addition, mathematical expressions are given that allow conversion of measured parameters to steam flow. A sample calculation illustrates the use of charts and tables for evaluating various parameters. The user is encouraged to consult the references for derivation of the expressions and for additional information on actual physical parameters for installing orifice meters in situations different from those discussed.

2. ORIFICE METERS

The orifice meter is essentially a flow-restricting device. When inserted into a conduit or pipe, it produces a pressure drop which varies with velocity and density of the fluid. The following discussion is presented for a flat plate square-edged orifice, a commonly used orifice plate in monitoring steam flow.

2.1. Basic relationships

In Fig. 7.1, a schematic of orifice plate installation into a pipe is shown. The following expressions are derived for calculating steam flow using an orifice plate installed into a pipe.

In the International System of Units (SI), a mathematical equality of physical quantities can be written:

$$W = C_f (D_2)^2 \alpha K Y_1 \sqrt{\varrho_1 h_w} \tag{1}$$

where W is the mass rate of steam flow through the pipe section (kg/s), D_2 orifice diameter at 16°C (mm), α metal thermal expansion factor (dimensionless), K orifice discharge coefficient (dimensionless), Y_1 expansion factor based on absolute static pressure at upstream tap (dimensionless) – see equation (10), ϱ_1 density of fluid flowing through orifice, upstream (kg/m^3), and h_w differential pressure across orifice (kPa); C_f is a dimensionless conversion factor:

Reference to a company or product name does not imply approval or recommendation of the product to the exclusion of others that may be suitable.

Chapter 7 references, p. 133.

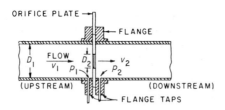

Fig. 7.1. A schematic of orifice meter installation.

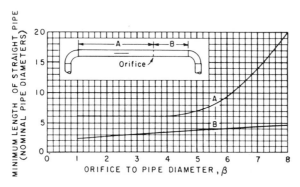

Fig. 7.2. Minimum length of straight pipe (times the value of nominal pipe diameter) for orifice preceded by a single elbow. A, upstream length; B, downstream length. (Adapted from Spink, 1958.)

35.11×10^{-6}, or 1.11 when diameters and pressures are expressed in basic units, m and Pa, respectively.

In the British Imperial System, equation (1) can be used for calculation of the numerical values of quantities. Then W is expressed in lb/h, D_2 in inch, ϱ_1 in lb/ft^3, and h_w in inches of water at 60°F; $C_f = 359.1$.

2.2. Location of orifice plate

In selecting a location for the orifice plate the following criteria should be followed:

(1) Uniform flow is essential to avoid erroneous measurements; surges and pulsations should be avoided if possible.

(2) The orifice plate should not be installed for pipes with diameters smaller than 50.8 mm (2 in). Individual calibration is necessary if pipe sizes are smaller than 50.8 mm (2 in).

(3) When an orifice plate is installed to measure wet stream flowing in a horizontal pipe, drain holes in the orifice plate near the bottom of the line should be provided.

(4) Maximum available length of straight pipe, both upstream and downstream from the orifice, should be selected. Sprenkle (1945) has given recommendations on minimum requirements for various piping arrangements both on the inlet and outlet sides of the orifice. Figure 7.2 shows the recommended orifice location when single fittings are present in the pipe. These straight pipe length requirements increase if a control valve, regulator, stop check valve or partly throttled gate valve closely follows the orifice. When these fittings are present, the length of the straight pipe section for the downstream should be 5 or 6 diameters instead of the usual 2 to 4 diameters.

2.3. Pressure taps

The three common types of pressure taps are flange taps, vena contracta taps and pipe taps. For flange taps the center of the upstream tap is exactly 25.4 mm

(1 in) from the upstream face of the plate; the center of the downstream tap is placed 25.4 mm (1 in) from the downstream face (see Fig. 7.1). The center of the upstream tap for vena contracta taps is located one internal pipe diameter from the upstream face of the plate, and the center of the downstream tap is located at the point of minimum pressure (Bean, 1971). For pipe taps the upstream tap is placed $2\frac{1}{2}$ nominal pipe diameters from the upstream face of the plate, and the center of downstream tap is placed 8 nominal pipe diameters from the downstream face of the plate.

2.4. Installation of orifice plates

The following rules must be observed in installing orifice plates:
(1) The sharp edge of the orifice must face upstream and the beveled edge downstream.
(2) For steam flow in horizontal pipes, the orifice tab or handle must be in the upright position to ensure that the drain hole (when present) is in the bottom-most location.
(3) The plate must not be shellacked.
(4) Both plate and gaskets must be placed concentric to the pipe; i.e., their centers are at the center of the pipe.
(5) Gaskets must not be wide enough to extend inside the inner periphery of the pipe. If they are too wide, metering errors may be caused and drain holes (if present) may be closed.
(6) Flange bolts must be pulled up evenly to prevent springing or buckling of the plate.

2.5. Measurements

The following measurements are required when orifice meters are used to measure steam flow.

Static pressure. The static pressure should be measured either upstream or downstream from the orifice plate.

Temperature. Using an appropriate sensor, temperature of the steam in the pipe should be determined accurately (within $\pm 1°C$) since it is used in calculating the physical properties.

Differential pressure. The differential pressure should be measured by a mercury manometer or a differential pressure cell.

Properties. Physical properties, such as viscosity μ, specific heat ratio k, and specific volume may be obtained from a handbook (Perry and Chilton, 1973). Steam quality is measured experimentally. Density is obtained from the following relationship:

$$\varrho_2 = \frac{1}{\text{(steam quality) (specific volume)}} \tag{2}$$

2.6. Calculations for steam flow rate

2.6.1. Orifice discharge coefficient
The orifice discharge coefficient K is obtained from empirical relationships based on experiments conducted by the American Gas Association, the American Society of Mechanical Engineers and the National Bureau of Standards

Chapter 7 references, p. 133.

TABLE 7.1

Values of A for orifices with flange taps

Diameter ratio	Nominal pipe diameter				
	50.8 mm (2 in)	76.2 mm (3 in)	101.6 mm (4 in)	152.4 mm (6 in)	203.2 mm (8 in)
0.100	160	220	270	380	480
0.125	180	240	300	420	520
0.150	200	260	320	440	550
0.175	210	270	330	450	550
0.200	220	280	340	450	550
0.225	220	290	340	450	540
0.250	230	290	340	440	530
0.275	240	300	350	440	520
0.300	250	300	350	440	510
0.325	260	310	360	450	520
0.350	270	330	380	460	530
0.375	290	350	400	490	560
0.400	310	370	430	520	600
0.425	330	400	460	570	660
0.450	360	450	510	640	750
0.475	400	490	570	720	850
0.500	440	550	610	820	970
0.525	480	610	720	930	1100
0.550	540	690	810	1100	1300
0.575	600	770	920	1200	1500
0.600	660	860	1000	1400	1700
0.610	690	900	1100	1400	1800
0.620	720	940	1100	1500	1900
0.630	740	980	1200	1600	2000
0.640	770	1000	1200	1700	2100
0.650	810	1100	1300	1800	2200
0.660	830	1100	1300	1800	2300
0.670	870	1200	1400	1900	2400
0.680	900	1200	1500	2000	2500
0.690	930	1200	1500	2100	2600
0.700	970	1300	1600	2200	2700
0.710	1000	1300	1700	2300	2800
0.720	1000	1400	1700	2400	3000
0.730	1100	1400	1800	2500	3100
0.740	1100	1500	1800	2600	3200
0.750	1100	1600	1900	2700	3300

When interpolating between values of A in this table, it is only necessary to read A correct to two significant figures. (From Stearns et al., 1951.)

(Stearns et al., 1951). The K-value is influenced by pipe size, diameter ratio β and Reynolds Number N_{Re}.

The K-value may be obtained using the following procedure for orifice plate with flange taps (Stearns et al., 1951).

Equation (1) can be expressed as:

$$W = N_1 K \qquad\qquad (3)$$

where N_1 is the product of all known factors.

Based on empirical data, a 'specific equation' is suggested for a particular value of K:

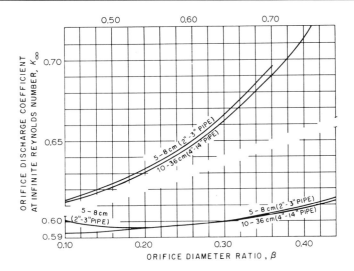

Fig. 7.3. Orifice discharge coefficient at infinite Reynolds Number for flange taps. (Adapted from Stearns et al., 1951.)

$$K = K_\infty (1 + A/N_{Re}) \qquad (4)$$

where K_∞ is the orifice discharge coefficient for infinite Reynolds Number (dimensionless), and A a variable number determined from Table 7.1 (dimensionless).

Equation (3) may be rewritten as:

$$W = N_1 K_\infty (1 + A/N_{Re}) \qquad (5)$$

However:

$$N_{Re} = \frac{4W}{\pi D_2 \mu} \qquad (6)$$

$$= N_2 K_\infty (1 + A/N_{Re}) \qquad (7)$$

where N_2 is again the product of known factors such that:

$$N_2 = \frac{4N_1}{\pi D_2 \mu} \qquad (8)$$

The parameter K_∞ is obtained from Fig. 7.3, as a function of β and pipe size. The following equation (9) is used to obtain a preliminary value of Reynolds Number, N'_{Re}:

$$N'_{Re} = N_3 K_\infty \qquad (9)$$

From Table 7.1, a value of A is selected on the basis of pipe diameter and β. The factor $(1 + A/N_{Re})$ is obtained from Fig. 7.4 using the values of A and N'_{Re}.

The actual flow rate and corresponding Reynolds Number are then calculated by substituting $(1 + A/N_{Re})$ in equations (5) and (7).

Typically, the value of K does not vary significantly with flow rate except for Reynolds Number $\approx 10^4$ and if the orifice diameter or the basic nature of fluid is not changed. Thus, only one computation is necessary.

2.6.2. Expansion factor

The expansion factor Y_1 accounts for density changes that occur due to change in velocity and pressure as steam flows through the orifice.

Empirical relationships have been developed for the determination of Y_1. For orifice installation with flange taps, the following equation is used (Stearns et al., 1951):

Chapter 7 references, p. 133.

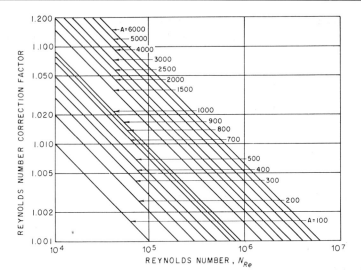

Fig. 7.4. Correction factor $(1 + A/N_{Re})$ for Reynolds Number. (Adapted from Stearns et al., 1951.)

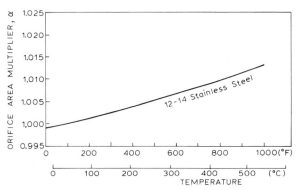

Fig. 7.5. Correction for thermal expansion of the orifice at different temperatures. (Adapted from Stearns et al., 1951.)

$$Y_1 = 1 - (0.41 + 0.35\beta^4)\frac{\Delta P}{kP_1} \tag{10}$$

where ΔP is the differential pressure across the orifice, $P_1 - P_2$ (kPa, psi) and P_1 the absolute static pressure at upstream pressure tap (kPa, psia).

2.6.3. Specific heat ratio

For steam, the specific heat ratio k varies almost linearly from 1.28 to 1.30, for a temperature rise from 95 to 260°C (200 to 500°F) (Bean, 1971).

2.6.4. Thermal expansion of the orifice

The metal thermal expansion factor α for the orifice plate can be determined from Fig. 7.5. This chart is for 12–14 Cr stainless-steel orifice plate. By knowing the steam temperature, the multiplier α can be obtained directly from the figure. For orifice plates made of other materials, appropriate figures should be consulted for the value of α.

2.7. Sample calculations (SI)

For steam flow measurements, the following parameters need to be measured: differential pressure, h_w (kPa); upstream pressure, P_1 (kPa); pipe diameter, D_1 (m); orifice diameter, D_2 (m); and steam quality (%).

The following parameters were measured for an orifice mounted with flange taps: h_w = 44 kPa; P_1 = 687 kPa; D_1 = 50.8 mm; D_2 = 30.5 mm; steam quality = 90%.

Calculate the steam flow.

Solution. From steam tables, at 687 kPa:

specific volume = 0.278 m³/kg, thus using equation (2):

$$\varrho = \frac{1}{0.9 \times 0.278 \text{ m}^3/\text{kg}} = 4 \text{ kg/m}^3$$

and

$$\mu = 0.01542 \text{ cP} = 1.542 \times 10^{-5} \text{ Pa s}$$

From Fig. 7.5, at 164.2°C:

$$\alpha = 1.003$$

From Section 2.6.3, also at 164.2°C:

$$k = 1.295$$

Further:

$$\beta = \frac{D_2}{D_1} = 0.6$$

Using equation (10):

$$Y_1 = 1 - (0.41 + 0.35 \times 0.6^4) \frac{44}{1.295 \times 687} = 0.978$$

From equation (1) and with

$$\varrho h_w = \left(4 \frac{\text{kg}}{\text{m}^3}\right)\left(44 \times 10^3 \frac{\text{kg m/s}^2}{\text{m}^2}\right) = 4 \times 44 \times 10^3 \frac{\text{kg}^2/\text{s}^2}{\text{m}^4}$$

follows:

$$W = 1.11(0.0305 \text{ m})^2 1.003K \times 0.978 \sqrt{4 \times 44 \times 10^3} \frac{\text{kg/s}}{\text{m}^2}$$

$$= 0.425K \text{ kg/s}$$

From Fig. 7.3:

$$K_\infty = 0.65$$

Using equation (8):

$$N'_{Re} = \frac{4 \times (0.425) \times 0.65}{\pi(0.0305) \times (1.542 \times 10^{-5})} = 7.48 \times 10^5$$

From Table 7.1:

$$A = 660$$

From Fig. 7.4, using A = 660 and N'_{Re} = 7.48 × 10⁵:

$$(1 + A/N_{Re}) \approx 1.00$$

Therefore:

$$K = 0.65 \times 1.0 = 0.65$$

and

$$W = 0.425 \times 0.65 \text{ kg/s} = 0.28 \text{ kg/s}$$

Chapter 7 references, p. 133.

2.8. Sample calculations (British Imperial System)

For steam flow measurements, the following parameters need to be measured: differential pressure, h_w (inches of water); upstream pressure, P_1 (psia); pipe diameter, D_1 (in); orifice diameter, D_2 (in); and steam quality (%).

The following parameters were measured for an orifice mounted with flange taps: $h_w = 175$ inches of water; $P_1 = 99.7$ psia; $D_1 = 2''$; $D_2 = 1.2''$; steam quality = 90%.

Calculate the steam flow.

Solution. From steam tables, at 99.7 psia:

specific volume = 4.451 ft^3/lb, thus using equation (2):

$$\varrho = \frac{1}{0.9 \times 4.451} = 0.2496 \text{ lb/ft}^3$$

and

$$\mu = 1.036 \times 10^{-3} \text{ lb/(ft s)}$$

From Fig. 7.5, at 327.6°F:

$$\alpha = 1.003$$

From Section 2.6.3, also at 327.6°F:

$$k = 1.295$$

Further:

$$\beta = \frac{D_2}{D_1} = 0.6$$

Using equation (10):

$$Y_1 = 1 - (0.41 + 0.35 \times 0.6^4) \frac{175 \times 3.613 \times 10^{-2}}{1.295 \times 99.7} = 0.978$$

From equation (1)

$$W = 359.1(1.2)^2 1.003 K \times 0.978 \sqrt{0.2496 \times 175}$$

$$= 3352.4 K$$

From Fig. 7.3:

$$K_\infty = 0.65$$

Using equation (8):

$$N'_{Re} = \frac{4 \times 3352.4 \times 0.65 \times 12}{\pi \times 1.2 \times 1.036 \times 10^{-5} \times 3600} = 7.44 \times 10^5$$

From Table 7.1:

$$A = 660$$

From Fig. 7.4, using $A = 660$ and $N'_{Re} = 7.44 \times 10^5$

$$(1 + A/N_{Re}) \approx 1.00$$

Therefore:

$$K = 0.65 \times 1.0 = 0.65$$

and

$$W = 3352.4 \times 0.65 = 2179 \text{ lb/h}$$

NOMENCLATURE

A	a variable number defined by (4)
A_1	inside pipe cross-sectional area at upstream pressure tap (ft^2)
A_2	orifice area at flow temperature (ft^2)
C_A	coefficient for Accutube (dimensionless)
C_D	coefficient of discharge (dimensionless)
C_f	dimensionless conversion factor, 1.11 (in basic SI units), 359.1 (in British Imperial units)
C_g	coefficient for Accutube sensor (dimensionless)
D_1	inside pipe diameter at upstream pressure tap (m, in)
D_2	orifice diameter at 16°C (m, in)
g	acceleration due to gravity (ft/s^2)
Δh	differential pressure across the orifice (ft of flowing fluid at upstream temperature and pressure)
H	enthalpy (Btu/lb)
h_w	differential pressure across orifice (Pa, inH$_2$O)
k	ratio of specific heat of steam at constant pressure to its specific heat at constant volume (dimensionless)
K	orifice discharge coefficient (dimensionless)
K_A	Annubar flow coefficient (dimensionless)
K_∞	orifice discharge coefficient at infinite Reynolds Number (dimensionless)
L	latent heat (Btu/lb)
m	weight (lb)
N_1	constant defined in (3)
N_2	constant defined in (7)
N_3	constant defined in (9)
N_{Re}	Reynolds Number (dimensionless)
N'_{Re}	a preliminary estimate of the Reynolds Number
P_1	absolute static pressure at upstream pressure tap (Pa, psi)
ΔP	pressure drop across orifice, $P_1 - P_2$ (Pa, psi)
S	sensible heat (Btu/lb)
V	velocity (ft/s)
V_f	velocity distribution factor (dimensionless)
W	mass rate of flow through pipe section (kg/s, lb/h)
Y_1	expansion factor (ϱ_2/ϱ_1) based on absolute static pressure at upstream pressure tap (dimensionless)
α	area multiplier (dimensionless)
ϱ_1	density of fluid flowing through orifice, upstream (kg/m^3, lb/ft^3)
ϱ_2	density of fluid flowing through orifice (lb/ft^3)
μ	viscosity of steam (Pa s, lb/(ft s))
β	orifice diameter ratio, D_2/D_1 (dimensionless)

3. PITOT-TUBE

Pitot-tubes are extensively used to measure velocity of a flowing fluid at a desired location in a pipe. Measurement involves two ports, one directly in the line of flow (for impact pressure) and the other at 90° from the first opening (for static pressure). The velocity is obtained from the differential pressure measured across the two sampling ports. Procedures are available to traverse the cross-sectional area of the pipe to obtain an average velocity. The pitot-tube causes virtually no pressure drop in the flowing stream. However, the accuracy is rather low, $\pm$ (0.5–5%). The following two commercial flow-sensing devices, based on the pitot-tube principle, have found wide acceptance for measuring steam flow.

3.1. Annubar® tubes

Annubar® sensors consist of two probes inserted in the pipe as shown in Fig. 7.6. One of the tubes faces the flow to sense velocity pressure. The second

Chapter 7 references, p. 133.

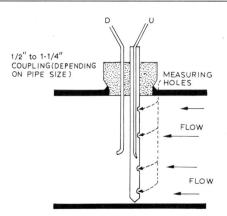

Fig. 7.6. Use of Annubar sensor to measure steam flow. D, downstream or low-pressure side. U, upstream of high-pressure side: inner tube in an interpolating element that averages the flow rates across the pipe.

probe faces downstream and allows determination of static pressure. The first probe has openings at four locations that allow sensing average pressure from four different regions in the cross-sectional area. An equalizing element provides average of the four pressures. The device has an accuracy of ± 0.5 to 1.5% over a wide range of pipe sizes. A major advantage of the Annubar is the ease of installation. Using 'hot taps' it can be installed in a line that may be under pressure.

3.1.1. Calculation procedure
In the British Imperial System, the equation used for calculating mass rate of flow is the following:

$$W = 8211.4 K_A A_1 Y_1 \sqrt{2g\varrho_2 \Delta P} \tag{11}$$

where K_A is the Annubar flow coefficient (dimensionless) obtained from Table 7.2. The parameter Y_1 is calculated as shown in Section 2.6.2.

3.2. Accutube®

Figure 7.7 shows an Accutube® installation in a pipe. In contrast to Annubar, this sensor contains only one sensing tube. Similar to Annubar

TABLE 7.2

Flow coefficient K_A for annubar

Sensor type 61		Sensor type 73		Sensor type 75/76	
Line size inner diameter (in)	K_A	Line size inner diameter (in)	K_A	Line size inner diameter (in)	K_A
1	0.915	2	0.678	6	0.592
$1\frac{1}{4}$	0.930	$2\frac{1}{2}$	0.711	8	0.621
$1\frac{1}{2}$	0.945	3	0.726	10	0.657
		$3\frac{1}{2}$	0.743	12	0.690
		4	0.764		
		5	0.740		

(From Dietrich Standard Corp., Boulder, CO.)

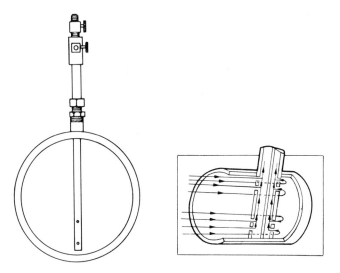

Fig. 7.7. An Accutube sensor for measuring steam flow.

TABLE 7.3

Values of C_g for various pipe sizes

Pipe size (in)	C_g	Pipe size (in)	C_g	Pipe size (in)	C_g
$\frac{1}{2}$[a]	0.507	2	0.763	10	0.828
$\frac{1}{2}$	0.453	$2\frac{1}{2}$	0.789	12	0.838
$\frac{3}{4}$[a]	0.582	3	0.794	14	0.846
$\frac{3}{4}$	0.510	4	0.796	16	0.850
1	0.642	5	0.804	18	0.862
$1\frac{1}{4}$	0.710	6	0.810	20	0.874
$1\frac{1}{2}$	0.748	8	0.814	24	0.882

[a]Marked values of C_g are for Bronze Cast Inline Sensors, Series 129; all other values are for Schedule 40 Pipe. (From Meriam Instrument, Cleveland, OH.)

elements, Accutubes are easy to install. A coupling is added to the pipe and the sensor can be introduced into a pressurized system without shutting down. The pressure differential measured across the ports is used in the following equation (in British Imperial units) to calculate steam flow:

$$W = 360.05 C_A D_i^2 \sqrt{\varrho h_w} \qquad (12)$$

where constant

$$C_A = C_g V_f. \qquad (13)$$

The values of C_g are given in Table 7.3. The parameter V_f, velocity distribution factor, equals 0.82 for turbulent and transitional flow.

4. STEAM QUALITY

Steam quality, at the point of consumption, must be known in order to calculate the energy delivered. A procedure used by Singh et al. (1979) is presented in the following sections.

Chapter 7 references, p. 133.

4.1. Materials required

Dewar flask with Styrofoam lid enclosed in a Styrofoam container;
0–100°C mercury thermometer;
1 m length of copper tubing insulated with fiberglass and duct tape;
precision balance with 10 kg capacity.

4.2. Method

The dry weight of the flask with lid and thermometer is determined and
noted with the date, time, location and steam pressure. The flask is then filled
two-thirds with cool tap water and reweighed. The weight of water is determined by difference and recorded with the water temperature. The insulated
tubing is connected to the tee connection in the high-pressure valve assembly
and the valve opened fully to equilibrate the line. The valve is then closed and
the uninsulated end ($\approx$ 10 cm) of the line is inserted through a hole in the
Styrofoam lid. (Three holes in the lid accommodate the tubing and thermometer, plus a small vent hole to allow escape of air displaced by condensed
steam.) The steam valve is then reopened carefully to obtain a satisfactory flow
of steam. Steam is allowed to flow into the flask until a temperature of about
75°C is obtained. The valve is then closed, the tube removed and the final
weight and temperature of the flask recorded.

Calculations are then made on the actual heat absorbed by the water compared to the theoretical values obtained from standard steam tables.

Each measurement is made in duplicate where practical to assume repro-
ducibility and repeated where discrepancies occur.

Deviations are usually traceable to operator error, most often due to variation in steam flow into the flask. The flow should be rapid enough to allow
bringing the water to temperature in 30–45 s, but not so rapid that steam
escapes through the vent hole or water bubbles over the top.

A sample calculation to estimate steam quality follows:

Location: Water heater
Steam pressure: 112 psig
Weight of flask + lid + thermometer (m_1) = 5.90 lb
Weight of flask + lid + thermos + water (m_2) = 12.72 lb
Weight of flask + lid + thermos + water + condensate (m_3) = 13.30 lb
Temperature of water (cold) (T_1) = 87.8°F
Temperature of water + condensate (hot) (T_2) = 161.6°F

4.2.1. Calculations

Weight of water (m_4) = $m_2 - m_1$ = 6.82
Weight of water + condensate (m_5) = $m_3 - m_1$ = 7.40
Weight of condensate (m) = $m_5 - m_4 = m_3 - m_2$ [=] lb = 0.58
Total heat of water (H_1) = (T_1 − 32) × m_4 [=] Btu = 380.56
Total heat of water + condensate (h_2) = (T_2 − 32) × m_5 [=] Btu = 959.04
Total heat of condensate (H) = $H_2 - H_1$ [=] Btu = 578.48
Total heat of condensate per pound of steam H/m [=] Btu/lb = 997.38
From saturated steam tables at measured steam pressure:

S = sensible heat (enthalpy of saturated water, H_f)
        [=] Btu/lb = 316.94

L = latent heat (enthalpy of vaporization, H_{fg})
        [=] Btu/lb = 874.4

$$\text{Steam quality} = \frac{(H/m - S)}{L} = \frac{(997.38 - 316.94)}{874.4} = 77.8\%$$

5. SUMMARY

The procedures useful in measuring steam flow with orifice meters, Annubar and Accutube sensors, have been discussed. Careful attention should be paid to install and operate these sensors for accurate results. There are other types of sensors not discussed in this paper, but available for measuring steam flow, such as vortex shedding meters and turbine flow meters. Each sensor offers a unique set of advantages and disadvantages that should be evaluated prior to their selection.

6. REFERENCES

Bean, H.S., 1971. Fluid meters, their theory and application. Report of ASME Research Committee on Fluid Meters, American Society of Mechanical Engineers, New York, NY, 263 pp.

Singh, R.P., Carroad, P.A., Chhinnan, M.S., Rose, W.W. and Jacob, N.L., 1979. Energy conservation in canning industry. Phase I – Identification and measurement of energy uses in food processing operations. Contract DE-AC07-78CS40191, Report to the Department of Energy, 150 pp.

Spink, L.K., 1958. Principles and Practices of Flow Meter Engineering. Foxboro Company, Foxboro, MA, 549 pp.

Sprenkle, R.E., 1945. Piping arrangements for acceptable flowmeter accuracy. Trans. ASME, 67: 345–360.

Stearns, R.F., Johnson, R.R., Jackson, R.M. and Larson, C.A., 1951. Flow Measurement with Orifice Meters. Van Nostrand, New York, NY, 337 pp.

Part III

Energy Consumption in Food Processing Systems

Chapter 8

Energy Management in Milk Processing

E.J. MILLER

1. INTRODUCTION

Milk processing involves many different operations in the manufacture of a diverse product range. Many of these operations are energy-intensive, and an indication of the importance of energy is given by the energy-use statistics presented in Table 8.1. When considered in conjunction with the total quantity of milk processed world-wide, these statistics indicate that milk processing is a major consumer of energy internationally. The actual significance of energy costs at a particular plant will depend on the type of products manufactured, the processing methods adopted and the relative price of energy. The objective of energy management must be to minimize the energy cost component of the production costs, but not at the expense of product quality or higher overall costs. It must always be remembered that energy is but one component of the production cost, albeit often a large one, and the drive for maximum energy efficiency will often be compromised in favour of other, equally important factors. The need for more attention to energy management has been high-lighted by several recently published surveys of energy use in milk processing operations. Nation-wide studies in the United Kingdom (Elsy, 1980), The Netherlands (Netherlands Institute for Dairy Research, 1983) and New Zealand (Vickers and Miller, 1983) all show large variations in the energy consumption per unit of production as recorded at plants manufacturing the same product. Yet energy management is neither difficult nor expensive.

In this chapter, the topic of energy management will be treated in two parts. The first part will provide reference material regarding the overall energy requirements for milk processing and the breakdown of those requirements between individual operations. The second part will present a practical, step-by-step energy management plan suitable for use in milk processing plants.

2. ENERGY USE IN MILK PROCESSING

2.1. Requirements for energy

As indicated in Table 8.1, the milk processing industry consumes fuel, electricity and vehicle fuel. Fuel is required predominantly for running the process, for cleaning duties and for space heating. Electricity provides motive power for pumps, fans, services equipment, etc. and, occasionally, process heat; vehicle fuel is used in the milk assembly operations. This latter energy con-sumption is a legitimate charge against milk processing operations since the milk processing concern generally owns and operates the milk collection vehicles.

Chapter 8 references, p. 153.

TABLE 8.1

Annual consumption of fuel, electricity and transport fuel (for milk collection only) per unit of milk processed in the dairy industries of selected countries

Country	Energy input per thousand litres of whole milk processed			Reference
	Fuel (GJ per 1000 l)	Electricity (GJ per 1000 l)	Transport fuel (GJ per 1000 l)	
Czechoslovakia	2.02	0.16	–	Tors (1980)
The Netherlands	1.48	0.18	–	Neth. Inst. Dairy Res. (1983)
New Zealand	1.81	0.12	0.09	Vickers and Miller (1983)
United Kingdom	1.15	0.15	0.12	Harris (1982)

TABLE 8.2

Recorded fuel consumption indices for selected dairy products

Product	Fuel consumption	
	Per tonne of production (GJ/t)	Per thousand litres of whole milk processed (GJ per 1000 l)
Pasteurized, bottled milk	0.88	0.91
Butter	4.27	0.25
Cheese – Cheddar varieties	4.44	0.53
Spray-dried milk powders	18.10	–
Roller-dried milk powders	30.87	–
Casein	25.45	0.74
Anhydrous milk fat	4.23	0.21
Caseinate	51.80	–

TABLE 8.3

Recorded electrical energy consumption indices for selected dairy products

Product	Electrical energy consumption	
	Per tonne of production (GJ/t)	Per thousand litres of whole milk processed (GJ per 1000 l)
Pasteurized, bottled milk	0.20	0.21
Butter	0.45	0.026
Cheese – Cheddar varieties	0.80	0.096
Spray-dried milk powders	1.38	–
Roller-dried milk powders	1.59	–
Casein	1.76	0.051
Anhydrous milk fat	0.53	0.026
Caseinate	4.71	–

2.2. Recorded energy consumptions

The consumption of fuel and electricity in the manufacture of different dairy products has been regularly assessed in the New Zealand dairy industry through the use of surveys. The most recently obtained estimates pertain to the 1979/1980 dairying season and these are presented in Tables 8.2 and 8.3 (Vickers and Miller, 1983). These estimates are averages for a whole year's operation and so they include all fuel and electricity use associated with that production.

The energy use indices quoted in Tables 8.2 and 8.3 are generally verified by information published elsewhere, but there are some discrepancies. For instance, in reporting an energy survey conducted in the United Kingdom liquid milk processing sector, Elsy (1980) reports an electrical energy consumption of 0.10 GJ/(1000 l) in the manufacture of pasteurized, bottled milk. This is slightly less than half the electrical energy consumption recorded in New Zealand for the same product. The reason for this difference is not immediately apparent. Similarly, a survey conducted in The Netherlands dairy industry (Neth. Inst. Dairy Res., 1983) indicates considerably lower energy requirements for butter production. This will be due largely to the fact that European butter makers, unlike their New Zealand counterparts, do not generally vacreate the cream prior to butter making. It is important to realize that these local variations do occur and must be taken into account when comparing energy consumptions in different dairy industries.

Cleland and Earle (1980) present energy consumption statistics for ice cream manufacture starting from a skim milk concentrate. These indicate a fuel requirement of 0.64 GJ per 1000 l of ice cream and an electrical energy requirement of 1.30 GJ per 1000 l. However, the available literature lacks consistent data on the energy requirements of the many other products which will be important in some countries. Important omissions include cartoned, pasteurized milk; UHT milk; many cheese varieties; cultured fresh milk products and milk fat/vegetable fat spreads such as bregott. It is important that these gaps be filled in the near future since such information is essential reference data for effective energy management. The unit of GJ per (metric) tonne has been adopted here for presenting energy-use statistics although many researchers do advocate the unit MJ/kg; the two units, however, have the same numerical value. It is recommended that in reporting energy-use data in the international literature, units based on fuel quantities, e.g., litres of oil per tonne, tonnes of coal equivalent per tonne, oil barrels per ton, be avoided since these are difficult to interpret given local variations in terminology and calorific values.

Recorded transport fuel inputs to milk collection operations, averaged over a year, have been published in the United Kingdom and New Zealand (refer to Table 8.1). These are 0.12 and 0.09 GJ per 1000 l collected, respectively. Such levels of energy input may be considered indicative, but obviously the energy consumption will be influenced by such things as the density of the milk collection area, the average volume of each pick-up and the extent to which bulk tankers have replaced churn collection.

2.3. Reasons for variations in energy efficiency

Numerous studies of the energy requirements in milk processing have reported large variations in the energy consumption per unit of production recorded at different plants. Elsy (1980), for example, indicated a range of approximately 0.25 to 2.65 GJ per 1000 l in the fuel requirement in pasteurized, bottled milk production. Some of this variation is undoubtedly due to an inattention or lack of concern to energy conservation, but there are also operational factors which may explain variations between plants. The more important of these are listed below.

(1) Age of the equipment installed. Equipment manufacturers are continually striving to reduce operating costs and so by a process of evolution, milk processing equipment is becoming more energy-efficient. However, not all milk processors will install the latest generation equipment immediately it becomes available with the result that there will always be a range of energy efficiencies recorded at different plants. On the other hand it has been noted that in

Chapter 8 references, p. 153.

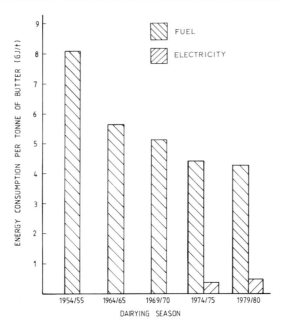

Fig. 8.1. Trends in the fuel and electricity consumption per tonne of butter produced in New Zealand. N.B. Electricity consumption data are not available prior to 1974/75.

New Zealand the mean consumption of electricity per unit of production is increasing. This is thought to be due to the increased complexity of the plants as a result of the increasing average size and the increasingly high levels of mechanization and automation, quality control and processing flexibility demanded. These trends are illustrated in Fig. 8.1 which shows the industry-wide mean fuel and electricity consumptions per tonne of butter produced in New Zealand as recorded since 1954.

(2) Cost of energy. A more expensive energy source will justify a greater expenditure on energy conservation and energy recovery equipment and hence it will encourage greater energy efficiency.

(3) Type of fuel available. The fuel type will have an effect on the efficiency with which that fuel can be used to generate process heat. Practical experience in the dairy industry has shown that the overall thermal efficiencies of coal-fired boilers are approximately 5% lower than for oil- or gas-fired boilers. The availability of gas may allow direct firing in air-heaters for spray powder plants, yielding heating efficiencies of 95–100%, and greater scope for flue-gas heat recovery due to the absence of sulphur compounds.

(4) Heat transfer medium employed. Where there is no demand for process temperatures above 90–100°C, as for example in the production of pasteurized milk and cheese, low-pressure hot water can replace steam as the heat transfer medium. This is more efficient due to the lower flue-gas heat losses from the hot-water generator, lower surface heat losses from piping and process plant surfaces, and the elimination of the energy losses associated with steam trapping, boiler blowdown and feed water de-aeration. Measurements from New Zealand factories operating on hot water indicate that fuel consumption reductions of approximately 30% for pasteurized, bottled milk and 15% for Cheddar cheese production are likely, with little or no increase in the electricity consumption, compared with steam-heated plants (Vickers and Miller, 1983).

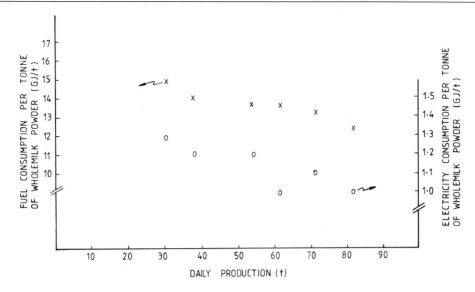

Fig. 8.2. Relationship between the energy consumption per unit of production and daily production in a spray-dried milk powder plant.

(5) Extent to which available plant capacity is used. Most milk processing equipment operates at peak efficiency under full-load conditions and should be operated that way. Those processes with a significant energy input to non-productive operation, e.g., start-up and cleaning, are most efficient when the processing time is longest. An example of this effect is in the evaporation step of milk powder manufacture. Regardless of how long the plant is operated each day, it must undergo a cleaning routine of 2.5–3.5 h during which it will draw approximately 75% of the steam load and 100% of the electrical power load required during productive running. Therefore, the cleaning component of the per unit production energy requirement is large and it will increase as the processing run time is decreased. This is illustrated in Fig. 8.2 which shows the relationship between the fuel and electricity requirements per tonne of whole milk powder and the daily production. These data were recorded at a 3.5-t/h plant recently commissioned in New Zealand. In countries where milk production shows a pronounced seasonal effect, the energy requirement per unit of production or per unit of milk processed at a particular plant will vary in accordance with these throughput changes.

2.4. Breakdown of the energy consumption in individual processes

Diagrams showing the major steps in the typical process together with the fuel and electricity allocation to those steps have been presented by Vickers and Shannon (1977) for the more common dairy products. These are reproduced here as Fig. 8.3–8.7. Figures 8.3–8.6 relate to pasteurized, bottled milk; creamery butter, Cheddar cheese, and acid casein, respectively, while Fig. 8.7 indicates the energy inputs to skim milk powder production when using an evaporation plant equipped with thermal vapour recompression. Figure 8.8 extends the coverage to include skim milk powder production using an evaporator with mechanical vapour recompression, while Figs. 8.9 and 8.10 show the energy inputs for whole milk powder production when using thermal and mechanical vapour recompression, respectively. The two processing variants are given for each milk powder type since the energy requirements are very different and the choice between the two options will be dictated by local conditions, particularly the fuel and electricity prices. The energy requirements

Chapter 8 references, p. 153.

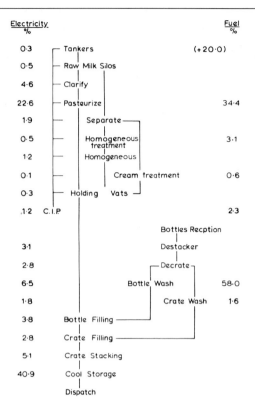

Fig. 8.3. Typical processing operations in the manufacture of pasteurized, bottled milk showing the percentage fuel and electrical energy consumption of each unit operation. (+) Additional items which require energy at some but not all plants. C.I.P., cleaning-in-place.

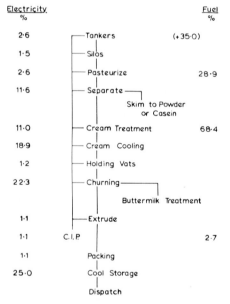

Fig. 8.4. Typical processing operations in the manufacture of creamery butter showing the percentage fuel and electrical energy consumption of each unit operation. (+) Additional items which require energy at some but not all plants.

of services equipment, e.g., air compressors, chilled water sets, are apportioned among the processing steps which they serve.

The information given for skim milk powder production may be considered valid for whey powder except that the evaporative load will be shared differently

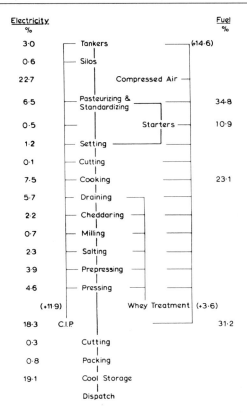

Fig. 8.5. Typical processing operations in the manufacture of Cheddar cheese showing the percentage fuel and electrical energy consumption of each unit operation. (+) Additional items which require energy at some but not all plants.

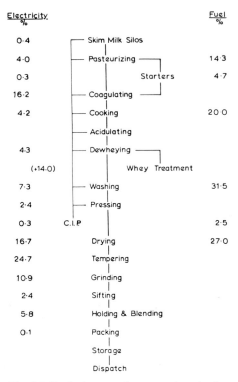

Fig. 8.6. Typical processing operations in the manufacture of acid casein showing the percentage fuel and electrical energy consumption of each unit operation. (+) Additional items which require energy at some but not all plants.

Chapter 8 references, p. 153.

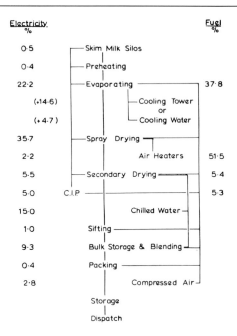

Fig. 8.7. Typical processing operations in the manufacture of spray-dried skim milk powder showing the percentage fuel and electrical energy consumption of each unit operation when using an evaporator equipped with thermal vapour recompression.

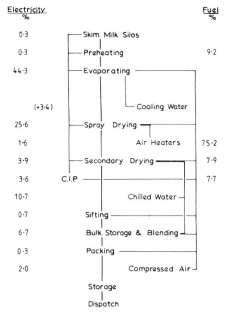

Fig. 8.8. Typical processing operations in the manufacture of spray-dried skim milk powder showing the percentage fuel and electrical energy consumption of each unit operation when using an evaporator equipped with mechanical vapour recompression. (+) Additional items which require energy at some but not all plants.

between the evaporator and the spray drier. This results from the lower total solids of the feed and the higher total solids achieved in the concentrate. In some cases a crystallization step may be included between the evaporator and the spray drier and this will consume a significant amount of electricity.

Figures 8.3–8.10 show the primary fuel inputs to the various steps of the 'typical' processes, but they do not show the considerable internal energy flows which result from heat recovery steps. Such information cannot be presented

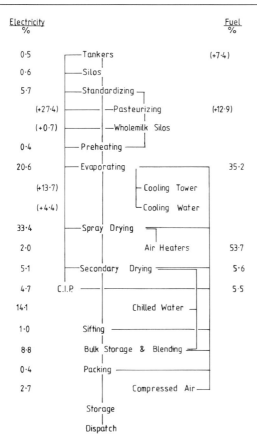

Electricity %		Fuel %
0·5	Tankers	(+7·4)
0·6	Silos	
5·7	Standardizing	
(+27·4)	Pasteurizing	(+12·9)
(+0·7)	Wholemilk Silos	
0·4	Preheating	
20·6	Evaporating	35·2
(+13·7)	Cooling Tower	
(+4·4)	Cooling Water	
33·4	Spray Drying	
2·0	Air Heaters	53·7
5·1	Secondary Drying	5·6
4·7	C.I.P.	5·5
14·1	Chilled Water	
1·0	Sifting	
8·8	Bulk Storage & Blending	
0·4	Packing	
2·7	Compressed Air	
	Storage	
	Dispatch	

Fig. 8.9. Typical processing operations in the manufacture of spray-dried whole milk powder showing the percentage fuel and electrical energy consumption of each unit operation when using an evaporator equipped with thermal vapour recompression. (+) Additional items which require energy at some but not all plants.

adequately here because there are so many variations in plants which are selected under different sets of conditions. Only one example will be presented and that is for the case of whole milk powder produced in a 'state-of-the-art' plant equipped with a seven-effect evaporator with thermal vapour recompression and a two-stage drying plant. The drying air is preheated using waste heat from the evaporator before passing through an indirect gas-fired air heater. The internal and external heat energy flows are shown in Sankey diagram form in Fig. 8.11 for which the enthalpy reference temperature is 0°C. Note that these are steady-state energy flows and therefore ignore the energy inputs to cleaning, non-productive running and non-process requirements.

2.5. Energy intensity of various processing options

Energy-use forecasters and planners often address the question of which production regime gives the minimum energy input for a given quantity of whole milk processed. This can be answered by combining the energy consumptions per unit of production, as given in Tables 8.2 and 8.3, with yield figures to determine the energy input per 1000 l of wholemilk processed for common product mixes. This has been done for New Zealand and the results are given in Table 8.4. Note that milk composition varies from region to region and so the yield factors used here may not be universally representative.

Chapter 8 references, p. 153.

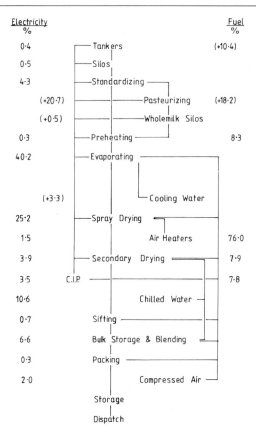

Fig. 8.10. Typical processing operations in the manufacture of spray-dried whole milk powder showing the percentage fuel and electrical energy consumption of each unit operation when using an evaporator equipped with mechanical vapour recompression. (+) Additional items which require energy at some but not all plants.

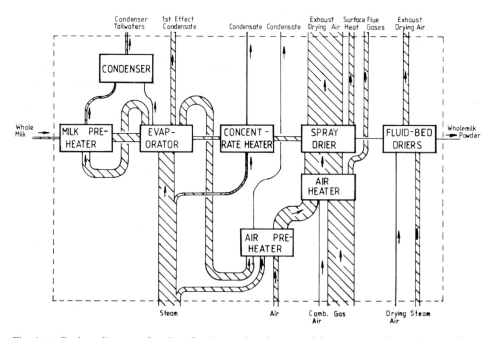

Fig. 8.11. Sankey diagram showing the internal and external heat energy flows in a modern spray-drying plant equipped with a 7-effect evaporator with thermal vapour recompression, and a 2-stage drier. N.B. The reference temperature for the enthalpy flows is 0°C.

TABLE 8.4

Fuel and electrical energy input per unit of whole milk processed for various product mixes encountered in the New Zealand dairy industry

Products	Quantity obtained from 1000 litres of whole milk (kg)	Energy input per 1000 litres of whole milk processed	
		Fuel (GJ/(1000 l))	Electricity (GJ/(1000 l))
Pasteurized, bottled milk	(1000 l)	0.91	0.21
Cheddar cheese	120		
Whey butter	4		
(Whey not processed)		0.55	0.10
Cheddar cheese	120		
Whey butter	4		
Spray-dried whey powder	43	1.33	0.16
Butter	59		
Spray-dried skim milk powder	83		
Spray-dried buttermilk powder	6	1.86	0.15
Butter	59		
Casein	29		
Spray-dried buttermilk powder	6		
Spray-dried whey powder	62	2.22	0.17
Spray-dried whole milk powder	130		
Butter	17	2.43	0.19
Anhydrous milk fat	49		
Spray-dried buttermilk powder	6		
Spray-dried skim milk powder	83	1.82	0.15

2.6. Likely changes in energy requirements

From a study of energy consumption in the New Zealand dairy industry over a period of 25 years, Vickers and Miller (1983) report an on-going decrease in the fuel consumption per unit of production, but also note a recent increase in electrical energy consumption per unit of production. The effect of the increasing thermal efficiency on the overall energy requirements will, however, be offset by the world-wide trend towards increased whey processing and the production of new, highly refined products requiring complex and energy intensive processing methods. The electrical energy consumption per unit of production is likely to continue increasing, but at a slowing rate, as the high cost of electrical energy becomes a limiting factor.

3. PRACTICAL ENERGY MANAGEMENT STEP BY STEP

To have on-going effectiveness, the energy management effort must be continuous and have clearly defined goals. That is, it must follow an overall energy management plan. There are at least seven steps in such a plan and these are shown in Fig. 8.12. Although there will be some overlap among the steps they should be taken in the approximate order shown.

3.1. Energy management team

Only the larger milk processing plants will be able to justify employing a full-time Energy Manager. However, in any plant it is essential that one person

Chapter 8 references, p. 153.

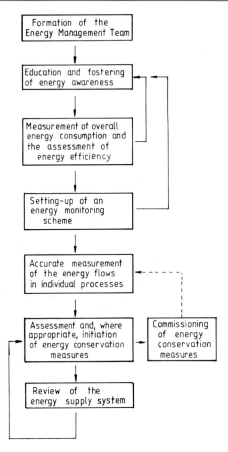

Fig. 8.12. Steps involved in an effective energy management plan for a processing plant.

takes overall responsibility for carrying out the various aspects of the energy management effort. This ensures continuity and that the routine tasks of energy monitoring and reporting are regularly carried out. This person should be supported by an Energy Group or Committee which sets the overall goals and reviews progress towards those goals. The Energy Group should comprise representatives of administration, production and engineering functions.

3.2. Fostering energy awareness

The formation of the Energy Group will go some way towards raising the level of energy awareness among staff. Such awareness will encourage co-operation at all levels, very necessary if energy management is to be effective. The Energy Manager should continue this education and make full use of the educational material which is generally available from governmental energy bodies. The use of training films, seminars and other devices should also be considered.

3.3. Initial energy audit

3.3.1. Measures of energy consumption
To set goals for the energy management effort, it is necessary to have a measure of the plant's energy efficiency. There are two such measures and these are the energy consumption per unit of production and the energy consumption per unit of milk processed. Whichever measure is used it should be determined separately for fuel, electricity and, where appropriate, transport fuel. The fuel

and electricity consumptions could be combined, but this would require a judgement regarding the primary energy input to electricity generation. This is often difficult to obtain and will vary from region to region. Therefore, the milk processor will find it best to treat fuel and electricity as separate entities.

Ultimately it will be essential that these energy-use indices are measured regularly and accurately. However, at an early stage of the energy management effort it is unlikely that the requisite instruments and reporting procedures will be in place. A useful first step is to calculate these indices from energy purchase records and production statistics. For liquid and solid fuels for which substantial on-site storage occurs, it is necessary to take stock level changes into account. The period over which the indices can be measured in this way will be quite long, probably of the order of weeks. If shorter review periods are required it may be possible to determine liquid fuel use by recording tank levels and solid fuel use by measuring the flow of fuel onto the site, perhaps by weighbridge, and by estimating the change in bunker contents. In both cases the inherent measuring errors will be significant compared with the daily fuel use for the smaller milk processing units and so the review period must be somewhat longer. Plants using natural gas and electricity only may be able to read the supply authority's meters on the incoming lines and so shorten the review periods to as little as 1 day.

If only one product, or one type of product, is manufactured, the energy consumption per unit of production can be determined quite easily. It is recommended that the unit of GJ/t be adopted for this measurement, but any consistent set of units may be used. Where more than one product is made the energy consumption per unit of production can only be determined if departmental monitoring of energy consumption occurs.

The energy consumption per unit of milk processed can also be used as a measure of energy efficiency, but it must be intepreted correctly. For a plant producing a relatively constant product mix, this measure will have some significance for comparative purposes and for multi-product plants without departmental energy monitoring it may be the only alternative. The recommended unit for this index is GJ per 1000 l.

3.3.2. Comparative statistics

Minimum theoretical energy consumptions are very difficult to define for any dairy process. For example in the pasteurization process it is theoretically possible to achieve heat regeneration levels approaching 100% and so the theoretical minimum heat energy consumption for this unit process is zero. However, to achieve such regeneration levels requires a prohibitively high capital investment and imposes high electrical loads for pumping duties. This highlights an important conflict. The achievement of the minimum heat energy consumption will generally preclude the achievement of the minimum electrical energy consumption and vice-versa. The correct energy consumption at any site will be defined by the compromise between energy costs, other operating costs and investment costs. Therefore minimum theoretical energy consumptions are largely irrelevant.

More meaningful bench-mark figures for comparison are the energy consumption indices recorded at similarly equipped plants producing the same or comparable products. These must be actual consumptions recorded over a period of time and include all non-productive energy use, such as used for plant cleaning, space heating, etc. It is suggested that where possible energy use statistics be obtained from within one's own industry since these will take local conditions into account. For example, in Sweden space heating is a large energy input which cannot be avoided. In contrast, space heating of milk processing buildings is virtually unknown in New Zealand where most of the

Chapter 8 references, p. 153.

milk processing is done during the summer period. Similarly, in those countries with cheap electricity there is likely to be an increased use of electricity and lesser use of heat energy as electrically driven heat pumps and mechanical vapour recompression plants become more viable. These local factors will have a large effect in determining what is a reasonable energy consumption. In the absence of local figures, those presented in Tables 8.2 and 8.3 should be used. These will be representative of a dairy industry similar to New Zealand's. That is, a large, well-established industry using 'state-of-the-art' processing equipment and methods.

3.3.3. 'energy-use' indices

The comparison of a plant's energy consumption per unit of production with a reference figure is quite straighforward if the plant manufactures one product only or if complete departmental energy monitoring exists. In all other cases it will require unsatisfactory guesswork to apportion the energy use. This can be avoided by considering the processing plant as a whole and by defining two 'energy-use' indices, one for fuel and one for electricity. These are defined by the equation:

$$\frac{\text{'energy-use'}}{\text{index}} = \frac{\text{actual consumption} - \text{anticipated consumption}}{\text{anticipated consumption}} \times 100\%$$

(1)

Both energy quantities in the above equation must be in the same units and the anticipated consumption is the sum of the products of production tonnages and estimates of the energy requirement per unit of production for that product. Again, where local data are not available, those estimates provided in Tables 8.2 and 8.3 should be used. The 'energy-use' indices have units of percent and can be literally interpreted as the percentage excess energy consumed in relation to industry averages. A negative index signifies higher than average efficiency while a positive index indicates a lower than average efficiency. The 'energy-use' indices are obviously suited to multi-product plants, but they are equally applicable to single-product factories.

3.4. Setting-up an energy monitoring system

An energy monitoring system can be considered as an energy management tool as well as energy conservation measure. It is an energy management tool in that it provides regular energy use statistics which gauge the effect of energy conservation measures and, if properly publicized, provides feedback and encouragement to staff. It is also an energy conservation measure since regular monitoring of energy ensures that diagnostic and corrective action is taken whenever the energy consumption rates change unexpectedly. It has often been suggested that the mere operation of an energy management system will reduce energy consumption by some 10% in an average plant.

The energy monitoring system need not be expensive since it can be made as sophisticated or as simple as desired. The top end of the scale is the computer-based system which continuously monitors meters and sensing elements and can provide a wide range of interpretive statistics. More in the scope of the average milk processing plant is the system based on manual readings of integrating meters located on the energy supply and reticulation system. The more meters fitted, the greater the breakdown of the energy flows within the plant. The absolute minimum is metering only the incoming energy flows. It is assumed that production management can provide accurate throughput and production statistics daily. If this is not so, a flow meter on the milk reception line may need to be incorporated in the energy management system. From these measurements of fuel, electricity and, if appropriate, tanker fuel and the production statistics it will be possible to calculate the daily energy consumption per unit of production or per unit of milk processed. The system can be extended by introducing departmental measurement of electricity, steam, hot water and primary fuel. It will also be worthwhile to meter major plant items individually, such as evaporators, and so record the specific energy consumption. If the total amount of steam or hot water supplied to the process as well as the fuel consumption of the boiler is recorded it is possible and desirable to define a steam or hot water generation efficiency. This would be expressed as the primary fuel input per unit of steam or hot water supplied. This is not a measure of thermal efficiency, but given some not too crucial assumptions regarding feedwater and combustion air temperatures this can be estimated. With a meter fitted in the boiler feedwater line it is possible to assess the efficiency of the condensate recovery system since the difference between the volume of feedwater and the volume of steam produced is an indication of the amount of steam used for feedwater preheating. One limitation of this is the relative inaccuracy of steam metering and it may be that the cumulative error in the steam metering may be greater than the amount of steam used in the preheating step.

It is strongly recommended that readings be taken daily, since this is the minimum period over which meaningful results can be obtained, but it provides a sufficiently fast response to changes. The meter reading duty should be entrusted to one person and the readings must take place at the same point in the processing cycle each day. One solution is to have the boiler operator record the meter readings before starting the boiler for the day's operation. If access to a computer is available it is suggested that this be used to analyse the measurements and generate the energy use report. It is important that the report be structured in such a way as to present the most relevant facts clearly, concisely and boldly. Only then is something likely to be done immediately.

The meters required for energy management need not be exact, it is more important that they give repeatable results since it is primarily changes that are of interest. Experience will dictate the actual types of meters used, but Table 8.5 may provide some guidance. When selecting meters for a manual monitoring system it is often wise to install those which either incorporate, or can later be modified to provide, a 4–20 mA output suitable for upgrading to a computerised system. In most cases this will not add to the cost, but it will increase flexibility. The total cost of setting up a simple energy monitoring system is not excessive and, once set-up, the labour requirement is unlikely to be more than 1 man-hour per day for most milk processing plants. Such an investment would surely be recouped in a short time for most operations.

3.5. Measurement of energy flows within the process

The energy flows within each process need to be fully understood. They need to be quantified so that energy recovery or energy conservation possibilities can accurately be assessed and the individual components of the total factory load need to be appreciated so that load shedding and process re-scheduling can be considered. The main purpose of an energy audit is to provide enough information to produce energy load diagrams, similar to Fig. 8.11, for the particular plant and process. Only then can one start to look at major changes as a means of reducing energy costs.

This information need not be monitored regularly, although those plants with a computer-based energy monitoring system may be able to do so at little extra cost. Generally it would be enough to measure the energy flows once and

Chapter 8 references, p. 153.

TABLE 8.5

Recommended meter types for manual energy monitoring in milk processing plants

Flow or condition	Meter or sensor type
Primary fuel flow	
Gas	Vortex meter
	Turbine meter
	(This volume flow measurement needs correction for temperature and pressure)
Oil	Positive displacement meter
	Accurate tank level sensor
Coal, woodwaste, etc.	Load cells on supply hopper
	Weighing conveyor
Hot water (district heat)	Energy meter incorporating volume flow and temperature differential elements
Electricity	Power transducer with kWh integrator
Process heat carrier flow	
Steam	Vortex meter
	Differential pressure meter (e.g., pitot, orifice plate)
Hot water	Vortex meter
	Turbine meter
Other	
Boiler feedwater flow	Vortex meter
	Turbine meter
Steam pressure	Pressure transducer[a]
Flue-gas composition	CO_2 sensor[a]
Temperature	Resistance bulb thermometer[a]
	Thermocouple[a]
Power factor	Power factor transducer[a]
Milk and product flows	Magnetic flow meter
	Vibrating-tube mass flow meter
Production	Check weighers on packing lines

[a]These sensors are not generally available with an integrating output and some form of averaging or recording will be necessary.

then only repeat the measurements when something is known to have changed. The energy flows should be measured over several days and an average taken since some day-to-day variation is bound to occur. The range of meters, and to a lesser extent the expertise, required to conduct such an energy audit may be out of the range of most milk processing plants. In such cases a consultancy or service organization equipped to do such work should be employed.

3.6. Assessment of energy conservation measures

Equipped with a thorough understanding of the present energy use situation, the Energy Manager is able to identify energy saving possibilities and assess the likely return from such measures. The decision to proceed with an energy conservation measure will hinge on the energy savings, the cost viability and practical suitability of the process or equipment change and the Energy Manager must ensure that all relevant personnel are consulted. As energy costs, processing parameters, etc., will change it is necessary regularly to reassess the hitherto rejected energy conservation possibilities to see whether the position of any has changed.

The international dairy community is well provided with reference material on energy conservation technologies and much of this information relates to actual experience. These references should be consulted for more detailed information as required. Several recent publications provide overviews of a wide range of energy conservation practices appropriate to the milk processing industry (Int. Dairy Fed., 1977; Danish Dairy Organisation and Danish Dairy Consumers Representation, 1980; Netherlands Institute for Dairy Research, 1983; Vickers and Miller, 1983). More detailed information is available on specific topics including hot water heating and heat recovery circuits (Vickers, 1977); evaporator condensate re-use, (Holmstrom, 1977); heat pumps, (Holmstrom, 1981; Anonymous, 1981), combined heat and electrical power generation (Lovell-Smith and Vickers, 1983) and heat recovery from spray drier exhausts (Jansen and Steenbergen, 1979; Brooks and Reay, 1982).

3.7. Evaluation of energy sources and purchase agreements

Once the process has been thoroughly studied and modified to reduce energy consumption to the minimum practical level, it is time to review the fuel and energy supply system. Obvious waste in this step should have been eliminated previously, but no major changes should take place until the energy use in the process is optimized since a reduction in energy use in the process will alter the viability of any changes in the supply system.

The factors to be considered include the type of fuel used, the contract conditions under which it is bought, the electricity tariff agreement and the possibility of shedding non-essential electrical loads to avoid incurring peak demand penalties. In-plant generation of electricity should also be considered at this point both as a means of reducing the peak demand and as a competitive supply of normal electricity requirements.

4. CURRENT SITUATION AND NEEDS FOR FURTHER INVESTIGATION

The information on energy use in milk processing presented in the first part of this chapter will have highlighted the variations in energy consumptions per unit of production which occur between countries and even between different plants in the same country. More research needs to be directed at explaining these variations since this will provide the lead for a greater overall energy efficiency. Such studies will ideally be supported by case histories which explain the different approaches and all their advantages and disadvantages. More information is also needed on the 'in the field' energy requirements for the manufacture of many dairy products.

The practical aspects of energy management are now well understood, but obviously not widely enough practised. Here too, the publication of case histories would be beneficial since examples of successful energy management programmes would help convince milk processors of the need and justification for more emphasis on energy management.

5. REFERENCES

Anonymous, 1981. Heat pumps in the dairy industry. Refrig. Air. Cond., 84 (April): 66–70.

Cleland, A.C. and Earle, M.D., 1980. Energy use in the ice cream industry. Publ. P22, New Zealand Energy Research and Development Committee, Auckland, 32 pp.

Danish Dairy Organisation and Danish Dairy Consumers Representation, 1980. Brancheenergianalyse. De Danske Mejeriers Faellesorganisation og Danske Konsummaelkmejeriers Faellesrepraesentation, 235 pp. (in Danish).

Elsy, B., 1980. Survey of energy and water usage in liquid milk processing. Milk Ind., 82 (10): 18–23.

Harris, P.S., 1982. Energy usage in the milk processing industry. In: Energy – use and conservation in the dairy industry. J. Soc. Dairy Technol., 35 (3): 81–82.

Holmstrom, P., 1977. Recirculation of evaporator condensates. In: Warsaw Sem. on Dairy Effluents – 2. Milk Ind., 79 (1): 15–19.

Holmstrom, P., 1981. Heat pumps in the Swedish dairy industry. Scand. Refrig., 10: 209–213.

Int. Dairy Fed., 1977. Energy conservation in the dairy industry. Doc. 102, International Dairy Federation, Bruxelles, 9 pp.

Jansen, L.A. and Steenbergen, A.E., 1979. Recovery of heat from exhaust air of spray driers in the dairy industry. In: Conf. on Energy Conservation in the Dairy Industry. Department of Industry, Commerce & Energy, Dublin, pp. 1–24.

Lovell-Smith, J.E.R. and Vickers, V.T., 1983. Cogeneration of heat and electricity in a spray drying plant. Rep. 86, New Zealand Energy Research and Development Committee, Auckland, 24 pp.

Netherlands Institute for Dairy Research, 1983. Sectoronderzoek energiebesparing in de zuivelindustrie (Section research energy saving in the dairy industry). Meded. M17, Nederlands Instituut voor Zuivelonderzoek, Ede, 225 pp. (in Dutch with English summary).

Reay, D.A., 1981. A review of gas–gas heat recovery systems. J. Heat Recovery Syst., 1: 3–X.

Tors, J., 1980. Energy in the dairy industry. Prum. Potravin, 31: 681–684 (In Czech).

Vickers, V.T., 1977. Dairy factory engineering services. N.Z. J. Dairy. Sci. Technol., 12: 219–231.

Vickers, V.T. and Miller, E.J., 1983. Energy use in the dairy industry 1979–80. Rep. 85, New Zealand Energy Research and Development Committee, Auckland, 26 pp.

Vickers, V.T. and Shannon, D.V., 1977. Energy use in the dairy Industry. Rep. 25, New Zealand Energy Research and Development Committee, Auckland, 54 pp.

Chapter 9

Energy Use in Food Freezing Industry

K. PORSDAL POULSEN

1. INTRODUCTION

Freezing involves lowering the temperature of a food item from ambient to temperatures below $-12°C$. In principle all temperatures below those of the surroundings should be considered when energy of freezing (chilling) is being discussed. In cold geographical regions, during winter periods, temperatures used for the storage of frozen foods might well be above outdoor temperatures; for products requiring distinct lower limits, this means that instead of cooling, heating may be required. In studies conducted in the U.S.A., heating of transport vehicles during the winter requires energy of the same order as cooling during summer periods. In the present survey, it is assumed that calculations can be based on average annual temperatures of the ambient which are higher than the temperatures inside stores and transportation vehicles. In this way we are operating in a 'cold chain' consisting of a number of different steps starting with the producer and ending at the home freezer. Many combinations exist, but the following is chosen as a typical example:

(1) production plant, possibly connected with storage
(2) (long-distance) transport
(3) wholesale stores
(4) (short-distance) transport
(5) retail stores
(6) home freezers
(7) consumption.

The different steps in this chain are heterogeneous with respect to the length of storage time and temperature. Consequently, additions to the total energy use vary from step to step for a given amount of product.

Most often the aim of energy analysis is to find ways of reducing energy consumption or conservation of energy and simple considerations whereby reductions in energy use can be achieved. For example, by:

(1) development of new foods which do not require low temperatures such as a combination of two or more ways of preservation, concentration (partly drying) and freezing being a well known example;
(2) reduction of the heat load which must be removed;
(3) improvement of the performance of equipment; and
(4) utilization of waste heat or renewable energy, e.g., solar energy.

Production of cold is an energy conversion process. The amount of electrical energy used for removing a quantity of thermal energy from a body at a temperature below that of the environment depends considerably on the actual circumstances. In studies where energy utilization for different freezing

Chapter 9 references, p. 177.

processes is compared with other methods of food preservation, the assumptions and preconditions must be indicated clearly, otherwise the results are of very limited value. In the recent literature on energy analysis new terms have appeared: the term *exergy*, which means energy in a convertible form; and *anergy*, which means energy in an unconvertible form. Electrical energy is 100% pure exergy whereas internal energy of the environment consists solely of anergy. The higher the proportion of exergy in any form of energy, the more valuable it is from a technical and economical point of view. Loss of exergy is a quantitatively calculable measure of the effectiveness of a process (see Chapters 4 and 5).

Analysis of energy use in food industry is important but it should never be forgotten that energy is only one of the several categories of costs. Other important parameters include nutritional value, sensory properties, range of application, and convenience.

2. REFRIGERATION CYCLE

The basis of mechanical refrigeration is the fact that at different pressures the condensation temperature of vapours is different. When pressure increases, the condensation temperature, or boiling point, also increases. This fact is applied in a cyclic process which can be followed on the pressure–enthalpy chart shown in Fig. 9.1. A refrigerant such as ammonia or a chloro-fluoro-methane, is adiabatically compressed from point B to point C. This gives superheated vapours at a high pressure. Condensation of the superheated vapours takes place at constant pressure following the saturation point D to full condensation at point E. From a receiver, liquid is expanded to point A where it is evaporated at a low temperature, for example $-25°C$. Latent heat of vaporization is extracted from the surroundings of the evaporator which can be a freezer store or a freezing tunnel. From point B the vapours are sucked into the compressor again. Quite often point B is in the superheated vapor area and point A is in the sub-cooled liquid area so that $H_B - H_E$ is larger than that shown on the chart.

The energy conditions of a refrigeration process are determined by the position of the enthalpy at points A, B, C and E.

The efficiency of a process can be indicated by the so called coefficient of performance (COP):

$$\text{COP} = \frac{H_B - H_A}{H_C - H_B} = \frac{Q}{W} \tag{1}$$

The numerator is the amount of heat which can be removed by the evaporator while the denominator represents the electrical power consumption of the compressor after correction for efficiency of the motor.

Heat of condensation $H_D - H_E$ and especially heat of $H_C - H_D$ can be partially recovered and utilized for heating water or for a similar purpose in the plant.

The minimum amount of exergy which is required to transport a given amount of heat Q from a temperature level T_0 to another level T_1 is given by the Carnot process:

$$W = \frac{Q(T_1 - T_0)}{T_0} \tag{2}$$

The real power consumption can be measured and compared with the theoretical consumption and the exergy efficiency can be found.

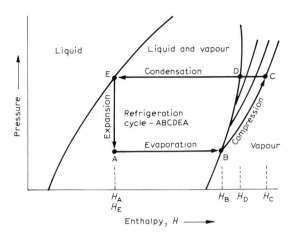

Fig. 9.1. Pressure–enthalpy chart for a refrigeration cycle.

Although power is mainly consumed in operating the compressor, large parts of the losses are due to inefficient heat exchange in evaporators and condensors. The increase in power due to poor heat exchange may be in the order of 100% in the case of cooling a cold store and even considerably more in small household refrigerators. It all depends on the size of the heat exchange surfaces. The Carnot efficiency is typically about 10% of the theoretical value, thus leaving plenty of room for improvements.

3. FREEZING OF FOODS

The amount of enthalpy which has to be removed from a given food when its temperature is about to be lowered from ambient to the temperature it has at the end of a processing line just prior to entering the freezer, can be found from enthalpy diagrams. By use of calorimetry, numerical values were determined in Karlsruhe, Federal Republic of Germany, in the 1950s and 1960s by Riedel (1957) and co-workers. These diagrams give good indications about the necessary requirements, especially for products having a natural water content. A modified diagram for beef is shown in Fig. 9.2. The amount of water converted into ice is indicated by the α lines.

The freezing process for the individual foods is complex due to the content of components which result in depressing the freezing point, often causing supercooling. The removal of latent heat is temperature-dependent. If a food is taken as a mixture of water and solids – and water is the dominant component of the majority of perishable foods which are going to be frozen – the enthalpy change can be considered to be a sum of enthalpy change of the solids (ΔH_s), enthalpy change of water before freezing (ΔH_w), enthalpy change of ice after freezing (ΔH_i) and the latent heat during freezing (ΔH_l):

$$\Delta H = \Delta H_s + \Delta H_w + \Delta H_i + \Delta H_l \tag{3}$$

The thermophysical properties are well known for water and reasonably well known for most solid components of foods. The solids content can be separated into proteins, carbohydrates and fats/oils. Edible oils solidify in the freezing range and more detailed information about enthalpy changes can be obtained from diagrams for peanut oil, sunflower seed oil, etc.

Freezing of pure ice, a typical food, and a sugar solution can be seen in Fig. 9.3.

Chapter 9 references, p. 177.

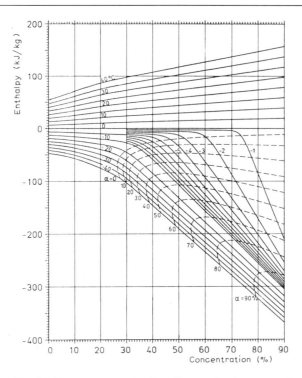

Fig. 9.2. Pressure–concentration diagram for lean meat. Data from Riedel (1957) as modified by Weisser and Zitzmann (1980). α = frozen water content.

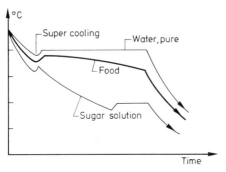

Fig. 9.3. Freezing curves of pure water, food and a sugar solution.

When pure water is cooled, 4.18 kJ are removed per kg for each degree Celsius change. After a possible supercooling, the temperature will stay at 0°C until freezing is complete. During the change of phase, a latent heat of 335 kJ kg^{-1} must be removed. Below freezing point, the specific heat is about 2 kJ kg^{-1}°C^{-1}. A corresponding amount of heat must be removed until the desired temperature is obtained.

For a 1-mol sugar solution the specific heat above freezing point is 3.2 kJ kg^{-1}°C^{-1}. Freezing point is − 1.9°C. After a probable supercooling, ice crystals are formed and 335 kJ removed for every kg. In the freezing period the remaining liquid part is becoming more and more concentrated in sugar and finally it all solidifies at the eutectic point. Below this point specific heat is changed to about 1.5 kJ kg^{-1}°C^{-1}. From a physical point of view most foods can be considered as dilute solutions in a solid matrix, and their freezing behaviour will follow curves between that of pure water and that of a sugar solution (see Fig. 9.3).

4. FREEZING METHODS

The choice of methods depends very much on the shape, size and character of the product to be frozen. There is a substantial difference between in-line freezing of small particles, such as peas, and the freezing of pig halves or large cartons of meat in batch tunnels.

Freezing equipment may be divided into the following groups with regard to the medium of heat transfer:
- direct contact: plate, band and drum freezers;
- air or other gaseous medium: blast freezers;
- liquids: immersion freezers;
- evaporating liquids/solids: liquid nitrogen, liquid fluorocarbon and liquid or solid carbon dioxide freezers.

While blast freezers are used for all kinds and sizes of products, the other methods require special packaging or a regular shape of the product.

The choice of freezer can have an important influence on the energy consumption.

For products such as fish fillets in parallelopiped packages, direct contact plate freezers or blast freezers might be used (Figs. 9.4 and 9.5).

In the plate freezer the product is pressed by metal plates which have internal channels for the refrigerant. This arrangement gives good heat transfer.

When an air blast freezer is used, a much lower evaporation temperature is required to achieve the same freezing rate as the one obtained in the plate freezer. This lower temperature must be chosen in order to compensate for the inferior heat transfer by the circulating air. In the blast freezer, additional energy is necessary to operate the fans and the resulting heat increases the refrigeration load. The total power per unit of product frozen might be 2 to 3 times higher in the blast freezer than in the plate freezer when the same freezing rate is desired.

Fig. 9.4. Vertical plate freezer (Gram Bros., Ltd.)

Chapter 9 references, p. 177.

Fig. 9.5. Blast freezer with automatic transport (Gram Bros., Ltd.)

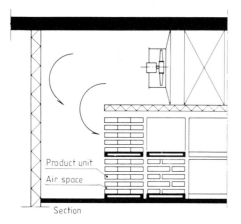

Fig. 9.6. Longitudinal section of the centre of a freezing tunnel.

4.1. Stacking in freezing tunnels

For a given installation the working practice might well have a good deal of importance to energy consumption. The following example worked out by Poulsen and Frederiksen (1984) illustrates the influence from improved flow conditions of the cooling air. In this study, wooden separators and plastic separators (Panther freezer separators) were compared.

Freezing tests were carried out in a 17-m long tunnel with a transverse measurement of 1.7 m × 2.7 m. Wind velocity was measured at 3.0 m/s before filling the tunnel. After filling, the velocity varied between 0.7 and 3.2 m/s depending on point of measurement. A simplified outline of a longitudinal section of the centre of the tunnel is shown in Fig. 9.6.

The following tests were carried out.

Test No. 1. A mixture of 21 158 kg of pork and beef distributed on 44 Euro-pallets (80 cm × 120 cm) was stacked using Panther Freezer Separators (Fig. 9.7).

Fig. 9.7. Stacking with Panther freezer separators.

Test No. 2. A mixture of 20 249 kg of pork and beef distributed on 44 Euro-pallets was stacked using wooden separators (Fig. 9.8).

Cardboard height varied from 11 to 15 cm. Thermocouples were placed centrally in pieces of meat so that core temperatures could be observed during the freezing period (Fig. 9.9).

In both tests, thermocouples were placed in lumps of ham on the pallets closest to the ventilator (sensor 2 on Fig. 9.10). Additional sensors were placed in boneless beef in the middle of the tunnel (such as sensor 6 on Fig. 9.10). Finally, sensors were placed in beef at points farthest from the ventilator (sensor 12 on Fig. 9.10). The sensors were placed centrally in the middle layer of the top row of pallets, so that fall in temperatures represents the warmest area of the respective pallets during freezing.

Air temperature was recorded in three places during freezing and product temperature in nine places. All twelve measuring points were identical during the two tests as regards to types of products and locations of measurement.

Panther Freezer Separators consist of a profiled plastic surface 50 mm high and with a dimension corresponding to half a Euro-pallet. Seen from one side, the separator consists of a number of trapezoidal profiles.

Chapter 9 references, p. 177.

Fig. 9.8. Stacking with wooden separators.

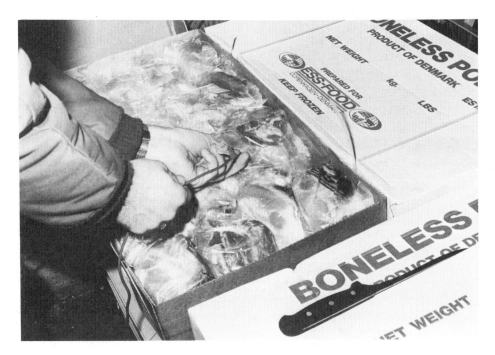

Fig. 9.9. Placing of thermocouples in lump of ham.

Wooden separators consist of three layers of 12-mm wooden fillets placed with 12 mm openings in between. The height of wooden separators is thus 36 mm.

The drop in temperatures in Fig. 9.10 indicates the typical development of cooling/freezing for the two tests with Panther Freezer Separators and wooden separators. Curves marked 2 and 12 represent pallets with quickest and slowest temperature decrease, respectively. Curve marked 1 indicates air temperature close to the ventilator. Curve 6 represent pallets in the middle of the tunnel.

Freezing periods have been calculated so as to obtain − 15°C at the centre, because at that temperature an average temperature of below − 18°C is

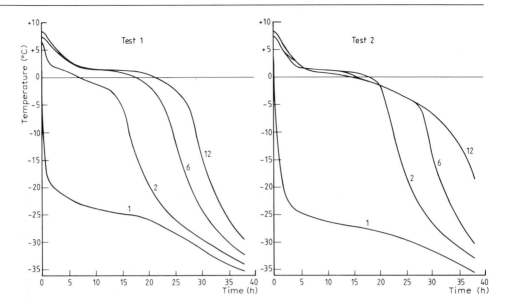

Fig. 9.10. Temperature as a function of time: test No. 1 with Panther freezer separators, test No. 2 with wooden separators. Curve 1 is air temperature, other curves are product temperatures.

guaranteed. For the front pallet − 15°C is achieved after 18.2 h in test No. 1 and 24.0 h in test No. 2. By changing from Panther Freezer Separators to wooden separators freezing period is prolonged by 31.9%. For the middle pallet similar freezing periods of 26.2 h and 30.0 h are found. Prolongation is 14.5%. For the hindmost pallet freezing periods are 30.5 h and 37.0 h, respectively, in other words a prolongation of 21.3%.

The differences in temperature drop are most pronounced when the air current is strongest, that means especially at the front of the tunnel and close to the ventilator. Consequently, at small loads greater advantages with regard to time will be achieved by the use of correct stacking and filling of the tunnel.

The increased capacity is valuable in itself, but the possible reduction of working time for compressors, fans, etc., saves 80 kWh per h in this freezing tunnel. By reducing layer thickness, even more favorable results may be achieved as the conditions of heat transfer at the surface will have a relatively greater influence.

4.2. Maximum surface heat transfer

Ideally, the total heat being removed by the refrigeration plant comes from the product, which is cooling down. As mentioned, blast freezing adds to the heat load due to the electrical energy supplied to the fans. In order to maintain the quality of the products and to achieve capacity it is often an aim to shorten the cooling period as much as possible. Within limits this is in agreement with energy conservation since efficient cooling practice requires uniformity of air velocity and temperature, and minimal resistance to heat flow.

As a general rule in chilling, and also a good guide in freezing, the Biot number, hl/k, which defines the ratio of the external heat transfer coefficient h to the internal heat transfer coefficient k (apparent heat conductivity), should not exceed a value of 5 according to Mattarolo (1976); l is a characteristic dimension of the body involved in the freezing operation – for a round shaped body l is the radius and for a flat shaped body l is half the thickness if we assume that cooling is taking place from all sides.

Chapter 9 references, p. 177.

TABLE 9.1

Comparison of freezing equipment

Equipment	Product	Product inlet temperature (°C)	Refrigeration load (MJ/h) at evaporating temperature (°C)		Electric power consumption (kW)
Blast freezing tunnel	meat in boxes, cardboard height 100–125 mm	10	460	−43	104
Spiral-belt (gyro) freezer	meat in boxes, cardboard height 100–125 mm	10	460	−43	100
Plate freezer	fish or meat in boxes, cardboard height 60 mm	10	380	−43	8
Rotating drum (contact) freezer	chopped spinach, product layer thickness 5 mmm	10	500	−45	120
Fluidized bed freezer	peas at 5 mm diameter	10	523	−43	125
Automatic blast freezer	chickens in cartons, cardboard height 100–125 mm	10	380	−43	92
	ready-made meals in aluminum trays, product height 40–45 mm	40	586	−43	125

For beef carcasses with a half thickness of 0.15 m, effective cooling is obtained in a low velocity air blast of 0.5–1.0 m/s ($h = 15$ W m^{-2} °C^{-1}). Higher velocities will only lead to small reductions in the cooling time, but require a large increase in fan energy resulting in extra heat load.

A small food product, such as peas, having a radius of about 0.5 cm can be frozen at very high air velocities or in spray or immersion freezers where heat transfer coefficients are as high as 300–400 W m^{-2} °C^{-1}.

4.3. Cryogenic freezing

Freezing with liquefied carbon dioxide or nitrogen is very costly in terms of energy compared with mechanical refrigeration systems. According to Darlington (1968/69) about 20 times as much work energy is required to produce a kilowatt of refrigeration at the temperature of liquid nitrogen (-196°C at normal pressure) as by conventional mechanical unit at -30°C. For carbon dioxide in the form of dry ice, the actual work energy per unit of refrigeration effect may be very much higher if the producer of carbon dioxide is burning fossil fuel in order to obtain CO_2, and the total energy requirement of the plant may range from 10 to 50 kW total energy per kW refrigeration. Many producers, however, utilize sources other than combustion, e.g., carbon dioxide from fermentation or from gas fields which sometimes contain nearly 100% pure carbon dioxide.

Justification for the use of cryogenic freezing is typically the flexibility of the system, low investment or a higher quality of the frozen product obtained by a high freezing rate.

4.4. A comparison between some freezing methods

Normally it is difficult to get exact information on energy consumption from manufacturers of freezing equipment. The various methods are suited for different sizes of product and many individual conditions can influence the selection of a system. The following is based on personal information (H.G. Vandall, Atlas Ltd., Ballerup, Denmark, 1980).

The basis is a freezing capacity of 1000 kg/h, the refrigeration energy and electrical energy are kept separate as conversion from electrical energy to refrigeration is liable to be influenced by the choice of equipment (Table 9.1).

All compressors use ammonia as the refrigerant. A further variable cost is the cooling water for the condensors which amounts to between 500 and 800 l/h. The price of a blast freezing tunnel is less than half of the price for a fluidized-bed freezer, so capital cost shows considerable variations. The demand for plant area is also very different for the different freezers: a rotating drum freezer occupies about 6.5 m^2 and the freezing tunnel described takes about 50 m^2. A fluidized bed freezer takes 8 m^2 and the other freezers between 15 and 25 m^2. It should be noted that several factors other than energy and capital cost influence the selection of freezers, e.g., dehydration loss during freezing, quality of the product, etc.

5. COST OF FREEZER STORAGE

In economical analysis it is convenient to consider the following four different categories:

energy cost
capital cost (interest and depreciation)
labour cost
packaging cost.

Chapter 9 references, p. 177.

TABLE 9.2

Dimensions and type of equipment (see Table 9.2) for the examined cold store volumes

Volume (m^3)	Height (m)	Width (m)	Type of equipment (see Table 9.3)
50 000	8	60	
20 000	8	36	
10 000	8	24	1, 2, 3
5 000	6	24	
1 000	6	8	
500	6	8	
300	6	8	4, 5
150	2.5	6	
100	2.5	5	
50	2.5	4	6, 7
10	2.5	2	

TABLE 9.3

Specifications for equipment used for the different volumes in Table 9.2

Identity number	Type of equipment	Stage	Refrigerant	Condenser
1	Large	1	R 717	
2	Large	2	R 717	Evaporative or
3	Large	2	R 502	shell and tube
4	Medium-sized	1	R 12	with water tower
5	Medium-sized	2	R 502	
6	Small	1	R 12	Air-cooled
7	Small	2	R 502	Air-cooled

To some extent the four types of cost can substitute each other. Energy, for example, can be saved by thicker insulation, but this means higher capital cost. A more expensive packaging can protect the product better so that a higher storage temperature can be allowed, that is replacing the energy cost by packaging cost.

In some countries which have mountains of a suitable rock material, there is the possibility of digging caves, which opens up interesting possibilities of underground storage. Such stores are low in capital cost and can also be low in energy cost. Wittersø (1983) describes how old mines are being utilized in Norway.

In order to get an overall understanding of the cost of freezer storage Borbely and Poulsen (1980) considered the following.

Total cooling costs for cold storage depend theoretically on three main factors: storage temperature; ambient temperature; volume of room. The aim of the calculations of Borbely and Poulsen was to obtain the total costs of cooling and energy consumption as a function of these factors.

Total costs include primarily:

energy consumption

machinery costs

insulation costs.

Costs not directly related to cooling are not included. Large variations of volumes were considered in order to get an overall view.

For the different room volumes different types of equipment were used (Table 9.2). Specifications for Table 9.2 can be found in Table 9.3.

Selection of equipment was based on the following conditions:

(1) Mean ambient temperature does not include the influence of solar radiation.

(2) Energy consumption values are mean values for a year.

(3) Specific energy consumption values of different parts of the equipment are taken at full heat load.

(4) The temperature difference was assumed to be 10°C between evaporation and storage, condensation and ambient temperatures, taking in the case of air-cooled condensers, the mean ambient dry bulb temperature, and in the case of recirculated water-cooled condensers, the wet bulb temperature. The following mean wet bulb temperatures were assumed as: 7, 16 and 25°C, corresponding to ambient temperatures of 10, 20, and 30°C.

(5) Since the heat transfer coefficient value of freons is smaller than that of ammonia, the condensers have a larger surface when freons are used. Furthermore, these air coolers show a larger energy consumption. The air coolers have 12-mm fin spacing for all temperatures.

5.1. Energy consumption

Typical machinery, such as compressors and air coolers, for the seven different categories, were chosen and information obtained from different manufacturers was used.

The equivalent value of water consumption was calculated and added to the electrical consumption.

5.2. Machinery costs

For the following calculations, 1978 prices were used. The cost of equipment was based on the sum of the prices of air coolers, condensers and compressors. The price of tubes and valves (15–20%), receivers and vessels (10%), transformer and electrical power transmission (30%), mounting (25%), and miscellaneous (10%), was added to the basic price to obtain the capital involved.

Costs per annum are:

$$C_y = C \frac{i(1 + i)^n}{(1 + i)^n - 1} + mC \tag{4}$$

where the interest rate is $i = 15\%$; depreciation period $n = 10$ years; maintenance costs $m = 8\%$.

To calculate the costs per h, the running time per year was assumed to be 5000 h considering that the equipment must be of such a size as to allow for peak demands.

Costs were calculated in kWh as units of money, 1 kWh being equivalent to 0.22 Danish Crowns (DKK). Some of the results can be seen in Fig. 9.11 where energy consumption and the sum of energy consumption and machinery costs are plotted against storage temperature. Ambient temperature is shown as an independent parameter.

From Fig. 9.11 it can be seen that when the temperature is lowered, the cost of the machinery increases more rapidly than the cost of energy consumption.

5.3. Insulation

Insulation costs depend also on storage and ambient temperatures, as well as on room-volumes.

Walls and roof. Sandwich panels of polyurethane hard-foam (thermal conductivity $k = 92$ J m^{-1}h^{-1}°C^{-1}) covered on both sides by metal sheets were used.

Chapter 9 references, p. 177.

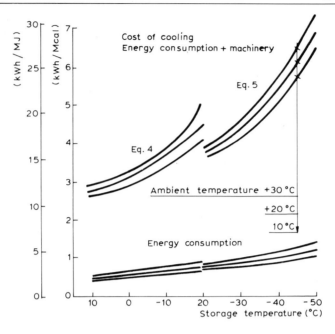

Fig. 9.11. Cost of cooling and energy consumption versus temperature for equipments 4 and 5 (see Table 9.3).

Prices including mounting:

Thickness (m)	0.05	0.1	0.125	0.15	0.18
Price (DKK)/m²	250	300	325	350	400

By using sandwich panels, parts of the construction costs are included, especially for smaller rooms.

Floor. Polystyrene slabs $(k = 167 \ \mathrm{J \, m^{-1} h^{-1} °C^{-1}})$ were used. The prices included mounting and use of a membrane (vapour barrier):

Thickness (m)	0.2	0.25	0.3	0.35
Price (DKK)/m²	250	290	325	360

For calculation of the costs the same formula was used for insulation as for the machinery, but by taking $i = 15\%$, $n = 15$ years, maintenance as 2%, and operating time as 8600 h per year.

5.4. Thickness of insulation

Walls and roof. Knowing specific energy (consumption and machinery) and insulation costs, the economic insulation thicknesses of the panels were determined by graphical methods for the seven types of equipment at three different ambient temperatures, using storage temperature as a parameter.

Commercial thicknesses were chosen close to the economic values, and further calculations were based on these thicknesses. Other factors, such as moisture condensation outside in case of high relative humidity, were not considered, as they only result in small changes in the summarized costs; furthermore it depends on the location and does not influence general trends.

The results show that panel thicknesses between 0.1 and 0.18 m in general are suitable. For storage at $+10°C$, a thickness of 0.05 m was found to be the

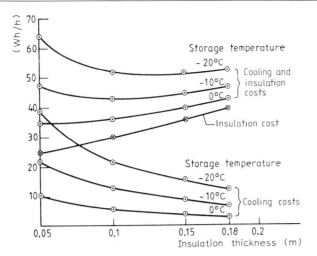

Fig. 9.12. Summarized costs of cooling (machinery plus energy) and insulation versus insulation thickness for equipment 6. Ambient temperature is + 10°C.

most economical, but as the curve showing the summarized expenses is rather flat in this case, an insulation thickness of 0.1 m was chosen also for this situation. For storage at − 50°C, a thickness of 0.18 m was chosen. This thickness, however, is not the economical optimum according to the graph, but as 0.18 m is the largest thickness which for the time being can be formed in one step, otherwise incurring an increase in price, which would indicate that the chosen thickness was optimal. Some of the results can be found in Fig. 9.12.

Floor. At storage temperatures below 0°C, the temperature of the heating layer under the floor was assumed to be + 5°C. At storage temperatures above 0°C insulation was chosen, so that heat flux would be the same as in the optimized situation for walls. Soil temperature was assumed to be the same as the ambient temperature.

5.5. Calculation of heat load

For the rooms given in Table 9.2 the following heat loads were calculated:
(1) transmission of heat through the walls and roof
(2) transmission of heat through the floor
(3) heat equivalent of lighting
(4) heat infiltration through doors
(5) heat load caused by air-cooler fans.
The operating time was assumed to be 40 h per week. After preliminary calculations the heat equivalence of operating trucks and personnel were neglected.

Heat loads 1 and 2 can be calculated on the basis of the above discussion. Heat load 3 was calculated as 10.5 kJ m^{-2}h^{-1}, referring to the basic area of the room. Heat load 4 can be calculated after Bäckström's formula:

$$Q_{\text{inf}} = 70\sqrt{\{V\}}\{\varrho\}\{I\} \text{ kJ per 24 h}$$

where $\{V\}$ is the numerical value of V, the room volume (m^3); $\{\varrho\}$ the numerical value of ϱ, the density (kg/m^3); and $\{I\}$ the numerical value of I, the enthalpy difference between the air inside and outside (kJ/kg). Taking for ϱ a medium value at 0°C, we get:

$$Q_{\text{inf}} = 3.8\sqrt{\{V\}}\{I\} \text{ kJ/h}$$

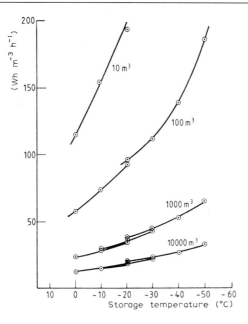

Fig. 9.13. Specific total cost (energy + machinery + insulation) versus temperature for four storage volumes.

Heat load 5 was taken into account by multiplying the sum of heat loads 1–4 by the factor $(1 + q)$, where q is the heat equivalence of energy consumption by the fans.

5.6. Energy consumption and cooling costs per volume

Knowing the specific energy consumption and the machinery costs for the different types of equipment and the heat load for each volume, the costs of energy consumption separately as well as the summarized costs of energy consumption, machinery, and insulation were calculated, and finally related to 1 m^3 of room volume.

In Fig. 9.13, the total costs, which are the sum of energy consumption, machinery and insulation, are plotted against the temperatures of storage for various volumes. Four characteristic volumes can be found in this figure where the ambient temperature is + 10°C. It is interesting to note how much the influence of the temperature is changed from one room volume to another.

Figure 9.13 shows that the cost per unit of cold store volume per hour is very much dependent on volume until sizes of about 10 000 m^3 are obtained. When these cold store volumes (or larger volumes) are operated, the effect of temperature variations is also reduced. This is in contrast to smaller volumes where specific costs are heavily dependent on temperature.

6. ADDITIONAL COST STUDIES FOR STORAGE

As it can be seen from the above discussion, it is more energy-expensive to run at lower temperatures than necessary, especially in the smaller volumes. It is the general practice to store all products together at a temperature of the order of − 25°C down to − 30°C. The temperature requirements of different groups of products are, however, very different and the standard level has been chosen with regard to the relatively small volumes of sensitive goods such as

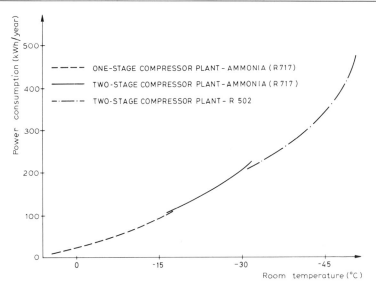

Fig. 9.14. Relations between power consumption and room temperature for a cold store of 8231 m³ volume.

fatty fish and ice cream. By storing these categories of products in separate low temperature rooms and handling the more tolerant products such as fruits, vegetables, pork, butter, etc., at higher temperatures, energy could be saved.

Other studies of power consumption in cold stores were undertaken by Poulsen and Jensen (1978). Total annual power consumption for the refrigeration plant was calculated in two cases: as a function of the temperature in the cold store for a given cold store volume; per unit of cold store volume at a fixed cold store temperature.

Power consumption was found on the basis of the cooling requirement as well as the number of operating hours of the entire refrigeration plant. Power consumption for compressors and condensers was based on information from manufacturers whereas power consumption for the fans in the cold store has been calculated on the basis of the amount of air circulating through the air coolers together with the corresponding pressure drop.

Total refrigeration demand included: transmission losses through walls, etc.; lights, trucks, etc.; infiltration due to door openings; and staff.

The following criteria were assumed: an annual mean ambient temperature of +8°C; an annual mean enthalpy of 23 kJ/kg dry air; an insulation thickness of 150 mm polyurethane; and five working days each of 8 h.

The power requirements have been found with the assumptions that: evaporating temperature is 10°C below cold store temperature; and the annual mean condensing temperature is +20°C.

In Fig. 9.14, relations between power consumption and room temperature are given for a specific cold store of the following dimensions:

length × width × height = 76.25 m × 17.00 m × 6.35 m (= 8231 m³)

Figure 9.15 indicates relations between power consumption per m³ per year and cold store volume at four different temperatures. Calculations have been based on the cold store dimensions as listed in Table 9.4. It should be noted that total refrigeration requirements depend on the relationship between length, width and height for a given cold store volume as the transmission losses may be minimized by adopting a cubic shape. Since, however, the interior height rarely exceeds 8 m for practical stacking reasons, the dimensions given can be regarded as representative.

Chapter 9 references, p. 177.

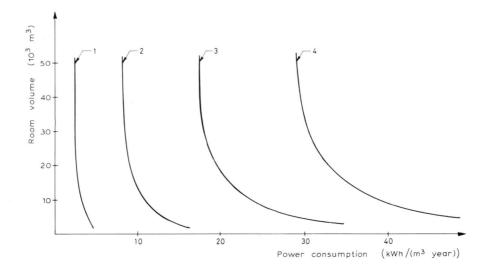

Fig. 9.15. Relations between power consumption, room temperature (1, 0°C; 2, − 15°C; 3, − 30°C; 4, − 45°C) and room volume.

TABLE 9.4

Cold store dimensions used in calculation for Fig. 9.15

Cold store volume (m³)	Length (m)	Width (m)	Height (m)
5 000	34.0	24.5	6.0
10 000	45.0	31.8	7.0
20 000	59.5	42.0	8.0
50 000	94.0	66.5	8.0

Power consumption decreases in Fig. 9.14 when the cold store temperature is raised and goes down to nothing when the annual mean ambient temperature, 8°C, is reached. For obvious reasons this can only be true if there are no variations in climate and day–night temperatures. If individual climatic conditions are considered, the situation becomes very complex.

6.1. Transport

Löndahl (1975) has calculated that additional energy to maintain the low temperature is about 10–15% of the basic energy of road transport. When specific energy costs for refrigeration are calculated, the transport unit can be considered to be a small volume store with an energy input of approximately 100 W per metric tonne. When this energy is generated mechanically by the motor of the truck the amount of diesel consumed corresponds to about 2 kW/t. This high energy consumption is due to the low combined efficiency of the combustion engine and the compressor.

6.2. Retail cabinets

The traditional method of exposing frozen products to allow viewing by customers is the worst possible method from the energy conservation stand-point. Even if large efforts have been made to reduce the energy demand by introducing night covers for the open top display cabinets and glass doors/ windows for the vertical types, it is still the most expensive step in the cold chain.

For the open-top cabinets it has been calculated that the heat load is one third by radiation from the surroundings, i.e., walls and ceiling. Depending on

Fig. 9.16. Display cabinets in a shop. Vertical cabinets with glass doors in the background (IWO A/S).

the emissivity of the frozen food packaging the heat radiation is absorbed by the upper layer which is consequently warmer than the circulating cold air, often by 10–15°C. Another third of the heat load is caused by infiltration of warm air from the shop. A large part of the remaining load is due to moisture condensation on the surface of the packages so that a very limited part is due to heat penetration through the insulation.

Another method of reducing energy consumption at the retail end is by the use of reflective packaging, such as aluminum foil, and by placing reflecting screens above the cabinets in order to reduce radiation from the surroundings.

In a few countries it is common practice to sell frozen goods from special shops where the packages cannot be seen and the customer has to open a tight cover to get the product. In other countries there is a door-step delivery system so that the orders are mailed after the customer has made a selection from a catalogue.

Information about energy consumption in display cabinets (Fig. 9.16) as given by J. Brinch (based on knowledge from IWO A/S, Copenhagen, 1984) is listed in Table 9.5. The figures are for total consumption from compressors, condensors, etc., with an average temperature of $-23°C$ in the circulating cooling air and $-20°C$ of the air returning to the evaporator. Hygrostatic control of heat in door-casings is based on temperature and relative humidity of the air in the shop.

6.3. Home freezers

In this step we have the most unfavorable surface to volume ratio, roughly 20 times larger than for an average commercial cold store. In addition, the insulation thickness is often down to 20 mm resulting in up to 50 times more heat leakage per unit volume than in industrial storage. Furthermore the

Chapter 9 references, p. 177.

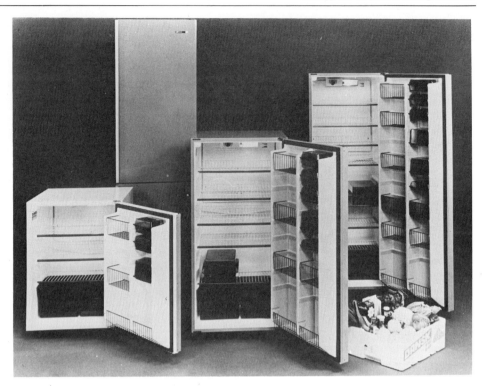

Fig. 9.17. Low energy home freezers (Gram Bros., Ltd.).

TABLE 9.5

Energy consumption in display cabinets

	(kWh/m^3 per 24 h)
Open-top cabinet, 1 m width, capacity 0.25 m^3 per m	
traditional use	32.6
supplied with night cover	19.0
with night cover and heat recovery	18.0
Open-top cabinet, 1.2 m width, capacity 0.34 m^3 per m	
traditional use	29.6
with night cover	17.0
with night cover and heat recovery	16.0
Vertical cabinet with glass doors, capacity 1.12 m^3 per section (per door)	
without automatic control of heat in door-casing	11.3
with hygrostatic control of heat in door-casing	8.5

power consumption per unit of refrigeration is much higher as a result of the very high temperature rise caused by small and inefficient heat transfer surfaces, poor motor efficiency and heavy compressor losses for a small machine at a high pressure ratio.

When it is considered that the total home refrigerator/freezer volume may be as high as 50% of commercial storage capacity, it must be concluded that it is important to improve this part of the cold chain.

It is said that the power used for home freezers is utilized for heating the house. This is true in the cold season in some countries, but in the summer and in warm climates where air-conditioning is used, additional energy is used to get rid of that extra heat.

Current research is being undertaken to lower the energy consumption. One example is Gram model FB 307 which has an insulation thickness of 75 mm and a power consumption of 0.92 kWh per 24 h according to O. Skak (personal information based on knowledge from Gram Bros., Ltd., Vojens, Denmark, 1984). Storage capacity is 307 l and the outer dimensions are: length × width × height = 110 cm × 69.5 cm × 85 cm.

In several countries, power consumption has been measured under standard conditions for refrigerators and freezers which were on sale locally. Lorentzen (1980) presented energy consumption data per 24 h for 36 refrigerators and freezers placed in a room at 25°C.

The highest consumption for a refrigerator operating at 5°C is 1.6 kWh per 24 h for a useful volume of 131 l, while the lowest consumption is 0.5 kWh per 24 h for a useful volume of 172 l.

In this study, freezers operating at − 18°C show even larger variations. The highest consumption is 3.6 kWh per 24 h for a useful volume of 253 l and the lowest consumption is 1.03 kWh per 24 h for a useful volume of 122 l.

Figure 9.17 shows some of the 'low-energy' freezers from Gram Bros. It has been calculated that the energy saving in 3 years for the better insulated home freezers are equal to the cost of a new freezer when Danish electricity prices are taken into consideration.

7. THE INTEGRATED COLD CHAIN

The total energy consumption for different preservation methods has been calculated by a number of researchers by adding up the energy values. These calculations normally accumulate the energy value of the food itself, and the energy values of the packaging material, distribution and preparation of the food for consumption for the first two 'energy levels', resulting in so-called gross energy requirements. Calculations are often based on differing assumptions and large uncertainties of operation, thus authors are bound to draw quite different conclusions. In the 1970s, some of the studies were used (and misused) to prove that the one preservation method or the other was less energy-consuming than the others. It is often impossible to compare the different studies, as they deal with different products which are sometimes unsuitable for the chosen freezing methods. Hallström (1980) compared three studies by use of a graph (Fig. 9.18).

As can be seen for all three studies, storage length in the retail step of the cold chain has a decisive influence on the result. If storage in home freezers had been included, an even higher energy consumption would have been shown.

If we look only at energy, it is advisable to keep the products for as long as possible in the large stores and then to consume them shortly after they have been bought. It must, however, be remembered that power consumption of a home freezer is independent of the load, so that when it is installed, it should also be utilized.

Löndahl's (1978) results indicate a lower consumption in retail than the two other investigators. This is because he assumes that heat produced by the cabinet is utilized for heating purposes.

For home storage the three studies give the following figures:

Reference	Days of storage	kWh per 1000 g
Löndahl (1978)	20	0.24
Olabode et al. (1977)	25	6.07
Poulsen and Raahauge (1979)	20	0.32

Chapter 9 references, p. 177.

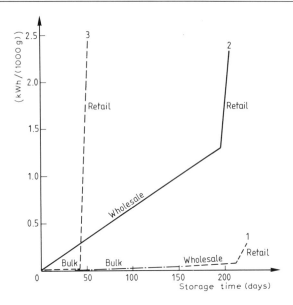

Fig. 9.18. Influence of storage time on energy consumption for 3 investigations: (1) green peas (Löndahl, 1978); (2) mashed potatoes (Olabode et al., 1977); (3) pea soup (Poulsen and Raahauge, 1979).

The freezing itself which entails lowering the product temperature from ambient to $-18°C$, consumes only 0.11–0.12 kWh per 1000 g product, when it is done properly in industry. One way of conserving energy is to leave this part of the job to industry.

8. TOTAL ENERGY USE IN FOOD FREEZING

About 25% of the world's production of perishable food is refrigerated and a vast network exists to handle this enormous amount of foodstuff.

The relative importance of energy use for refrigeration in the individual countries varies with climate, development of the food freezing industry and other industries especially energy-intensive industries, e.g., metal works. In Denmark, where light industry dominates and food freezing is important, as much as 15–20% of the electricity is estimated to be used for refrigeration. In the neighbouring country, Norway, which has much more heavy industry, only 2% of the electricity is used for the refrigeration of food.

In private households in Denmark about 30% of the electricity is used for the freezing and refrigeration of foods.

This chapter does not deal with improvements in the mechanical equipment used for refrigeration, or new methods, such as stepwise freezing, in order to lower temperature differences between evaporators and the product. Attempts are currently under way to avoid crystal formation by the use of inhibitors, such as sugars and polyhydric alcohols (so called cryoprotectants). If phase transitions can be avoided, then considerable savings will be achieved in freezing energy, whereas storage will be unaffected. The book *Saving of Energy in Refrigeration* (IIR, 1980), gives many practical hints, especially about mechanical parts.

In planning cold store operations the optimum should be considered, i.e., the conditions which consider both economy and quality. The systematic approach is to plot energy consumption or total cost and quality loss calculated as functions of temperature. The optimum is found at the intersection of the two lines (see Fig. 9.19). This method is of more theoretical interest than of

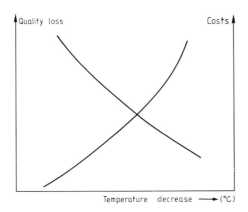

Fig. 9.19. Cost and quality loss as functions of temperature. Temperature optimum is found at the intersection between the lines.

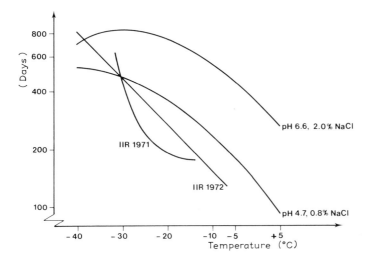

Fig. 9.20. Practical storage life of Danish butter compared with recommendations from International Institute of Refrigeration, Paris.

practical value due to the many unknowns in product mix and storage length and the fact that the price of a product is not directly related to its quality.

A thorough knowledge of the relationship between storage temperature and storage life is also essential before optimization can be attempted. One example of the discrepancies between the recommendations issued by the International Institute of Refrigeration and experimental data was shown by Poulsen et al. (1976) (see Fig. 9.20). At lower temperatures, the storage life may vary by several hundred days.

More information about the storage life of frozen foods and better performance of home freezers and retail cabinets are urgent areas for future research.

9. REFERENCES

Borbely, P. and Poulsen, K.P., 1980. Relations between total costs, energy, insulation, volume of cold stores, and temperatures. Scand. Refrig., 9: 137–140.

Darlington, M.E., 1968/69. The use of liquid nitrogen in the field of refrigeration. Proc. Inst. Refrig., 65: 59–71.

Hallström, B., 1980. Food freezing – do we have the energy? Paper presented at the 2nd International Frozen Food Industries' Conference, Monaco.

IIR, 1980. Saving of energy in refrigeration. International Institute of Refrigeration, Paris, 207 pp.

Lorentzen, G., 1980. Energy saving in refrigeration systems. Proc. Int. Symp. Energy and Food
    Industry, 1980, Madrid. CIIA, Paris.
Lorentzen, G., 1983. Energy and refrigeration. Int. J. Refrig., 6: 262–273.
Löndahl, G., 1975. Energy consumption in food preservation. In: Proc. 14th Int. Congr. Refrigera-
    tion, Moscow, Vol. IV, pp. 278–287.
Löndahl, G., 1978. Energy conservation in frozen food distribution. Annexe 1978-2, International
    Institute of Refrigeration, Paris, pp. 355–359.
Mattarolo, L., 1976. Technical and engineering aspects of refrigerated food preservation. Annex
    1976-1, International Institute of Refrigeration, Paris, pp. 49–69.
Olabode, H.A., Standing, C.N. and Chapman, P.A., 1977. Total energy to produce food servings as
    a function of processing and marketing modes. J. Food. Sci., 42: 768–774.
Poulsen, K.P. and Frederiksen, R.B., 1984. Freezing tests with Panther freezer separators. Techni-
    cal University of Denmark, Lyngby.
Poulsen, K.P. and Jensen, S.L., 1978. Quality–economy relations of frozen foods. Annexe 1978-2,
    International Institute of Refrigeration, Paris, pp. 85–94.
Poulsen, K.P. and Raahauge, L., 1979. Ready made meals made by freezing and other preservation
    methods – a cost comparison. Scand. Refrig., 8: 325–328.
Poulsen, K.P., Danmark, H. and Mortensen, B.K., 1976. Time–temperature-tolerance of Danish
    butter varieties. Annexe 1976-1, International Institute of Refrigeration, Paris, pp. 133–140.
Riedel, L., 1957. Enthalpie–Konzentrations-Diagramm für mageres Rindfleisch. Kältetechnik, 9
    (Heft 2).
Weisser, H. and Zitzmann, W., 1980. Rechnerunterstützt gereichete Enthalpie–Konzentrations-
    Diagramme fettarmer Lebensmittel. ZFL, 31: 352, 361.
Wittersø, F., 1983. Bunes Fryselager A/L. Scand. Refrig., 12: 297–300.

ADDITIONAL READING

Romero, R. and Singh, R.P., 1982. Energy accounting of frozen food plants. Paper presented at the
    1982 Summer Meeting of the American Society of Agricultural Engineers, Madison, WI.

Chapter 10

Energy Accounting in Food Canning Industry

R. PAUL SINGH

1. INTRODUCTION

The canned fruits and vegetable industry is the largest energy-consuming food industry in the State of California. In terms of energy intensity, or energy consumed per unit mass of product processed, this industry ranks second behind beet sugar processing. In 1978, the U.S. Department of Energy initiated a comprehensive research project to examine energy use in the canning industry located in California. The project included energy accounting studies conducted in tomato, peach and spinach canning plants. The results from this project have been reported by Singh et al. (1979, 1980), Carroad et al. (1980) and Chhinnan et al. (1980). This chapter presents an overview of this comprehensive study.

2. SPINACH CANNING

An energy accounting study in a spinach canning plant was conducted in summer 1978 as part of a comprehensive research funded by the U.S. Department of Energy. The overall objective of the energy accounting study was to identify energy-intensive operations in spinach canning. Although only small quantities of spinach are canned in the U.S.A., most of the processing operations in spinach canning are similar to canning of other fruits and vegetables.

2.1. Data collection

A spinach canning plant located in northern California was selected for this study. Spinach processing in this plant was divided into ten unit operations to assist in data collection. These ten operations were: product receiving, dry reel cleaning, washing, blanching, sorting, filling, heating in exhaust boxes, can seaming, retorting, and palletizing. All of the above operations, except retorting, were operated on a continuous basis. The retorts for sterilization purposes operated in a batch mode.

An inventory of all electric motors was made. The motors were identified by location, and name plate information such as amperage, horsepower, number of phases and voltage was recorded. At the main junction boxes, electric watt transducers (Ohio Semitronics) were wired in-line between the motor and the circuit breaker as shown in Fig. 10.1. The output of this type of a transducer is in millivolt, which can be converted to electrical power consumed by the motor at a given load.

Chapter 10 references, p. 190.

Fig. 10.1. An electric watt-transducer installed to measure electric energy consumption.

Fig. 10.2. An orifice plate installed in a steam pipe.

In addition to electrical energy, steam is used in the spinach processing line. Steam is consumed in the blancher, exhaust box, retort and in the can seamer. Steam consumption by the retort and the blancher was measured with the use of orifice plates mounted in steam pipes as shown in Fig. 10.2. In the case of the exhaust boxes, the water was heated by steam supplied to a common heat exchanger. In addition, steam headers present in each exhaust box helped maintain a steam vapor atmosphere. The steam requirements of the exhaust boxes were determined by installing orifice plates at the two locations, to

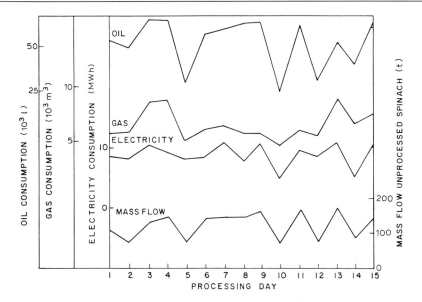

Fig. 10.3. Daily energy and mass flow profiles for spinach processing (Chhinnan et al., 1980). t, (metric) tonne = 10^3 kg.

measure steam flow to the heat exchanger, and the live steam flow to the exhaust box. It was found that the steam flow to the exhaust boxes was quite steady, therefore a pneumatic differential pressure transmitter with a circular chart recorder was used. At other locations steam flow was measured by first converting the output of the differential transmitter into a milliampere signal which was then recorded on an automatic data logger (Autodata 9, Accurex).

2.2. Data analysis

The energy accounting data were analyzed on the basis of an 8-h shift. During this shift there were 1.7 h of lunch and coffee breaks when some of the equipment operated idle.

The electrical consumption data for all electric motors were obtained whether these motors operated idle or under load. It was found that on the average, during an 8-h shift, the motors operated for 410 min under load and during the 1.7 h break time these motors operated idle for 35 min.

The steam consumption by the blancher was calculated for periods when the product was conveyed through the unit and also for the period when the blancher was operated empty to maintain it at desired temperature. In the case of the exhaust boxes, as mentioned previously, steam was used to heat water in an indirect heat exchanger in addition to providing live steam in the individual boxes. The hot water from the heat exchanger was supplied to the four exhaust boxes. The total steam consumption by the exhaust boxes was determined by measuring steam flow to the heat exchanger as well as the four individual boxes. The batch retorts use considerable steam during the venting period. The steam flow was measured both for the venting period and the remaining cook period.

2.3. Results and discussion

Analysis of data on total energy consumption by the plant provides useful information on the types of fuel requirements. As seen in Fig. 10.3 the plant consumed electricity, natural gas and fuel oil. The plant processed around 150 t

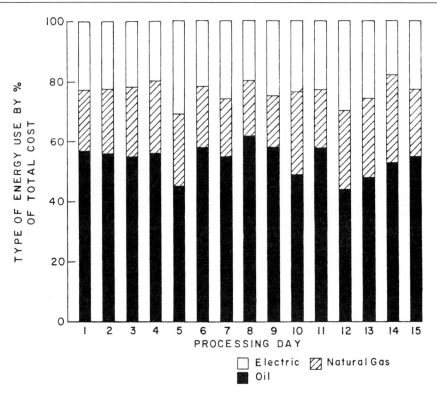

Fig. 10.4. Type of energy use by percentage of total cost in spinach processing (Chhinnan et al., 1980).

of spinach per day. The total processing season was only 15 days long. This emphasizes the importance of fuel supply during the processing season. Since spinach is a perishable commodity, any disruptions in energy availability during the 15-day period would have serious implications to this industry.

Using the daily energy consumption data, the electrical energy intensity may be calculated as 0.072 kWh per kg of raw spinach. Assuming an energy conversion factor of 11.0769 MJ/kWh for fossil fuel equivalence (Gries, 1975), the electrical consumption was 0.8 MJ/kg of raw spinach. For thermal energy, obtained from natural gas and fuel oil the intensity value is 6.5 MJ/kg of raw spinach. The electrical energy consumption represented about 11% of total energy consumption.

The daily energy bills were analyzed to determine the relative differences in cost of various types of energy. Natural gas and fuel oil together represent about 80% of the energy cost (Fig. 10.4). These results are common to other fruit and vegetable canning plants. The average energy cost for canning spinach was calculated to be $0.0181 per kg of raw spinach.

The above results obtained from the total energy consumption by a plant are useful to develop energy use profiles. However, these data do not identify energy intensive operations for the purposes of energy conservation. Detailed energy accounting of a processing line is necessary to quantify energy consumption by individual unit operations. An energy accounting diagram based on symbols suggested by Singh (1978) was developed as shown in Fig. 10.5. The energy consumption data are shown for an 8-h shift. Clearly processing equipment associated with three unit operations can be identified as energy-intensive, namely: blancher, exhaust box and retort. These operations are major users of steam. Concerning the electric consumption, the washing operation is most important. Spinach requires a considerable amount of washing to remove dirt and insects.

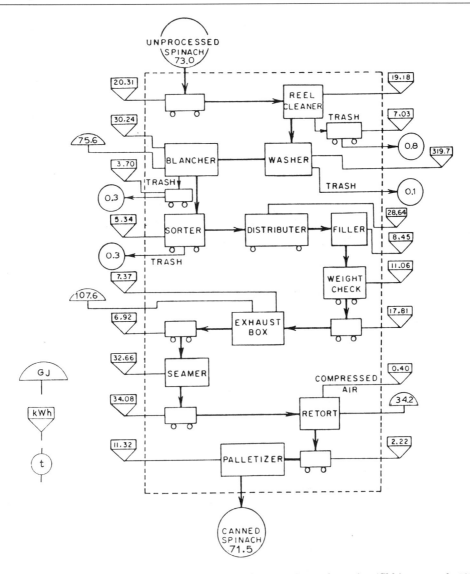

Fig. 10.5. Energy accounting diagram for spinach processing and canning (Chhinnan et al., 1980).

Energy consumption as a percent of the total energy is shown in Table 10.1. The values given in the table include the total energy consumed by two reel cleaners, two washers, two blanchers, four exhaust boxes and six retorts during an 8-h shift. It is evident that the exhaust boxes required almost half of the total energy consumed in canning spinach. It was estimated that the cost of steam in 1978 to operate these exhaust boxes was $13 000 per season. Alternative procedures such as the use of mechanical vacuum, may be more energy efficient than the use of exhaust boxes.

Opportunities for energy conservation include modifications of the blancher. Data analysis indicated that this blancher operated at a 31% efficiency. Incomplete steam condensation in water, hot water overflow, condensate discharge into drain, and surface losses from the blancher accounted for the major causes of energy loss. At times when no product was being conveyed through the blancher, 1895.1 kg/h steam was being used. This emphasizes considerable 'wastage' of energy during lunch and coffee breaks.

In batch retorts, considerable steam was wasted during venting. Although venting is a necessary procedure to assure safe processing conditions, venting for periods longer than necessary should be avoided. Similarly, attempts

TABLE 10.1

Energy intensity by unit operations for a typical 8-h shift for processing 73 t of spinach (Chhinnan et al., 1980)

Unit operation	Energy			Percent of total energy
	Electrical (kWh)	Thermal (GJ)	Total (GJ)	
Receiving	20.3	–	0.22	0.1
Dry reel cleaning	26.2	–	0.29	0.1
Washing	319.7	–	3.54	1.1
Blanching	33.9	108[a]	108.38	34.2
Sorting	5.3	–	0.06	0.0
Filling	48.2	–	0.53	0.2
Exhaust box	25.2	154	154.28	48.6
Seaming	73.7	–	0.82	0.2
Retorting	0.4	48.8	48.8	15.4
Palletizing	13.5	–	0.15	0.1
Total energy	566.4[b]	310.8	317.07	100

[a] Boiler efficiency assumed at 70%.
[b] An additional 3424 kWh were consumed by pumps to operate the water well, the waste water handling system, the operation of the boiler and accessories and lighting during the 8-h shift.

to recover energy from vented steam, for use in heating water, should be explored.

In summary, the study of the spinach canning operation revealed that canning a kg of raw spinach required 6.5 MJ of natural gas and fuel oil and 0.072 MJ of electricity. Exhaust boxes, blanchers and retorts are the most energy-intensive equipment. Attempts should be made to modify these equipments to make them more energy-efficient. For maximum energy utilization, uniform product flow through various processing steps is essential. This is particularly true for product processed in the energy-intensive equipment.

3. CANNING OF TOMATO PRODUCTS

An energy accounting study of canning tomato products was conducted in 1979 in a diversified processing plant located in Sacramento, CA. The tomato products studied included whole peeled tomatoes, tomato juice and tomato paste.

The plant processed 1200–1350 t of raw tomatoes per day in three 8-h shifts. The entire processing line was divided into 15 sections to facilitate data acquisition. This division was determined by the location of electrical panels. The electrical consumption by various processing and handling equipment was measured with the use of electric watt transducers (Model PC 76-1, Ohio Semitronics). Steam flow to the processing equipment was measured with the use of orifice plates mounted in the steam lines. The pressure drop caused by the orifice plate was transmitted to an electronic differential pressure transmitter (Foxboro). An automatic data acquisition system (Autodata 9, Accurex) was used to record data from the various differential pressure transmitters as well as electric watt transducers.

A computer program was written to average acquired data on steam flow and electric consumption. Care was taken to account for the times when electric motors were not operating such as during breakdowns and lunch breaks. Details on energy monitoring and computer programs are available in a report by Singh et al. (1979).

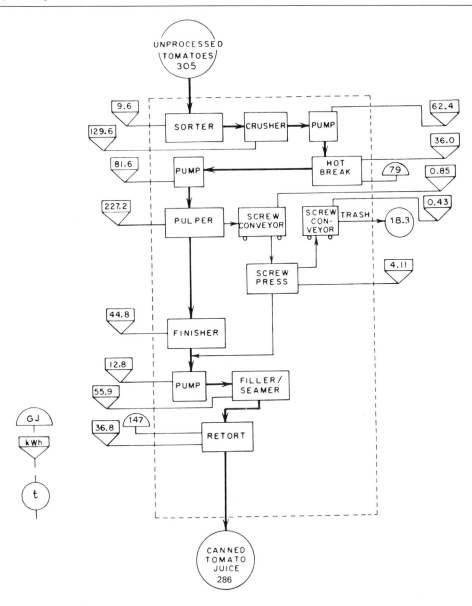

Fig. 10.6. Energy accounting diagram of tomato juice canning (Singh et al., 1980.) Basis: 8-h shift.

3.1. Results and discussion

The energy intensity of tomato processing can be obtained from the daily amount of tomato received by the plant and the total daily energy consumption. Using data from 6 days of processing, a thermal energy intensity value of 1251.4 kJ per kg of tomatoes received was calculated. This value represents processing of tomatoes into the three products manufactured in this cannery. The electrical energy intensity value was calculated to be 0.025 kWh/kg of raw tomatoes. The electrical intensity value was obtained from energy consumption data for 1 month, during which time some processing of pears and peaches was also conducted. However, tomatoes constituted over 95% of the products processed. It should be noted that in this plant tomato paste was packaged in drums which were subsequently frozen. This practice is not very common in the Californian canning industry.

Chapter 10 references, p. 190.

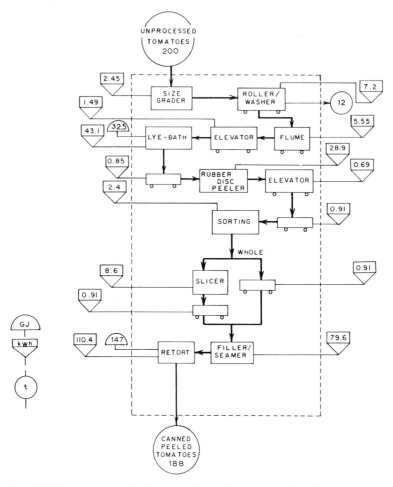

Fig. 10.7. Energy accounting diagram of peeled tomato canning (Singh et al., 1980). Basis: 8-h shift.

3.2. Energy accounting of receiving operations

In California, 99% of tomatoes destined for processing are harvested using mechanical harvesters. After harvest, the tomatoes are loaded directly into 25-t gondolas for transportation. Each truck hauls two gondolas to the canneries.

In the cannery, where this project was carried out, at the receiving station the tomatoes were removed from the gondolas with the use of water. The water containing field dirt of tomatoes was pumped to a mud settling tank. The tomatoes were conveyed in a hydraulic flume for additional washing and initial inspection. Water was recirculated in the hydraulic flume. The receiving station had the capacity to handle approximately 600 t in an 8-h shift. The majority of the electrical energy at the receiving station was consumed by the pump conveying water to the mud settling tank. The energy intensity of the receiving operations was calculated to be 0.32 Wh/kg of raw tomatoes received.

3.3. Tomato juice

Production of tomato juice involved crushing tomatoes, heating them rapidly to inactivate enzymes, filling juice into cans, and retorting the cans. The energy accounting diagram for tomato juice production is shown in Fig. 10.6. It is evident that most operations consume electricity. Hot-break heaters, necessary to inactivate enzymes, and retorts used steam. Combining the thermal energy and electrical energy data to similar base units of kJ, the

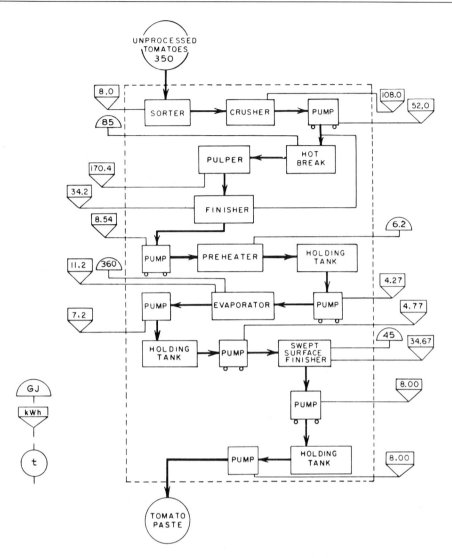

Fig. 10.8. Energy accounting diagram of tomato-paste manufacturing (Singh et al., 1980). Basis: 8-h shift. A + B + C + D = 36 t of waste.

hot-break heaters and retorts accounted for almost 97% of the energy consumed in the processing line. For the equipment included in the system boundary in Fig. 10.6 the energy intensity of tomato juice production was calculated to be 1086.2 kJ/kg of raw tomatoes.

3.4. Canned peeled tomatoes

Processing of canned peeled tomatoes required lye-peelers to facilitate peel removal and retorts to sterilize the canned product and conveying equipment. As shown in Fig. 10.7, lye-bath peelers and retorts consumed steam, whereas all other equipment operated with electricity. These two operations also accounted for almost 99% of total energy consumed by the equipment indicated in Fig. 10.7. The energy intensity was calculated to be 1300.2 kJ/kg of raw tomatoes.

3.5. Tomato paste

The energy accounting diagram of tomato paste production is shown in Fig. 10.8. Several operations such as sorting, pulping and finishing were similar to tomato juice production. Steam was used in vertical heat exchangers to preheat tomato juice. A large quantity of steam was used in the evaporator. The energy use by the energy-intensive equipment as a percent of total energy consumption is shown in Fig. 10.8. The evaporator and the heat exchanger used in preconcentration accounted for the majority of steam consumption. The energy intensity of tomato paste production for the equipment studied was 1307.2 kJ/kg of raw tomatoes.

4. PEACH CANNING

A study on energy use in a peach canning plant was conducted in 1978 in a cannery located in northern California. The operations studied included washing, shaking, grading, pitting, inspecting and lye peeling. Data on energy use in retorting was estimated from equipment used in processing tomatoes.

Steam and electricity were measured at six monitoring locations. Peach canning involved receiving peaches in bins, dumping fruit into a water tank and then elevating it out with a conveyor. The peaches were then graded for size, rinsed in water and pitted. After pit removal, the peach halves were orientated cup down on a belt conveyor and conveyed to a lye-bath peeler. After exposure to caustic solution for a predetermined time, the fruit was again rinsed. The fruit was allowed to orientate cup up, again inspected, size-graded and then filled into cans along with syrup. The canned fruit was then heated in retorts to achieve the desired sterilization.

Steam flow was measured with the use of orifice plates mounted in steam pipes. In this study only steam flow to lye-bath peeler was monitored. The pressure drop caused by the orifice plate was measured using an electronic differential pressure transmitter (Foxboro). The electrical signal from the differential pressure transmitter was recorded by a data-logger (Autodata 9, Accurex).

The electrical energy was measured using electric watt transducer (Ohio Semitronics). The transducers were installed into the circuit between motor and circuit breaker. The peach processing line contained 167 electrical motors, 17 motors were selected as representative and wired with watt transducers.

The mass flow of peach halves into the lye-bath was determined by taking photographs of the belt conveyor, and counting the number of peach halves on the belt. Knowing the belt speed and the weight of a representative sample of peach halves, the mass flow rate to the lye-bath peeler was determined. The calculated mass flow rates were compared with the cannery records on shipments received and processed.

5. RESULTS AND DISCUSSION

An energy accounting diagram for peach canning is shown in Fig. 10.9. As previously mentioned, steam flow to the retorts was estimated from other studies conducted as part of the comprehensive research program. Nine retorts were used in processing peaches, the total energy used in retorting was estimated to be 263.3 GJ per 8-h shift.

Within various operations, transport of fruit and waste consumed most electricity. It was determined that 23% of the total electric consumption occurred in dry conveying whereas 38% was consumed in pumping water to convey fruit and waste products.

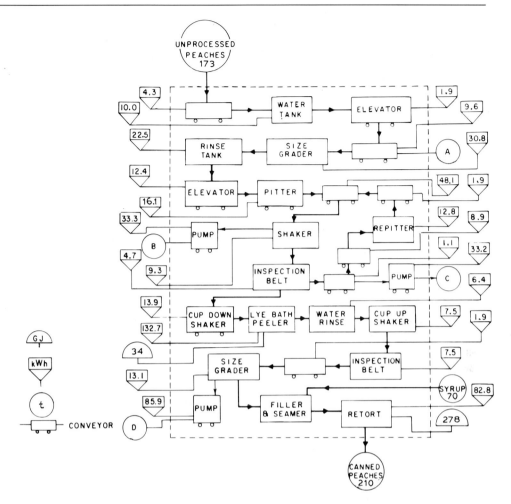

Fig. 10.9. Energy accounting diagram of peach canning (Carroad et al., 1980). Basis: 8-h shift.

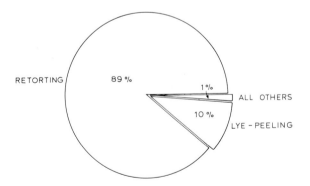

Fig. 10.10. Energy consumption in peach processing and canning.

Steam quality to the lye bath peeler was determined to be 86.3%. The steam consumption by the three lye-bath peelers was determined as 28.5 GJ.

Using fossil-fuel equivalent factor, the energy requirement as a percent of the total consumption is shown in Fig. 10.10. It is clear that retorting and lye-bath peeling are the most energy consumptive unit operations. Equipment associated with these two operations are prime candidates for modifications that would allow energy conservation in peach canning.

Chapter 10 references, p. 190.

6. SUMMARY

The data presented in the preceding paragraphs provide a quantitative description of energy use in canning different fruits and vegetables. Since most of the unit operations are similar in the canning industries, these data should provide good estimates for products other than those studies in this project. These data are also useful in identifying energy intensive operations and energy conservation opportunities in the canning industry.

7. REFERENCES

Carroad, P.A., Singh, R.P., Chhinnan, M.S., Jacob, N.L. and Rose, W.W., 1980. Energy use quantification in the canning of clingstone peaches. Presented at 39th Annual Meeting of Institute of Food Technologists, 10–13 June 1979, St. Louis, MO. J. Food Sci., 45: 723–725.

Chhinnan, M.S., Singh, R.P., Pederson, L.D., Carroad, P.A., Rose, W.W. and Jacob, N.L., 1980. Analysis of energy utilization in spinach processing. Trans. ASAE, 23: 503–507.

Gries, V., 1975. The energy spectrum, a comparison study of appliances. Marketing Conf., American Gas Association, Atlanta, GA, 18 pp.

Singh, R.P., 1978. Energy accounting in food process operations. Food Technol., 32 (4): 40–46.

Singh, R.P., Carroad, P.A., Chhinnan, M.S., Rose, W.W. and Jacob, N.L., 1979. Energy conservation in the canning industry. Phase I – Identification and measurement of energy uses in food processing operations. A Project Report. Department of Agricultural Engineering, University of California, Davis, CA, 150 pp.

Singh, R.P., Carroad, P.A., Chhinnan, M.S., Rose, W.W. and Jacob, N.L., 1980. Energy accounting in canning tomato products. J. Food Sci., 45: 735–739.

Chapter 11

Energy Use in Evaporation of Liquid Foods

T.R. RUMSEY

1. INTRODUCTION

Evaporation of liquid foods is a major consumer of energy in certain types of food processing plants. Schwartzberg (1977) estimated that the concentration of liquid food products in the United States required the equivalent of 11.6 million barrels of oil or about 70 PJ per year, which was nearly 4.4% of the energy used to process food. The beet sugar industry alone required the equivalent of 2.58 million barrels of oil or about 16 PJ annually.

Much of the original work on evaporation was done for the sugar and salt industries (Standiford, 1963). Evaporation of liquid foods is most commonly accomplished using multiple-effect evaporators. Norbert Rillieux is credited with the invention of multiple-effect evaporation in vacuum (Staub and Paturau, 1963). Double and triple-effect evaporators developed by Rillieux were used in the sugar cane industry in Louisiana during the early 1840's.

The data on evaporator energy use presented in this chapter are from articles found using a computer literature search of several data bases. Only a few publications documenting evaporator performance have appeared in technical journals since the energy crisis of the 1970's. A large portion of the data available are from publications in trade journals. Often these articles tend to be advertisements for new makes or models of evaporators with data supplied by the manufacturer.

Actual in-plant evaporator performance data are relatively scarce. There are at least two reasons for this. First of all, companies are reluctant to publish data which could possibly help a rival and secondly, the data are often difficult and time-consuming to obtain. Smith and Taylor (1981) make the following comment: "Our involvement with evaporator testing over the past few years has perhaps taught us more about the difficulties and dangers of this activity than it has produced concrete and reliable data. Nonetheless we now have a better feel for what happens in this important unit operation of sugar manufacture."

Methods of performance testing are covered in the next section. These are useful for designing tests to measure evaporator energy use, and include techniques to interpret the results and analyze possible causes for poor performance.

2. PERFORMANCE TEST METHODS

Several publications give detailed accounts of procedures for evaluating the performance of evaporators. Some of the measurement and analytical techniques given are described below.

Chapter 11 references, p. 201.

TABLE 11.1

Calculation of two-effect evaporator performance

No.	Measured							Calculated		
	T_0 (°C)	T_1 (°C)	T_2 (°C)	T_F (°C)	X_F (%)	X_p (%)	Feed (kg/h)	U_1 (W/(m^2°C))	U_2	V_0 (kg/h)
1	118	70	48	87	5.7	28.2	21550	1108	570	8907
2	118	67	45	83	5.8	28.1	22700	1099	601	9384
3	114	74	53	63	5.0	34.0	27250	1895	859	12631
4	107	74	51	63	5.0	34.0	24300	2051	697	11184

2.1. Measurement techniques

The equipment test committee of the American Institute of Chemical Engineers has prepared a guide for the performance evaluation of evaporators (AlChE, 1979). Sections are included on test planning, instruments and methods of measurement, test operation, computation of results and interpretation of results. Their technique involves measurements of both steam flow and feed flow rates to the evaporator. One of these flow rates along with other measured data are used to calculate theoretical heat balances and a theoretical estimate of the other measured flow variables. The evaporator is assumed to be performing satisfactorily if the measured and theoretical flow rates are approximately the same. Overall heat transfer coefficients are also calculated to examine the possibility of fouling or the occurrence of noncondensable gases in the steam side. The publication gives a set of example calculations for several test cases.

The United State Department of Energy (ERDA, 1977) presents a detailed account of the data and measurement techniques required to make performance evaluations of evaporators. They suggest using plant operating data to determine the theoretical steam requirements for the evaporator operating under ideal conditions. Data necessary for the calculations include: (a) first-effect steam pressure; (b) feed temperature and composition; (c) temperature and pressures in each effect (or liquor compositions and temperatures); and (d) product flow, temperature and composition. Theoretical heat and mass balance calculations are then made using the data. If the difference between the measured and calculated steam flow is within 5%, the evaporator is assumed to be performing satisfactorily.

Seven major sources of energy losses are listed by ERDA (1977): excessive venting, radiation and convection losses, poor vacuum system performance, air leakage, water leakage, fouling, and poor separator efficiency. Methods are given to estimate or measure the magnitude of each of these losses.

Baker (1977) summarizes the information necessary for the operational performance test of an on-line evaporator. Table 11.1 is taken from this chapter, and is repeated here as an example of the type and amount of data that is needed for such a test. The data required are similar to those recommended by AlChE (1979). The minimum period for gathering data is 2 h, with readings taken every 10–15 min. Baker does a sample heat balance for the performance test of a four-effect evaporator using data collected according to the procedure given. The data are analyzed to investigate an abnormally low overall heat transfer coefficient in the first effect. Baker notes that: "Instruments used in obtaining test data must be sensitive enough to detect significant changes and must be properly calibrated. The number of manhours wasted and false conclusions drawn from the use of bad instruments is almost beyond belief."

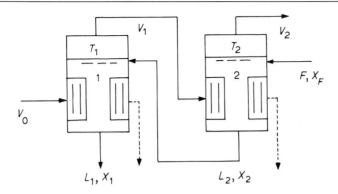

Fig. 11.1. Schematic diagram of a two-effect evaporator with backward feed.

2.2. Analytical techniques

Steady state heat and mass balances can be used to analyze evaporator performance. An example of such an analysis will be given. The technique used is that given by Holland (1975). This method has been used previously to analyze sugar evaporators (Radovic et al., 1979) and tomato paste evaporators (Rumsey et al., 1984).

A two-effect tomato paste evaporator (Rumsey and Scott, 1982) is used to illustrate the technique. The evaporator uses forced circulation in its first effect and natural circulation in its second effect. In the analysis, it is assumed that the boiling point elevations are negligible. The equations for the first effect shown in Fig. 11.1 are (see Nomenclature):

NOMENCLATURE

A_i	surface area of heat exchanger for ith effect (m²)
$C_p(X_i)$	specific heat of product in ith effect (kJ/(kg °C))
F	feed flow rate (kg/h)
$H(T_i)$	vapor enthalpy for ith effect (kJ/kg)
$h(T_i)$	condensate enthalpy for ith effect (kJ/kg)
$h(T_i, X_i)$	product enthalpy in ith effect (kJ/kg)
L_i	product flow from ith effect (kg/h)
Q_i	heat transfer rate from vapor to product in ith effect (kJ/h)
T_i	temperature in ith effect (°C)
U_i	overall heat transfer coefficient in ith effect (W/(m² °C))
V_i	vapor flow rate from ith effect (kg/h)
X_i	mass fraction of solids in ith effect

Overall mass balance:

$$L_2 = V_1 + L_1$$

Solids mass balance:

$$L_2 X_2 = L_1 X_1$$

Steam side energy balance:

$$V_0 H(T_0) = Q_1 + V_0 h(T_0)$$

Product side energy balance:

$$L_2 h(T_2, X_2) + Q_1 = V_1 H(T_1) + L_1 h(T_1, X_1)$$

Heat transfer rate:

$$Q_1 = U_1 A_1 (T_0 - T_1)$$

Chapter 11 references, p. 201.

The equations for the second effect are derived in a similar manner:

Overall mass balance:

$$F = V_2 + L_2$$

Solids mass balance:

$$FX_F = L_2 X_2$$

Vapor side energy balance:

$$V_1 H(T_1) = Q_2 + V_1 h(T_1)$$

Product side energy balance:

$$F h(T_F, X_F) + Q_2 = V_2 H(T_2) + L_2 h(T_2, X_F)$$

Heat transfer rate:

$$Q_2 = U_2 A_2 (T_1 - T_2)$$

Curve fits of steam table properties are used for the steam and condensate enthalpies. The product enthalpies are calculated by equations in the form:

$$h(T_i, X_i) = C_p(X_i)(T_i - T_{ref})$$

The following variables are assumed to be known or measured: A_1, A_2, F, T_F, T_0, T_1, T_2, X_F and X_1. The ten equations above are used to solve the following ten unknowns: L_1, L_2, Q_1, Q_2, U_1, U_2, V_0, V_1, V_2 and X_2. A computer subroutine that solves simultaneous nonlinear algebraic equations was used to solve the equations. The results for a sample set of calculations are given in Table 11.1. The data are from measurements on the same model evaporator at two different processing plants.

3. PERFORMANCE TEST RESULTS

The results presented are grouped by product. This list is not meant to be all-inclusive. For example, no data were found for corn syrup, which is listed by Schwartzberg (1977) as having a high energy requirement. The section dealilng with tomato products is more lengthy than the others because of this author's work with evaporators in this area.

3.1. Citrus products

The performance of citrus juice evaporators has been analyzed in several publications by personnel at the University of Florida's Agricultural Research and Education Center. Almost 90% of the evaporation capacity in Florida's citrus industry is supplied by evaporators of the long tube, falling film type (Chen, 1982). These evaporators employ the high temperature short time principle, and are commonly known as TASTE (thermally accelerated short time) evaporators. They have from four to seven effects, with an average evaporating capacity of 15 550 kg h. The schematic of a four-effect, six-stage TASTE evaporator is shown in Fig. 11.2 (Chen, 1982). Typical residence time for a seven-effect TASTE evaporator is just over 7 min.

The energy requirements for a TASTE citrus evaporator were measured by Chen et al. (1979). The evaporator had four effects and seven stages during the first tests. Further tests were performed after it was modified to five effects and eight stages.

Because of the low residence times and steady operating nature of the evaporator, the test lengths were 12 min each. Product concentrations were

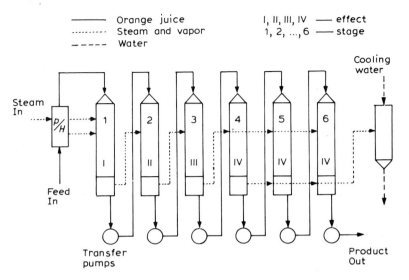

Fig. 11.2. Schematic diagram of a multiple-effect citrus evaporator.

TABLE 11.2

Summary of citrus evaporator data

Number effects	4	5	6	6
Feed concentration (°Brix)	11.8	12.2	4.85	4.65
Feed rate (kg/h)	21220	22120	9785	9620
Feed temperature (°C)	44.6	43.3	a	a
Product concentration (°Brix)	59.4	60.4	57.3	58.5
Steam flow (kg/h)	7180	4795	1955	1815
Steam economy	2.4	3.7	4.58	4.88

[a]Data not available.
°Brix = % sucrose (w/w).

a refractometer at the start and middle of the test run. The feed rate was measured by noting the change in level in a feed tank over a four minute period during middle of the test run. Steam flow was determined at the start and mid-point of the test run by measuring condensate flow diverted into a container.

Representative data were given for one run in each configuration. A summary of these test data is given in Table 11.2. In its four-effect configuration, the evaporator concentrated juice from 11.8 to 59.4°Brix. The feed rate was measured at 21 220 kg/h and the steam flow rate measured 7180 kg/h. Using these data, the steam economy was calculated to be 2.4. The economy on subsequent tests of the evaporator in this configuration ranged from 2.2 to 2.7. Vacuum leakage was suspected as the cause of the low steam economy and capacity.

The evaporator was subsequently modified by the addition of a fifth effect, and a new set of performance tests was conducted. The data are summarized in Table 11.2. The feed rate was measured at 22 120 kg/h, with a composition of 12.2°Brix and the product had a composition of 60.4°Brix. The steam flow was measured at 4790 kg/h and the steam economy was calculated to be 3.7. A typical operating season for these evaporators is 3000 h. It was estimated that upgrading from four to five effects would save enough energy to pay back the cost of the upgrade in less than two and a half seasons.

Carter and Chen (1982) monitored the performance of a commercial six-effect TASTE evaporator. The evaporator was used to concentrate orange pulpwash, a by-product of organce juice concentrate production. Two modes of operation

Chapter 11 references, p. 201.

TABLE 11.3

Summary of data needed for performance analysis of four-effect evaporator

Item or effect	Body				
	1	2	3	4	Condenser
Steam of chest (kg/h)	M	C	C	C	C
Steam pressure (Pa)	M	M	M	M	
Steam latent heat (kJ/kg)	R	R	R	R	
Steam temperature saturated (°C)	R	R	R	R	
Liquid in temperature (°C)	M	C	C	C	
Liquid out temperature (°C)	C	C	C	C	
Boiling point rise (°C)	R	R	R	R	
Vapor temperature (°C)	R	R	R	R	
Vapor pressure (kPa)	M	M	M	M	M
Vapor latent heat (kJ/kg)	R	R	R	R	
Liquid flow in (kg/h)	M	C	C	C	
Liquid flow out (kg/h)	C	C	C	C	
Evaporation (kg/h)	C	C	C	C	
Product concentration in (%)	M	M	M	M	
Product concentration out (%)	M	M	M	M	
Heating surface (m^2)	M	M	M	M	
Overall heat transfer coefficient (W/(m^2°C))	C	C	C	C	

M, Measured test; C, calculated; R, data from reference tables.

were investigated: manual and automatic control of the steam flow and feed flow. Steam condensate temperature was used to control steam flow to the evaporator. The product vapor temperature in the fifth stage was used to indicate product concentration for control of the feed to the evaporator. The set points for the steam and product temperature were 100 and 68.5°C, respectively. A microcomputer was used for data acquisition and control. A Basic language program was implemented to accomplish proportional, integral and derivative control.

Feed rates were measured using feed tank level difference and a positive displacement, mechanical register flow meter. Steam flow was determined by measuring condensate flow two to three times during the test period. Product concentrates were measured with a refractometer.

Several tests were conducted in each mode, although data are only given for two representative tests. The data are summarized in Table 11.3. Test lengths were approximately two hours each. During the manual control tests, the feed had an average composition of 4.85°Brix and the feed rate averaged 9790 kg/h. The product was concentrated to 57.3°Brix and used 1960 kg/h of steam for a steam economy of 4.58. This was 90% of its theoretical steam economy. Under automatic control, the feed composition was 4.65°Brix and feed rate was 9620 kg/h. Measured output concentration was 58.5°Brix and steam flow was 1815 kg/h. The steam economy was calculated at 4.88, which was 6.6% greater than that for manual control.

3.2. Dairy products

The dairy industry uses evaporation of whole milk, skimmed milk, butter milk and whey. There are several trade journal articles concerning evaporators used for dairy products. Most of the data given appear to be based on the expected performance as supplied by the evaporator manufacturer rather than on actual measurements.

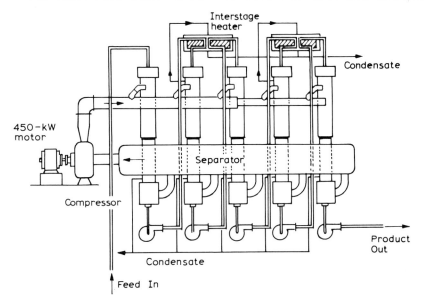

Fig. 11.3. Schematic diagram of a five-stage milk evaporator with mechanical vapor recompression (Anonymous, 1980).

A two-stage falling film plate evaporator with mechanical vapor recompression (MVR) has been installed at a milk processing plant (Anonymous, 1979). Its 150-kW rotary compressor is electrically powered. After start-up, no boiler steam is used by the evaporator. The evaporator has a design capacity of 5445 kg/h when used to concentrate buttermilk and skim milk to 25% solids. It has produced 2690 l/h of skim milk at 25% solids for runs of over 15 h without any drop in capacity. The steam economy was reported to be 6, and this was claimed to be equivalent to an 8 to 30-effect conventional evaporator, depending on the cost of fuel. The estimated fuel savings were expected to be enough to amortize the rotary compressor in less than 1 year.

A five-stage evaporator with MVR has been in operation at a milk plant for several years (Anonymous, 1980). Figure 11.3 is a schematic diagram of the evaporator. During its first 2 years of operation, the evaporator saved nearly $350 000 annually over the conventional three-effect system that it replaced. The evaporator has the capacity to concentrate 23 750 kg/h of 8.5% solids skim milk up to 45% solids. The MVR system compresses approximately 19 200 kg/h of vapor at 71°C from the separator and introduces it back into the five-stage heaters at 75°C. A 450-kW electric motor is used to run the centrifugal compressor.

Standfort (1983) describes a seven-effect MVR evaporator used in a milk receiving plant. The evaporator can concentrate whole whey, pre-concentrated whey, skim milk and whole milk. It is a falling film type evaporator. Steam is recompressed from the first and fourth effects by the turbocompressor. The compressor is driven by a multiple-stage steam turbine. The first effect is heated by both the recompressed vapors and discharge steam from the turbine. It removes 17.5 kg of water from the feed for each kg of steam supplied to the turbine. The evaporator runs at essentially constant capacity for 20 h, and 4 h are allowed for cleaning each day.

3.3. Beet and cane sugar

Much has been written on evaporation in the beet and cane sugar industries. The text on sugar by Honig (1963) contains chapters on the principles of steam

Chapter 11 references, p. 201.

TABLE 11.4

Summary of sugar evaporator data

Effect no.	Original configuration		Upgraded configuration			Temperature (°C)
	Area (m²)	Vapor bleed	Temperature (°C)	Area (m²)	Vapor bleed	
1	995	Yes	126	995	No	129
2	1009	Yes	111	1609	Yes	123
3	702	Yes	93	1439	Yes	115
4	598	No	75	598	Yes	97
5	None	None	None	550	Yes	82

economy in evaporation, the chemistry of the evaporation process and the cleaning of evaporators. The review article by Zagrodzki and Kubasiewicz (1977) contains a wealth of engineering information on sugar evaporation.

Computer programs have been written specifically for the sugar industry to evaluate multiple-effect evaporator systems (Radovic et al., 1979; Hoekstra, 1981). Such computer programs have been used to help analyze the steam needs of entire sugar mills (Reid and Rein, 1983) and to calculate overall heat transfer coefficients in fouling studies (Smith and Taylor, 1981).

The text book type installation of multiple-effect evaporators is rarely seen in sugar plant operations (Hoekstra, 1981). Often there are four to five effects with more than one vessel per effect which are plumbed together in various parallel and series configurations. Vapor is often bled from several of the effects for use in other process operations. Baikow (1982) illustrated the benefits of bleeding vapor by using steady state heat and mass balances to analyze a four-effect sugar evaporator with and without vapor bleeding. The vapors were withdrawn from the first and second effects to preheat juice and run vacuum pans. As bleeding the vapors is similar to venting, the steam economy of the evaporator fell from 3.98 to 1.99 kg water evaporator per kg of steam. However, there was a 19.66% savings of steam overall by using the vapor bleeds rather than boiler steam to preheat the juice and run the vacuum pans.

Karren and Rychkun (1981) presented operational data concerning improvements made on a multiple-effect beet sugar evaporator. In its original condition it had four effects with the areas listed in Table 11.4. In 1980, a fifth effect was added to the evaporator. Additional heating surface area was added to the second and third effects by adding two additional bodies. The areas of the heat exchangers which used vapors from the various effects were also changed. These changes resulted in higher temperature vapors being available at each effect. Vapors could now be bled from the last four effects instead of the first three, and so more efficient use was made of the steam from the boiler. In the original configuration, 1.69 kg of water were evaporated per kg of steam. The improvements to the system increased this number to 2.21. Because of vapor bleeding from several of the effects, these values are lower than the approximate expected values of 4 and 5 for the four- and five-effect evaporators.

The performance of a mechanical vapor recompression unit installed at a cane sugar plant is discussed by Allan et al. (1983). The unit was set up to compress the vapors from the first effect of a five-effect evaporator. A flow diagram of the installation is shown in Fig. 11.4. The compressor is powered by a steam turbine. Steam that passes through the turbine is used in another vessel in the first effect, as shown in the diagram. The vapor is compressed from 145 to 196 kPa. The amount of vapor recompressed was approximately 31 000 kg/h. It was estimated that the unit saved approximately 6000 kg/h of

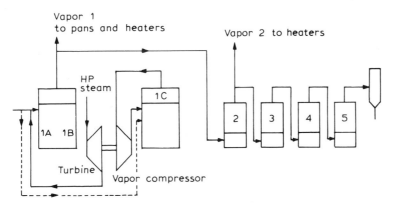

Fig. 11.4. Steam flow diagram of a cane sugar evaporator using mechanical vapor recompression (Allan et al., 1983). HP, high pressure.

high-pressure steam. The yearly savings in steam was nearly one-sixth of the total installed cost of the unit.

3.4. Tomato products

Evaporators are used to produce tomato products with varying degrees of concentration. The primary products are classified as purees and paste (Goose and Binsted, 1964). Tomato puree ranges in solids content from 11% (light puree) to 22% (heavy puree) while tomato pastes range from 28% (light paste) to 45% (heavy paste).

The tomato paste industry has become energy conscious as can be seen by the introduction of evaporators with an increasing number of effects. Snyder et al. (1969) described a new double-effect evaporator designed for heat-sensitive products such as tomato paste. An energy-saving modification to this evaporator was described by Attiyate (1978). The modification consisted of a factory built third effect which was added to increase evaporator capacity while keeping the steam consumption the same. Rogers (1976) described a tomato paste processing plant which utilized three new triple-effect evaporators. At present, there are at least two plants using four-effect evaporators to manufacture tomato paste.

A number of energy audits on tomato product evaporators have been performed (Rumsey et al., 1981, 1984). The audits were conducted over a 2-year period under a grant from the U.S. Department of Energy. Single, double and triple-effect evaporators were monitored at several processing plants.

The evaporators used in the industry are the recirculating type, and almost all employ forced circulation. The operation of the evaporators encountered was similar. The concentration of the product out of the evaporators was controlled automatically. In-line instrumentation measured total solids in the final stage, and this was used to control the rate of product removal. Level controllers were used to control the flow rate of paste between stages and the feed into the evaporator.

The primary measurements taken were steam and feed flow rates and temperatures in each effect. Steam flows were measured to each evaporator using differential pressure flow meters. Two independent measurements were made of the steam flow to the evaporator in most tests. Raw juice flow was measured with a portable ultrasonic flow meter. Temperatures were measured with copper constantan thermocouples attached to evaporator surfaces with tape and covered with two layers of insulation. All data were recorded using a portable digital data logger. Data were recorded on magnetic and paper tape

Chapter 11 references, p. 201.

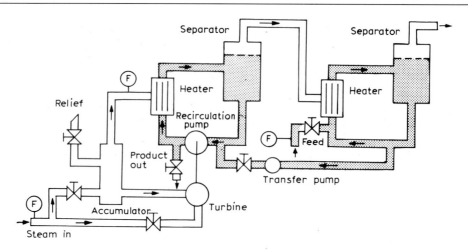

Fig. 11.5. Schematic diagram of a double-effect tomato paste evaporator (Rumsey et al., 1981).

TABLE 11.5

Average performance for tomato paste evaporators

Evaporator	Effects	Solids			Measured			Theory	
		Time (h)	In (%)	Out (%)	Feed (kg/h)	Steam (kg/h)	Economy (kg/kg)	Steam (kg/h)	Economy (kg/kg)
A	2	18	5.9	28.1	20900	11000	1.38	7950	1.91
A	2	24	5.4	28.1	22800	12400	1.50	9550	1.93
B	2	24	5.0	40.5	18000	11400	1.25	8950	1.89
B	2	24	5.0	40.5	20950	12150	1.55	9800	1.87
C	3	24	5.0	30.0	32950	10600	2.60	10300	2.67
C	3	23	5.0	30.0	28250	9700	2.46	8600	2.69
D	3	24	5.0	35.4	38150	14250	2.30	12200	2.69
D	3	24	5.2	44.6	42250	15450	2.42	14850	2.51

at 10-min intervals. All flow data were averaged over each time interval. A microcomputer was used to reduce and analyze the data. The results for one double-effect and two triple-effect evaporators are summarized here.

A schematic diagram of the double-effect evaporator is given in Fig. 11.5. It is the same model evaporator described by Snyder et al. (1969). The evaporator uses forced circulation in the first effect and natural circulation in the second. Power for the centrifugal pump in the first effect is supplied by a steam turbine. During normal operation, measurements indicated that about 50% of the total steam for evaporation goes through the turbine and 50% is in the form of makeup steam through the control valve. The variation in feed flow rate was typical of the data gathered on this model evaporator. The variation was caused by the opening and closing of the feed valve which was responding to the level controller in the second effect.

Average measured feed and steam flows for two of the double-effect evaporators are given in Table 11.5. The data were averaged over a full operating day whenever possible because of fluctuations in feed rate to the evaporators. Theoretical steam flows and economies were calculated using the method covered in the analytical techniques section of this chapter. The theoretical economies calculated ranged from 1.87 to 1.93. These were in agreement with a value of 1.82 given in the evaporator manufacturer's literature. Measured values of steam flow were higher than theoretical values by about 23%, which is outside the maximum range of 5% suggested by ERDA (1977). One possible reason for the difference was the amount of venting from the first effect heater. This was set manually with valves on the outside of the heater, and it was noticed that at times the amount of venting seemed excessive.

Data for two models of triple-effect evaporators are also given in Table 11.5. The first one, evaporator C in Table 11.5, is the same model as described by Attiyate (1978). One forced circulation effect was added to the two-effect evaporator model previously discussed. Manufacturer's literature gave a steam economy of 2.63 which is close to the theoretical economies of 2.67 and 2.69 calculated for the two test runs listed. The measured economies were 2.60 and 2.46, respectively, with measured steam flows 2.8 and 11.3% greater than theoretical. No extensive effort was made to track down the reason for the difference between the measured and theoretical values. This was because the measurements were usually within the 5% tolerance specified by ERDA (1977).

A triple-effect evaporator similar to that described by Rogers (1976) was monitored, and the results are given in Table 11.5 as evaporator D. This evaporator has a rated capacity of 55 000 kg/h water evaporated as compared to 31 000 kg/h for evaporator C. Its rated economy is 2.75 from maufacturer's literature. The measured economies of 2.30 and 2.42 were slightly below the theoretical values of 2.69 and 2.51. Measured steam flows were 14.4 and 3.88% greater than theoretical. Again, as for the double effect, it appeared that excess venting was the probable cause for the difference.

5. REFERENCES

Allan, G.N., Kedian, M.R. and Trattles, D.E., 1983. Mechanical vapor recompression at Pongola. Proc. S.Afr. Sugar Technol. Assoc., 57: 79–84.

AIChE, 1979. AIChE Equipment Testing Procedure – Evaporators – A Guide to Performance Evaluation (2nd Edition). American Institute of Chemical Engineers, New York, NY.

Anonymous, 1979. MVR evaporator provides $60 000 annual fuel cost savings. Food Process., 40 (1): 92.

Anonymous, 1980. Energy efficient evaporation. Food Eng., 52 (1): 104–105.

Attiyate, Y., 1978. Modified evaporator boosts tomato processing output. Food. Eng., 50 (11): 98–100.

Baikow, V.E., 1982. Manufacture and Refining of Raw Cane Sugar (2nd Edition). Elsevier, Amsterdam, 588 pp.

Baker, T.W., 1977. Evaporation and heating. In: G.P. Meade and J.C. Chen (Editors), Cane Sugar Handbook, Wiley, New York, NY, pp. 185–234.

Carter, R.D. and Chen, C.S., 1982. Microcomputer control of citrus juice evaporation saves energy. Food Technol., 36 (5): 239–244.

Chen, C.S., 1982. Citrus evaporator technology. Trans. ASAE, 25: 1457–1463.

Chen, C.S., Carter, R.D. and Buslig, B.S., 1979. Energy requirements for the TASTE citrus juice evaporator. In: R.A. Fazzolare and C.B. Smith (Editors), Changing Energy Use Futures, Vol. IV. Pergamon Press, New York, NY, pp. 1841–1848.

ERDA Technology Applications Manual, 1977. Upgrading existing evaporators to reduce energy consumption. Technical Information Center, Oak Ridge, TN, 91 pp.

Goose, P.G. and Binsted, R., 1964. Tomato Paste. Food Trade Press, London.

Heldman, D.R. and Singh, R.P., 1981. Food Processing Engineering (2nd Edition). AVI, Westport, CT.

Hoekstra, R.G., 1981. A computer program for simulating and evaluating multiple effect evaporators in the sugar industry. Proc. S.Afr. Sugar Technol. Assoc., 55: 43–50.

Holland, C.D., 1975. Fundamentals and Modeling of Separation Processes. Prentice-Hall, Englewood Cliffs, NJ.

Honig, P., 1963. Principles of Sugar Technology, Vol. 3. Elsevier, Amsterdam.

Karen, B. and Rychkun, M., 1981. Energy conservation at a Canadian sugar beet factory. Sugar Azucar, 76: 46–47, 50–53.

Radovic, L.R., Tasic, A.Z., Grozdanic, D.K., Djordjevic, B.D. and Valent, V.J., 1979. Computer design and analysis of a multiple effect evaporator system in the sugar industry. Ind. Eng. Chem. Process Res. Dev., 18: 318–323.

Reid, M.J. and Rein, P.W., 1983. Steam balance for the new Felixton II mill. Proc. S.Afri. Sugar Technol. Assoc., 57: 85–91.

Rogers, H.T., 1976. That's a lot of tomato paste! Am. Veg. Grower, 24 (5): 14, 42, 44.

Rumsey, T.R. and Scott, E.P., 1982. Measurement of heat transfer coefficients in multiple effect evaporators. ASAE Pap. 82-6029, Summer Meeting, June 1982, Madison, WI. American Society of Agricultural Engineers, St. Joseph, MI.

Rumsey, T.R., Conant, T.T., Pedersen, L.D. and Rose, W.W., 1981. Energy conservation in the food processing industry: measurement of energy used in evaporation of tomato products. Final Report, National Food Processors Association, Department of Energy Contract DE-AC07-78C540191, 97 pp.

Rumsey, T.R., Conant, T.T., Fortis, T., Scott, E.P., Pedersen, L.D. and Rose, W.W., 1984. Energy use in tomato paste evaporation. J. Food. Process Eng., 7 (3): 111–121.

Schwartzberg, H.G., 1977. Energy requirements for liquid food concentration. Food Technol., 31 (3): 67–76.

Smith, I.A. and Taylor, L.A.W., 1981. Some data on heat transfer in multiple effect evaporators. Proc. S.Afr. Sugar Technol. Assoc., 55: 51–55.

Snyder, B., Lerner, G., Witmer, C., Malvick, A. and Robe, K., 1969. Lowers evaporator temperature for tomato paste 40 F. Food. Proc., 30 (3): 42–44.

Standfort, P., 1983. A milestone in evaporation systems. Dairy Rec., 84 (7): 89–90, 92, 94, 96, 98.

Standiford, F.C., 1963. Evaporation. Chem. Eng., 70 (25): 157–176.

Staub, S. and Paturau, M., 1963. Principles of steam economy in evaporation. In: P. Honig (Editor), Principles of Sugar Technology. Elsevier, Amsterdam, pp. 38–104.

Zagrodzki, Sk. and Kubasiewicz, A., 1977. Heat economy in beet sugar factory evaporation. Sugar Technol. Rev., 4: 1–154.

Chapter 12

Energy Requirements in Food Irradiation

CHRISTIAN TRÄGÅRDH

1. INTRODUCTION

The commercial energy input in the food-producing system has increased tremendously in the last few decades. This is especially true for the industrialized parts of the world, but it also applies to the developing parts, where there is an increasing energy demand. The reasons may vary from country to country and from area to area, but they have in common demands for higher yields in the agricultural sector, as well as a more efficient post-harvest system to enable storage and distribution of the products obtained under various conditions and for longer periods of time. The development of the existing systems took place, to a large extent, under conditions when natural resources, specially energy, were considered to be relatively cheap. Relatively little consideration was given to the influence of added chemicals (biocides, fertilizers, preservatives, etc.) and food processing on human health. However, the situation is changing so that natural resources as well as human welfare have gradually increased in importance. The search for less demanding systems which still give high efficiency as well as high nutritional quality thus seem to be a high priority.

Irradiation (X-ray, electrons beams, γ-radiation) ($\lambda \approx 10^{-11}$–10^{-13} m) has often been claimed as the 'new' preservation method with a lower energy demand than conventional ones. Looking at the preservation only this is true, but this technology, however, influences other operations in the food chain, such as packaging, transport, storage, etc., as well as influencing product losses. In this chapter, results are presented where a comparison is made between conventional food preservation techniques and food irradiation, with respect to energy requirements for the total post-harvest system. In cases where differences in product losses also appear, the energy demand in the agricultural sector is also taken into account.

The results in themselves are not of primary interest, as they only reflect arbitrary and perhaps superficial situations. Of interest, is how these comparisons and analyses are performed using the available energy data found in the literature. Thus, in Table 12.1, energy data are collected from the references for those processes and items under consideration here. In certain cases recalculations based on theoretical considerations and practical assumptions must be done. Examples are cooling and hot water treatments. Also the energy demand for exchange of air in potato and onion storage are calculated in this way. It is of great importance to check that the energy data are relevant to the actual situation, data found in the literature and in this book often differ as a consequence of the type of equipment used, operating practice, ambient temperature, local infra-structure, training of staff, etc. The energy accounting system and practice also result in differences even for almost equivalent cases.

TABLE 12.1

Energy consumption by different food preservation methods

---

(1) Transport
    (a) Truck
        – short distance: 2.7 MJ km^{-1}t^{-1}
        – long distance: 1.4 MJ km^{-1}t^{-1}
        – here used: 2 MJ km^{-1}t^{-1}
    (b) Train: 0.22 MJ km^{-1}t^{-1}
    (c) Air cargo: 12 MJ km^{-1}t^{-1}
    (d) Ship
        coast traffic: 0.7 MJ km^{-1}t^{-1}
        canal: 0.15 MJ km^{-1}t^{-1}
    (e) Cold transport: addition of 20–30% depending on ambient temperature and transport system.

(2) Production of chemicals (active ingredient)
    (a) CIPC: 158 MJ/kg
    (b) Methyl bromide: 52 MJ/kg
    (c) Ethylene dibromide: 36 MJ/kg
    (d) Ethylene oxide: 65 MJ/kg

(3) Preservation
    (a) Irradiation
        – sprout inhibition with 0.10 kGy $\triangleq$ 0.012 MJ/kg
        – insect disinfestation with 0.25 kGy $\triangleq$ 0.007 MJ/kg
        – hygienization with 2.5 kGy $\triangleq$ 0.021 MJ/kg
        – radappatization with 30 kGy $\triangleq$ 0.157 MJ/kg
    (b) Heat sterilization of retort pouches
        – heat: 0.29 MJ/kg
        – electricity: 0.02 MJ/kg
    (c) Blanching of fish and meat products in pouches: 0.25 MJ/kg
    (d) Freezing to -20°C (0.99 MJ/kg) to -30°C (1.2 MJ/kg)
    (e) Heating of spices: 0.36 MJ/kg
    (f) Drying: 6 MJ/kg removed water

(4) Energy for cold storage
    Electricity to compressors:

Temperature difference (°C)	5	10	15	20	35	50
Energy demand (10^3 W/kg)	1.25	3.75	5.0	6.25	13	20

In potato and onion storage exchange of air requires following energy input (10^{-3} W/kg):

Temperature difference (°C)	Storage temperature (°C)				
	5	10	15	20	25
5		5.57			24.0
10	2.56			20.9	
15			12.5		

In potato storage, circulation of air requires 1.4×10^{-3} W/kg

(5) Energy for packaging
    (a) Package material:
        – polypropylene 120 MJ/kg
        – paper 50 MJ/kg
        – LD-polyethylene 88 MJ/kg
        – laminates for retort pouch: 61 MJ/kg
        – carton for pouch 13 MJ/m^2
    (b) Form fill and seal of retort pouch:
        – electricity: 0.066 MJ/kg
        – thermal energy: 0.11 MJ/kg

The next step is to make up a scheme like those in Figs. 12.1–3. This should be as detailed as possible in order actually to describe a 'real' situation under the actual premises. The flow sheets presented in Table 12.1 do not serve as models in this respect. Here, they only serve as a basis for calculations. Besides, the important thing in these calculations was to discover differences and important factors about the alternatives.

Examples of steps in the flow sheets in Figs. 12.1–3 that must be carefully evaluated are the transport situation and packaging. Conditions of vehicles and roads, transport distances and transport structure very much influence the specific energy demand; for example, for short-distance truck transport the energy consumption is 2.7 MJ km^{-1}t^{-1}, with long-distance truck transport it is 1.4 MJ km^{-1}t^{-1}. Packaging is concerned with size, thickness, choice of materials, re-use, etc.).

2. EVALUATED POST-HARVEST SYSTEMS

The following systems are selected in consultation with the International Atomic Energy Agency, Joint FAO/IAEA Division of Isotope and Radiation Applications of Atomic Energy for Food and Agricultural Development, Food Preservation Section, Vienna, for evaluation.

(1) Sprout inhibition of:
  (a) Potatoes through cold storage ($\leqslant 5°C$ treatment by CIPC (28 g/m^3) or irradiation at a dose of approximately 0.10 kGy (Fig. 12.1a).
  (b) Onions and ginger roots through cold storage or irradiation at a dose of approximately 0.10 kGy (Fig. 12.1b).

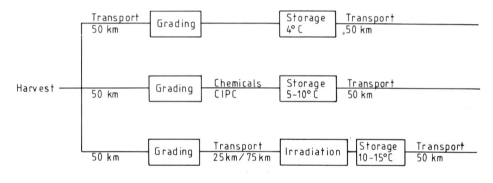

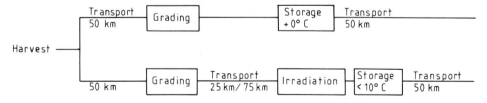

Fig. 12.1. Sprout inhibition.

(a) Potato handling and storage. Storage capacity = 10 000 t, storage time = 6 months; chemical treatment (CIPC, isopropyl-*N*-3-chlorophenyl-carbamite) is performed at a ratio of 28 g/m^3. The energy demand for grading and mechanical handling is assumed to be negligible. Air circulation and exchange of air due to respiration and water evaporation is required. Truck transport is assumed.

(b) Onion handling and storage. Storage capacity = 10 000 t, storage time = 6 months. The energy demand for grading and mechanical handling is assumed to be negligible. Exchange of air due to respiration and water evaporation is needed. Truck transport is assumed.

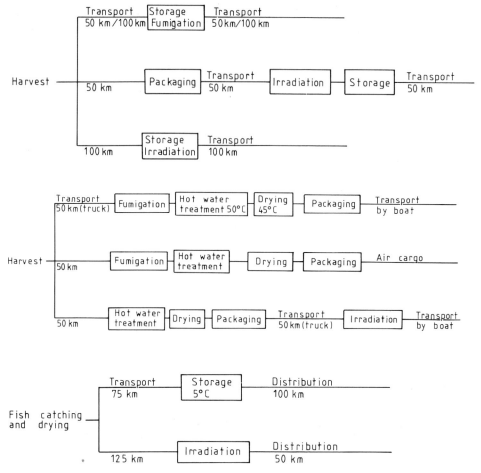

Fig. 12.2. Insect disinfestation.

(a) Systems for insect disinfestation of cereals and pulses. Packaging is done in 50-kg bags of polypropylene with a thickness of 0.07 mm. Fumigation with methyl bromide is here assumed to be performed twice for the storage period (12 months) at 48 g/m^3. Irradiation of the products is performed once for the storage time assumed. Truck transport is assumed.

(b) Systems for insect disinfestation of tropical fruits. Fumigation with ethylene dibromide at 8 g/m^3. The packaging material is an insect-resistant paper carton (23 kg size). Transport distance for the processed product is assumed to be 5000 km at a temperature < 10°C.

(c) Insect disinfestation and storage of dried fish. Transport and distribution by truck. The packaging material is assumed to be insect-resistant and returnable.

(2) Insect disinfestation of:
    (a) Cereals and pulses through fumigation by methyl bromide (48 g/m^3) or irradiation at a dose of approximately 0.50 kGy (Fig. 12.2a).
    (b) Tropical fruits through fumigation by ethylene dibromide (8 g/m^3) or irradiation at a dose of approximately 0.50 kGy (Fig. 12.2b).
    (c) Dried fish through irradiation at a dose of approximately 0.50 kGy compared to cold storage (5°C) (Fig. 12.2c).

(3) Hygienization of:
    (a) Spices through fumigation by ethylene oxide (900 g/m^3) or irradiation at a dose of approximately 3.00–5.00 kGy (Fig. 12.3a).
    (b) Fresh fish, poultry and ground meat (shelf-life extension) through irradiation at a dose of 1.0–3.0 kGy (Fig. 12.3b).
    (c) Frozen fresh fish and poultry through irradiation at a dose of 2.00–5.00 kGy (Fig. 12.3c).

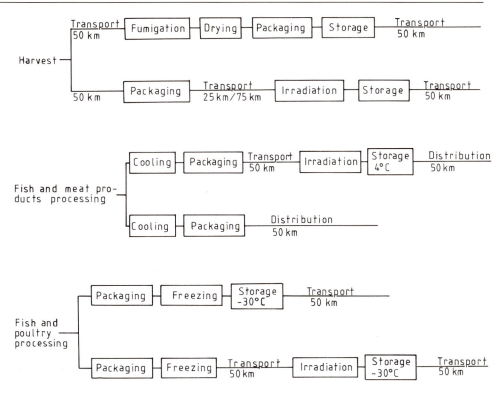

Fig. 12.3. Hygienization.

(a) Spices. Truck transport; storage at ambient temperature; simple packaging in 50-kg sized polypropylene bags. Fumigation is performed with ethylene oxide 900 g/m^3.

(b) Shelf-life extension of fresh fish, poultry and ground meat. Distribution is assumed at low temperatures. Distribution is assumed to be more rational in the case of shelf-life extension. Storage is calculated for 4 weeks at 4°C. Packaging is calculated on very simple LD–PE foil in consumer-sized packages.

(c) Frozen fresh fish, shellfish and poultry. Cold transport; storage time here is calculated for 6 months. Packaging is calculated on simple LD–PE foil only of freezing quality in consumer-sized packages (1 kg).

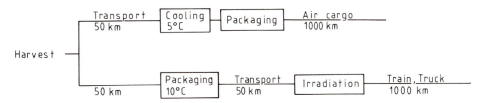

Fig. 12.4. Refrigerated distribution system: shelf-life extension of strawberries.

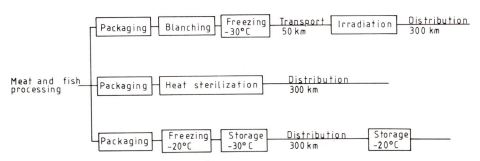

Fig. 12.5. Long-range preservation systems. These systems using an advanced packaging technology including an inner foil or laminate and an outer carton in 300 to 500-g packages. The distribution and storage system is assumed to be of a large scale with a centralized production giving long transport distances (300 km) and differentiated storage. Storage time is 6 months.

TABLE 12.3

Energy demands for storage and handling of onions in bulk at different conditions and storage prolonging methods

Energy input (MJ/kg) for	Cold storage	Irradiation + cold storage
Production of onions	2	2
Transport	0.10	0.15 ‾‾‾‾ 0.25
Sprout inhibition	–	0.012
Storage (el)	0.04/0.31/0.56	0/0.15/0.51
Transport	0.10	0.10
Total	2.34/3.25/4.10	2.26/2.77/4.00 ‾‾‾‾‾‾‾‾‾‾ 2.36/2.87/4.10
Losses (%)	50	20
Total for the available product	4.67/6.51/8.21	2.83/3.47/5.00 ‾‾‾‾‾‾‾‾‾‾ 2.95/3.59/5.12

Energy inputs for storage are calculated at the ambient temperatures of 5, 15 and 30°C. Two distances to the irradiator are compared.

The energy requirement for irradiation and the chemical systems are approximately the same, but probably biased towards the former. The low-temperature storage system differs more from the other two with a higher energy demand.

4.1.2. Onion storage and handling

The conditions here are different from those of potato storage, as, for the storage period considered, a low temperature cannot prevent a high degree of spoilage (up to 50%). Besides even radiated products have to be stored at a relatively low temperature. There is no really effective commercial chemical available for sprout inhibition. If the assumption regarding product losses after 6 months of storage is correct, irradiation seems to be favourable in all cases, calculated on the available commercial product, as seen in Table 12.3.

Even small differences in storage spoilage make the radiation treatment favourable.

For both potato and onion storage it is important to treat only those parts which are meant for later use. Otherwise the energy figures would change drastically as that would result in efforts such as additional transport, refrigeration, chemicals, radiation (which all cost energy), being used without any gain.

4.2. Insect disinfestation

4.2.1. Cereals and pulses

Two systems are considered here: (a) a small or medium-sized local silo; (b) a large-scale operation in a central elevator. It is decided here that packaging is only required for irradiation on a small scale while on a larger scale, the seed is continuously radiated and then stored in a silo. Fumigation is performed twice for this storage period.

Table 12.4 gives the energy demand under the circumstances chosen. The method of disinfestation only has a marginal influence on the total energy demand. Transport and packaging are those operations which have a considerable influence on the total energy input. The high transport energy input for

TABLE 12.4

Insect disinfestation of cereals and pulses: influence on energy demand of disinfestation methods and handling system

Energy input (MJ/kg) for	Fumigation (methyl bromide)		Irradiation	
	Local storage	Central elevator	Local storage	Central elevator
Production of cereals	4	4	4	4
Transport	0.10	0.20	0.20	0.20
Packaging	0.20	–	0.20	–
Disinfestation	0.007	0.007	0.007	0.007
Transport	0.10	0.20	0.10	0.20
Total post-harvest	0.41	0.41	0.51	0.41

TABLE 12.5

Energy demand for processing and distribution of fresh tropical fruits: irradiation in comparison with fumigation as a method of insect disinfestation

Energy input (MJ/kg) for	Fumigation (ethylene dibromide)	Irradiation	Air cargo
Transport	0.10	0.20	0.10
Hot water treatment	0.04	0.04	0.04
Drying	0.05	0.05	0.05
Disinfestation	0.02	0.02	0.02
Packaging	0.90	0.90	0.90
Storage (el)	0.015	0.015	0
Transport	2.50	2.50	60
Total	3.66	3.76	61.11
Losses (%)	50	10	10
Total for available product	7.32	4.18	67.9

local storage of irradiated products is dependent on that, as a central multi-purpose radiator is assumed here. As the energy figures are rather close, changes in the conditions from those assumed here can easily alter the situation.

Thus from an energy point of view it does not seem favourable to use radiation as a method of insect disinfestation when considering a local system. However, there could be other advantages which should not be forgotten, but they are not in the scope of this investigation. (Methyl bromide is prohibited in the U.S.A. due to its assumed hazardous effect as a mutagenic or carcinogenic substance left in the food product.) On the other hand, irradiation could be advantageous in the large-scale system, as the mechanical handling is reduced and the grain is not exposed to chemicals (the total energy input is almost equal for the systems compared).

4.2.2. Tropical fruits

The situation here is very similar to that of onion handling; energy is added for an effective and product-gentle treatment (irradiation has the effect both of insect disinfestation and of delaying ripening). The irradiation system as compared to fumigation is thus more energy-intensive, but taking into account the reduced losses for the assumed time of storage and distribution it is more feasible, as seen in Table 12.5. The figures for the air cargo alternative speak for themselves. Note that no figures are available for the agriculture, which, if included, would have changed the results.

TABLE 12.6

Disinfestation and storage of dried fish

Energy input (MJ/kg) for	Cold storage	Irradiation
Production of dried fish	200	200
Transport	0.15	0.25
Disinfestation	–	0.007
Storage (el)	0.068–0.136	0
Transport	0.10	0.10
Total excluding fish catching and drying	0.48–0.71 (0.32–0.39)	0.36 (0.36)

Figures in parentheses are those where the electricity values are multiplied by a factor of 1.0 instead of 3.4.

TABLE 12.7

Hygienization of spices: energy demand for selected microbial disinfection system

Energy input (MJ/kg) for	Fumigation (ethylene oxide)	Irradiation
Transport	0.10	0.15/0.25
Packaging	0.85	0.85
Microbial disinfection	0.06	0.03
Drying	0.30	–
Transport	0.10	0.10
Total	1.41	1.13/1.23

4.2.3. Dried fish

These treatments are not directly comparable, as cold storage does not disinfest the insects, but during the cold period it has the same effects as insect dormancy; this is the reason for the comparison. When removed from cold storage, insect activity will, of course, continue.

The total energy input for the two systems of cold storage and radiation followed by storage at ambient temperature favours of the former, as shown in Table 12.6. However, the situation may easily change, depending on local conditions.

Small changes in transport demand, storage time, specific energy demand for storage, etc., easily favour one system more than the other. Thus an energy analysis for a given specific situation is the only way to find the best system with respect to energy demand.

4.3. Hygienization

4.3.1. Spices

The process for microbial disinfestation, including the process for restoring the moisture activity to its original acceptable level, dominates the total energy input for these systems, as seen in Table 12.7. These circumstances favour the radiation process so that even a high energy demand in other links for this system does not overrule the basic advantages. Radiation is a low energy demanding process which can be performed on packed product under dry conditions which the other cannot. Thus, product quality reasons also favour the irradiation alternative, as it does not involve thermal drying.

TABLE 12.8

Energy demand for an irradiation system as hygienization and shelf-life extension of fresh fish, poultry and ground meat

Energy input (MJ/kg) for	Direct marketing	Irradiation
Production of meat incl. slaughtering	45	45
Cooling (el)	0.65	0.65
Packaging	0.45	0.45
Transport	–	0.16/0.21
Irradiation	–	0.02
Storage (el)	–	0.01/0.02
Transport	0.16/0.21	0.08/0.11
Total processing	1.86/1.91	1.99/2.11
Energy content of the products	6	6

Two ambient temperatures, 15 and 30°C, are considered. Various transport and distribution situations are encountered.

4.3.2. Shelf-life extension of fresh fish, poultry and ground meat

Here, there are really two situations. First, that of heating the product to make it acceptable for human use if, for one reason or other, the hygienic standard is below the legislative limits. Second, where a treatment could mean a longer shelf-life with its positive effects on distribution demand and a reduction of eventual losses due to unsold products. The assumption made here that irradiation system itself means additional energy inputs but with products having a longer shelf-life than those destined for direct marketing, as indicated in Table 12.8. Here the difference between the two systems is very sensitive to the transport situation. A change compared to the situation here assumed could very easily alter the favourable alternative. Thus it is not possible to say anything which is generally valid. Note that a rationalization in the distribution is assumed for the irradiation system.

If on the other hand losses or conversion into animal feed in certain situations are the alternative – the conversion in itself is energy-demanding (ranging between 1 and 2 MJ/kg) – then the situation is different. In that case irradiation, if effective, is an energy 'saving' treatment. A risk or probability that calculus could possibly give an answer to if this is a good approach. However, radiation if properly used could naturally contribute to an improved public health standard.

4.3.3. Frozen fresh fish, shellfish and poultry

The introduction of irradiation as a normal procedure in processing frozen products where *Salmonella* could be a public health problem also means an additional energy input of 0.2 MJ/kg depending on local conditions. This is only an addition of 5% calculated on the 'post-harvest' energy demand and could thus be considered as marginal, but of course it is anyway somewhat unnecessary. In an acute situation irradiation is, even from an energy point of view, a most satisfactory solution. Both the energy already spent plus additional energy (for the compulsory conversion processes to a product of low value) would greatly exceed any of those figures presented in Table 12.9.

TABLE 12.9

Energy input for hygienization of frozen fresh fish, shellfish and poultry

Energy input (MJ/kg) for	Normal handling	Hygienization through irradiation
Freezing (el)	1.2	1.2
Packaging	1.4	1.4
Transport	–	0.16/0.20
Irradiation	–	0.02
Storage (el)	0.28/0.39	0.28/0.39
Distribution	0.16/0.20	0.16/0.20
Total	6.59/7.01	6.77/7.23

Two ambient temperatures are considered: 15°C and 30°C.

TABLE 12.10

Influence on energy demand of shelf life extension for a strawberry handling system

Energy input (MJ/kg) for	Air cargo	Irradiation
Transport	0.10	0.25
Cooling (el)	0.10	0.10
Packaging	0.40	0.40
Irradiation	–	0.02
Transport	12	Train 0.5 + 0.1 Truck 2.5
Total	12.84	Train 1.61 Truck 3.51

Two alternatives for long-distance transport are considered

4.4. Shelf-life extension of strawberries

The systems compared here are somewhat peculiar. It is the long-distance (1000 km) supply of strawberries where air cargo is compared to train or truck cold transport. As air cargo is extremely energy-intensive the advantages of irradiation could well be recognized, as shown in Table 12.10. Thus if a radiation source is available within a limited time or transport distance it is a good alternative, probably also from an economic point of view.

4.5. Long-range preservation of meat and fish products

The presumption for these systems is a relatively advanced and demanding consumer pattern which is reflected in the high packaging and distribution energy costs.

Note that the energy input for packaging is a crucial point and the ultimate choice here affects the final result.

The total energy demands for these systems are rather close. This makes a final comparison very difficult due to small variations in specific energy demands for the different operations and changes in various assumptions. Examples are:

(1) The package material for the radiation process is assumed to require less heavy quality as it is not retorted which might be wrong because the material quality may be governed by other factors, such as storage conditions coupled to material permeability.

TABLE 12.11

Energy demand for selected long-range preservation systems. Considered products are meat and fish. Compared preservation methods are heat sterilization freezing and cold storage and radiation sterilization.

Energy input (MJ/kg) for	Heat sterilization in retort pouches		Freezing	Radiation sterilization using flexible pouches	
Blanching		–	–		0.25
		15.00	4.00		10.00
Packaging	(el)	0.07		(el)	0.07
Transport		–	–		0.20
Preservation		0.29		(el)	1.2 freezing
	(el)	0.02	1.2 (el)		0.16 irradiation
Warehouse storage	(el)	0.01	0.28/0.39		0.01
Distribution		0.60	0.70/0.78		0.60
Retail and home (el)		0	2.60/3.80		0
Total		16.23	18.57/23.1		15.56
		(15.98)	(8.78) (10.17)		(12.49)

Figures in parentheses represent those where the electricity factor of 1.0 is used instead that of 3.4. Two amount temperatures are considered: 15 and 30°C.

(2) The information about the energy demand for the freezing operation as well as cold storage vary the most, which, in combination with (in this evaluation) the fact that the electricity consumption is multiplied by a factor of 3.4 for conversion to oil equivalents, makes a final judgement hard and sensitive.

(3) The choice of the electricity conversion factor depends on how the energy is converted and the efficiency of the conversion, if heating is accomplished in the power generation, etc. This factor influences the preferable system, which is also seen in Table 12.11. Thus it is not possible to make any general statements. Only a thorough evaluation of a specific situation where all assumptions are defined could give an 'energy answer' as a guidance for choice.

It should also be noted that the resulting products are not comparable, as two of them mean heating of the products to a level above the denaturation temperature and thus do not give the same price, use, etc. A frozen product of meat or fish is normally not blanched unless a boiled product is required.

5. ACKNOWLEDGMENTS

This work was financially supported by the International Atomic Energy Agency, Vienna. An original draft was kindly commented on by Dr. A. Brynjolfsson, U.S. Army Research and Development Command, Natick, MA. U.S.A. The results were thoroughly evaluated together with Mr. Jan van Kooij and Mr. Paison Loaharanu, IAEA, Food Preservation Section, Vienna.

A report was revised in 1982 after discussions with Dr. Dick Langerak, ITAL, Wageningen, The Netherlands, after the Research Coordination Meeting on Pre-Commercial Scale Radiation Treatment of Food held in Colombo, Sri Lanka, February 1982, where an original report covering the results presented here, was presented and discussed. This chapter is based on a revision of the report presented in Colombo.

6. LITERATURE CONSULTED

Balázs-Sprincz, V., 1977. Evaluation of the economic feasibility of radiation preservation of selected food commodities. At. Energy Rev., 153: 407–457.

Baraldi, D., 1978. Technological tests at the preindustrial level on irradiated potatoes. In: Food Preservation by Irradiation. Proc. Symp., Wageningen. 2 Volumes, IAEA, Vienna, pp. 155–166.

Borbely, P. and Poulsen, K.P., 1980. Relations between total costs, energy, insulation, volume of cold stores and temperatures. Scand. Refrig., 9: 137–140.

Brodrick, H.T. and Tomas, A.C., 1978. Radiation preservation of subtropical fruits in South Africa. In: Food Preservation by Irradiation. Proc. Symp., Wageningen. 2 Volumes, IAEA, Vienna, pp. 167–178.

Brynjolfsson, A., 1978. Energy and food irradiation. In: Food Preservation by Irradiation. Proc. Symp., Wageningen. 2 Volumes, IAEA, Vienna.

Brynjolfsson, A., 1981. Food-energy-developing countries – food irradiation. Combination Processes in Food Irradiation. Proc. Symp., Colombo. IEAE-SM250/26, IAEA, Vienna, 8 pp.

Bäckström, M., 1970. Kylteknikern. Almqvist & Wiksell, Stockholm/Uppsala, 928 pp. (in Swedish).

Dollar, A.M. and Hanaoka, M., 1973. Commercial disinfestation treatment of fruit by ionizing radiation. In: Radiation Preservation of Food. Proc. Symp., Bombay. IAEA, Vienna, pp. 617–628.

Elias, P.S., 1979. Food irradiation and food packaging. Chem. Ind., 19 May: 336–341.

Farkas, J., Beczner, J. and Incze, K., 1973. Feasibility of irradiation of spices with special reference to paprika. In: Radiation Preservation of Food. Proc. Symp., Bombay. IAEA, Vienna, pp. 389–402.

Härrod, R.A., 1977. AECL gammasterilization facilities. Radiat. Phys. Chem., 9: 91–111.

Hylmö, B. and Sparks, W.C., 1976. Expressing the need of ventilation of a potato pile. Potato Res., 19: 253–256.

Hylmö, B., Persson, T., Wikberg, C. and Sparks, W.C., 1975. The heat balance in a potato pile. Acta Agric. Scand. 25: 81–91.

Kahan, R.S. and Howker, J.J., 1978. Low-dose irradiation of fresh non-frozen chicken and other preservation methods for shelf-life extension and for improving its public-health quality. In: Food Preservation by Irradiation. Proc. Symp., Wageningen. 2 Volumes. IAEA, Vienna, pp. 221–242.

Leach, G., 1976. Energy and Food Production, IPC, Guildford, Great Britain, 137 pp.

Lidgren, K., Jönsson, G., Arvidsson, L., Backman, M. and Hocking, C., 1979. Energi och förpackningar (Energy and packages). Medd. 52, ID Nr. 142512, Svenska Förpacknings forsknings institutet, Spånga, Sweden (in Swedish), 135 pp.

Löndahl, G., 1976. Food preservation and energy consumption. Scand. Refrig. 6: 174–178.

Löndahl, G., 1977. Fryskonservering – jämförelse ur energisynpunkt med andra konserveringsmetoder (Freeze preservation – an energy comparison with other preservation methods) 10. Nordiska Kylkongressen, Helsingfors, 5–8 June, 15 pp. (in Swedish).

McCulloch, A., 1981. ICI Ltd, Mond Division, Runcorn, Great Britain. Personal communication.

Olsson, P., 1979. Systemstudie för livsmedelssektorn (Energy study of the food sector). STU-Rapp. 77-6552, Swedish National Board for Technical Development (STU), Stockholm (in Swedish).

Olsson, P., 1980. Energy accounting in food process operations. Paper presented at the Symp. Energy and Food Industry, Madrid, 6–8 October.

Ramler, W.J., 1977. Electron beam facilities. Radiat. Phys. Chem., 9: 69–89.

Singson, C.C., De Guzman, Z.M., Mendoza, E.B., Lustre, A.O., Roncal, R., Villaruel, F. and Dolendo, A.L., 1978. Use of gamma irradiation for the extended commercial storage of Philippine onions and other agricultural products. In: Food Preservation by Irradiation. Proc. Symp., Wageningen. 2 Volumes, IAEA, Vienna, pp. 133–153.

Steffe, J.F., Williams, J.R., Chnimon, M.S. and Black, J.R., 1980. Energy requirements and costs of retort pouch vs can packaging systems. Food Technol., 34 (9): 39–43.

Thomas, P., Srirangarajan, A.N., Padwal-Desai, S.R., Ghanekar, A.S., Shirsat, S.G., Pendharkar, M.B., Nair, P.M. and Nadkarni, G.B., 1978. Feasibility of radiation processing for post-harvest storage of potatoes under tropical conditions. In: Food Preservation by Irradiation. Proc. Symp., Wageningen. 2 Vols., IAEA, Vienna, pp. 71–82.

Trägårdh, C., Solmar, A. and Malmström, T., 1980. Energy relations in some Swedish food industries. In: P. Linko, Y. Mälkki, J. Olkku and J. Larinkari (Editors) Food Process Engineering. Vol. 1. Applied Science Publishers, London, pp. 199–206.

Wohlgemuth, R., 1979. Protection of stored foodstuffs against insect infestation by packaging. Chem. Ind., 19 May: 330–334.

Chapter 13

Energy Use in Food Blanching

T.R. RUMSEY

1. INTRODUCTION

Blanching is an important unit operation in the pretreatment of fruits and vegetables. It is used prior to freezing, canning and dehydration. Lee (1958) lists two objectives for blanching in the preparation for freezing: (a) to inactivate enzymes in the tissues; and (b) to shrink the material to conserve space in packing. Vegetables frozen without the blanching pretreatment develop off-flavor, odor and colors. The objectives for blanching prior to canning are: (a) the removal of tissue gasses; (b) the shrinking of the materials for adequate can fill; and (c) the heating of the materials to obtain a vacuum after canning and processing. Blanching is used prior to the dehydration process to help to sterilize the product, to inactivate enzymes and to prevent off-flavor, odor and colors (Lazar, 1973). Blanching also has a favorable effect on the rate of drying.

The blanching process is a relatively fast process. A list of approximate time and temperature requirements for vegetables is given in Table 13.1 (Farrall, 1976). Blanching time is a function of piece size, heating medium and its temperature and material packing in the blancher (Lazar, 1973). As indicated in Table 13.1, the two most common heating media are steam and water. Schematic diagrams of water and steam blanchers are shown in Figs. 13.1 and 13.2.

Lee (1958) summarized a number of studies concerning the relative merits of water blanching versus steam blanching. Steam blanching is more effective for conserving soluble nutrients, but under certain conditions leaves undesirable flavors.

2. ENERGY CONSERVATION IN BLANCHER DESIGN

Concerns over energy use have resulted in a number of innovative new blancher designs and energy conserving modifications to existing blanchers. Since the mid-1970's, reports on such designs have appeared in various trade publications. In most cases, the energy performance is based on data supplied by the manufacturer.

Havighorst (1973) described a new steam blancher for which it was claimed that steam requirements could be reduced by 50% over conventional steam and water-curtain blanchers. This was accomplished by using venturi nozzles inside the steam chamber to recycle steam that was normally vented to atmosphere. A schematic diagram of the blancher is shown in Fig. 13.3. The interior of the blancher is sealed with a water steam-seal loop around the base of the blancher hood and a water steam-dam at each end of the blancher. The basic

---

Chapter 13 references, p. 224.

TABLE 13.1

Blanching time and temperatures

Product	Heating medium	Blanch time (min)
Asparagus	Steam	3.5–5
Broccoli	Steam	3.5
Carrots	Water (99°C)	2–3
Cauliflower	Steam	4–5
Corn (on the cob)	Steam	6–11
Corn	Steam	3
Lima beans	Steam	3–4
Lima beans (baby)	Water (99°C)	2.5
Peas (green)	Water (99°C)	0.8–1
Snap beans (cross-cut)	Steam	2–4
Spinach	Steam	2–3

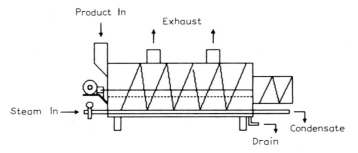

Fig. 13.1. Water blancher (Farrall, 1976).

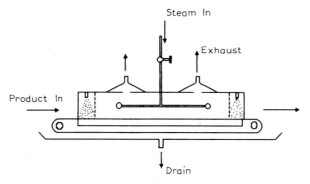

Fig. 13.2. Steam blancher with water curtains (Farrall, 1976).

unit is 2.1 m high, 1.4 m wide and 20.7 m in length. Product is conveyed through the blancher on a woven stainless-steel belt. The blancher has a rated capacity of 11 400 kg/h for leafy vegetables and 6800 kg/h for vegetables such as broccoli, cauliflower and brussel sprouts.

Articles on a hydrostatically sealed steam blancher have appeared in several publications. The blancher is similar in appearance to the one described above, but uses a different method of introducing steam into the blanching chamber. Two factors were given for its high energy efficiency: (a) an effective water seal enclosing the steam chamber; and (b) water moving in a counterflow direction through the blancher from the cooling section to the seal area and on to the washing section. Ray (1975) described an installation of this unit at a frozen food plant. Steam consumption was reported to be 0.077 kg steam per kg of product when blanching 2950 kg/h of broccoli. It was claimed that this was 50% of the normal value of 0.155 kg steam per kg of product required for conventional exhaust type steam blanchers. Layhee (1975) wrote of the installation of

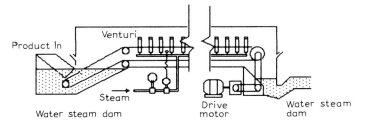

Fig. 13.3. Steam blancher with venturi tubes (Havighorst, 1973).

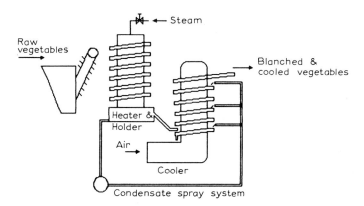

Fig. 13.4. Schematic diagram of vibratory spiral blancher-cooler (Bomben et al., 1978).

the same model blancher at a different frozen food plant. It was used to process spinach and cauliflower. The engineering department at this plant estimated that the blancher reduced energy requirements by 50%, cutting the steam consumption from 1 kg to 0.5 kg steam per kg product. The installation of a larger model of the same blancher was described by Rodriguez and Robe (1978). It was being used at a frozen-food plant to blanch broccoli. The conveyor belt was modified so that it could handle chopped broccoli on one side and broccoli heads on the other. The blancher's capacity was between 5000 and 6000 kg/h. The operating efficiency was again estimated at 0.5 kg steam per kg product.

A prototype vibratory spiral blancher (Fig. 13.4) was described by Bomben (1976). Product was moved through the steam chamber and cooling section of the blancher using a vibratory spiral conveyor. The entrance and exit to the steam chamber is sealed and the chamber is insulated. The blancher was installed at a frozen food plant and its performance was evaluated on a number of types of vegetable. Steam consumption for this blancher averaged 0.145 kg steam per kg product. A detailed account of the performance of this blancher including energy efficiency and effluent generation is given by Bomben et al. (1978).

The performance of an efficient new steam blancher was reported by Cumming (1980) and Dunlop (1981). A unit was successfully operated at a vegetable processing plant. The blancher uses the individual quick blanch (IQB) technique. The product is heated in a single layer at it passes through the heating section. It is then put through a holding section where the product is piled up in buckets. In this adiabatic holding section, the heat penetrates into the product and it is held for the required time. Rotary valves are used to prevent steam escaping from these sections. Steam use by the system varied from 0.14 to 0.25 kg steam per kg product depending on product throughput. The high efficiencies are achieved by recirculation of uncondensed steam and the proper sealing of the heating chamber. Products that were successfully blanched

Chapter 13 references, p. 224.

included chopped broccoli, carrots, brussel sprouts, whole green beans, cut beans, yellow beans and peas.

Thermal recompression of exhaust steam was used to improve the efficiency of three direct steam injection blanchers (Hoezee et al., 1982). The blanchers were used by a baby food manufacturer to blanch vegetables and fruit before pureeing in finishers. The screw cooker blanchers were each 0.46 m in diameter and 15.2 m long. Steam was directly injected at 0.15-m intervals along the bottom of the blancher. A vapor recyling system was installed to recover waste steam from the vapor space above the product. A steam jet thermocompressor was used to capture the vapor and inject it back into the blanchers. Steam consumption prior to the modification was reported to be 0.50–0.90 kg steam per kg product. With the thermocompression system, this was reduced to 0.14–0.22 kg steam per kg product.

The successful operation of a new high-temperature-short-time (HTST) steam pressure blancher was reported (McGowan et al., 1984). Operating in a batch mode, the blancher processed up to 17 250 kg/h of cob corn. The unit handles 450-kg batches at a time which are conveyed into a special steam pressure vessel. Measurements of steam flow indicated that the blancher used 0.12 kg steam per kg product.

3. ANALYSIS OF ENERGY USE IN BLANCHING

Theoretical estimates of energy requirements for blanching can be made using steady-state energy balances (Bomben, 1977). Ignoring heat losses, an energy balance on the blancher shown in Fig. 13.1 yields the following ratio of steam use per quantity of product:

$$W_s/W_p = C_p(T_{po} - T_{pi})/(H(T_0) - h(T_0)) \qquad (1)$$

In this equation, W_s and W_p are the mass flow rates of steam and product, respectively. The specific heat of the product is denoted by C_p, and the inlet and outlet product temperatures are T_{pi} and T_{po}. The enthalpy of the saturated and condensed steam, both at temperature T_0, are $H(T_0)$ and $h(T_0)$. Using nominal values of specific heat, $C_p = 4.18$ kJ/(kg °C), product inlet and outlet temperatures, $T_{pi} = 16°C$ and $T_{po} = 88°C$, and steam temperature $T_0 = 100°C$, the ratio of steam to product flow is 0.133 kg steam per kg product. The heat balance equation provides a means of evaluating steam consumption data as well as estimating heat losses. The difference between steam flow rates estimated by the above equation and measured data should be due to heat losses.

4. ENERGY AUDITS OF BLANCHERS

Several studies concerning energy use have been conducted on commercially operating blanchers. Data have been gathered on both steam and water blanchers.

4.1. Steam blanchers

Scott et al. (1981) presented energy use data on four different operating steam blanchers. Data were presented for a conventional steam blancher without end seals, a steam blancher with water curtains similar to the schematic diagram in Fig. 13.2, a steam blancher with hydrostatic water seals and a steam blancher with hydrostatic water seals and venturi nozzles similar to the one shown in Fig. 13.3. All blanchers were monitored over several operating shifts to provide representative data.

TABLE 13.2

Summary of energy audit results for steam blanchers[a]

Blancher	Measured				Theory		
	Product flow (kg/h)	Steam flow (kg/h)	Steam/ product (kg/kg)	Thermal energy/ (MJ/kg)	Steam/ product (kg/kg)	Thermal energy (MJ/kg)	Thermal efficiency (%)
Steam, conventional	5490	5180	0.944	2.12	0.120	0.219	10.3
Steam, water curtain	4830	3090	0.640	1.56	0.109	0.221	14.2
Steam, hydrostatic	12800	4960	0.388	0.953	0.127	0.259	27.1
Steam, hydrostatic	5900	2180	0.369	0.910	0.138	0.311	34.1

[a]Scott et al. (1981)

Data taken during the audits included steam flow rate to the blancher and mass flow rate of product through the blancher. Steam flows were measured with a differential pressure meter and recorded with a portable digital data logger. Steam temperature, pressure and quality were also measured. Mass flows of product were determined by periodically weighing samples from the product line into the blanchers.

Temperatures of the blancher surfaces, steam and water were recorded on the data logger. Product mass average temperatures were measured by collecting product samples in an insulated beaker and taking their temperature with a thermometer.

The conventional steam blancher consisted of a conveyor with a stainless-steel hood. Water seals enclosed the sides, but there were no seals at the ends where the product entered and exited from the blancher. Thus unit was 15.2 m long and 1.3 m wide. The hood had 0.5 m high vertical sides and a sloped top. Power to run the mesh conveyor was supplied by a 1.5-kW electric motor.

A summary of the energy audit data for this blancher is given in Table 13.2. Spinach was being blanched at a rate of 5490 kg/h. The blancher used 0.944 kg steam per kg of product. The residence time in the blancher was 1.5 min. The product temperature at entry was 25°C, and it was blanched at a set temperature of 96°C. Steam to the blancher had a temperature of 159°C at 0.60 MPa with a quality of 76%. Its flow rate averaged 5180 kg/h which was equivalent to a thermal energy input rate of 11.63 GJ/h. Thermal efficiency, defined as the ratio of theoretical to actual thermal energy required to heat the product up to blanch temperature, was 10.3%. An energy balance for this blancher is given in the first column of Table 13.3. Steam losses from the unsealed entrance and exit amounted to 79.7% of the energy input to the blancher. A considerable amount of uncondensed steam was observed to be escaping from these points during the tests.

The steam blancher with end seals was similar in design to the conventional blancher above. Water sprays were positioned inside the ends of the blancher to condense steam that might escape. They also served to help cool the product at the exit. The blancher was 15.2 m long, but because of the water sprays, the effective blanching length was 12.2 m. The blancher width and hood dimensions were the same as the conventional unit. A 0.75-kW electric motor was used to drive the mesh conveyor belt which carried the product through the blancher.

TABLE 13.3

Energy balances for steam blanchers

	Conventional	Water curtains	Hydrostatic seals	Hydrostatic seals
Energy to raise product temp (%)	13.2	19.0	27.2	30.9
Convection losses (%)	0.5	0.5	0.7	1.1
Radiation losses (%)	0.2	0.4	0.3	0.6
Condensate losses (%)	2.0	10.9	16.7	16.2
Conveyor reheated (%)	4.4	3.2	0	0
Unaccounted losses (%)	79.7	66.0	55.1	51.2

Results of the energy audit data for this blancher are given in Table 13.2. The product being processed was green beans. The production rate was 4830 kg/h with a blanch time of 3.75 min. The ratio of measured steam flow rate to product flow rate was 0.640. The steam was saturated with a pressure of 0.55 MPa and quality of 85%. The product entered the blancher at a temperature of 20°C and the blanching temperature was set at 99°C. Water was sprayed at a rate of 8160 kg/h and its temperature was 12°C. The water combined with steam condensate and exited through a single pipe at a temperature of 36°C. The surface temperature of the blancher averaged 90°C and the ambient air 21°C. Thermal energy input rate to the blancher was 7.56 GJ/h and the thermal efficiency was 14.2%. Distribution of the energy flows for the blancher are given in Table 13.3. The unaccounted losses, 66% of the input energy, were primarily due to uncondensed steam that escaped through vent ducts in the top of the hood. This also includes energy consumed in heating the water sprays which accounted for 6.8%.

The steam blancher with hydrostatic water seals conveyed product into and out of the steam chamber on dunking and discharge belts which passed the product through water seals. Steam could not escape the blancher directly although it could condense and exit via overflow lines on the water seals. The blancher was 25.6 m long, 0.79 m high and 1.7 m wide. Small electric motors were used to run the conveyor that moved the product through the blancher.

During the audit, spinach was being processed at a rate of 12 800 kg/h. A summary of the energy audit data is given in Table 13.2. Steam at 0.80 MPa and 85% quality was measured at a flow rate of 4960 kg/h for a ratio of steam to product of 0.388. The thermal energy input rate was measured at 12.2 GJ/h and the thermal efficiency 27.1%. Product entered at 33°C and the blanching temperature was 98°C. The average blancher surface temperature was 86°C and the ambient air temperature was 23°C. Residence time in the blancher was 1.5 min. As seen in Table 13.3, the unaccounted for losses were still large, representing 55.1% of the total energy input.

The final steam blancher audited was similar to that described by Havighorst (1973) and shown schematically in Fig. 13.3. It had hydrostatic end seals and used venturi nozzles to recycle steam in the steam chamber. The blancher was 12.2 m long, 0.79 m high and 1.6 m wide. Two 7.5-kW pumps were used to recirculate water in the seal area, and small 0.75-kW and 0.2-kW motors were used to operate paddles to submerge product entering and exiting from the

TABLE 13.4

Summary of energy audit results for water blanchers

Blancher	Measured				Theory		
	Product flow (kg/h)	Steam flow (kg/h)	Steam/ product (kg/kg)	Thermal energy/ (MJ/kg)	Steam/ product (kg/kg)	Thermal energy (MJ/kg)	Thermal efficiency (%)
Water (tubular)[a]	4980	1094	0.220	0.543	0.118	0.242	44.5
Water (screw conveyor)[a]	2845	1075	0.378	0.910	0.143	0.284	31.2
Water tank[b]	9130	4720	0.517	1.03	0.161	0.322	31.4

[a]Rumsey et al. (1981).
[b]Chhinnan et al. (1980).

blancher. A 2-kW motor ran the product conveyor on the blancher. Measurements of power usage for all the motors showed that they required less than 2% of the total energy input.

A summary of the audit results is given in Table 13.2. Spinach was being processed at a rate of 5900 kg/h. The steam at 0.86 MPa and 99% quality was measured at 2180 kg/h for a ratio of steam to product of 0.369. The thermal energy input rate was 5.37 GJ/h and thermal efficiency was 34.1%. The product entered at 24°C and the blanching temperature was 93°C. Average surface temperature of the blancher was 93°C and ambient air temperature was 28°C. The energy balance given in Table 13.3 is similar to that for the hydrostatic blancher without the recirculating venturi nozzles. A total of 51.2% of the total input energy was unaccounted for losses.

4.2. Water blanchers

Rumsey et al. (1981) presented energy consumption data on two commercial operating water blanchers. A detailed account of the energy audits for these blanchers is given by Scott (1980). The measurement procedures and data collection equipment were the same as those described above (Scott et al., 1981). One of the blanchers was a tubular unit and the other utilized a screw conveyor.

The tubular blancher consisted of a convoluted stainless-steep pipe, 488 m in length and 0.10 m in diameter. Product and water were pumped through the unit by a 7.5-kW centrifugal pump. The water was heated by steam injection at a point 19.5 m from the pump. At the blancher exit, the product was separated from the hot water with a sieve. The hot water was returned to a supply tank at the entrance of the blancher via a 52.7 m long, 0.15 m diameter pipe. Make up water was added to the tank as needed. The product was added to the system at the supply tank and pumped from the tank to the blancher.

During the energy audit of the tubular blancher, lima beans were being processed at a rate of 4980 kg/h. A summary of the audit results is given in Table 13.4. Flow rate of water in the tube was measured to be 51 700 kg/h. Steam flow averaged 1094 kg/h at a temperature of 158°C and quality of 86%. Thermal energy input rate was 2.71 GJ/h and thermal efficiency was 44.5%, the highest of all blanchers tested. The average residence time of beans in the system was 6.8 min, of which approximately 1.5 min was spent in the holding tank and 1–1.5 min in the cooling trough at the blancher exit. Beans entered the blancher at 18°C and exited to the cooling section at 40°C. Blanch temperature

Chapter 13 references, p. 224.

TABLE 13.5

Energy balances for water blanchers

	Tubular	Screw conveyor
Energy to raise product temp (%)	44.0	31.4
Reheat water (%)	44.4	31.1
Convection losses (%)	5.0	1.0
Radiation losses (%)	3.9	0.5
Unaccounted losses (%)	2.7	35.0

was 96°C. An energy balance for the blancher is summarized in Table 13.5. Only 2.7% of the total input energy rate was unaccounted for.

The screw conveyor water blancher was a 0.114-m^3 vessel through which product was conveyed with by a turning screw. The vessel was rectangular with a rounded bottom with a length of 5.1 m, a width of 1.0 m and a height of 1.25 m. A 0.56-kW variable speed electric motor controlled the speed of the product through the blancher. The blancher was fed by product that was conveyed with water through a piping system. A sieve was used to separate the water out. A vibrating screen separated product from water at the blancher exit. The discharge water was pumped back to the blancher inlet. Steam was injected into the blancher water via steam spargers at the bottom of the unit.

The blancher was processing cauliflower cuts at a rate of 2845 kg/h. Product temperature at the inlet was 20°C. The blanching temperature was 93°C. Steam flow into the unit was 1075 kg/h with a temperature of 168°C and a quality of 82%. The total input energy rate was 2.59 GJ/h. Energy audit data are presented in Table 13.4 for this blancher. Its thermal efficiency was 31.2%. Residence time for the product in the blancher was 2.25 min. The average surface temperature of the blancher was 93°C and ambient air temperature was 18°C. The thermal energy balance for the blancher is summarized in Table 13.5. A total of 35% of the input energy was assumed lost as uncondensed steam and leaking discharge water. The escaping steam was visible from the unsealed product entrance and exit.

Chhinnan et al. (1980) gave energy accounting data on a commercial blancher at a spinach processing plant. The blancher processed 9130 kg/h of spinach and used 4720 kg/h of steam for a ratio of steam to product of 0.517. The product entered at 15°C and exited at 96°C. Residence time in the blancher was 3 min. It was calculated that 31% of the energy input went to heating up the product and 69% was lost through incomplete condensation of steam, hot water discharge to the drain and heat losses by convection and radiation.

5. REFERENCES

Bomben, J.L., 1976. Vibratory blancher-cooler saves water, heat and waste. Food Eng. Int., 1(7): 37–38.

Bomben, J.L., 1977. Effluent generation, energy use and cost of blanching. J. Food Process Eng., 1: 329–341.

Bomben, J.L., Hudson, J.S., Dietrich, W.C., Durkee, E.L., Farkas, D.F., Rand, R. and Farquhar, J.W., 1978. Vibratory spiral blancher-cooler. EPA-600/2-78-206, U.S. Environmental Protection Agency.

Chhinnan, M.S., Singh, R.P., Pedersen, L.D., Carroad, P.A., Rose, W.W. and Jacob, N.L., 1980. Analysis of energy utilization in spinach processing. Trans. ASAE, 23: 503–507.

Cumming, I.B., 1980. The development of a new blanching system. J. Can. Diet. Assoc., 41: 39–44.

Dunlop, J., 1981. New blancher needs 90% less steam and produces 90% less effluent. Food Can. 41(2): 20–21, 24, 26.

Farrall, A.W., 1976. Food Engineering Systems, Vol. 1. AVI, Westport, CT.

Havighorst, C.R., 1973. Venturi tubes recycle heat in blancher. Food Eng., 45 (6): 89–90.

Hoezee, D., Argyres, G. and Robe, K., 1982. Vapor recycling in screw cookers reduces steam consumption by 72%. Food Process., 43 (6): 112–114.

Lazar, M.E., 1973. Dehydration plant operations. In: W.B. van Arsdel, M.J. Copley and A.I. Morgan (Editors), Food Dehydration, Vol. 1 (2nd Edition). AVI, Westport, CT.

Layhee, P., 1975. Engineered FF line yields 5 big production benefits. Food Eng., 47 (2): 61–62.

Lee, F.A., 1955. The blanching process. In: E.M. Mrak and G.F. Stewart (Editors), Advances in Food Research. Academic Press, New York, NY, pp. 63–109.

McGowan, R.W., Brown, G.L., Hansen, N. and Robe, K., 1984. HTST pressure blancher cuts steam costs $3600/day. Food Process., 45 (1): 88–89.

Ray, A., 1975. Steam blancher uses 50% less energy. Food Process., 36 (1): 64.

Rodriguez, R. and Robe, K., 1978. New processing line boosts productivity 21%. Food Process., 39 (1): 90–91.

Rumsey, T.R., Scott, E.P. and Carroad, P.A., 1981. Energy consumption in water blanching. J. Food. Sci., 47 (1): 295–298.

Scott, E.P., 1980. Energy analysis and conservation in steam and water blanchers. Unpublished M.Sc. Thesis, University of California, Davis, CA.

Scott, E.P., Carroad, P.A., Rumsey, T.R., Horn, J., Buhllert, J. and Rose, W.W., 1981. Energy consumption in steam blanchers. J. Food Process Eng., 5: 77–88.

Chapter 14

Energy and Water Consumption in Catering Establishments in Sweden

CHRISTINA SKJÖLDEBRAND and EINAR MATTHIASSON

1. INTRODUCTION

In 1978 and 1979 a study was carried out at the Division of Food Engineering, Lund University, Sweden, concerning, among other things, energy and water consumption in Swedish catering establishments. This study was divided into two parts. In the first part an inventory was made to obtain information about food residue generation, water consumption and energy use (Malmström et al., 1980). This information was determined to find where unnecessary and abnormal losses occur. In order to make the investigation as representative as possible, six institutional kitchens were chosen with respect to certain factors that were considered to influence the amount of waste, energy and water.

In the second part of the study, water consumption and energy use were measured for some selected apparatus. Three of the above-mentioned kitchens were chosen and within them particular equipment. This was a follow-up from the first part (Andersson et al., 1980).

Dishwashing was excluded in the second part, but not in the first. This part has been treated further in a separate project.

This study was part of a Swedish project called 'Catering 1990'. In this the Swedish National Board of Technical Development has given 20 million Swedish Crowns ($\approx$ US$ 1.6 million) spread out over 6 years (1978–1984) on technical research and development for the Swedish catering establishments.

2. PRESENTATION OF THE ESTABLISHMENTS INVOLVED IN THE STUDY

Table 14.1 gives a presentation of the kitchens chosen. The type of kitchen indicates the working method that was used. The number of dishes served at each meal is an indication of the kind of equipment used. The number of portions gives an indication of the amount of food material that the kitchen deals with. The level of readiness of the food gives an indication of the kind and amount of treatment that takes place in the kitchen.

A catering kitchen is a composite of the basic principle of work and flows of material. Figure 14.1 shows a basic plant layout of the production flow.

This layout gives an indication of the kind of treatment that takes place in the kitchen. The different steps are the following:
- cleaning and rinsing: removal of dirt and removable parts, for example, egg shells and potato peel;
- preparation: mechanical treatment of foods, e.g., grinding, slicing, mixing;
- heat conversion: transforming the foods chemically and physically by heating, e.g., frying, boiling, baking;

Chapter 14 references, p. 237.

TABLE 14.1

Presentation of the different kitchens involved in the study

Kitchen	Type of kitchen	Number of meal times per day	Number of main dishes	Number of portions served daily	Level of readiness of the food (percentage ready-to-cook and ready-to-serve foods
A	p (personnel kitchen) built 1971	1	1	160–200	35.5
B	p (restaurant) built 1972	3	> 1	200–500	56.7
C	m (school)	1	1	500	88.0
D	p (regimental)	3	1	500–1000	31.3
E	c (hospital)	3	1	1100–1500	54.5
F	p (hotel)	3	> 1	400–900	< 30.0

p, production kitchen (cooking and serving foods).
m, convenience foods kitchen (using ready-to-serve foods).
c, central kitchen (cooking and distribution foods).

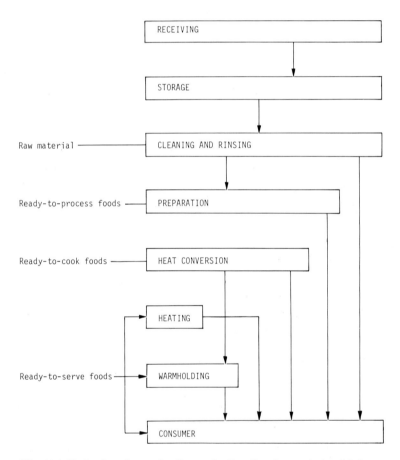

Fig. 14.1. Basic plant layout for the production flow in a catering kitchen.

    – heating: tempering and/or thawing of the foods; and
    – keeping warm: keeping food at eating temperature.
In the inventory all the equipment was studied, but storage facilities were excluded.

    In the second part, three kitchens out of the six were chosen. The requirement was that they should, as far as possible, represent Swedish catering

TABLE 14.2

Equipment on which the energy and water measurements were carried out (second study)

Apparatus	Number[a]	Water	Energy
Frying table	1 (B)		×
Stove	1 (B)		×
Convection oven	1 (D)		×
Oven	1 (B)		×
Boiler for potatoes	1 (B)	×	×
Pressure cooker	2 (D, A)	×	×
Steam jacketed kettle	2 (D, A)		×
Fryer	1 (B)		×
Equipment for warmholding	1 (D)		×
Heating plates	1 (D)		×
Potato peeler	1 (A)	×	
Vegetable rinsing machine	1 (D)	×	

[a]Kitchen where the equipment was located is indicated in parentheses.

establishments in general. This is not possible, however, but these may be considered to represent the most common ones if the size and the characteristics are taken into account.

The kitchens selected in the second part were the restaurant kitchen (B in Table 14.1), the hospital kitchen (E in Table 14.1), and the personnel kitchen (A in Table 14.1). Table 14.2 shows a summary of the equipment on which the energy and water measurements were carried out and in which kitchen they were located. This is related to the second study.

2.1. Water

Water was used in the kitchens as both hot and cold water. Since there were at least 20 to 40 locations in the kitchen where water was used, it was difficult to control them. This means that consumption at some places was measured prior to others.

Our first study focused on the following six water-consuming places.

(1) Washing. A continuous dishwasher was used in all of the kitchens. The dishwashers were all provided with a final rinsing zone from which the used water was used for renewing the water in the tanks of the other parts of the dishwasher.

(2) Pot washing was done using a pot washing machine in kitchens B, D and E. It was partly manual in kitchen D and completely manual in kitchens A and C.

(3) Process machines were washed manually in all the kitchens.

(4) In cleaning and rinsing, water was used for removal of soil from root crops and vegetables.

(5) In the heat conversion section, water was used as heat transfer medium.

(6) Water was used to clean the floors.

In the second study the water consumption was measured for some specific apparatus, i.e., the potato-boiling pan, the two steam pressure cookers, the potato peeler and the vegetable-rinsing machine.

2.1.1. Measuring methods

The water consumption was measured using integrating flow meters, wherever this was possible. In other cases the filling time of buckets or the technical data of the machine were used. When it was impossible to use any of these methods, estimates were made.

Chapter 14 references, p. 237.

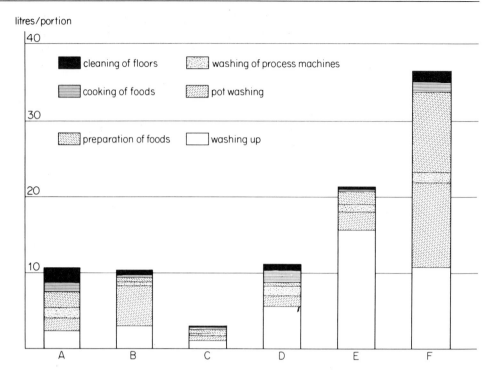

Fig. 14.2. Water consumption in the six different kitchens.

2.1.2. Results

As stated earlier, water consumption takes place mainly during the six different operations in the kitchen. The hot water has, in general, a temperature of 60°C. In kitchen D the temperature was 70°C, in kitchen E 90°C. In the latter, a heat exchanger was used to decrease the temperature to 40–60°C.

A general result of this inventory was that 75% of the total water consumption was used for some kind of washing. Figure 14.2 shows the results of the measured water consumption in this six kitchens.

The difference in water consumption per portion during washing depended partly on whether the pre-rinsing was automatic or not and partly on how many dishes were used by the customer. In all of the cases studied here, manual pre-rinsing was also used, but this represents only a small portion of the total water consumption during washing. Kitchen E was an exception, where the manual pre-rinsing used 90% of the total dishwashing consumption because of continuous cleaning of the waste collector.

It is important to make the dishwashing machines more efficient without reducing the hygienic standard. One method that is used in some dishwashers is countercurrent washing. Another method is to improve the pre-rinsing and the final rinsing by making the spray assemblies more efficient. A research project was started in 1980 to study the dishwashing machines for catering from the above mentioned aspect (A. Malmborg, unpublished results, 1985).

Pot washing was done, as indicated before, with the aid of special machines in kitchens B, E and F. In kitchen B, this was done partly manually and in the other two kitchens (A and C) it was done manually. In all the kitchens, burnt-on-soil had to be removed manually. The water consumption is somewhat greater with pot washing machines than with manual washing for the same number of dishes. It is primarily the number of kitchen utensils required for cooking that governs the amount of water used.

In the hospital kitchen (E), transport vehicles were used for transporting food to the different patients. These were washed afterwards using 1.4 l of water.

In the second study, one particular potato peeler was studied in more detail; it was located in a personnel restaurant (A). Three different peeling operations were examined. Regulation of water flow was manual and here one peeling operation is reported. The process started with 20.6 kg potatoes: 9.4 kg (46%) of the potatoes were peeled in the abrasive potato peeler and 1.3 kg (6%) were trimmed away manually; 9.9 kg (48%) of the potatoes were left.

For the operation, 125 kg water were used for rinsing: more than 30 kg for cleaning potatoes, and 70 kg for cleaning of the peeler. Totally more than 225 kg water were used, which corresponds to about 10.9 kg per kg of unpeeled potatoes. About the same results were found for the other two trials.

Also a rinsing machine for vegetables was studied. This was located in the restaurant. It was used also for potatoes and fish. During rinsing, water and product were loaded into the machine to a certain level. The result was that 6.4 kg water per kg vegetables was used for the total operation.

2.2. Energy

Since the energy crisis, the costs for energy have accounted for a large proportion of the production costs.

The inventory, i.e., the first part of this study, was carried out to determine if energy losses occur, and if so, where. The goal was also to see if something could be done to save energy.

Energy enters the kitchens as hot water, electricity or gas, and is used for cooking, keeping dishes warm and washing. The energy leaves the kitchen as hot air, hot water, steam or hot food. The energy intake depends on the type of kitchen and the number of dishes per day.

2.2.1. Methods

The electrical energy use in the kitchen was measured as a total for the whole kitchen and for special apparatus during use. In the second study, only special apparatus were chosen and a total energy balance was made. The energy was measured partly by existing electric meters and partly by clip-on ammeters connected to a plotter. In some cases, the rated output was just multiplied by the used time.

The energy in water and food was measured using measured temperature and quantity.

The amount of energy in water is calculated by means of:

$$Q = mc_p(t - t_0)$$

where t is the measured temperature (K); Q the energy use (J); t_0 a reference temperature, here 0°C (273.16 K); c_p specific heat (J/kg); and m the quantity of water (kg).

The energy use in the food was calculated by means of:

$$Q = m \int_{t_0}^{t} c_p \, dt$$

Here c_p was calculated from the equation (Sörenfors, 1978):

$$c_p = 1600 + 2600 \, w + 0.15 \, F\{t\} \text{ kJ/kg}$$

where w is the water content; F the fat content; and $\{t\}$ the numerical value of the temperature expressed in °C.

The energy loss can be described by: convection from hot surfaces, radiation from hot surfaces, steam from the products and media, leakage of hot air when doors are opened. The leakage was very hard to determine. Convection and

Chapter 14 references, p. 237.

radiation from hot surfaces were calculated by means of surface temperature and were registered during a long period as a function of the time. The surface temperature was measured by means of thermocouples.

The radiation was calculated by (Bankvall, 1969):

$$Q = h_s A(t_s - t_a)$$

in which

$$h_s = 0.04 \times 0.09\varepsilon \times 5.7 \,[\{T_m\}/100]^3 \,\mathrm{J\,s^{-1}\,m^{-2}\,K^{-1}}$$

and

$$T_m = [\tfrac{1}{2}(t_s - t_a) + 273.16] \,\mathrm{K}$$

where Q is the total energy (J); h_s the radiation heat transfer coefficient; A the surface area ($\mathrm{m^2}$); t_s, t_a surface and ambient temperature, respectively (K); T_m the mean temperature of surface and ambient; and ε the emission factor.

As for convection, the following equation was used:

$$Q = h_c A(t_s - t_a)$$

in which

$$h_c = 2.66[\{t_s\} - \{t_a\}]^{1/4} \,\mathrm{W\,m^{-2}\,K^{-1}}$$

where h_c is the convective heat transfer coefficient.

The water evaporated from the product and water surfaces was more difficult to measure. The only possible measurement is that of the amount of water before and after cooking. The difficulties also occur due to the fact that errors easily arise, as 1 kg of water needs as much as 0.6 kWh to be evaporated. Usually the water loss via steam is as low as 1%. There are also some losses of water due to other factors.

2.2.2. Results

The hotel restaurant used about three times as much energy as the normal restaurant. This is mainly due to the fact that in the hotel restaurant the customer usually eats three dishes per meal, but in the restaurant he eats just one dish, the main dish. Another factor is the level of readiness of the raw material which was much lower here.

The energy use did not differ very much between a production kitchen and a central kitchen. The reasons are that the boundary line between them is very hazy. The energy use in the convenience food kitchen differs very much from the others. This is an illusory picture because in this case a great amount of energy has been used in the food industry to make the convenience food. Figure 14.3 shows a summary of the energy use in the six different kitchens. In catering establishments, the energy is almost entirely consumed in four different operations.

Preparation of foods uses electrical energy for a number of different electrical motors, which means that the consumption is low (less than 1% of the total electrical energy demand). Water is used for cleaning and rinsing but as this water is not heated, no energy is used here.

Heat conversion used 40–80% of the total energy demand of the kitchen. The main part of this energy was used for boiling, frying, baking and so on, i.e., for physical and chemical changes of the food. The heat was transferred to the food, i.e., electrical energy was transferred to heat which, in turn, was transferred to the food. The energy losses were mainly in the form of: hot water to the sewer; heat from hot surfaces; evaporation from product and heating media; heat transmission; heated air; and leakage when doors are openened. The first four sources give the greatest losses. Only 10% of the energy input leaves with the foods.

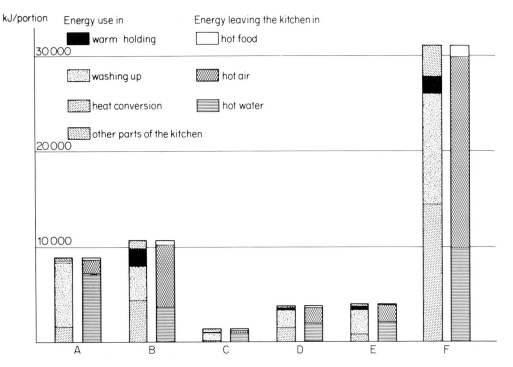

Fig. 14.3. Energy use in the six different kitchens.

TABLE 14.3

Energy losses for some equipment studied in the investigation

	Energy losses as a percentage of the total				Energy input (kWh/day)
	Transmission	Steam	Heating	Hot water	
Frying table	88	1	5	–	70
Steam boiling kettle	35	47	1	7	30
Steam boiling cupboard	18	1	0.8	71	70
Stove	92	3	1	–	200

The size of the losses varies from one piece of equipment to another. The amount of equipment varies between the different kitchens. The biggest difference is between one establishment that serves one dish and one that serves several. A convenience food kitchen is differently equipped, due to the fact that only thawing and reheating occur.

The energy losses are mainly in the form of hot water, from pressure steamers, and by means of transmission in frying tables and kitchen ranges. The losses of energy from steam boiling kettles are normally through transmission and leakage of vapor.

The power consumption is dependent on who is operating the equipment and how the routines of the kitchen are working.

Table 14.3 shows the energy losses for the heat conversion equipment that used the most energy during this investigation.

For example, the frying tables have a hot surface, with a temperature of about 250°C. They are often on for 0.5–1 h before usage. The heating time is 10–15 min. The rest of the time there is just a waste of energy.

Chapter 14 references, p. 237.

TABLE 14.4

Energy use during potato frying (kWh/kg) for 9 min

In		Out	
Electricity energy	0.26	Potatoes (4.7 kg)	0.07
Potatoes	0.01	Steam (0.7 kg)	0.09
		Miscellaneous	0.11

Energy to the product was $\dfrac{0.26 - 0.04}{0.95} \times 100\% = 23\%$, losses were $\dfrac{0.39}{0.95} \times 100\% = 41\%$.

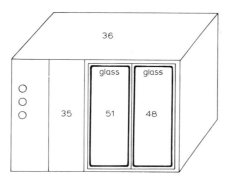

Fig. 14.4. Measured surface temperature (°C) on the different walls of the convection oven.

The stove is a major energy user. This equipment is used mostly in restaurants that produce several dishes. These stoves are often on for the whole day even if they are not used.

Keeping the dishes warm was carried out in hot cupboards, hot shelves and bain-maries. The energy consumption is almost exclusively electrical. Of the total electrical energy demand, 5–10% was used in keeping dishes warm and the remaining energy is lost to the surroundings in hot water, hot air and vapor.

Washing uses an average of 50% of the total energy input. Electrical energy is used for heating water, keeping the water warm, pumps, and conveyor drive. The energy losses are mainly in hot water to the sewer. Manual pot washing only uses energy as hot water while a pot washing machine uses 7% as hot water and 93% as electrical energy.

In the second part of our investigation some of the heat converting equipment was studied more in detail. Some energy balances are shown here.

The frying table in the restaurant had a frying surface of 700 mm × 550 mm. No insulation was found. The heating time for the table was 10 min. The energy used was 1.5 kWh and the temperature was 150–170°C. For 103 out of 250 min, the table was not used and the energy use during this time was 1.7 kWh. This energy was counted towards the losses.

Table 14.4 shows the heat balance for frying potatoes. Two other studies were carried out simultaneously, and in total, the energy losses were found to be 46%. The energy used for the product was 29%. The energy use for heating of the table and the time it was not in use was calculated to be 12% of the total energy demand.

The convection oven was used in the hospital kitchen. This one had two carts with ten shelves on each. The oven was preheated for about 5 min to 150°C. Two different products were baked in our investigation. During the measurements, 69% of the total energy was lost and 15% was used by the product. Figure 14.4 shows the oven and the temperature measured on its outer surface.

TABLE 14.5

Energy balance for the cooker (kWh/kg)

In		Out	
Electricity energy	0.19	Product	0.1
Product (101.8 kg)	0.02	Water	0.04
Shelves (24 kg)	0	Shelves	0.004
Water (28 kg)	0.009	Miscellaneous	0.05

Losses were 51%, energy used by the product 49%.

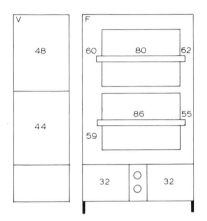

Fig. 14.5. Schematic diagram of the pressure cooker. The surface temperatures (°C) are shown.

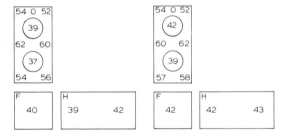

Fig. 14.6. A schematic diagram of the heating equipment for plates used in the hospital kitchen. The temperature (°C) at different times and different locations are shown: 71 min after heating (left) and 157 min after heating (right).

A pressure cooker in the restaurant was studied. Figure 14.5 shows a schematic diagram of the equipment. It has two different ovens. Steam was produced in a separate boiling pan. The pressure was 1.35–1.4 bar which corresponds to about 108–109°C. The cooker was used for 87 min in total and for 29 min of this the oven was empty.

Table 14.5 shows an energy balance for the cooker. Heating equipment for plates was studied. In the hospital kitchen, eight of these pieces of equipment were found. Sixty to 65 plates could be placed in each of two sites. Recommendations are that plates should be heated to 80°C. Figure 14.6 shows the temperature at different times at different areas of the equipment.

It was found that only 12% of the energy was taken up by the plates.

3. CONCLUSIONS

The abrasive potato peelers increase both the amount of food preparation waste and the water consumption. If a process scheme is made for handling of

Chapter 14 references, p. 237.

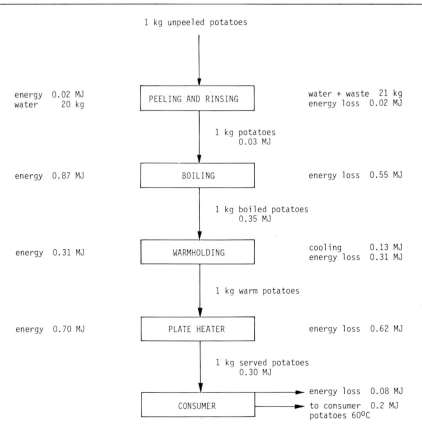

Fig. 14.7. Process scheme for handling of potatoes. The energy use and water consumption are shown.

potatoes, the following figures are found for energy use and water consumption (see Fig. 14.7). The figure shows a summary of the waste and the water consumption for 20 kg of potatoes handled in the kitchen.

The results show that it is important to find better and new methods for rinsing and peeling. It is not possible to solve the problem by using prepared potatoes because the industry uses similar methods and the utilization of the raw material is almost as bad. Another reason for not using prepared potatoes is related to the quality. The cleaning of root crops and vegetables, in some of the kitchens, is rather excessive, for example, cleaning of potatoes for half an hour under running water.

Water is used as a heat carrier or as part of the foods. It is worth mentioning that the kitchens serving coffee and tea have a higher water consumption in the heat conversion step than the others.

Electricity, which is very expensive, was the main source of energy in heat conversion. It is therefore important to minimize its use. Transmission energy can easily be decreased by insulation of the equipment. Insulation also leads to better working conditions, because the surface temperature of the apparatus is reduced. The ventilation can also be reduced as a consequence of insulation. Heat radiation from hot frying tables and stoves, among other things, is more difficult to decrease. There is a possibility of using lids during shorter breaks, but that does not really solve the problem. Frying tables and especially kitchen ranges should be developed for better utilization of energy.

The energy during warmholding is used for keeping the temperature of the foods constant. A reduction could be made if the equipment was better insulated and if the keeping-warm time was reduced.

Washing used 75% of the water consumption and 50% of the total energy demand use in kitchens studied.

Our two investigations have shown that there is a great need for research and development of equipment for the catering establishments.

4. REFERENCES

Andersson, E., Skjöldebrand, C. and Trägardh, C., 1980. Energi-vattenförbrukning i storkök (Energy demand – Water use in catering). STU Inf. 223-1981, Swedish National Board of Technical Development, Stockholm (in Swedish).

Bankvall, N., 1969. Varme. Kompendium i byggnadsteknik (Heat transfer). Report, Institute for Building Material, Lund (in Swedish).

Malmström, T., Matthiasson, E., Sivik, B. and Sköldebrand, C., 1980. Water consumption, energy use and food residue generation in Swedish catering establishments. In: G. Glew (Editor), Proc. 2nd Hanogabe Conf., 1979. Applied Science Publishers.

Sörenfors, P., 1978. Värma och masstransport vid stekning av färsprodukter. Ph.D. Thesis, Lund University (in Swedish with English summary).

Chapter 15

Energy Consumption in Membrane Processing of Foods

BENGT HALLSTRÖM

1. TERMINOLOGY AND DEFINITIONS

Membrane technology involves two types of processes. Ultrafiltration (UF) means fractionation of high molecular solutions from water containing smaller molecules; an example is the separation of proteins and salts. In reverse osmosis (RO), also sometimes called hyperfiltration (HF), only water can pass through the membrane; an example is the desalination of sea water. RO requires a more tight membrane resulting in a rather high feed pressure, while UF uses a more open membrane also therefore needing a lower pressure of the feed. The diagram in Table 15.1 shows the filtration areas for RO and UF in comparison to other techniques.

In membrane processes the feed is separated into two streams: the retentate or the concentrate held back by the membrane, and the permeate being the fraction passing through the membrane. This is illustrated in Fig. 15.1. With the symbols used in the figure the following factors are defined:

– concentration factor

$$\frac{c_c}{c_f}$$

– rejection factor

$$\frac{c_f - c_p}{c_f}$$

There is a wide range of membranes available in the market, and the development of new materials is very fast. Originally most membranes were made from cellulose acetate, but today synthetic materials are dominating. Different types are available with regard to fractionation ability, but also with regard to mechanical, thermal and chemical resistance. This is especially important in the food industry where there is a need for cleaning and sometimes sterilization of the equipment.

The membrane structure as such means a restriction for the flow passing through the membrane, i.e., the permeate. This property defines the relationship between the flow of permeate and the pressure drop. However, in processing of food liquids a layer of molecules is formed on the surface of the membrane (fouling). Also on the top of this layer a concentration gradient of the substance to be concentrated is developed in the neighbourhood of the surface; this is called concentration polarization. Both these phenomena, the layer of molecules on the membrane surface and concentration polarization

---

Chapter 15 references, p. 244.

TABLE 15.1

Useful ranges of various separation processes

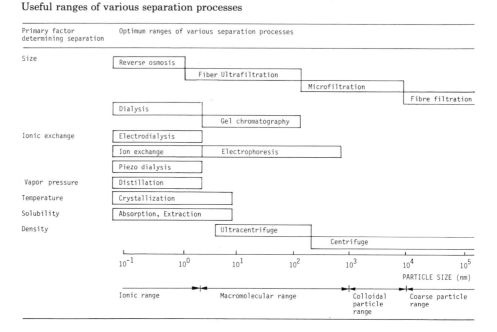

cause additional resistance to the permeate flow. This resistance is in fact greater than the resistance of the membrane itself and is furthermore increasing during the operation of the plant.

2. EQUIPMENT

The membranes are built into units called membrane modules. Different geometries have been developed and as the conditions are similar to those in heat exchangers similar configurations are present in the market. Consequently there are tubular, spiral, plate & frame and hollow fibre modules available (Fig. 15.2).

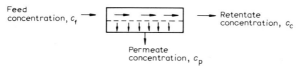

Fig. 15.1. Principal sketch of a membrane process.

3. PLANT ARRANGEMENTS

In principle the following arrangements are possible (Fig. 15.3): batch process; 'once-through' principle; multi-stage recirculation plant.

Batchwise processing is the simplest and also the cheapest. It is especially convenient for small capacities and it is also very flexible. A drawback is of course the rather long retention time.

In the 'once-through' plant the retention time is brought to a minimum, but this system is applicable only to high capacities. In this type of plant it is more difficult to control the final concentration.

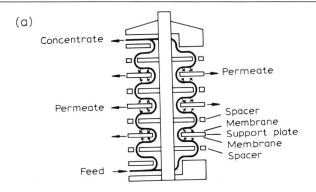

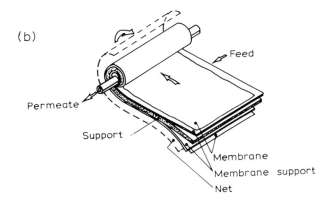

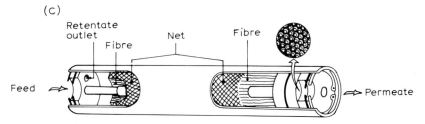

Fig. 15.2. Principles of different membrane modules: (a) plate and frame module; (b) spiral module; (c) hollow fibre module.

Therefore, the most common system especially for a high concentration ratio, is the multi-stage recirculation. This plant needs a feed pump and a recirculation pump for each stage.

4. ENERGY REQUIREMENT

A break-down of the energy requirements for a commercial membrane processing plant includes the following: feed pump and recirculation pumps; pretreatment, if any; heat treatment, if present; cleaning and sterilization; and control equipment.

The feed pump energy requirement is dependent on the flow, i.e., the capacity of the plant. Furthermore, the physical properties of the liquid are of importance, mainly viscosity. The size and the energy consumption of the recirculation pumps are related to the recirculation flow and the pressure drop of the modules. This pressure drop varies for different types of modules and manufacturers. The concentration of the liquid should be considered as this is

Chapter 15 references, p. 244.

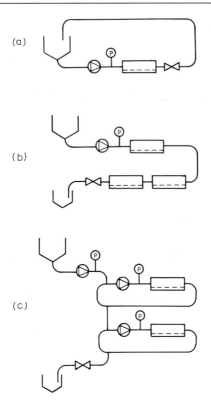

Fig. 15.3. Plant arrangement: (a) batch process; (b) single pass or 'once-through'; (c) multi-stage recirculation plant.

increasing towards the final stage of the process and the corresponding viscosity increase means a higher pressure drop.

Sometimes heating of the feed flow is done in order to improve the capacity. The corresponding energy should then be considered. As the recirculation pumps involve a slight temperature increase of the liquid, this may need a cooler to be installed after the final stage incurring a further energy requirement.

Like all other food processing equipment, these plants need cleaning at intervals. CIP facilities are mostly included in the plants and certain routines are recommended. However, the corresponding energy requirement should not be neglected in the total calculation.

A general equation for the total energy requirement will consist of two main terms. The first corresponds to the feed pump and the second to the recirculation pump or pumps. The first term is proportional to the feed and the pressure in the first recirculation stage; this pressure is dependent on the final concentration to be reached in the plant. The second term depends on the recirculation rate in each stage and this is in turn a function of the plant capacity. Furthermore, the second term depends on the final concentration, as the pressure drop of the modules is a function of the final viscosity. As a result, for the same type of plant and equipment and for the same food product the specific energy consumption is only a function of final concentration.

5. EXAMPLES

5.1. Reverse osmosis

Some typical examples of the specific energy requirements given in the literature are presented in Table 15.2 (see Glueckstern, 1982; Pepper and

TABLE 15.2

Energy requirement in reverse osmosis

Product	Dry matter content (%)	Energy requirement (kWh per kg of water)
Whey	6–12 ⎫ 6–28 ⎭	0.005–0.007
Skim milk	9–22 ⎫	0.006–0.012
Whole milk	12–28 ⎭	
Apple juice	10–20	0.005
Desalinating seawater		0.005 (desalted water)

Orehard, 1982; Rubin, 1982a,b; S. Kristensen, DDS, Nakskov, Denmark, personal communication, 1982; data from Paterson Candy International, Ltd., Loverstone Mills, Great Britain). As a comparison, an up-to-date figure for sea water desalination is also given. It should be observed that in the figures of Table 15.2 only the energy consumed by the pump(s) is included.

5.2. Ultrafiltration

In ultrafiltration the energy requirement is more specific to the duty and as these vary considerably it is difficult to compare figures. No literature data have been found.

6. COMPARISON OF ENERGY REQUIREMENTS BETWEEN REVERSE OSMOSIS AND EVAPORATION

RO requires only electrical energy if heating processes are excluded in these calculations. There are, however, different types of evaporation plants with regard to the energy required. A multi-stage plant needs mainly thermal energy, but also power for all pumps. These plants are mostly provided with one or more thermal compressors and they are therefore often called thermal vapour recompression (TVR). The other option is the mechanical vapour recompression (MVR) plant, requiring mainly electrical energy. However, steam is needed to start it up.

Both types of energy are not directly comparable and must therefore be transformed into an equivalent energy form. Thermal energy is generated from oil at very high efficiency, 80–90%. To produce electrical/mechanical energy from oil means a much lower efficiency, normally in the range of 30%. To add these energy forms together to a total (steam) equivalent energy input, electrical energy input has to be multiplied by a ('heat-to-power') factor. In the literature between 2.8 (Thijssen, 1974) and 3 (Schwartzberg, 1977) are mostly used. Here a value of 3 has been chosen for the calculations. Table 15.3 compares the energy consumption for some types of plants.

The figures in the table are the energy requirements per kg of water evaporated or transferred. The steam and power requirements for the evaporation plants are cited from the literature (Voisin, 1982; Von Loon, 1982; Wiegand, 1982).

This way of calculating and comparing energy is mainly of theoretical interest. The processing industry has to calculate in money as there are great variations in electrical and thermal energy costs both geographically and from time to time. Further local conditions have to be considered. Therefore the table above should be converted into costs and some examples of such calculations are given in Table 15.4.

Chapter 15 references, p. 244.

TABLE 15.3

Comparison of energy consumption in different plants

Type of plant	Direct energy input		Equivalent energy input (kWh/kg)
	Steam (kg/kg)	Power (kWh/kg)	
Evaporation			
TVR 3 effects	0.20 –0.25	0.003	0.17 –0.20
5 effects	0.13 –0.17	0.003	0.11 –0.14
7 effects	0.077–0.13	0.003	0.07 –0.10
MVR	0.002	0.010–0.030	0.046–0.11
Reverse osmosis		0.005–0.012	0.015–0.048

TABLE 15.4

Energy consumption costs in different plants and countries

Type of plant	Direct energy input		Energy cost		
	Steam (kg/kg)	Power (kWh/kg)	(DM/kg)	(FF/kg)	(US$/kg)
TVR 3 effects	0.22	0.003	0.014	0.031	0.00307
7 effects	0.10	0.003	0.0066	0.014	0.00151
MVR	0.02	0.020	0.0052	0.0085	0.00166
Reverse osmosis	–	0.010	0.0020	0.0029	0.0007

F.R.G.: DM 60 per metric tonne of steam $\triangleq$ DM 0.20 per kWh (1 DM $\triangleq$ US$0.40).
France: FF 135 per metric tonne of steam $\triangleq$ FF 0.29 per kWh (1 FF $\triangleq$ US$0.13).
U.S.A.: US$ 13 per metric tonne of steam $\triangleq$ US$ 0.07 per kWh.

7. REFERENCES

Glueckstern, P., 1982. Comparative energy requirements and economics of desalting processes based on current and advanced technology. Desalination, 40: 63–74.
Pepper, D. and Orehard, A.D., 1982. Improvements in the concentration of whey and milk by reverse osmosis. J. Soc. Dairy Technol., 35: 49–53.
Rubin, J., 1982a. Umkehrosmose von Molke-eine Alternative zum Eindampfen? Dtsch. Molk. Ztg., 2: 49–51.
Rubin, J., 1982b. Umkehrosmose von Molke-ein Weg zur Einsparung von Transportkosten. Dtsch. Molk. Ztg., 17: 535–538.
Schwartzberg, H.G., 1977. Energy requirements for liquid concentration. Food Technol., March: 67–76.
Thijssen, H.A.C., 1974. Fundamentals of concentration processes. In: A. Spicer (Editor), Advances in Preconcentration and Dehydration of Foods. Applied Science Publishers Ltd., London, pp. 13–44.
Voisin, M., 1981. Concentration de lactosérum: évaporation simple effect recompression mechanique de vapeur. Tech. Lait., 957: 47–49.
Von Loon, J., 1982. Neuentwicklungen beim Eindampfen von Milch und Milchprodukten. Dsch. Molk. Ztg., 2: 42–48.
Wiegand, 1982. Leaflet: Eindamfanlagen mit mechanischer Brüdenverdichtung. Wiegand GmbH, Karlsruhe.

Part IV

Energy Generation and Heat Recovery in the Food Industry

Chapter 16

Energy Generation from Direct Combustion of Solid Food Processing Wastes

STEVEN A. SARGENT and JAMES F. STEFFE

1. INTRODUCTION

Food processing plants require large quantities of energy for processing operations and in turn generate sizable amounts of solid and liquid waste materials. Rising costs for both energy and disposal have dramatically increased production costs in recent years and as a result represent a major concern to management. While the types and quantities of wastes generated by food plants vary widely, the potential exists for in-plant conversion of currently unusable or under-utilized wastes with fuel potential into recoverable energy, or more specifically, steam and hot water. Energy recovery by these means, if proven feasible, could result in significant savings for the industry in terms of reducing the amount of fossil fuel purchased and savings in waste disposal. Characterization and analysis of energy and disposal costs are dependent upon a basic understanding of several parameters, most importantly:

(1) operating conditions representative of food processing plants;
(2) biomass types, fuel potential and availability:
(3) replacement equipment for handling and combustion of biomass which is readily available and reasonably priced; and
(4) a cost analysis method capable of determining the feasibility potential.

2. ENERGY CONSUMPTION TRENDS

In 1981, the U.S. Food and Kindred Products Industry (FKPI) Group ranked sixth of all industry groups in terms of fuel and electrical energy consumption, purchasing 963.3 PJ, or 7.8% of the total consumption of 12 198.6 PJ (U.S. Bureau of the Census, 1983a). The average energy cost was $4.53 per GJ for all industry groups, ranging from $3.52 to $7.85 per GJ for 1981. Energy costs for the FKPI Group were $4.56/GJ, up 17.6% from 1980 costs. Regarding the value of product shipments, the FKPI Group ranked first, with a value of $272 136.6 million, or 13.5% of the total of $2 017 542.5 million (U.S. Bureau of the Census, 1983b).

Several trends in energy usage can be noted during the period of 1967–1981 (Table 16.1). U.S. energy consumption peaked in 1971 at 1088.1 PJ before declining to 1011.6 and 963.3 PJ in 1974 and 1981, respectively. The decrease during that 10-year period partly reflects energy conservation practices which were initiated as a result of the increased fossil fuel costs beginning in the 1970s. Greatest cost increases were for petroleum fuels, with 1029%, 956% and

Chapter 16 references, p. 264.

TABLE 16.1

Trends in energy costs by fuel type for major U.S. industry groups and the Food and Kindred Products Group, 1967–1981

Fuel purchased	U.S. industries energy costs ($ per 10^6 Btu)			Food and kindred products group (% usage)			
	1981	1967	% Change	1981	1974	1971	1967
Electrical energy	11.23	2.55	340	15.5	13.2	11.7	9.3
Distillate oil	6.55	0.62	956	2.7	8.0	7.4	6.6
Residual oil	4.74	0.42	1029	6.6	7.8	7.3	8.2
Coal	1.58	0.28	464	13.0	9.5	13.6	24.0
Coke and breeze	4.21	0.71	493	0.2	0.2	0.2	0.2
Natural gas	3.14	0.32	881	51.6	57.1	57.9	49.8
Other fuels	–	–	–	10.4	4.2	1.9	1.9
				100.0	100.0	100.0	100.0
Total energy consumption trends in FKPI							
(10^{12} Btu)				913.1	958.8	1031.3	899.6
(PJ)				963.3	1011.6	1088.1	949.1

10^{12} Btu $\approx 1.055 \times 10^{15}$ J $= 1.055$ PJ.
Adapted from U.S. Bureau of the Census, 1983a,b; Casper, 1977.

881% rises for residual oil, fuel oil and natural gas, respectively. Coke and breeze, coal and electrical energy had price increases of 493%, 464% and 340%, respectively, during this period.

Within the FKPI Group, electrical energy usage increased markedly from 9.3% to 15.5% of all energy purchased during 1967–1981. The use of 'other' fuels (including liquid petroleum gases) also increased from 1.9% to 10.4%. Use of coal dramatically decreased from 24.0% to 13.0%, while distillate and residual oil usage decreased only slightly and there was no change in the use of coke and breeze. Natural gas usage increased from 49.8% to 57.9% in 1971, before gradually declining to 51.6% in 1981.

Energy consumption for the industries within the FKPI group ranged from 161.7 PJ for 'grain mill products' to 53 PJ for 'bakery products' (Table 16.2). 'Preserved fruits and vegetables' ranked third with 119.9 PJ, behind 'sugar and confectionery products' with 134.8 PJ. Energy costs for this group ranged from $3.44/GJ for 'sugar and confectionery products' to $5.77/GJ for 'miscellaneous foods and kindred products'. These costs for the nine industries were fairly dependent upon total energy consumption; the larger operations generally had lower overall costs per heat unit than did the smaller ones due, in part, to the economy of scale of operation (larger plants normally have a higher output per unit of total cost than do smaller plants).

In terms of the value of product shipment, 'meat products' were ranked first, with a total value of $65 909 million in 1981. Second and third were 'dairy products' and 'beverages', with $36 942 and $36 075 million, respectively. Least valued shipments were from 'sugar and confectionery products', with $16 283 million. 'Preserved fruit and vegetables' ranked fifth in value at $27 719 million.

From this overview, energy costs are substantial for the FKPI Group. It was the sixth largest energy purchaser in 1981, utilizing almost 8% of the total energy, and ranked sixth most efficient in terms of cost per heat unit. This industry shipped the highest valued products of all industry groups.

TABLE 16.2

Energy consumption and costs and the value of product shipments for industries within the Food and Kindred Products Group, 1981

Industry	Energy consumption and costs					Value of product shipments	
	$(10^{12}$ Btu$)$	PJ	Rank	($ per 10^6 Btu)	($/GJ)	(Million $)	Rank
(1) Grain mill products	153.3	161.7	8	4.11	3.90	31 914.7	4
(2) Sugar and confectionary products	127.8	134.8	9	3.63	3.44	16 282.7	9
(3) Preserved fruit and vegetables	113.6	119.9	4	5.41	5.13	27 719.5	5
(4) Beverages	111.9	118.1	6	4.90	4.64	36 074.9	3
(5) Fats and oils	109.1	115.1	7	4.32	4.10	17 948.8	7
(6) Meat products	103.4	109.1	5	5.32	5.04	65 909.0	1
(7) Dairy products	87.3	92.1	2	5.65	5.36	36 941.6	2
(8) Miscellaneous FKPI[b]	56.4	59.5	1	6.09	5.77	22 443.5	6
(9) Bakery products	50.2	53.0	3	5.61	5.32	16 904.9	8
FKPI	913.1	963.3		$\bar{x} = 4.81$	4.56	272 139.6	
All U.S. industry groups	11 562.7	12 198.6		$\bar{x} = 4.78$	4.53	2 017 542.5	

[a]Adapted from U.S. Bureau of the Census, 1983a,b.
[b]Includes seafoods, coffee, macaroni, food preparations.

Chapter 16 references, p. 264.

3. FOOD PROCESSING WASTE GENERATION

3.1. Food wastes

In 1968 the Office of Solid Waste Management, U.S. Environmental Protection Agency, conducted the first survey of solid waste disposal by U.S. food processors. The areas covered in the survey were for canned, frozen and dehydrated foods, and later the following conclusions were published (Hudson, 1978):

(1) The U.S. food processing industry produces approximately 8437×10^6 kg of solid residual per year.

(2) Of this amount, fruit and vegetable processors generate 93% of the residuals, or 7802×10^6 kg. Speciality processors (baby foods, soup, stew, TV dinners, spaghetti) account for 4% or 336×10^6 kg, while seafood processors account for 3% or 254×10^6 kg.

(3) An additional 289×10^6 kg are disposed of as liquid waste by these industries, or approximately 16% of the total wastes generated.

The type and size of processing plant operation will greatly influence the kinds of wastes produced. For example, for each 1000 kg of raw apples processed, the following wastes are generated: 20 861 l of waste water containing 2.5 kg of suspended solids, and 300 kg of solid residuals. From citrus processing, however, 12 517 l of waste water are produced for each 1000 kg of raw fruit, along with 2.5 kg of suspended solids and 220 kg of solid residuals (Woodruff and Luh, 1975).

Processing operations produce solid residues, such as peelings, trimmings, cores, stems, pits, culls of undesirable fruits or vegetables, nut shells, kernel fragments and grain hulls. The physical properties of these wastes are discussed in Section 7. Liquid wastes arise from several processing operations. Waste water with low levels of suspended solids arises from hydro-handling systems and product cleaning operations, which require periodic replacement to remove accumulated field and chemical contamination. This may be disposed of in sewage or irrigation systems, provided that no toxic chemical levels are present. Liquids containing toxic constituents, such as salt brines from pickling cucumbers or lye from caustic peeling operations, must be detoxified prior to disposal.

Peeling operations generate the largest amount of liquid wastes in the food industry, followed by blanching operations (White, 1973). Both of these latter contain high amounts of suspended solids and require some treatment before being released to the environment.

The moisture content (MC) for fresh fruits and vegetables has a range of 77–96%, wet basis. Pomaces or presscakes (the processed wastes resulting from production of juices) may have a MC as low as 52% for grape pomace to over 70% for apple pomace, depending upon the method and efficiency of the press (Ben-Gera and Kramer, 1969; White and Plaskett, 1981).

Disposal of high MC solid wastes is a significant concern since they cannot be left in the plant. The high moisture content and presence of soluble sugars in fruit and vegetable processing wastes promote rapid fermentation, providing an excellent medium for microbial pathogens, insects and other pests, as well as objectionable odors (Smock and Neubert, 1950).

3.2. Non-food wastes

Non-food processing wastes are generated from shipping, canning, maintenance and office operations, most importantly packaging materials, but also

TABLE 16.3

Consumption of packaging wastes for the U.S. industries

	$(10^9$ kg)	(%)
Paper, paperboard	33.5	57
Glass	10.8	19
Metals	7.6	13
Wood	4.0	7
Plastics	2.3	4
Total	58.2	100

Mantell, 1975.

assorted solid wastes such as office trash, floor sweepings and garbage. In some instances field residues from cleaning, or from nearby pruning or harvest operations must also be disposed of. The food industry is the largest consumer of packages (44%), the next being the beverage industry (13%). The 1976, total packaging materials consumption was estimated at 58.2×10^9 kg, nationally (Table 16.3).

4. WASTE UTILIZATION AND DISPOSAL

Physical characteristics, governmental discharge restrictions and disposal costs are the primary determinants for the method of waste disposal for the processor. Returning to the data published by Hudson (1978):

(1) For the food industry as a whole 79% of the residuals or 6622×10^6 kg are utilized as by-products, with the remaining 21% disposed of as waste.

(2) About 97% or 6441×10^6 kg of the residuals utilized as by-products are fed to animals.

(3) Of the 1814×10^6 kg disposed of as solid waste, 50% is placed in landfills (both sanitary and open), 49% is spread on the land and 1% is burned on-site.

(4) Liquid wastes, which carry 16% of the total wastes (289×10^6 kg), are disposed of as follows: 50% released untreated into streams, lakes, rivers, or oceans, with lesser amounts disposed of in public sewer systems. Very few plants utilize on-site treatment or irrigation.

These data are summarized in graphic form (Fig. 16.1).

Public concern and government legislation over environmental contamination has reduced the number of wastes which are considered safe for disposal (Hills and Roberts, 1981). Buried processing and municipal wastes (refuse tips) may produce temperatures up to 150°C as well as gases such as methane, carbon monoxide and hydrogen sulfide due to microbial decomposition under anaerobic conditions. Methane may accumulate and begin to seep from the tip, creating the danger of explosion. A pilot project to recover such gases was initiated prior to 1979 at a municipal landfill in the Los Angeles area, with estimates of recovery of 17×10^6 m^3 per year over a 15-year period (Burnett, 1979). Several other examples of by-product disposal practices and utilization follow.

Cannery wastes sometimes make a very palatable and nutritious animal feed supplement. Often the wastes are transported and fed in the same form as when they are produced. Such wastes may have high MC (above 50%) originating from screening, trimming, peeling and pressing operations. Potato and corn by-products are sold as cattle feed (Licht and Revel, 1981), while apple pomace

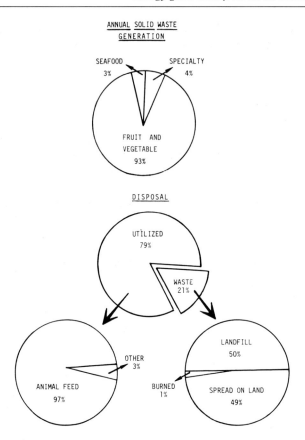

Fig. 16.1. Waste generation and disposal in the U.S. food processing industry.

is given to cattle operators for the cost of transportation. The pomace is fed to beef cattle as a fiber substitute. Feeding to pregnant cows is not recommended, however, since those fed on pomace supplemented with non-protein nitrogen gave bith to dead or weak calves, of undetermined cause (Fotenot et al., 1977).

Prepared animal feeds are made from sugar beet pulp and citrus pomace, which are dried, treated with nutrient additives and packaged prior to shipment (Hendrickson and Kesterson, 1965). These wastes account for the greatest portion of wastes utilized as feed and have the advantage of longer storage periods and reduced loss of nutrients when compared to high MC feeds, due to less microbial action (Pugsley, 1975). Recently, apple pomace became available as a flavor/fiber ingredient for the baking industry. Other residues are by nature of low MC, and include grain pieces and rice hulls; rice hulls, while added to feed rations, are not recommended for use as a solitary feed due to possible abrasion in the digestive tract of the animal (Hsu and Luh, 1980).

Some waste by-products have strong economic importance, most notably production of pectin from citrus wastes (Hendrickson and Kesterson, 1965), bedding from hulls and shells and extraction of chemicals (e.g., furfural from corn cobs, Arnold, 1975). Additional information for upgrading waste products may be found in Ledward et al. (1983).

Soil incorporation of tomato and fruit cannery wastes has been demonstrated by first spreading the wastes on the topsoil at rates up to 250 000 kg/ha, followed by disking. No soil or groundwater contamination by heavy metals occurred at these rates (Noodharmcho and Flocker, 1975; Timm et al., 1980). Conversion of high MC wastes to humus is feasible by composting (Rose et al., 1965; Toth, 1973). Many growers dispose of apple pomace as a mulch on their orchards, but must periodically neutralize the acidity added by the pomace by incorporating lime into the soil. The fresh pomace left in the orchard acts as a potential host for disease organisms, and adds to weed control problems due to seeds which germinate the following spring.

5. ENERGY CONVERSION METHODS

Several processes exist which can transform biomass into energy. Selection of the appropriate process is dependent upon several factors: the physical state of the biomass (initial moisture content, the heat value, physical properties), the efficiency of the energy conversion process, energy demands of the plant and economic feasibility. The following methods have proven technically feasible for a wide spectrum of processing wastes: anaerobic digestion, in which microorganisms breakdown biomass materials to produce methane gas and carbon dioxide; fermentation, in which yeasts ferment simple sugars into ethanol; and thermochemical conversion, in which heat is released by thermochemical reaction (White and Plaskett, 1981).

Anaerobic digestion and fermentation are best suited for conversion of wet processing residues to fuels, such as cannery wastes (Lane, 1979). Citrus juice extractor residues (peel, pulp, seeds) and the press liquor resulting from dewatering of these residues, show potential for utilization as substrates to produce fermented products (Graumlich, 1983). Of the three, thermochemical conversion produces the highest amount of heat per unit of fresh product (Hall, 1981), and has proven cost-effective on an industrial scale for conversion of a variety of waste materials into usable energy, such as process steam or electricity (Table 16.4). With assistance from governmental funding, a U.S. apple processor has demonstrated the possibility of converting apple pomace into process steam and cogenerating electricity by direct combustion (Schwieger, 1982).

Conversion of industrial solid wastes to useful energy is growing in acceptability. In 1977 it was estimated that approximately 15% of non-wood processing wastes were converted into energy, equivalent to 94.9 PJ (Tillman, 1977). In 1980, a plant in Cheboygan, MI began combusting plastics, cellulose fibers and factory and office trash, generating up to 29.5 GJ/h and saving over \$350 000 annually in fossil fuel costs and over \$550 000 per year in disposal costs (Reason, 1982b).

Municipal solid wastes (MSW) are converted to produce approximately 43.400 PJ per year in the U.S.A. (Tillman, 1977). Composition of MSW was estimated to be 80% organic combustibles (food wastes, paper, plastics, leather, rubber, wood) and 20% inorganic non-combustibles (glass, metal) (Baum and Parker, 1973). Conversion of MSW requires extensive presorting to remove the inorganic residues and has proven cost-effective on a municipal scale basis.

There are three methods of thermochemical conversion of biomass. Direct combustion occurs when the biomass is oxidized with air in excess of

TABLE 16.4

Industrial conversion of by-products into usable energy by direct combustion

By-product	Resultant energy produced	Location	Reference
Walnut hulls	Steam, electricity	Stockton, CA	Anonymous, 1981
Pecan shells	Steam	Florence, SC	Howard, 1981
Apple pomace	Steam, electricity	Orrtanna, PA	Schwieger, 1982
Plastic, paper waste	Steam	Charlevoix, MI	Reason, 1982b
Solid municipal waste	Steam, electricity	Saugus, MA	Cheremisinoff et al., 1980
Sugar cane bagasse	Steam, electricity	Kauani, HI	Reason, 1982a

Chapter 16 references, p. 264.

stoichiometric requirements and held above the ignition temperature, assuring complete combustion. The stoichiometric requirement is the theoretical amount of oxygen necessary to completely oxidize the carbon, hydrogen, sulfur and trace elements in the biomass to produce primarily carbon dioxide, water vapor and heat (Fryling, 1966). Derived fuels are obtained when the combustion air is sub-stoichiometric (gasification) or absent (pyrolysis, or carbonization). Gasification produces biogas, or producer gas, while pyrolysis produces charcoal or char liquid, both of low-to-medium heat value.

The derived fuels (methane, ethanol, biogas, charcoal and char liquid) contain more heat value per unit of final fuel weight and are therefore – if pressurized – more economical to transport and store than the raw residue, but direct combustion results in the highest heat value per unit of raw biomass material (Hall, 1981). The wood products industry has utilized direct combustion for years to produce steam and heat for drying kilns, and more recently to cogenerate electricity (Jamison, 1979).

Conversion efficiencies of direct combustion, anaerobic digestion and submerged microbial fermentation were determined for apple and grape pomace (Kranzler et al., 1983). Direct combustion releases a net energy of 1750 kJ/kg of fresh apples, whereas anaerobic digestion and fermentation release 920 and 90 kJ/kg, respectively. Heat values for grape pomace were 1280, 550 and 30 kJ/kg of fresh grapes for direct combustion, anaerobic digestion and fermentation, respectively. Of the three methods, it was concluded that direct combustion is the most efficient means to convert pomace and least complicated method to retrofit to existing steam generating systems. Anaerobic digestion was considered viable, although less efficient, while fermentation was a decidedly disadvantageous alternative for pomace conversion due to the low heat value and complex equipment required. Solid-state fermentation of apple pomace produced approximately 4.3% alcohol by weight, and increased protein in the remaining pomace by 50%, improving the animal feed value (Hang et al., 1981). A combination of anaerobic digestion and composting has also been suggested as a means of recovering energy from apple pomace (Jewell and Cummings, 1984).

In summarizing energy conversion methods, thermochemical conversion by the direct combustion process may be the optimal method for in-plant conversion of fruit and vegetable processing wastes to recoverable energy for the following reasons:

(1) direct combustion generates the most heat per unit fresh biomass;
(2) in-plant production and combustion is more energy-efficient than other conversion processes;
(3) efficient biomass combustion boiler systems are readily available to the industry and have a less complex operation than those for other conversion process;
(4) the ash by-product of combustion accounts for a small portion of the initial volume, greatly reducing disposal costs, and has potential for utilization as a fertilizer (Hsu and Luh, 1980) and as a component for ornamental plant media (Regulski, 1983).

6. DIRECT COMBUSTION OF SOLID WASTES

6.1. Solid fuel combustion theory

A review of combustion theory will provide better understanding of the fuel characteristics of the biomass wastes. In order for sustained combustion of a solid material to occur, three conditions must be satisfied–proper temperature,

TABLE 16.5

U.S. stationary source emission performance standards

Source	Pollutant	Standard
(A) Coal; coal/wood	Particulate	0.043 kg/MJ
Residue-fired[a]	Opacity	20%; 40%, 2 min/h
boilers over	SO_2	0.516 kg/MJ
264 GJ/h	NO_x	0.301 kg/MJ
(B) Gas; gas/wood	Particulate	0.043 kg/MJ
Residue-fired[a]	Opacity	20%; 40%, 2 min/h
boilers over	NO_x	0.086 kg/MJ
264 GJ/h		
(C) Incinerators	Particulate	0.18 g per dry standard m³,
over 45.4 × 10³ kg/day		corrected to 12% CO_2

Olexsey, 1980.

time and turbulence. The fuel must be confined for an adequate residence time above the ignition point, the latter being that temperature at which combustion becomes self-sustaining. Turbulence ensures that sufficient oxygen is available to combine with hydrogen, carbon, sulfur and trace elements released during the combustion reaction. Once these conditions are met, the three-stage combustion process begins (Elliott, 1980).

During the first stage any remaining moisture is evaporated from the fuel. This represents a net energy loss, since the heat required to raise the water to the boiling point and the heat of vaporization is equal to roughly 2600 kJ/kg of water and the fuel temperature is held near the 100°C. Upon vaporization the second, or flaming combustion, stage begins in which volatile gases evolve from polymeric compounds within the biomass as temperatures rise from 150 to 540°C. This phase releases great amounts of heat as the ignition point is surpassed and the process becomes self-sustaining. Gases released include carbon monoxide (later oxidized to carbon dioxide), the paraffin series (e.g., methane), the olefin series (e.g., ethylene), the aromatic series (e.g., benzene), and other, including sulfur compounds and water vapor (Perry and Chilton, 1973). Finally, the remaining fixed carbon is oxidized during the glowing combustion stage, releasing carbon dioxide and leaving ash. The principal reactions concerning direct combustion are described by the following equations (Babcock and Wilcox, 1978):
– for carbon

$$C + O_2 \rightarrow CO_2 + 32\,797 \text{ kJ/kg}$$

– for hydrogen

$$2H_2 + O_2 \rightarrow 2H_2O + 142\,119 \text{ kJ/kg}$$

6.2. Combustion emissions considerations

Particulate emissions are the principal pollutants arising from combustion of biomass materials. The amount of fly ash carried by the stack gases varies with the method of combustion, the biomass and the combustion system being employed. U.S. standards for stationary sources relevant to biomass fuel combustion are 0.043 kg/MJ for particulates in either coal/wood or gas/wood-fired boilers (Table 16.5). An excellent review of particulate collectors can be found in the special report by the editors of Power (1980). The cyclone collector is

Chapter 16 references, p. 264.

commonly used to remove larger particulates and may be adequate for efficient combustion systems. Baghouse collectors can be added if emissions are not met by the cyclone collectors, removing greater than 99.9% of the fly-ash. Wet scrubbers remove fines, but require substantial post-treatment of the waste water. Electrostatic precipitators are also widely used where biomass is burned in conjunction with coal.

The most toxic gaseous pollutants to economic crops are sulfur dioxide, hydrogen fluoride, ozone, nitrogen dioxide and peroxyacetal nitrate. The principal mode of action is by disruption of biochemical reactions upon pollutant uptake through open stomata (Tibbitts and Kobriger, 1983). Only sulfur dioxide and nitrogen oxides (NO_x) emissions are restricted by the federal government; however, these latter pollutants pertain normally to fossil fuels since biomass fuels contain miniscule amounts of sulfur and nitrogen. Conversion of atmospheric nitrogen to NO_x occurs only when combustor temperatures exceed 1650°C (Babcock and Wilcox, 1978).

6.3. Sources of heat loss

As stated previously, adequate turbulance is essential to ensure that stoichiometric requirements are met. This is accomplished by introducing excess air into the combustion chamber. Excess air is measured as the percentage of ambient air added above the stoichiometric requirement, and varies with the fuel, MC and combustor design. Inadequate excess air causes incomplete combustion, resulting in unburned carbon and carbon monoxide leaving the stack and carbon remaining in the ash. Seventy-two percent of the heat value of carbon is lost if carbon monoxide is not oxidized. Too much excess air results in fly ash being carried in the exhaust gases, severe cooling of the combustion chamber and excessive heat loss, since the air will be heated and exhausted to the atmosphere (Hughes, 1976). Thus, precise monitoring of the combustion system is fundamental in establishing and maintaining optimal combustion conditions.

Combustion chamber temperatures must likewise be controlled, since ash becomes molten when heated above the respective fusion temperature. As the ash cools, it congeals into a solid, glass-like substance known as slag. Deposits of slag within a combustor or boiler create costly maintenance problems and greatly reduce heat transfer efficiency (Schwieger, 1980). Ash fusion temperatures have been determined for fuel candidates and should be consulted prior to fuel/air adjustments of combustion systems, since the fusion temperatures vary between ash types.

Stack temperatures range from 200°C to over 370°C. Although any exhaust gases above the ambient temperature represent an energy loss, a minimum of 200°C should be maintained in order to avoid inadequate updraft and condensation which causes corrosion in the heat exchanger and stack (Bender, 1964). These heated gases are the major source of heat loss for power boilers, with lesser amounts being lost to hot ash removal, radiation losses from the system and blowdown (flushing of hot water from boilers as a maintenance routine.

6.4. Waste heat recovery

Recovery of waste heat is possible from these sources, and methodology for energy accounting of food processing operations has been described in detail by Singh (1978). A study of food processing plants in the northwestern U.S. identified exhaust gases to discharge up to 18% of the total energy lost, followed by dryer exhausts and condenser cooling water (Davis et al., 1980). Significant savings in energy costs have been realized by recovering waste heat from exhaust gases from the dehydration of citrus wastes (Bryan, 1977) and from waste water discharged to a drain (Combes and Boykin, 1981).

As noted previously in Table 16.4, besides producing steam or hot water many plants are also cogenerating electricity. In several cases the processor changed from that of an electrical importer to that of an exporter to the local power grid. The pulp and paper industry has shown particular promise, with estimates of 791 PJ in energy savings per year (Johanson and Sarkanen, 1977).

7. COMBUSTION CHARACTERISTICS OF SOLID WASTES

Many processing wastes have significant energy potential (Table 16.6). Most cellulosic residues have heat contents in the range of 13 950–23 260 kJ/kg (dry weight), which includes paper and wood packaging wastes, nut shells, fruit pits and field residues. Plastics, rubber, fats and oils have higher heat contents due to the higher proportion of hydrogen and carbon per unit. The greater percentage of oxygen in biomass materials as compared to plastics, reduces the heat content of these materials, since the carbon and hydrogen are already partly oxidized (White and Plaskett, 1981).

Combustion of plastics increases heat recovery substantially, but requires special attention. Sudden flare-ups in the combustion chamber can occur with flow rates in excess of 10% of the total fuel (Kut and Hare, 1981). Combustion of polyvinyl chloride (PVC) plastic results in the release of chlorine, which combines with hydrogen to form hydrochloric acid (HCl). Severe corrosion occurs in the heat exchanger when HCl condenses on the surfaces. Chlorine is also released from the burning of salt in food processing wastes and paper products. As long as the temperature in the heat exchanger and stack is maintained above the condensation point of HCl (150–350°C) corrosion problems will be minimized (Baum and Parker, 1973). The sulfur content for plastics (1–2%) is not significant.

Biomass wastes with the highest ash contents are sugar beet and potato foliage (21.2 and 13.5%, respectively). All other reported values are below that for peanut shells at 8.8% (Table 16.6). The most likely fuel candidates for processing firms are within the range for adequate emission control; values for cherry and peach pits are less than 1%.

Ash fusion temperatures for paperboard, textiles, paper and plastics will not be reached under normal operating conditions in a biomass boiler, and therefore will produce little or no slag (Table 16.7).

Combustion of these residues would require the same emission standards as those for waste-fueled combustors listed previously (Table 16.5). Although limits for HCl-emission have not been set at the federal level, the State of Michigan (U.S.A.) allows a maximum of 0.07 mg/m^3 when measured at the property line of the plant. Fly ash absorbs some HCl while being carried in the flue gas, and any excess HCl can be removed satisfactorily by water scrubbers (Baum and Parker, 1973). It should be repeated that HCl is produced only by combustion of PVC plastics.

Ash, fly ash and slag residues have been utilized in several manners. Ash from a gasifier combustion system was determined to be very compatible with peat as a container medium for the nursery industry (Regulski, 1983). Fly ash from coal combustion has proven acceptable as a component for stabilizing aggregates for use as a highway paving (NRC, 1976). Recently, coal cinders were evaluated for use as a container medium component, and found to contribute significant amounts of micronutrients to growing plants; heavy metals were also added, the possible toxic effects on the plants to be determined later

Chapter 16 references, p. 264.

TABLE 16.6

Combustion characteristics of selected processing wastes and residues

	Heat content (dry basis)		Ash (%)
	(Btu/lb)	(kJ/kg)	
(A) *Packaging wastes*[a]			
**(1) Corrugated paper boxes	7 429	17 280	5.3
(2) Brown paper	7 706	17 924	1.1
(3) Paper food cartons	7 730	17 980	6.9
(4) Waxed milk cartons	11 732	27 289	1.2
(5) Plastic coated paper	7 703	17 917	2.8
(6) Newspaper (packing)	8 480	19 724	1.5
**(7) Polyethylene, polypropylene	19 000	44 194	0.0
(8) Polystyrene	17 250	40 123	–
(9) Polyamides (nylon)	12 750	29 657	–
(10) Polyesters	12 000	27 912	–
(11) Polyurethane	11 500	26 749	–
(12) Polystyrene foam	18 120	42 147	–
(13) Polyvinyl chloride (PVC)	8 250	19 189	2.1
(14) Vinyl	8 830	20 539	0.0
(15) Softwood (pine)	9 150	21 283	0.1
(16) Hardwood (oak)	8 682	20 194	0.1
(B) *Field residues*[b]			
(1) Barley straw (spring)	7 739	18 000	5.3
(2) Barley straw (winter)	7 653	17 800	6.6
(3) Bean straw	7 739	18 000	5.3
(4) Oat straw	7 696	17 900	5.7
(5) Pea straw	7 696	17 900	7.7
(6) Potato foliage	7 438	17 300	13.5
(7) Rape straw	7 739	18 000	4.5
(8) Rye straw	7 825	18 200	3.0
(9) Sugar beet tops	6 621	15 400	21.2
(10) Wheat straw	7 567	17 600	7.1
(11) Corn stover (35% MC, w.b.)[c]	4 613	10 730	4.0
(12) Corn cob (15% MC, w.b.)[c]	7 997	18 600	1.4
(13) Cotton gin trash (12.5% MC)[d]	8 072	18 775	–
(C) *Nut shells and fruit pits*[e]			
(1) Almond (soft)	8 360	19 445	3.1
(2) Black walnut	8 000	18 608	0.3
(3) Chestnut	7 900	18 375	n.a.*
(4) English walnut	8 000	18 608	0.8
(5) Filbert	8 300	19 306	0.7
(6) Peanut	8 800	20 469	8.8
(7) Pecan	8 950	20 818	1.8
(8) Apricot	8 520	19 817	0.7
(9) Cherry	7 800	18 143	0.8
(10) Peach	8 200	19 073	0.4

			Moisture content (as received wet basis)
(D) *Assorted solid wastes*[a]			
(1) Paper	7 572	17 612	10.2
(2) Wood	8 613	20 033	20.0
(3) Grass	7 693	17 894	65.0
(4) Brush	7 900	18 375	40.0
(5) Greens	7 077	16 461	62.0
(6) Leaves	7 096	16 505	50.0
(7) Leather	8 850	20 585	10.0
(8) Rubber	11 330	26 353	8.2
(9) Plastics	14 368	33 420	2.0

TABLE 16.6 (*continued*)

	Heat content (dry basis)		Moisture content (as received, wet basis)
	(Btu/lb)	(kJ/kg)	
(10) Oil, paints	13 400	31 168	0.0
(11) Linoleum	8 310	19 329	2.1
(12) Rags	7 652	17 798	10.1
(13) Dirt	3 790	8 815	3.2
**(14) Wet fruit wastes	8 484	19 734	80.0
(15) Fats	16 700	38 844	0.0

[a]Baum and Parker, 1973.
[b]White and Plaskett, 1981.
[c]Claar et al., 1981.
[d]Oursborn et al., 1978.
[e]Mantell 1975.
*Not available.
**Used in this analysis.

TABLE 16.7

Ash fusion temperatures for selected processing wastes

Ash	Temperature (°C)
Mixed waste	1205
Paperboard, textiles	1227
Plastics, rubber	1261
Coal	1330

Kut and Hare, 1981; Kranzler et al., 1983.

(Neal and Wagner, 1983). These residues are sterile and inexpensive by-product sources.

An analysis was made for the technical and economic feasibility of combusting wastes generated by apple juice processors in the state of Michigan (Sargent et al., 1983a, b). Apple pomace, or presscake, is the solid waste resulting from pressing operations of juice and cider. It has unique combustion properties due to the presence of rice hulls, which are often added as a press aid to improve juice extraction efficiency.

The primary constituent of apple pomace is cellulose. Volatile and fixed carbon amount to 95.99% of bone-dry pomace with the remaining 4.0% as ash and 0.1% as sulfur and trace elements (Table 16.8). Ash and sulfur contents are much lower for pomace and other biomass wastes than for coal, and sulfur is also less than that for #2 fuel oil. Natural gas produces virtually no ash or sulfur. Rice hulls contain an average of 17.4% ash, and when present in pomace, will raise the overall ash content by less than 1%.

Analyses of ash (Table 16.9) reveal a high level of silicon in rice hulls (95.8%), which affects the handling characteristics. The presence of rice hulls in the apple pomace is reflected by the high percentage of silicon, as compared to wood or coal ash. Silicon is very abrasive, and would restrict use of pneumatic handling of dried pomace containing rice hulls. Rice hulls are alternately used as industrial abrasives for cleaning metal parts (Schwieger, 1982).

Bone-dry apple pomace has a heat content of 18 000 kJ/kg, similar to that for wood, and approximately 60% that for coal, since it contains less fixed carbon (Table 16.9). Rice hulls have a heat content of 13 390 kJ/kg. The ash fusion temperature of apple pomace is 1482°C, higher than that for bituminous coal.

Chapter 16 references, p. 264.

TABLE 16.8

Ash analyses for selected biomass and fossil fuels

	Percent ash				
	Apple pomace[a]	Rice hulls[b]	Grape pomace[a]	Wood[c]	Coal[c]
Silicon dioxide	83.0	95.8	19.3	33.8	37.6
Iron oxide	0.3	–	1.9	1.6	29.3
Aluminum oxide	0.0	–	23.7	2.6	20.1
Magnesium oxide	1.4	–	5.2	4.7	1.3
Potassium oxide	9.0	–	16.9	0.1	1.6
Calcium oxide	2.2	–	18.9	56.5	4.3
Sodium oxide	0.2	–	1.1	0.5	0.8
Barium oxide	0.0	–	0.2	0.0	0.0
Titanium oxide	0.0	–	0.0	0.2	0.8
Sulfur trioxide	0.7	–	4.4	0.0	0.0
Phosphorus pentoxide	2.3	–	7.7	0.0	0.0
Undetermined	0.9	4.2	0.7	0.0	4.3
Total	100.0	100.0	100.0	100.0	100.0
Percent ash produced by combustion	4.0	17.4	2.7	0.1	10.3
Ash fusion temperature					
(°F)	2700	–	2400	2580	2450
(°C)	1482	–	1315	1415	1343

[a]Kranzler et al., 1983.
[b]Nelson et al., 1950.
[c]Babcock & Wilcox, 1978.

TABLE 16.9

Comparison of selected analyses for apple pomace and fossil fuels

	Apple pomace[a]	Rice hulls[b]	Coal[c]	No. 2 fuel oil[d]	Natural gas (95% methane)[e]
Ultimate analysis (%)					
Carbon	44.6	39.2	75.5	87.3	74.9
Hydrogen	6.2	5.0	5.0	12.6	25.1
Oxygen	44.8	32.7	4.9	0.004	–
Nitrogen	0.4	2.0	1.2	0.006	–
Sulfur	0.05	0.1	3.1	0.22	–
Ash	4.0	17.4	10.3	–	–
H_2O	–	3.6	–	–	–
Heat content					(liquid)
(Btu/lb)	7 780	5 760	13 000	18 670	23 885
(kJ/kg)	18 096	13 398	30 238	43 427	55 557

Ash fusion temperature	Bituminous coal[c]	Apple pomace[f]	Grape pomace[f]
(°F)	2450	2700	2400
(°C)	1343	1482	1315

[a]Kranzler and Davis, 1981.
[b]Singh et al., 1980.
[c]Elliott, 1980.
[d]Perry and Chilton, 1973.
[e]Hsu and Luh, 1980.
[f]Kranzler et al., 1983.

With combustion chamber temperatures held below the fusion temperature slag deposits will be minimized. The heat content of pomace, as with other biomass fuels, is inversely related to MC. As MC increases from 0–20 to 65%, the heat content decreases from 18 100–12 330 to 3950 kJ/kg, respectively.

8. SELECTION OF HANDLING/COMBUSTION SYSTEM COMPONENTS

8.1. Handling system

Handling system components should be evaluated and selected from pertinent references and conversations with industrial representatives, followed by sizing according to the waste flow rate. Criteria for selection of system components should be based upon four general considerations:
  (1) waste availability, including quantities produced, length of processing season and plant processing schedule;
  (2) types of handling equipment available to the industry;
  (3) characteristics of the combustion furnaces, including dependability, combustion efficiency, retrofit potential and multi-fuel capability;
  (4) investment costs relating to purchase, installation; and operating costs relating to maintenance.

Bulk densities for processing plant wastes must be known for accurate sizing of conveying systems. Values for several wastes range from 16.0 kg/m^3 for expanded polystyrene to 770.0 kg/m^3 for oak (Table 16.10).

The handling components should include a hammermill for size reduction of non-particulate wastes prior to conveyance to a rotary drier. The drier should have the capability for efficient drying of particulate, high MC materials, and the flexibility for use in batch or continuous operations. The drier would combust a fossil fuel, but the potential exists to reduce drying costs by recovering waste heat from the boiler stack and introducing into the drier. Wastes requiring no drying would pass through the hammermill and by-pass the drier.

Packaging wastes typically have a MC below 15%, which is favorable for in-plant storage; however, other handling problems are created. Nails, staples and wire bindings must be removed from such items as pallets, crates and paper boxes in order to avoid excessive wear on equipment. Metallic objects have been reported to ignite dry biomass from sparks generated by handling equipment, especially hammermill size reducers (Kut and Hare, 1981). Removal of metal fasteners would increase hand labor costs, while loose metal objects could be removed by an in-line metal detector/removal system prior to any

TABLE 16.10

Bulk densities for selected industrial wastes

	(kg/m^3)	(lb/ft^3)
(1) Folded newspapers, cardboard (packed or baled)	500	31.2
(2) Loosely crumpled paper	50	3.1
(3) Loose waste paper (in sacks)	20	1.2
(4) Uncompacted vegetable waste, separated food wastes (70–80%)	200	12.5
(5) Cotton gin trash	56	3.5
(6) Oak (14% MC)	770	48.1
(7) Pine (15% MC)	570	35.6
(8) Polystyrene (expanded)	16	1.0

Kut and Hare, 1981; Beck and Halligan, 1980.

Chapter 16 references, p. 264.

operations. Plastics likewise require no drying (2% MC), although ambient temperatures must be maintained below the melting point in order to prevent blockage and untimely maintenance shutdown.

It would be advantageous to dry wet wastes prior to combustion for several reasons. With a lower initial MC, more heat would be available to produce steam; any moisture in the fuel must be evaporated prior to combustion, therefore more heat is lost with higher MC fuels. Handling dry wastes requires much less power and has fewer equipment problems than wet pomace and may be stored as a stable biological product prior to combustion. Also, several biomass boilers require a dry fuel for efficient energy conversion. Wood chips are typically stored and combusted at 35% MC (Schwieger, 1980), while 20% MC was suggested for apple pomace as a compromise between net heat content and drying costs (Kranzler and Davis, 1981). Pelletizing wastes would produce a dense fuel with a higher heat content per unit mass, but is very energy intensive (Swint, 1980).

Clumps passing through the drier would be separated, fed again through the hammermill and reintroduced into the drier. The clumps may case-harden at the surface, thereby reducing drying efficiency, since the dry surface acts as an insulating barrier, hindering moisture diffusion from the inside. Clumps could also block subsequent waste flow and disrupt the combustion process in the combustion chamber.

Upon drying, the waste would be transported by belt conveyor or bucket elevator to a bulk collector for short-term storage. Pneumatic handling would be advisable only for non-abrasive waste in order to avoid premature wear of transport piping. In the case of apple pomace, which often contains abrasive rice hulls, the hulls could first be separated from dried pomace by air classification. This would permit pneumatic handling of the pomace and allow the hulls to be recycled on a daily basis as a press aid.

A bulk collector would be located outside of the building and adjacent to the boiler room. The purpose of the collector would be for protection against adverse weather with overflow capacity. The handling/combustion system was designed for a continuous production schedule; storage would be necessary to prevent accumulation of wastes within the plant in the event of brief shutdowns of the boiler. Screw augers at the base of the collector would transport and meter the wastes to the boiler. Bridging in the bin can be avoided with an appropriate removal system (Fig. 16.2).

8.2. Combustion systems

Several multi-fuel combustors are available for direct combustion of biomass fuels, fossil fuels and co-firing these fuels. Many of these combustors can be retro-fitted to existing boilers or purchased as an integral part of a package boiler. Retrofit combustors require less capital investment than the package boiler systems; however, the heat recovery efficiency for retrofit applications decreases by as much as 25% through heat losses between the combustor and the heat recovery boiler. Package boilers (those produced at the factory with the combustor and heat exchanger boiler as a single unit) have heat recovery efficiencies of 65–85%, depending on the method of construction and flame adjustment.

Three package boiler systems representing the distinct combustion technologies of pile burning, suspension firing and fluidized-bed combustion were selected for consideration in this work. The boilers are of the fire tube design and would be sized by the anticipated waste flow rates. Pile burning and suspension firing systems have been extensively used by the wood products industry for combusting wastes ranging from hogged brush to sawdust fines

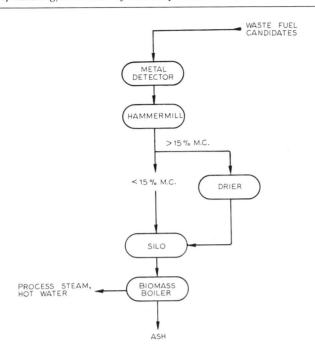

Fig. 16.2. Mass flow scheme for waste fuel candidates.

(Bullpit, 1980). Fluidized-bed combustion is a relatively new technology used for burning coal and municipal wastes on a power-house scale, but also showing excellent promise for use on a smaller scale for combusting biomass.

In pile burning systems solid fuel is introduced into the combustion chamber through the bottom grate by a screw auger, forming a pile as it is pushed outward. It may also be pneumatically fed into the chamber from above, where it partially burns in suspension before falling onto the grate. The fuel accumulates in a thick bed pile with combustion occurring at the surface of the pile. This permits fuels of 50–60% MC and of non-uniform size to be combusted, since the extended residence time facilitates drying in the combustion chamber. Furnace designs are the dutch oven, fuel cell, cyclone, wet cell, inclined water-cooled pinhole grate, traveling-grate spreader-stoker and vibrating grate (Perry and Chilton, 1973).

Dry, particulate fuels (15% MC) are required by suspension firing systems, in which the fuel is pneumatically fed into the combustion chamber. Nearly complete combustion occurs by proportionally metering the air with the fuel flow rate. These systems have been installed in powerhouse operations, and pulverized coal is routinely co-fired with biomass fuels to increase heat output. Furnace designs are the cyclonic and solid fuel burners (O'Grady, 1980).

The current interest in fluidized-bed combustion systems has developed because of the capability of burning a variety of fuels up to 55% initial MC at non-uniform sizes. The combustion air is forced upward through a bed of preheated sand maintained at approximately 927°C by fossil fuel. The air causes the sand particles to become fluidized at which time the waste fuel is introduced into the bed, dried and combusted by the continuous agitation from the hot sand particles. Heat generated by the waste during firing will maintain the bed temperature, permitting reduction or elimination of the fossil fuel. Addition of lime to the sand allows combustion of high sulfur coals, the lime acting to absorb sulfur compounds before release to the exhaust gases (LePori et al., 1981).

Due to the higher amounts of ash derived from thermochemical conversion of cellulosic materials, a rigid schedule must be maintained for removal of ash

TABLE 16.11

Differences between direct combustion systems

System	Advantages	Disadvantages
Pile burning	(1) Use of high MC fuels (2) Non-uniform fuel size (3) Simple design and operation	(1) High refractory repair costs (2) Slow response to load changes (3) Manual ash removal (some systems)
Suspension firing	(1) Low particulate emission (2) Rapid response to load changes	(1) Low MC fuels only (2) Uniform fuel particles (3) Pneumatic handling only (4) Very accurate air control required
Fluidized-bed combustion	(1) Use of high MC fuels (2) Non-uniform fuel size (3) Package boilers available	(1) Slow response to load changes (2) Preheat bed with fossil fuel (3) Clinker formation in bed

Schwieger, 1980; Bullpit, 1980.

from the combustion chamber to prevent slag formation. The trend has been to design combustors which have automatic ash removal systems in the grate area which permit continuous operation by elimination of frequent manual cleaning. Several systems also separate unburned char pieces from the ash and reinject them into the combustion zone, improving efficiency up to 7%.

These systems were selected to provide a greater choice for the processor considering investment in waste conversion technology. Each had advantages and disadvantages (Table 16.11), and selection of a particular combustor is dependent upon several technical factors, including size of operation, MC of the fuel, need for multi-fuel combustion, energy form required for processing (e.g., steam, hot water, hot air) and presence of abrasive materials in the waste stream.

Fossil fuel and purchased electrical energy represent costs to food processors. As restrictions increase for solid waste disposal, disposal costs also become a significant management concern. The potential exists for processors to realize substantial savings in energy and disposal costs through in-plant combustion of processing wastes.

9. REFERENCES

Anonymous, 1981. Walnut shells to fuel diamond walnut plant. Calif. Grape Grower, 2(2): 46.
Arnold, L.K., 1975. The commercial utilization of corncobs. In: C.L. Mantell (Editor), Solid Wastes: Origin, Collection, Processing, and Disposal. Wiley, New York, NY, pp. 393–403.
Babcock & Wilcox, Inc., 1978. Steam – Its Generation and Use. New York, NY.
Baum, B. and Parker, C.H., 1973. Solid Waste Disposal. Vol. 1, Incineration and Landfill. Ann Arbor Science, Ann Arbor, MI, 397 pp.
Beck, S.R. and Halligan, J.E. 1980. Thermochemical conversion of agricultural residues. In: M.L. Schuler (Editor), Utilization and Recycle of Agricultural Wastes. CRC Press, Boca Raton, FL, pp. 197–236.
Bender, R.J., 1964. Steam generation. Power (special report) 108(6), 48 pp.
Ben-Gera, I. and Kramer, A., 1969. The utilization of food industries wastes. Adv. Food Res., 17: 77–152.
Bryan, W.L., 1977. Recovery of waste heat from drying citrus by-products. In: C.J. King and J.P. Clark (Editors), Water Removal Processes: Drying Concentration of Foods and Other Materials. AIChE Symp. Ser. 163, American Institute of Chemical Engineers, New York, NY, pp. 25–32.
Bullpit, W.S., 1980. Retrofitting fossil-fuel boilers. In: M.P. Levi and M.J. O'Grady (Editors), Decisionmakers Guide to Wood Fuel for Small Energy Users. SERI/TR-8234-1, Solar Energy Research Institute, Golden, CO, pp. 99–108.

Burnett, J.M., 1979. Waste materials as fuels. In: P.W. O'Callaghan (Editor), Energy for Industry. Pergamon Press, Oxford, pp. 91–109.

Casper, M.E., 1977. Energy Saving Techniques for the Food Industry. Noyes Data Corporation, Park Ridge, NJ, 657 pp.

Cheremisinoff, N.P., Cheremisinoff, P.N. and Ellerbusch, F., 1980. Biomass: Applications, Technology and Production. Marcel Dekker, New York, NY, 221 pp.

Claar, P.W., Buchele, W.F. and Marley, S.J., 1981. Development of a concentric-vortex agricultural residue furnace. In: Agricultural Energy, Vol. 2. Publ. 4-81, American Society of Agricultural Engineers, St. Joseph, MI, pp. 349–356.

Combes, R.S. and Boykin, W.B., 1981. Heat recovery/thermal energy storage for energy conservation in food processing. In: Agricultural Energy, Vol. 3. Publ. 4-81, American Society of Agricultural Engineers, St. Joseph, MI, pp. 610–613.

Davis, D.C., Romberger, J.S., Pettibone, C.A. and Kranzler, G.A., 1980. Waste heat from food processing plants in the Pacific Northwest. Trans. ASAE, 23: 498–502, 507.

Elliot, R.N., 1980. Wood combustion. In: M.P. Levi and M.J. O'Grady (Editors), Decisionmakers Guide to Wood Fuel for Small Energy Users. SERI/TR-8234-1, Solar Energy Research Institute, Golden, CO, pp. 73–78.

Fotenot, J.P., Bovard, K.P., Oltjen, R.R., Rumsey, T.S. and Priode, B.M., 1977. Supplementation of apple pomace with nonprotein nitrogen for gestating beef cows. I. Feed intake performances. J. Anim. Sci., 46: 513–522.

Fryling, G.R. (Editor), 1966. Combustion Engineering. Combustion Engineering, Inc., New York, NY.

Graumlich, T.R., 1983. Potential fermentation products from citrus processing wastes. Food Technol., 37 (12): 94–97.

Hall, C.W., 1981. Biomass as an Alternative Fuel. Government Institutes, Rockville, MD, 267 pp.

Hang, Y.D., Lee, C.Y., Woodhams, E.E. and Cooley, H.J., 1981. Production of alcohol from apple pomace. Appl. Environ. Microbiol., 42: 1128–1129.

Hendrickson, R. and Kesterson, J.W., 1965. By-products of Florida citrus. IFAS Bull. 698, University of Florida, Gainesville, FL, 76 pp.

Hills, D.J. and Roberts, D.W., 1981. Conversion of cannery solid wastes into methane gas. Pap. 81-6008, American Society of Agricultural Engineers, St. Joseph, MI, 21 pp.

Howard, T., 1981. Nutshells replace oil as fuel for generating steam at a pecan plant. Food Process., 2 (11): 116.

Hsu, W.H. and Luh, B.S., 1980. Rice hulls. In: B.S. Luh (Editor), Rice Production and Utilization. AVI, Westport, CT, pp. 736–763.

Hudson, J.T., 1978. Solid waste management in the food processing industry. In: Proc. 9th National Symposium on Food Processing Wastes, 29–31 March, Denver, CO. EPA 600/2-78-188, U.S. Environmental Protection Agency, Washington, DC, pp. 637–654.

Hughes, A.D., 1976. Fueling around the boiler room. For. Prod. J., 26 (9): 33–38.

Jamison, R.L., 1979. Wood fuel use in the forest products industry. In: K.V. Sarkanen and D.A. Tillman (Editors), Progress in Biomass Conversion, Vol. 1. Academic Press, New York, NY, pp. 27–52.

Jewell, W.J. and Cummings, R.J., 1984. Apple pomace energy and solids recovery. J. Food Sci., 49: 407–410.

Johanson, L.N. and Sarkanen, K.V., 1977. Prospects for co-generation of steam and power in the forest products industry. In: D.A. Tillman, K.V. Sarkanen and L.L. Anderson (Editors), Fuels and Energy from Renewable Resources. Academic Press, New York, NY, pp. 197–212.

Kranzler, G.A. and Davis, D.C., 1981. Energy potential of fruit juice processing residues. Pap. 81-6006, American Society of Agricultural Engineers, St. Joseph, MI, 7 pp.

Kranzler, G.A., Davis, D.C. and Mason, N.B., 1983. Utilization of pomace for fruit juice processing energy requirements. Pap. 83-6003, American Society of Agricultural Engineers, St. Joseph, MI, 9 pp.

Kut, D. and Hare, G., 1981. Waste Recycling for Energy Conservation. Architectural Press, London, 326 pp.

Lane, A.G., 1979. Methane from anaerobic digestion of fruit and vegetable processing wastes. Food Technol. Aust., 31 (5): 201–207.

Ledward, D.A., Taylor, A.J. and Lawrie, R.A., 1983. Upgrading Wastes for Feeds and Food. Butterworth, Stoneham, MA, 321 pp.

LePori, W.A., Anthony, R.G., Lalk, T.R. and Craig, J.D., 1981. Fluidized-bed combustion and gasification of biomass. In: Agricultural Energy, Vol. 2. Publ. 4-81, American Society of Agricultural Engineers, St. Joseph, MI, pp. 330–334.

Licht, L.A. and Revel, J.L., 1981. Case history: utilization of food processing by-products. Pap. 81-6501, American Society of Agricultural Engineers, St. Joseph, MI, 13 pp.

Mantel, C.L. (Editor), 1975. Solid Wastes: Origin, Collection, Processing, and Disposal. Wiley, New York, NY, 1127 pp.

Neal, J.C. and Wagner, D.F., 1983. Physical and chemical properties of coal cinders as a container media component. HortScience, 18: 693–695.

Nelson, G.H., Talley, L.E. and Aronovsky, S.I., 1950. Chemical composition of grain and seed hulls, nut shells, and fruit pits. Am. Assoc. Cer. Chem. Trans. Cer. News, 8: 58–68.

Noodharmcho, A. and Flocker, W.J., 1975. Marginal land as an acceptor for cannery wastes. J. Am. Soc. Hortic. Sci., 100: 682–684.

NRC, 1976. Lime-fly ash-stabilized bases and sub-bases. Publ. 37, Transportation Research Board, National Research Council, Washington, DC, 57 pp.

O'Grady, M.J., 1980. Grate, pile, suspension and fluidized-bed burning. In: M.P. Levi and M.J. O'Grady (Editors), Decisionmakers Guide to Wood Fuel for Small Industrial Energy Users. SERI/TR-8234-1, Solar Energy Research Institute, Golden, CO, pp. 115–127.

Olexsey, R.A., 1980. Environmental impact of conversion of refuse to energy. In: T.C. Frankiewicz (Editor), Energy from Waste, Vol. 1. Ann Arbor Science, Ann Arbor, MI, pp. 197–206.

Oursborn, C.D., LePori, W.A., Lacewell, R.D. and Schacht, O.D., 1978. Energy potential of Texas crops and agricultural residues. Misc. Publ. 1361, A & M University, College Station, TX, 80 pp.

Perry, R.H. and Chilton, C.H. (Editors), 1973. Heat generation, transport and storage. Section 9 in: Chemical Engineer's Handbook (5th Edition). McGraw-Hill, New York, NY.

Power, 1980. Controlling particulate emissions from utility and industrial boilers. Power (special report) 124(6), 20 pp.

Pugsley, E.B., 1975. Beet sugar. In: C.L. Mantell (Editor), Solid Wastes: Origin, Collection, Processing and Disposal. Wiley, New York, NY, pp. 455–474.

Reason, J., 1982a. Bagasse provides 90 percent of Hawaii's sugarmill energy. Power, 126: 102.

Reason, J., 1982b. Factory wastes burned to cut fuel consumption, save land fill costs. Power, 126: 144.

Regulski, F.J., 1983. Physical properties of container media composed of a gasifier residue in combination with sphagnum peat, bark, or sand. J. Am. Soc. Hortic. Sci., 108: 186–189.

Rose, W.W., Chapman, J.E., Roseid, S., Katsuma, A., Porter, V. and Mercer, W.A., 1965. Composting fruit and vegetable waste. Compost Sci., 3: 13–25.

Sargent, S.A., Steffe, J.F. and Tennes, B.R., 1983a. Technical and economic feasibility of utilizing apple pomace as a boiler feedstock. DE-FG02-81R510307, Final Report U.S. Department of Energy, 100 pp.

Sargent, S.A., Steffe, J.F. and Pierson, T.R., 1983b. Economic feasibility of using apple pomace as a boiler feedstock. ASAE Pap. 83-6544, American Society of Agricultural Engineers. St. Joseph, MI, 23 pp.

Schwieger, R., 1980. Power from wood. Power (special report) 124(2), 32 pp.

Schwieger, R., 1982. Cogeneration, waste-fuel firing cut company's costs. Power, 126: 88.

Singh, R.P., 1978. Energy accounting in food process operations. Food Technol., 32(4): 40–46.

Singh, R., Maheshwari, R.C. and Ojha, T.P., 1980. Development of a husk fired furnace. J. Agric. Eng. Res., 25: 109–120.

Smock, R.M. and Neubert, A.M., 1950. Apples and Apple Products. Wiley, New York, NY, 486 pp.

Swint, W.H., 1980. Fuel storage: wood pellets, shavings, sawdust, and other dry residues. In: M.P. Levi and M.J. O'Grady (Editors), Decisionmakers Guide to Wood Fuel for Small Industrial Energy Users. SERI/TR-8234-1, Solar Energy Research Institute, Golden, CO, pp. 67–72.

Tibbetts, T.W. and Kobriger, J.M., 1983. Mode of action of air pollutants in injuring horticultural plants. HortScience, 18: 675–680.

Tillman, D.A., 1977. Uncounted energy: the present contribution of renewable resources. In: D.A. Tillman, K.V. Sarkanen and L.L. Anderson (Editors), Fuels and Energy from Renewable Resources. Academic Press, New York, NY, pp. 23–54.

Timm, H., Flocker, W.J., Akeson, N.B. and O'Brien, M., 1980. Mineralization of soil-incorporated tomato solid waste. J. Environ. Qual., 9: 211–214.

Toth, S.J., 1973. Composting agricultural and industrial organic wastes. In: G.E. Inglett (Editor), Symp. Processing Agricultural and Municipal Wastes. AVI, Westport, CT, pp. 172–182.

U.S. Bureau of the Census, 1983a. 1982 Census of manufactures. Fuels and electric energy consumed. MC82-S-4-1, 2, U.S. Government Printing Office, Washington, DC, 57 pp.

U.S. Bureau of the Census, 1983b. 1981 Annual survey of manufactures. M81(AS)-1, 2, U.S. Government Printing Office, Washington, DC, 11 pp.

White, J.W., 1973. Processing fruit and vegetable wastes. In: G.E. Inglett (Editor), Symp. Processing Agricultural and Municipal Wastes, 27–28 August 1972, New York. AVI, Westport, CT, pp. 129–142.

White, L.P. and Plaskett, L.G., 1981. Biomass as Fuel. Academic Press, London, 211 pp.

Woodruff, J.G. and Luh, B.S., 1975. Commercial Fruit Processing. AVI, Westport, CT, 710 pp.

Chapter 17

Low-Temperature Waste-Heat Recovery in the Food Industry

D.B. LUND

1. OVERVIEW

Several generalities apply to energy utilization within the food industry. First, boilers generally operate in the 5.5 to 10-atm overpressure range $(6.5–11 \times 10^5$ Pa, 80–150 psig), since most of the process heating is carried out at temperatures less than 135°C (270°F). This is necessary because of the product quality's sensitivity to higher temperatures. Secondly, most of the process heat is applied to the product indirectly. That is, generally the product is packaged before heating (as in thermal processing of canned products) or is heated in heat exchangers or vats (as in pasteurization of fluid milk or partial cooking of meat products). The resultant waste stream is therefore usually condensate or hot water not highly contaminated by product, and as such offers some potential for recovery of its waste heat. Finally, because of the heating medium's relatively low temperature, the waste-heat streams are generally high-volume, lower-temperature sources. Waste-heat streams are often co-mingled to reduce the mass-average temperature to a value acceptable for disposal. Successful application of waste-heat recovery systems would therefore require segregation of waste-heat sources in some operations.

Before describing food process operations in greater detail, one essential criterion must be established: the food industry's primary objective is to produce safe, nutritious, wholesome foods for trusting consumers. Thus, any consideration of waste-heat recovery projects should include a hazard analysis. In this, the potential benefits are weighed against the potential risk of product contamination or impact on consumer safety. For example, if an ammonia leak in a refrigeration system developed as a result of a waste-heat recovery project, it could result in a freezer full of tainted ice cream. The main point is that energy is only one factor used to evaluate food processing systems. Product quality and consumer safety are more important, particularly in on-going systems, and must remain foremost in designs of new systems.

2. PROCESS DESCRIPTIONS

Although each food processing facility is unique in layout, the unit operations applied to transform raw agricultural commodities into consumer-acceptable products are fairly standard. Table 17.1 (and Figs. 3.3, 3.7, 3.8, 3.10 and 3.12) present generalized energy and material flow charts for several of the 4-digit SIC 20 (Standard Industrial Classification) industries (Casper, 1977). From these diagrams and from the industrial cooperators on the project, it is possible to identify the waste heat sources that may be used in heat recovery schemes.

Chapter 17 references, p. 280.

TABLE 17.1

Characteristics of waste heat sources and acceptor streams in the canning and meat processing and dairy industry

(a) Canning processing

Source	Characteristics				Hydraulic load[a]		Temperature		Reference
		(lb/sh tn)		(kg/t)	(gal/sh tn)	(l/t)	(°F)	(°C)	
Water blanching									
Snap beans	BOD	1.38		0.69	29.8–80.2	124–335	190	90	Weckel et al., 1968
	SS	0.26		0.13					
Lima beans	BOD	1.30		0.65	197	822	190	90	Bomben, 1977
Peas	BOD	2.8–6.0		1.4–3.0	57.6–92.2	240–385	190	90	
Steam blanching									
Snap beans	BOD	1.1		0.55	30.0–36.0	125–150	190	90	
	SS	0.04		0.02					
Lima beans	BOD	7.0		3.5	27.1–57.1	113–238	190	90	
Peas	BOD	8.6		4.3	45.8–75.1	191–313	190	90	
Vibratory spiral blancher									
Snap beans	BOD	1.06		0.53	6.48	27	190	90	
	SS	0.17		0.08					
Lima beans	BOD	1.80		0.90	6.07	25	190	90	
	SS	1.08		0.54					
Brussels sprouts	BOD	0.86		0.43	3.60	15	190	90	
	SS	0.15		0.08					
Broccoli	BOD	0.50		0.25	2.62	11	190	90	
	SS	0.18		0.09					
Cauliflower					0.72	3	190	90	

Source	Characteristic				Temperature (°F)	Temperature (°C)	Reference
Steam blanching including water cooling							
Snap beans							
(steam blanching)		BOD 1.84	36.0	150	190	90	Estimate (this study)
(water cooling)		BOD 3.2	1183.2	4937			
Lima beans		BOD 2.2	27.1	113	190	90	
		BOS 6.8	1190.4	4967			
Peas		BOD 5.4	45.8	191	190	90	
		BOD 5.8	1190.4	4967			
Cooker condensate	—		28–50	117–210	250	120	
Cooling water	—		60–100	250–415	130	55	
Can topping water overflow	Dilute salt solution		40–50	165–210	200	95	
Boiler feed water	—		380–450	1590–1880	60	15	

(b) Meat processing

Source	Characteristic	Hydraulic load		Temperature (°F)	Temperature (°C)	Reference
Hog production		(gal per hog)	(l per hog)			
Clean-up	—	9.6	36	140	60	Davis and Connor, 1976
Primary chicken processing		(gal/sh tn)[a]	(l/t)[a]			
Scalding water overflow	Water and feathers	147–103	613–430	140	60	Dwyer et al., 1976
Defeathering	Water and feathers	136	568	68	19	
Primary chill	—	226	943	70	21	
Slaughter		(gal/sh cwt)[b]	(l/t)[b]			
Condensate from heating water	—	16	668	210	99	Estimate (this study)
Boiler feed water	—	6	250	60	15	

Chapter 17 references, p. 280.

Table 17.1 (continued)

Source	Characteristic	Hydraulic load		Temperature		Reference
		(gal/sh cwt)[b]	(l/t)[b]	(°F)	(°C)	
Manufacture						
Condensate from heating water	—	40–50	1670–2100	210	99	Estimate (this study)
Boiler feed water		15–25	625–1045	60	15	
(c) Milk processing		(gal/sh tn)[c]	(l/t)[c]			
Cooling stages	Sweet water–water cooled by ice	1100	4590	42	5	Knopf et al., 1978
	Glycol	660	2754	32	0	
Cottage cheese clean-up	Water	195	814	140	60	Estimate (this study)
Ice cream room clean-up	Water	371	1548	140	60	
Pasteurizer overflow or condensate		3–4	12.5–17	160	70	
Clean-up	—	50–60	210–250	150	65	
Boiler feed water	—	8–10	33–42	60	15	
Cheese processing						
Whey	Whey	238	993	100	38	Lund et al., 1978
Clean-up water	Water	60–130	250–545	140	60	
Pasteurizer overflow water		3.2	13	160	70	Estimate (this study)
Condensate curd/whey heating		7	29	200	95	
Boiler feed water		36	150	60	15	

BOD, biochemical oxygen demand.
SS, suspended solids.
[a]Water volume by mass of raw commodity.
[b]Water volume by mass of live weights.
[c]Water or whey volume by mass of raw milk.

In meat processing (meat packing SIC 2011, poultry processing SIC 2016, and processed meats SIC 2013) waste-heat streams are generated from: (1) hog dehairing, (2) edible and inedible rendering, (3) clean-up, (4) boiler blow-down, (5) condensate from indirect heating, (6) refrigeration condensers and compressors including water from water-cooled condensers, (7) poultry scalding and defeathering, (8) thawing and tempering, and (9) retorting (thermal processing) (see Fig. 3.3).

For canning fruits and vegetables (see Fig. 3.12), the major sources of waste heat are: (1) blanching water, (2) topping water (water added to the can after the produce has been added), (3) retort condensate, (4) can-cooling water, (5) clean-up water, (6) boiler blowdown, and (7) venting of still retorts.

Finally in dairy processing, the major waste-heat sources are: (1) pasteurizer condensate or overflow, (2) refrigeration condensers and compressors, (3) whey, (4) clean-up water, (5) vapor from evaporators (referred to as cow water), (6) exhaust from spray driers, and (7) wastewater from membrane processing systems (see Figs. 3.7, 3.8 and 3.10).

To assess the potential for heat recovery from these streams, it is necessary to characterize each stream's composition, temperature, and flow rate. These data for most of these waste streams are summarized in Table 17.1. The data were obtained from several sources, including the five industrial contacts on this project. Obviously, these data generally apply to specific plants and therefore only indicate order of magnitude estimates for some streams. Like the energy use profile, the waste-heat sources are unique to each plant. Thus, these data are presented only as examples. The data are presented on a per unit-of-production basis because most plants are using that basis in reporting data directly or indirectly to the U.S. Department of Energy and because that basis facilitates scaling the data to different plant capacities.

Potential for heat exchanger fouling by stream components is an important consideration in heat recovery from waste streams in the food industry. Constituents of these waste streams such as proteins, sugars and other soluble organic compounds, and inverse solubility salts (e.g., calcium and magnesium phosphates and sulfate) readily interact with negatively charged heat exchanger surfaces; this may result in deposition and reduction in heat exchanger efficiency. These deposits are generally tenacious, and their removal requires the use of chemical cleaning agents. Unfortunately, the fouling characteristics of these streams are not known and there is an insufficient data base to predict their fouling behavior. In some streams, such as clean-up water in meat processing, heat is potentially recoverable, but fouling characteristics necessitate using more energy in cleaning the heat recovery system than is recovered by that system. In such cases, a settling tank and skimmer could be used as a pretreatment to reduce the fouling potential.

Despite a risk of oversimplification, some generalities can be made about the fouling potential for waste streams from food processing. First, because waste streams are being cooled, inverse solubility salts should not present fouling problems, and generally the solubility of other mineral salts will not be exceeded through the limited temperature drop waste streams normally experience. Secondly, waste streams containing sizable quantities of animal fat should probably go through a settling tank with skimmer before indirect recovery to avoid potential problems of crystallizing on the exchanger surface. Thirdly, water from vegetable processing operations, even though relatively high in organic material, should present no difficulty in waste-heat recovery because the stream's temperature is being reduced. Fourthly, waste-heat streams resulting from indirect heat exchange with food products should require only the normal precautions necessary for use as boiler feed water (i.e., settling tank, skimmer, deaerator, etc.).

Chapter 17 references, p. 280.

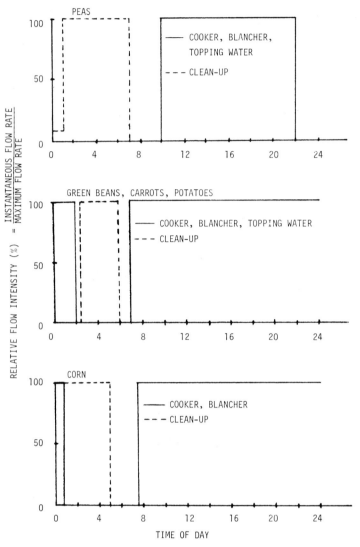

Fig. 17.1. Relative flow rates in a 24-h period in various canning operations (From Foell et al., 1980b).

One important characteristic of aqueous streams from food processing is that the temperature of these streams is 38–95°C (100–200°F). A common acceptor stream for indirect heating is boiler feed water which is usually 10–21°C (50–70°F). Other acceptor streams, however, can be identified. In meat processing clean-up, water used in dehairing, and water used for thawing or tempering can serve as acceptor streams. In each case only the make-up water can be preheated, because the unit operation is conducted at temperatures greater than that of the waste-heat source stream. In canning, acceptor streams are boiler feed-water, can topping water, and clean-up water. Blancher feedwater is not considered as an acceptor stream because blanching operations can be carried out using direct steam condensate as the sole source of overflow. It is desirable to have some blancher overflow to control the build-up of solids in blanching water. Using direct steam heating appears to generate a desired rate of blancher overflow. In the dairy industry, acceptor streams are boiler feed-water and clean-up water.

Maximum waste-heat recovery occurs when waste stream availability exactly coincides with acceptor stream demands. It is essential, therefore, to determine the time frame for both waste and acceptor streams. Figures 17.1, 17.2 and 17.3 show representative processing schedules for canning plants: a

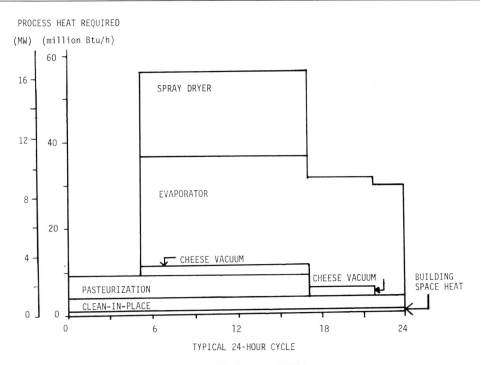

Fig. 17.2. Cheese plant load profile (from Foell et al., 1980b):

spray dryer:	12 h at 5.9 MW (20 million Btu/h)
evaporation:	19 h at 7.3 MW (25 million Btu/h)
cheese vacuum:	17 h at 0.6 MW (2 million Btu/h)
pasteurization:	17 h at 1.5 MW (5 million Btu/h)
clean-in-place:	24 h at 0.9 MW (3 million Btu/h)
building space head:	24 h at 0.3 MW (1 million Btu/h).

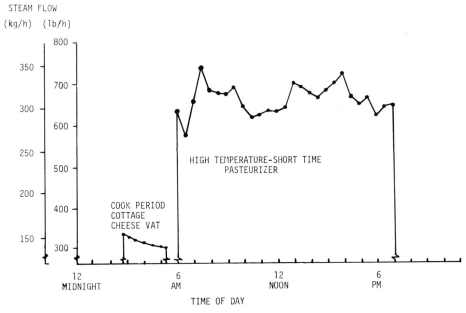

Fig. 17.3. Daily Steam demand at a milk plant (from Knopf et al., 1978).

cheese plant with dryer, and a fluid-milk plant with cottage cheese production. In canning plants, clean-up water is generally required out-of-phase with waste-heat sources, but boiler feedwater demand is in-phase, making it the primary acceptor stream for waste heat. For peas, green beans, potatoes, and

Chapter 17 references, p. 280.

carrots, topping water is also a potential acceptor stream. One striking characteristic of both acceptor and source streams is that they are basically on/off streams. This is a characteristic of most food industry process streams. Raw product is usually accumulated, as far as possible, so the plant runs at maximum capacity. (Figure 17.1 presents the 24-h cycle for canning plant operation.) Production is dependent on availability of raw material, which is highly variable. In general, Wisconsin plants run on an average of 6 days per week. Peas are processed from mid-June through July, green beans from mid-July to September, corn from mid-August through September, and root crops (potatoes, carrots and beets) from October to late November.

In dairy and meat processing, operations are not as strikingly seasonal. Production schedules are shifted from one product to another, but energy demands are fairly constant. Figures 17.2 and 17.3 present the processing energy demands on a 24-h period in a cheese plant with whey concentration and drying capability, and a fluid-milk plant, respectively. The demands are basically on/off, similar to canning plant demands. Meat processing plants operate on a pattern similar to dairy plants. Production is relatively constant throughout the year and waste-heat streams are generally compatible with acceptor streams, with the exception of plant clean-up. In canning, dairy and meat processing, most plant clean-up hot water is used during non-production hours.

3. POTENTIAL WASTE-HEAT RECOVERY

3.1. Canning industry

Several waste-heat streams, as previously explained, present some potential for waste-heat recovery in the canning industry. In the thermal process, steam is condensed on the outside of cans to heat the product to temperatures between 115 and 130°C (240 and 265°F), and after the scheduled process time the heat is extracted from the container and its contents by using cold water as a heat sink. This process generates two large waste-heat streams: (1) condensate from the heating process, which is under pressure and at the corresponding condensing temperature, and (2) cooling water, which is at 38–55°C (100–130°F). In both cases, the waste-heat source is relatively clean.

Before investigating the potential for waste-heat recovery from these and other streams, however, several observations made by the industrial cooperators should be noted. First, energy conservation measures may be the primary prerequisite to using waste heat. By reducing the flow rates of the waste-heat streams, more heat could be extracted from them using the same flow rates as the acceptor streams. Conservation measures could also include insulation of retorts, thereby reducing the rate of condensation. Second, blancher overflow may be one of the largest waste-heat streams in a canning plant. As previously mentioned, there is evidence that direct steam heating of blancher water provides sufficient overflow to control solids buildup in the blancher water. Thus there is no need for additional make-up water to the blancher. Third, can topping is currently one of the more inefficient water transfer operations, with as much as one-third of the 95°C (200°F) water lost as waste. Undoubtedly mechanical handling designs exist which would essentially eliminate topping water waste. Finally, venting of still retorts is established by the Food and Drug Administration. Two opportunities for energy conservation exist here. The first involves designing retort steam distributor systems which feed steam to the top of the retort and vent from the bottom (since air is heavier than steam). The second involves designing of vent systems using vented steam as a heat source.

Several waste-heat recovery systems are already being used in the canning industry. Examples include:

(1) using cooker (retort) condensate to provide boiler feed water, to preheat topping water, and to defrost freezing tunnels where freezing operations are run parallel to canning operations;

(2) using waste heat from refrigeration compressors to preheat water used to defrost freezing tunnels;

(3) using boiler blowdown to preheat feedwater to the boiler;

(4) using can cooling water to provide boiler feed water and to preheat can topping water.

Currently it is not possible to estimate the extent to which these systems are used in the canning industry.

To estimate the potential for waste-heat recovery, the project team developed three scenarios. Several assumptions were made in setting up the calculations. First, only liquid–liquid heat exchangers were considered for waste-heat recovery. In the canning industry, nearly all waste-heat streams are liquid. For meat processing and dairy operations, this is not necessarily the case. Waste heat from hair singeing in hog processing and in smoke house operations could be recovered; in dairy plants, waste heat from spray drying offers potential for recovery. These were not included, however, because the first line of heat recovery would be from liquid streams, and because generally the economics of heat recovery from gas streams is not favorable. Secondly, the liquid–liquid heat exchangers operate at 75% effectiveness. Effectiveness is defined as

$$\varepsilon = \frac{[\dot{m}C_{\mathrm{p}}(T_{\mathrm{in}} - T_{\mathrm{out}})]_{\mathrm{hot\,or\,cold}}}{(\dot{m}C_{\mathrm{p}})_{\mathrm{min}}(T_{\mathrm{hot\,in}} - T_{\mathrm{cold\,in}})}$$

With a stream capacitance ratio of about 1.0 and countercurrent flow, this effectiveness value is in the practical range. Thirdly, all of the recovered heat is used to preheat boiler feedwater. Generally the waste stream is much smaller than the boiler feed stream, with the exception of can cooling water in canning plants. Thus increasing the flow rate of the acceptor stream will not result in large increases in recovered heat. Fourthly, in unit operations using indirect heating with steam, potentially 75% of the condensate could be recovered and returned to the boiler as feedwater. This figure was ascertained in consultation with the industrial cooperators and seems to be representative of experience for the food industry. The losses are due to vents, steam traps, and flashing in non-pressurized return lines, etc. It was assumed that the clean-up water was the only waste-heat stream which could be used as a waste-heat source. Generally for canning, meat processing, and dairy processing, clean-up with hot water sufficient for sanitizing is used during non-production hours. As the boiler demand at that time is small, the potential for waste-heat recovery is minimal.

The calculations in these three scenarios illustrate several important points on waste-heat recovery in canning plants. Generally there are sufficient quantities of partially-heated water which can serve as boiler feedwater. The two most apparent sources are can-cooling water and cooker condensate. By using heat recovery schemes and condensate recycle it would be possible to reduce boiler energy requirements by 5–10%.

Situation I

The assumptions are:

(1) condensate to the boiler is not recycled;

(2) blowdown is 10% of the boiler feed rate;

Chapter 17 references, p. 280.

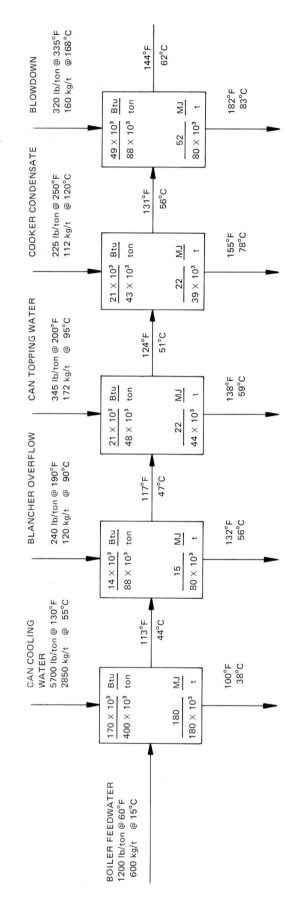

Fig. 17.4. Systems diagram for a canning plant, Situation I (from Foell et al., 1980b).

(3) all waste streams are compatible with acceptor streams; and

(4) no direct use is made of a waste stream as boiler feedwater.

These assumptions result in the waste-heat recovery scenario illustrated in Fig. 17.4. The data are for a canning plant processing 13 tons of raw peas per hour. The boiler feed water is preheated by indirect heat exchanger with successively warmer waste-heat streams. The waste-heat streams are: (1) can-cooling water at 55°C (130°F), (2) blancher overflow at 90°C (190°F), (3) can topping water at 95°C (200°F), (4) cooker condensate at 120°C (250°F), and (5) boiler blowdown at 170°C (335°F). Based on a 75% heat exchanger effectiveness, the extracted heat from each waste stream is given by the numerator in the ratio expressed in the respective box. The denominator is the heat energy that could be extracted if the waste-water stream could be cooled to 15°C (60°F). Thus the ratio represents the fraction of heat which can be removed from the waste-heat stream. The temperature of each waste-heat stream after heat extraction is calculated, as is the temperature of the boiler feed stream after each operation.

In this situation the net result is preheating the boiler feedwater from 15 to 62°C (60–144°F) by indirect exchange with the waste-heat streams. Approximately 320 MJ of waste-heat per metric tonne (275 × 10^3 Btu per short ton) of raw peas is recovered in this scheme, accounting for about 45% recovery based on a reference temperature of 15°C (60°F). Assuming the boiler operates at 8.6 atm over pressure (9.6 × 10^5 Pa) and 170°C (125 psig, 335°F), the enthalpy contributed by the waste-heat sources represents 7.3% of the total enthalpy required in the boiler.

Situation II

The assumption are:

(1) condensate returned to the boiler is 75%;

(2) blowdown is 10% of the boiler feed rate;

(3) all waste streams are compatible with acceptor streams; and

(4) direct use is made of some acceptable waste streams as boiler feedwater.

The resulting scenario for waste heat recovery is presented in Fig. 17.5. In this case, can cooling and cooker condensate were assumed to be acceptable boiler feedwater streams. Since the can-cooling water flow rate was larger than the boiler feed rate, nearly 47% of the can-cooling water would be discharged from the plant. For this situation then, the boiler feedwater is available at 55°C (130°F). After indirect exchange with blancher overflow, can topping water and boiler blowdown streams, the boiler feedwater is preheated from 55 to 69°C (130–156°F). Cooker condensate water is then mixed with the boiler feedwater, resulting in an average boiler feedwater temperature of 72°C (161°F). This is 10°C (17°F) higher than that achieved in Situation I. The heat recovered by indirect heat exchange represents 72% of the recoverable heat based on a reference temperature of 55°C (130°F). This recovery scheme would reduce the enthalpy requirement in the boiler by 8.8%.

Situation III

The assumptions are:

(1) condensate return to the boiler is 75%;

(2) there is no blowdown for heat recovery;

(3) clean-up wastewater is not compatible with acceptor streams; and

(4) direct use is made of some acceptable waste streams as boiler feedwater.

Chapter 17 references, p. 280.

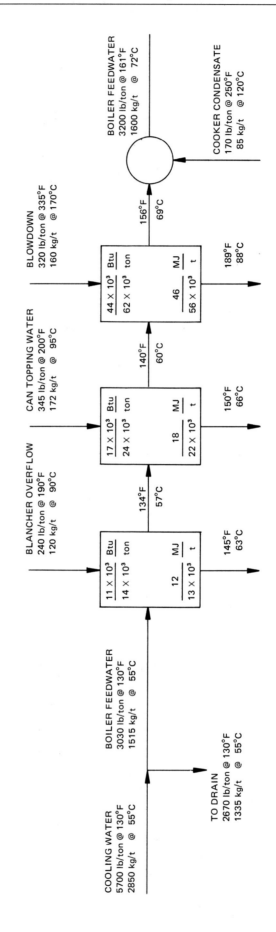

Fig. 17.5. System diagram for a canning plant, Situation II (from Foell et al., 1980b).

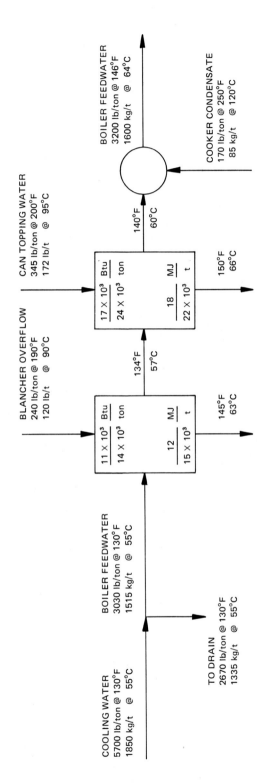

Fig. 17.6. System diagram for a canning plant, Situation III (from Foell et al., 1980b).

Chapter 17 references, p. 280.

TABLE 17.2

Summary of waste heat recovery potential under various scenarios

Food industry subsector	Situation					
	I		II		III	
	PRE(%)[a]	BFE(%)[b]	PRE(%)	BFE(%)	PRE(%)	BFE(%)
Canning	45	7.3	72	8.8	74	7.5
Meat processing	72	4.4	75	4.3	–	2.9
Fluid milk	59	7.9	69	7.7	69	2.6
Cheese	23	7.3	16	8.8	10	5.1

[a]PRE(%), potentially recoverable energy expressed as a percent of the energy content of the waste streams relative to the temperature of the boiler feedwater as a reference.
[b]BFE(%), boiler feedwater energy contributed by indirect waste heat recovery expressed as a percent of the total energy for the boiler.

Figure 17.6 presents the analysis of this situation. As in Situation II, can cooling water and cooker condensate are used as boiler feedwater, while blancher overflow and can topping water are used for indirect heat exchange. In this case, the boiler feed is heated from 55 to 64°C (130–146°F) with a resulting 74% energy recovery from the blanching overflow and can topping water (relative to a reference temperature of 55°C). Boiler energy requirements could be reduced 7.5% in this scenario.

4. CONCLUSION

The potential exists for waste heat recovery in the food processing industry. In canning, meat processing and manufacturing, and dairy processing, waste-heat streams can be identified which can be used directly as boiler feedwater. There are also several opportunities for indirect heat exchange using waste streams generated simultaneously with the demand for boiler feedwater and hot water for processing. A summary of waste heat recovery potential under various scenarios is given in Table 17.2. Based on our analysis, it is possible to reduce boiler energy requirements from 15 to 50% if all waste heat could be extracted from the heat sources, that is, by reducing the temperature to boiler feedwater temperature. In most cases this would require identifying acceptor streams outside the plant or using other means of recouping and storing the heat from the waste stream. In practice, it is more likely that for the food processing industry it is technically feasible to recover heat energy from waste streams either directly or indirectly, and by doing so reduce boiler energy requirements from 3 to 10%.

5. REFERENCES

Bomben, J.L., 1977. Effluent generation, energy use and cost of blanching. J. Food Proc. Eng., 1: 329–341.

Casper, M.E. 1977. Energy Saving Techniques for the Food Industry. Noyes Data Corporation, Park Ridge, NJ, 657 pp.

Davis, G.A. and Connor, L.J., 1976. A simulation study of decision strategies for hog processing plants constrained by energy supply regulations. Department of Agricultural Economics, Michigan State University, East Lansing, MI, 47 pp.

Dwyer, S.J., Unklesbay, K., Unklesbay, N. and Dunlap, C., 1976. Identification of major areas of energy utilization in the food processing/food service industry. Final Report for NSF Grant No. NSF-51A 75 16222, University of Missouri, Columbia, MO, 225 pp.

Foell, W.K., Huennekens, J.R., Lindsay, M.A., Stevenson, R.E. and Ten Wolde, A., 1980a. Industrial energy use in Wisconsin: consumption patterns and conservation measures. Div. State Energy Spec. Monogr., ERC Rep. 80-102, IES Rep. 110, University of Wisconsin, Madison, WI, 195 pp.

Foell, W.K., Lund, D., Mitchell, J.W., Ray, D., Stevenson, R. and Ten Wolde, A., 1980b. Low temperature waste-heat recovery in the food and paper industries. Report for Contract No. 31-109-38-5235. Argonne National Laboratory. U.S. DOE Industrial Energy Conservation Program, 202 pp.

Knopf, F.C., Wilson, P.W. and Okos, M.R., 1978. Energy utilization in a dairy processing plant. ASAE Pap. 78-6521. Department of Agricultural Engineering, Purdue University, West Lafayette, IN, 17 pp.

Lund, D.B., Duffie, J.A., Buelow, F. and Singh, R., 1978. Utilization of solar energy in cheese processing operations. Final Report, Department of Food Science, University of Wisconsin, Madison, WI, 76 pp.

Weckel, K.G., Rambo, R.S., Veloso, H. and von Elbe, J.H., 1968. Vegetable canning process wastes. Rep. 38, College of Agricultural and Life Sciences Research, University of Wisconsin, Madison, WI, 20 pp.

Wilson, P.W., Marks, J.S. and Okos, M.R., 1979. Energy utilization in dehairing and rendering processes of the pork industry. ASAE Paper No. 79-6023, Department of Agricultural Engineering, Purdue University, West Lafayette, IN, 41 pp.

Chapter 18

Cogeneration in Food Processing Plants

ARTHUR A. TEIXEIRA

1. INTRODUCTION

This chapter reviews developments in the use of industrial cogeneration as a means of energy conservation in food processing plants. In the context of industrial energy systems, the term 'cogeneration' refers to the harnessing of multiple forms of useful energy that would otherwise be wasted from an energy conversion system when dedicated only to a single task. Perhaps the most common example of centralized industrial cogeneration is the on-site concurrent generation of electricity with process steam as a more efficient use of fuel to meet both the electrical and thermal energy requirements of an industrial process plant. Historically, the use of cogeneration had been a common practice in industrial plants when low-cost electricity was not readily available from the vast network of public utility grids that exist today. Since then both the availability and low cost of purchased electricity, oil, and natural gas have popularized the use of small 'package' boilers to generate process steam alone while electricity is purchased separately from local utilities. In the face of such plentiful low-cost energy, it was difficult to economically justify the greater capital costs for industrial systems, and their popularity has gradually declined over the years.

Recently, the food industry faced a total 'about-face' in the cost and availability of energy, which has created a new set of ground rules in establishing capital spending priorities for improving energy efficiency in most industrial processing plants. Recognizing the inherent fuel efficiency of cogeneration systems, the U.S. Department of Energy, through its Division of Industrial Energy Conservation, has been funding programs directed towards identifying opportunities for the increased use of cogeneration in various sectors of U.S. industry – including the food processing industry. Because of this increasing new interest in cogeneration, this chapter presents a brief discussion of just what it is, how it should save energy, and what use it has had and could have in the food processing industry. Specific case study examples are given to show how opportunities for cogeneration have been identified and evaluated for potential application in a soy bean oil mill, malt beverage brewery, and citrus processing plant.

2. WHAT IS COGENERATION AND HOW DOES IT SAVE ENERGY?

One way to appreciate the energy-saving potential of cogeneration is to understand the basic inefficiency that is inherent in the generation of electricity alone. In a typical power plant, electric generators are driven by gas or steam turbines with such pressure requirements that the exhaust heat or steam from these turbines contains approximately two-thirds of the energy originally delivered to the turbine. Since fuel is burned to provide the energy needed in driving these turbogenerators, roughly 3 kWh of fuel energy are required to produce 1 kWh equivalent of electric energy. Unless the utility can sell some of its exhaust steam or heat to a process plant located close by, this inefficiency must be reflected in the price of the electric power sold to its customers.

More frequently, however, this inefficiently produced electricity is purchased by industrial process plants to meet their electric power demand, while burning fuel themselves to generate steam for their process heat requirements. The process heat requirements in many industrial processing plants can be more than adequately met by the exhaust steam from a turbo-generator, and since little additional fuel is required to produce the necessary power steam at higher pressure, industrial processing plants are being encouraged to examine on-site cogeneration of their own electric power. In this way, fuel already being consumed for industrial process heating can do double duty by producing electricity as well, while reducing total industrial demand for purchased electricity.

Although the discussion above tends to describe cogeneration in terms of its energy-saving benefit to society, it can also offer real economic benefits to the processing plant itself. These economic benefits stem from the principle that a plant using cogeneration produces its own electricity 'free', as it would produce nearly the same amount of steam to meet its process heating requirements whether cogenerating electricity or not. Therefore, the cost for purchasing this electricity from an outside utility would be saved. In actual practice, this savings is approximately 15% less than theoretical because of slightly increased fuel requirements and operating costs for a cogeneration power plant over a boiler alone.

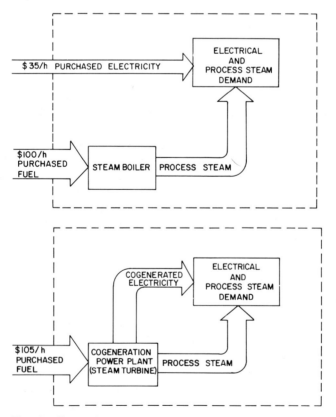

Fig. 18.1. Economic rationale for the use of industrial cogeneration.

Figure 18.1, from Teixeira (1979), illustrates this economic rationale for the use of industrial cogeneration. The schematic illustration at the top of the figure suggests a hypothetical processing plant which is purchasing electricity to meet its electric power demand, and purchasing fuel to generate its process steam requirement. The costs per hour for these purchases are shown as $35.00 and $100.00 for electricity and fuel, respectively, for a total energy cost of $135.00 per h. If the same processing plant could meet both the electrical and process steam demand from an on-site cogeneration system as shown in the bottom of the figure, then the plant would purchase no electricity, and total energy cost would be approximately $105.00 per hour for purchased fuel only – suggesting more than 20% savings in total energy costs.

The above discussion is a very simplistic view of cogeneration, which has been aimed towards providing some understanding of why it should command new interest. There are various complicating issues and problems concerning cogeneration that limit both its technical and commercial feasibility in many industrial process applications, some of which are discussed later. In the following section, various cogeneration schemes are described in order to appreciate the degree of flexibility that can be achieved with cogeneration.

3. ALTERNATE COGENERATION SCHEMES

Numerous schemes have been devised for cogeneration systems in order to provide flexibility in accommodating various processing plant situations. In fact, any energy conversion system which produces shaft power, heat, and/or electricity in meeting the energy demand of a processing plant can be called a cogeneration system. Three of the more common cogeneration schemes, which represent the use of steam turbines, gas turbines, and reciprocating engines, are described below (Teixeira, 1980).

3.1. Steam turbine systems

The use of a high-pressure boiler with a steam driven 'topping' turbine is probably the most commonly known system used for industrial cogeneration of steam and electricity. A schematic diagram of such a steam topping system is given in Fig. 18.2. At the heart of this system is an industrial steam boiler capable of delivering steam at sufficiently high pressure to drive the steam turbogenerator, which provides electric power to the plant. The low-pressure exhaust steam from the turbine is then delivered throughout the plant to provide the plant with all of its process steam requirements. The diagram also describes the various heat recovery systems used in preheating the returning condensate, make-up water, and combustion air to the boiler.

3.2. Gas turbine systems

In the steam turbine systems described above, steam is generated first, then used to drive the turbine. In gas turbine systems, the turbogenerator is driven first by combustion gases from the burning fuel–air mixture. The hot exhaust gas from the turbine is then used as the heat source in a low-pressure waste heat boiler to provide process steam to the plant. A simplified schematic diagram of such a gas turbine system with waste heat boiler is shown in Fig. 18.3. These systems are often attractive to smaller plant operations, since large high-pressure steam boilers are not required.

Chapter 18 references, p. 302.

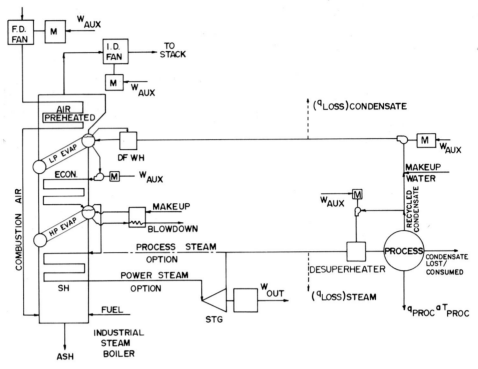

Fig. 18.2. High-pressure steam boiler for cogeneration applications with steam turbine system (courtesy, Westinghouse Electric Corp.).

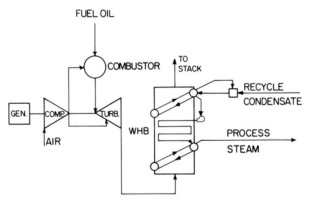

Fig. 18.3. Oil-fired gas turbine energy cogeneration system with waste-heat boiler (courtesy, Westinghouse Electric Corp.).

3.3. Reciprocating engine systems

A third alternative to the steam and gas turbine systems described above is a system based on the use of a reciprocating engine as shown in Fig. 18.4. In this type of system, the basic power plant is a diesel or other internal combustion engine which drives the electric generator delivering electric power to the processing plant. The exhaust gases from the engine are then supercharged with compressed air and used as the heat source in a low-pressure waste heat boiler to provide process steam, just as with the gas turbine system described above. At the same time, heat is recovered from the hot coolant that recirculates through the engine's cooling jacket to preheat the condensate returning to the boiler for maximum efficiency.

The three systems described above are only simplified examples of the various configurations and combinations of cogeneration schemes that are

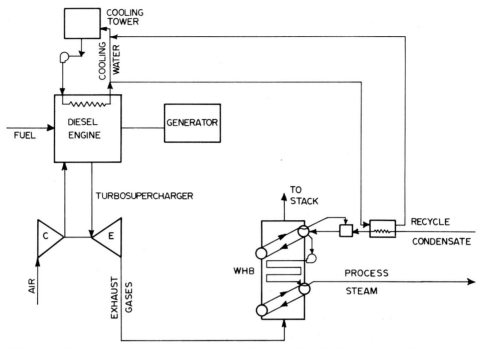

Fig. 18.4. Diesel engine cogeneration system with waste-heat boiler (courtesy, Westinghouse Electric Corp.).

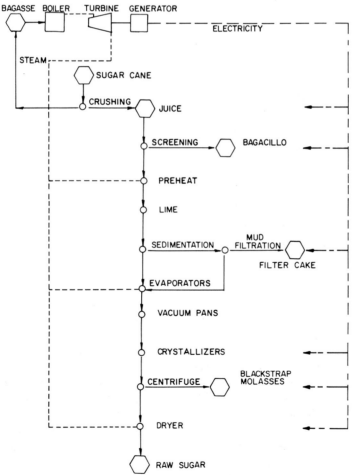

Fig. 18.5. Material and energy flow for a typical raw cane sugar mill showing use of cogeneration (from DPRA, 1974).

Chapter 18 references, p. 302.

possible. The specific scheme most suitable for any given processing plant would depend on a variety of factors such as the total demand and demand profile for the plant's thermal and electric energy requirements, process steam temperature and pressure requirements, cost and type of fuel available, physical layout and space requirements, as well as all the economic considerations involved in the selection of a new or replacement utility system. Discussion of these factors and how they would dictate that choice of particular cogeneration schemes is covered in the specific case study examples. A brief discussion of how cogeneration has been used in our food industry and its outlook for future use is given below.

4. USE OF COGENERATION IN THE FOOD INDUSTRY

The use of cogeneration in the food industry has generally been confined to the processing of bulk commodities where highly energy-intensive operations are required, such as in the beet sugar processing, corn wet milling, and cane sugar processing and refining industries. Many of the processing plants in these industry subsectors are quite large, and require huge amounts of steam to evaporate the millions of pounds of water from dilute sugar and starch solutions that are processed daily, as well as electric power to drive heavy

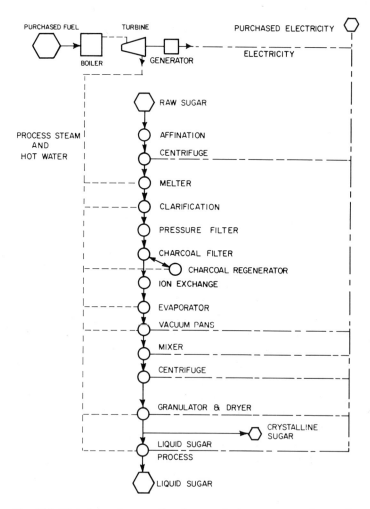

Fig. 18.6. Material and energy flow for a typical cane sugar refinery showing use of cogeneration (from DPRA, 1974).

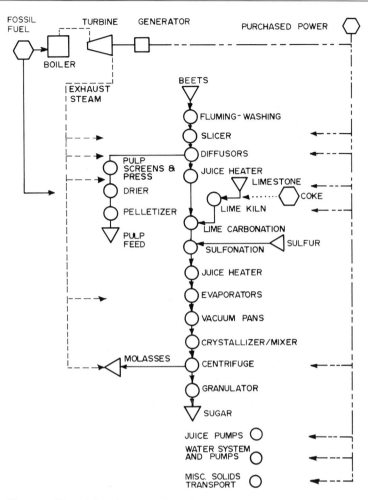

Fig. 18.7. Material and energy flow for a typical beet sugar processing plant showing use of cogeneration (from DPRA, 1974).

machinery. Unlike most of the food industry, which is relatively less energy-intensive, the cost of energy in these processing plants represents a significant part of the cost to manufacture these bulk commodities. Figures 18.5–18.8 contain material and energy flow diagrams for typical processing plants in the raw cane sugar, cane sugar refining, beet sugar and corn wet milling industries. These diagrams show how cogeneration is commonly used in these highly energy-intensive subsectors of our food processing industry, and were taken from a report to the Federal Energy Administration by DPRA (1974).

In the rest of the food industry, where most processing operations are considerably less energy-intensive, the historic availability of low-cost fuels and electricity has created a large dependence on the use of purchased electricity and small package boilers to provide process steam. Therefore, with the exception of a few scattered processing plants involving breakfast cereal, gelatin and canning operations, there has been little use of cogeneration in the rest of the food industry. In almost all cases where cogeneration is being used, the systems are based on steam driven 'topping' turbines with high-pressure steam boilers. Also, because cogeneration is nothing new, there has been little research or development on this topic reported in the technical or scientific literature.

Because of the dramatic changes occurring in the cost and availability of energy, the future outlook for cogeneration in the food industry may be quite

Chapter 18 references, p. 302.

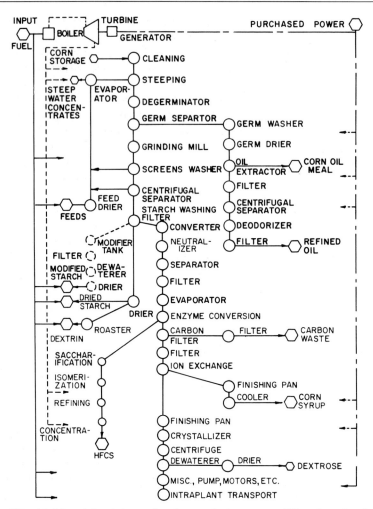

Fig. 18.8. Material and energy flow for a typical corn wet milling plant showing use of cogeneration (from DPRA, 1974).

different from the situation we see today. The energy and energy cost savings potential of cogeneration systems can be expected to take on new economic significance in choosing industrial utility systems for replacement or plant expansion programs in the U.S. food industry. Cogeneration is already being closely examined in at least three other subsectors of the food industry – the soybean oil mills, malt beverages, and citrus processing industries. The fairly steady demand profile (hourly, daily, and monthly variations in steam and power demand), and appropriate balance between steam and electricity that is found in existing process plants within these subsectors makes them likely candidates for the future use of cogeneration. In some cases, key decision-makers have already anticipated their future use of cogeneration by specifying high-pressure steam boilers with a power steam option in their new plant expansion programs. With these boilers already in place, the turbogenerators can be installed at a later date whenever the decision to cogenerate is made.

5. EVALUATING OPPORTUNITIES FOR COGENERATION

Although most of the previous discussion tends to suggest that opportunities for cogeneration can be identified with respect to food product categories or industry subsectors, that suggestion is misleading. The opportunity for using cogeneration in any given food processing plant has little to do with the specific product being manufactured. Instead, these opportunities should be evaluated by examining three basic criteria: appropriate balance between demand profiles for steam and electricity; economic justification based on price for purchased electricity and capital investment required; and procurement of a satisfactory standby agreement with the local utility.

Once these basic criteria can be met for any given processing plant, then further cogeneration should be considered regardless of the type of product being manufactured or the specific industry subsector in which the plant may operate. In fact, some food processing plants operate a variety of product lines under one roof which may span across different food industry subsectors, such as plants which produce both canned and frozen foods.

It must be emphasized, however, that meeting the criteria shown above is only a first step in evaluating opportunities for cogeneration. Beyond this first step, which establishes only technical and economic feasibility, lies a host of complex 'soft' issues which need to be addressed. As implied by the third criterion above, these issues begin with the need to establish some workable relationship with the local utility. Even in the most well-balanced industrial cogeneration plants, there are periods of time when the plant's demand for power may exceed its ability to generate it, or when the power being generated exceeds demand. Ideally, the industrial cogenerator would like to both buy and sell power to the local utility on an 'as-need' basis while no longer serving the utility as a steady customer. The utility companies, of course, find it difficult to agree with such arrangements without high-priced standby or demand contracts that could tend to diminish the incentives for cogeneration.

Other issues may involve joint ownership of a cogeneration power plant by a group of companies who operate processing plants in close proximity to each other. In such an arrangement, all of the plants in the group share in the use of steam and power from the cogenerating power plant, while benefiting from the economy of scale for a single facility. Still other ownership arrangements can involve the local utility company as owner of the cogeneration power plant as a means of dealing with the complex standby agreements discussed above. Finally, there is the question of whether an industrial processing plant really wants to get into the business of generating electric power. This includes the need for plant personnel to become familiar with cogeneration systems components, and systems operation and maintenance, as well as the inherent personnel resistance to change or breaking tradition.

Recognizing that these issues can be seen as strong disincentives for industrial cogeneration, the U.S. Department of Energy and its Federal Energy Regulatory Commission have taken steps towards establishing new rules and guidelines regarding rates and exemptions for qualifying cogeneration and small power production facilities. These steps are intended to help promote the increasing use of industrial cogeneration as an important part of the total industrial energy conservation program. The food industry should do its part in this program by encouraging key decision makers to evaluate the opportunities for using cogeneration in their food processing plants.

6. ECONOMICS OF GENERATION FOR A SOYBEAN OIL MILL AND MALT BEVERAGE BREWERY

Perhaps the most recent comprehensive study on identifying and evaluating opportunities for industrial cogeneration is contained in a report from USDOE, (1980). The report includes a study on the economics of optimum cogeneration systems designed for a soybean crushing mill and a malt beverage brewery as

Chapter 18 references, p. 302.

examples of food industry applications for cogeneration. The report also includes similar case studies for eight additional non-food industry processing plants. The approach to evaluating the economic feasibility of cogeneration in all these plants was based on examining the following three topic areas: plant energy demand profiles in terms of hourly, daily, and seasonal variations of electric power, steam, and other thermal requirements; cogeneration systems to meet the energy demand based on commercially available and proven system components; economic analysis from the viewpoint of an industrial plant owner looking at incremental investments needed for cogeneration and the savings that would accrue from implementing such a system.

6.1. Energy demand profiles

Most industrial processing plants that are large enough to be considered practical candidates for cogeneration systems, have a demand for electric power in the range of 1–100 MW. It should be recognized that these are small when compared with public utilities where standard units of 1000–2000 MW are common.

The energy demand profiles for the two food industry plants are shown in Figs. 18.9 and 18.10 for the soybean oil mill and malt beverage brewery, respectively. Although smallest among all the industrial plants that were considered, the profiles, themselves, are representative of typical processing plants. The soybean oil mill, for example, operates continuously around the clock providing an essentially constant demand for steam, heat, and electricity on an hourly and daily basis, with only slight seasonal or monthly fluctuations. The only interruption in these demand profiles occurs during two planned

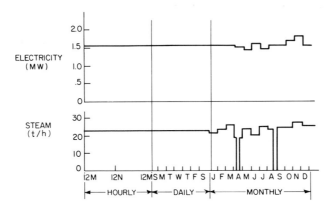

Fig. 18.9. Hourly, daily, and monthly energy demand profiles for a Midwest soybean oil mill.

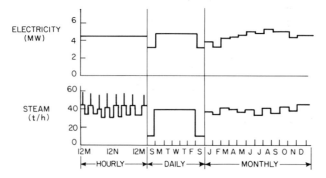

Fig. 18.10. Hourly, daily and monthly energy demand profiles for a Northeast malt beverage brewery.

shutdown periods for routine boiler maintenance in April and August. Also (not shown), is an additional heat demand of 2000 kWh in the form of propane or natural gas to operate direct-fired soybean dryers that are external to the mill.

In the case of the malt beverage brewery (Fig. 18.10), there is cyclical fluctuation in steam demand within any 24-h period reflecting brew-house operations, in which brewing cycles are repeated roughly every three hours. Steam demand fluctuations of this type can be accommodated by the use of a steam accumulator in the design of the cogeneration system. Although there is some seasonal variation in electric power demand reflecting increased production during summer vacation months, seasonal steam demand remains essentially constant as reduced space heating requirements offset increased production requirements in the summer.

6.2. Cogeneration systems

All cogeneration systems that were considered in the study are state-of-the-art technology and commercially available today. These include topping cycles, like back-pressure steam turbines supplying exhaust process steam; and bottoming cycles, such as a gas turbine generating electric power with a waste heat boiler generating low-pressures process steam from the turbine exhaust gases. The steam and gas turbines are the only two systems found to be practical in the size range of 1–100 MW for application in industrial processing plants. Throughout, it was assumed that the plant steam requirements have to be met, and the plant would take any electric power that the cogeneration system can generate. Typically, the electric power so generated does not satisfy all of the plant's energy requirements. As a result, there is seldom any need to face the problem of selling excess cogenerated electric power.

Block flow diagrams describing the cogeneration systems proposed for each of the two food plants are shown in Figs. 18.11 and 18.12 for the soybean oil mill

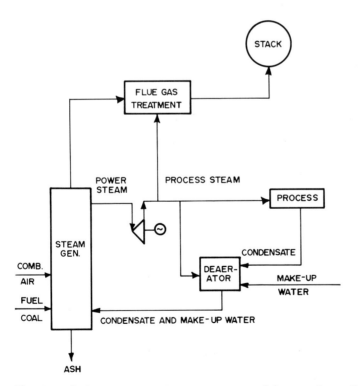

Fig. 18.11. Optimum cogeneration system proposed for a soybean oil mill (USDOE 1980 with courtesy of Westinghouse Electric Corp.).

Chapter 18 references, p. 302.

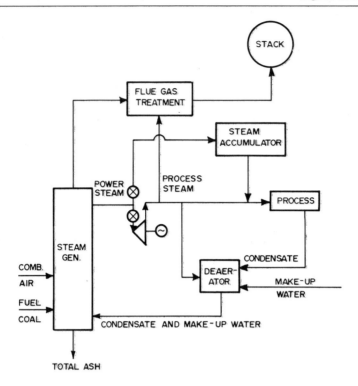

Fig. 18.12. Optimum cogeneration system proposed for malt beverage brewery, (USDOE, 1980, with courtesy of Westinghouse Electric Corp.).

and malt beverage brewery, respectively. The cogeneration facility chosen for the soybean oil mill is a stoker-fed boiler firing No. 3 seam coal. Steam generated at 62.2 atm (6.3 MPa) and 470°C is expanded through a back-pressure steam turbine, producing a gross power output of 2.1 MW. The exhaust steam, at 11.2 atm (1.13 MPa) is used to deaerate the condensate return flow, to reheat the flue gas treated in the flue gas desulfurization system, and to supply the soybean oil mill with 26 000 kg/h of usuable process steam, part of which is used to heat drying air indirectly, to the external soybean dryers.

The facility chosen for the malt beverage brewery is also a stoker-fed boiler firing No. 8 seam coal. The generated power steam at 62.2 atm and 470°C is expanded to 9.2 atm (0.93 MPa) through the back-pressure turbine, producing a gross power output of 3.4 MW. After extracting streams are taken off to supply energy for flue gas reheat and condensate deaeration, the exhaust steam is piped to the brewery operations as process steam. A small fraction of the high-pressure power steam is used to store energy in the hot water contained in the high-pressure accumulator to meet the cyclical steam demand from the brewhouse operations.

6.3. Economics

Both capital investments and operating costs were developed on an incremental basis for those plants that would have to replace process steam boilers in any event. In considering cogeneration, the net incremental investment over and above the process steam boiler replacement is the investment needed to generate electric power. These incremental investments contain two parts: the cogeneration system would have capital investments in an electric power generator; and the cogeneration boiler would operate at a higher pressure than the process steam boiler demanding better water quality. Each of these parts represents approximately 50% of the total incremental investment.

TABLE 18.1

Economics of industrial cogeneration

Cost/Savings item	Symbol notation
Investment (incremental)	ΔI
Net savings	
Savings on purchased electricity	ΔE
Use more fuel	ΔF
Increase other operating and maintenance costs	$\Delta[O \& M]$
Net savings	$\Delta E - \Delta F - \Delta[O \& M]$

TABLE 18.2

Fuel utilization and energy costs for soybean oil plant with and without industrial cogeneration

Energy consumption and cost	Existing separate generation	Industrial cogeneration	
		Coal-fired	Oil-fired
Gas (MWh/year)	158 000	–	188 000
Cost @ $12.00/MWh	1 900 000	–	2 240 000
Electricity (MWh/year)	14 347	–	–
Cost @ $40.00/MWh	575 000	–	–
Cost @ $80.00/MWh	1 150 000	–	–
Coal (MWh/year)	42 000	188 000	–
Cost @ $6.85/MWh	(used to generate purchased electricity above)	1 282 000	–
Total fuel (MWh)	200 000	188 000	188 000
Total cost ($ millions)	2.5–3.0	1.3	2.2
Energy savings (MWh/year)	–	12 000	12 000
Cost savings in purchased energy ($ millions/year)	–	1.2–1.7	0.3–0.8

In calculating potential savings, the on-site production of this cogenerated electric power saves on purchased electricity (ΔE in Table 18.1). Compared to an electric utility, a system that is cogenerating electric power and supplying process steam will use more fuel, approximately 0.149 kWh of additional fuel per kWh of electricity generated. This incremental fuel (ΔF in Table 18.1) concomitantly increases other operating and maintenance costs ($\Delta[O \& M]$ in Table 18.1), and both of these must be subracted from the net savings in purchased electricity as shown in the table. This adjustment typically amounts to approximately 15% of the net savings in purchased electricity.

Fuel requirements for each of the two food plants with and without cogeneration are shown in Tables 18.2 and 18.3 for the soybean mill and brewery, respectively. The tables also show assumed costs for purchased fuels and electricity in order to illustrate the magnitude of cost savings that can typically be realized from cogeneration for these plants. Both plants presently purchase all of their electricity from a local utility and separately generate their process steam using either gas- or oil-fired boilers. Although both plants would probably convert to the use of coal as part of a cogeneration implementation project, the tables also show the fuel cost savings associated with a gas- or oil-fired cogeneration system for the purposes of comparison. This also allows a distinction to be made between cost savings that result purely from cogeneration versus cost savings that also accrue as a result of switching to a less expensive fuel (coal).

Chapter 18 references, p. 302.

TABLE 18.3

Fuel utilization and energy costs for malt beverage brewery with and without industrial cogeneration

Energy consumption and cost	Existing separate generation	Industrial cogeneration	
		Coal-fired	Oil-fired
No. 6 Oil (MWh/year)	189 000	–	212 000
Cost @ $15.00/MWh	2 900 000	–	3 260 000
Electricity (MWh/year)	16 600	–	–
Cost @ $40.00/MWh	665 000	–	–
Cost @ $80.00/MWh	1 330 000	–	–
Coal (MWh/year)	48 600	212 000	–
Cost @ $6.85/MWh	(used to generate purchased electricity above)	1 450 000	–
Total fuel (MWh)	238 000	212 000	212 000
Total cost ($ millions)	3.6–4.2	1.5	3.3
Energy savings (MWh/year)	–	26 000	26 000
Cost savings in purchased energy ($ millions/year)	–	2.1–2.7	0.3–0.9

In the case of the soybean oil mill as an example (Table 18.2), the existing fuel requirement under separate generation consists of: (1) natural gas purchased by the plant to generate process steam and direct heat to dryers (158 000 MW annually); and (2) coal used by the local utility to supply the plant with the amount of purchased electricity that could be replaced by the proposed cogeneration system (42 000 MW annually). Thus, the total fuel required amounts to 200 000 MW annually. Under cogeneration there would be no fuel consumed for purchased electricity, while the plant would increase its purchase of fuel (in the form of either coal or natural gas) to 188 000 MW annually to supply both process steam and electricity. This would affect a net fuel savings of 12 000 MWh annually (approximately 6% energy savings).

The cost savings that can be realized are strictly a function of the difference in costs between purchased electricity that the plant would save and the purchased fuel required to cogenerate. For example, unit fuel costs for gas, oil and coal were chosen that would be typically representative in a first year of operation. In the case of purchased electricity, two cost figures were chosen to reflect the wide regional variation that exists in electricity costs, as well as to illustrate the sensitivity of purchased electricity costs in the economic analysis. Based on these unit costs, potential energy cost savings for the soybean oil mill (Table 18.2) are in the range of $1.2–1.7 million for a coal-fired cogeneration system versus $0.3–0.8 million for a gas-fired system. In the case of the larger malt beverage brewery (Table 18.3), these savings range from $2.1–2.7 million for a coal-fired system versus $0.3–0.9 million for an oil-fired system. Both cases illustrate the greater savings contribution made by coal conversion over cogeneration per se, in which the unit cost for purchased fuel remains unchanged. These savings do not reflect increased operating costs, which have been assumed to be negligible. However, the cost of invested capital could be a significant factor which was not considered in this simplified analysis.

In spite of these simplifying assumptions, however, the capital investment required for equipment, engineering and construction for cogeneration systems that were considered, is still quite high, as shown in Tables 18.4 and 18.5 for the soybean mill and malt beverage brewery, respectively. In the case of the

TABLE 18.4

Soybean oil mill estimated capital costs for industrial cogeneration system

Cost item	Cost ($ millions)	
	Coal-fired	Gas-fired
Steam boiler	5.5	2.5
Turbine generator	2.3	2.3
Flue gas treatment	1.0	–
Total direct costs	8.8	4.8
Engineering and construction	4.0	2.2
Interest and escalation (3 years)	3.5	2.0
Total capital cost	16.3	9.0
Incremental capital cost	15.3	8.0
Annual cost savings in purchased energy[a]	1.2–1.7	0.3–0.8
Payback period (years) from cost savings in purchased energy	8–12	10–26

[a]Does not include cost of invested capital.

TABLE 18.5

Malt beverage brewery estimated capital costs for industrial cogeneration system

Cost item	Cost ($ millions)	
	Coal-fired	Gas-fired
Steam boiler	6.6	3.2
Turbine generator	2.6	2.6
Flue gas treatment	1.5	–
Total direct costs	10.7	5.8
Engineering and construction	4.7	2.5
Interest and escalation (3 years)	4.6	2.5
Total capital cost	20.0	10.8
Annual cost savings in purchased energy[a]	2.1–2.7	0.3–0.9
Payback period (years) from cost savings in purchased energy	7–9	12–36

[a]Does not include cost of invested capital.

soybean oil mill in Table 18.4, for example, a breakdown of estimated capital costs for both a coal-fired and gas-fired cogeneration system is shown. The incremental capital investment in both cases has been estimated at $15.3 and $8 million, respectively, allowing a credit of $1 million for the scheduled replacement of the plant's low pressure, gas-fired process steam boiler. Dividing these incremental capital costs by the respective first year's purchased energy cost savings in each case results in crude payback periods based on these purchased energy savings in the range of 8–12 years for a coal-fired system, and 10–26 years for a gas-fired system, depending on the unit cost of purchased electricity saved in each case. As noted in the tables, this payback analysis does not include the cost of invested capital, which could be equal in magnitude to the energy cost savings at typical interest rates. A similar analysis for the malt beverage brewery is shown in Table 18.5. In the case of the brewery, there were no plans to replace existing process steam boilers. This required consideration of total capital investment rather than an incremental investment in the analysis.

Chapter 18 references, p. 302.

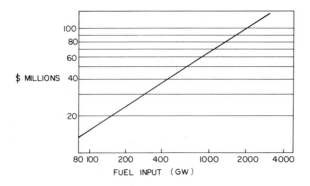

Fig. 18.13. Estimated capital investment versus energy requirement for industrial cogeneration systems (USDOE, 1980).

By most capital project evaluation criteria, these payback periods would suggest only marginal economic feasibility at best. However, the economics of cogeneration can vary considerably depending on various site-specific situations. For example, cogeneration can be economic when incremental capital investments are low compared to electric energy prices. This means that in regions where electricity energy prices are high, such as in and around large cities, cogeneration should probably be considered. Cogeneration can also show a good return on investment in situations where fuel costs are low compared with electricity prices. An example might be where fuel can be derived from a waste or by-product, such as in raw cane sugar processing where the spent cane stalks (bagasse) can be used as the boiler fuel to operate the cogeneration system, or a paper mill that can make use of wood wastes as fuel.

In general, however, it still takes site-specific situations to make cogeneration economic today. However, energy costs are changing rapidly, and small changes in the relative prices of fuels and electricity, tax incentives, and new developments in small-scale power generating technology are examples of the kinds of situations that the astute project engineer should be closely following in order to effectively re-examine the opportunity for industrial cogeneration in site-specific plant situations.

Based on experience in considering the application of cogeneration to a variety of industrial processing plants with different levels of energy demand, a predictable relationship has been observed between the size of the cogeneration system and the capital investment required (USDOE, 1980). This relationship is shown in Fig. 18.13 in which the cogeneration investment (expressed in $ million) is plotted against the fuel energy input required by the cogeneration system (expressed in thousands of megawatts). Note that both axes in Fig. 18.6 are labeled with non-linear scales, and the curve represents a best-fit relationship among the plants that were considered. By reference to Fig. 18.13 and the methodology for estimating cost savings described earlier in this section, it should be possible to make a crude preliminary economic analysis for a proposed cogeneration system of any size within the range studied based on an understanding of the energy demand profile of the processing plant to be considered, and the ratio of process steam to electricity shown in the two cogeneration systems described.

The case studies presented have focused on relatively large-scale centralized systems designed to meet the total energy requirements of the plant. The economics for small-scale systems designed for specific unit operations within a plant can be more attractive as discussed in the following section on potential applications for cogeneration in citrus processing plants.

7. COGENERATION IN CITRUS PROCESSING

In a study on opportunities for energy conservation in citrus processing, Leo (1982) investigated the use of cogeneration as both a central plant utility system as well as for specific unit operations involving citrus peel drying and citrus juice evaporation. For a central plant system, he investigated a Brayton cycle (gas turbine) and Rankine cycle (steam turbine) cogeneration system (shown schematically in Figs. 18.14 and 18.15, respectively), as well as a reciprocating internal combustion engine, as discussed previously under alternate cogeneration schemes.

According to Leo (1982), the basic characteristics of the three types of engines when used for cogeneration can be summarized as shown in Table 18.6. The gas turbine shows the highest overall energy savings at 29%, which represents an energy cost saving of 42%. The reciprocating engine carries the greatest initial cost per kilowatt, and is clearly uneconomical. The gas and steam turbines have essentially the same payout time, but differ dramatically in their heat-to-power ratio. These ratios are helpful in deciding the best engine to use in order to match a particular heat load, as discussed previously. Although the energy savings reported for these systems is in the same order of magnitude as those reported for the soybean oil mill and malt beverage brewery in the previous case studies, there is insufficient data available to explain the wide differences in economic payback other than the inherent variability of site-specific situations and assumptions discussed throughout this chapter.

In considering localized use of cogeneration with specific unit operations, Leo (1982) examined the potential case of a gas turbine in connection with citrus peel drying and with juice evaporation using a dual-mode evaporator. Figure 18.16 shows the essential components of a typical peel dryer. About half of the exhaust is recirculated back to the furnace to save fuel and maintain humidity in the exhaust. The remaining exhaust serves as a good source of energy for the waste-heat evaporator. Figure 18.17 shows how a gas turbine can be placed in front of the dryer furnace to provide supplemental heat to the dryer while generating electricity for general plant use.

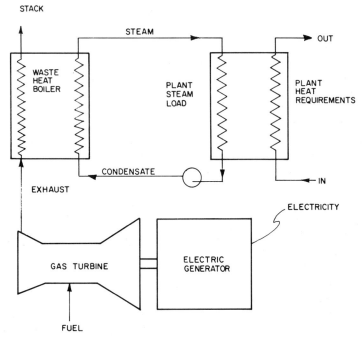

Fig. 18.14. Central Brayton cycle (gas turbine) cogeneration flow diagram (from Leo, 1982).

Chapter 18 references, p. 302.

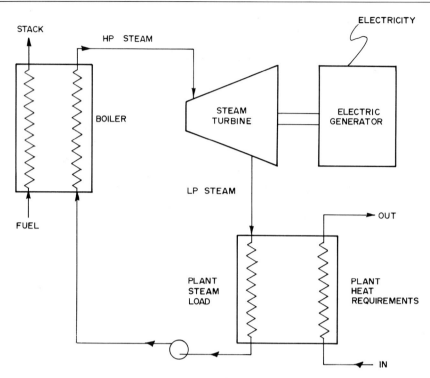

Fig. 18.15. Central Rankine cycle (steam turbine) cogeneration flow diagram (from Leo, 1982). HP, high pressure; LP, low pressure.

TABLE 18.6

Characteristics of three types of engines used for central cogeneration

Type of engine	Overall energy saving[a] (%)	Energy cost saving (%)	Capital cost ($/kW)	Payout time (years)	Output $\left(\dfrac{\text{kWh-heat}}{\text{kWh-electricity}}\right)$
Gas turbine (Brayton)	29	42	578	2.7	1.67
Steam turbine (Rankine)	10	34	465	2.6	7.30
Reciprocating engine	12	38	1165	17.0	0.54

Source: Leo, 1982.
[a]Compared to a standard boiler system.

The modular cogeneration system proposed for the 'dual mode' evaporator system is shown in Fig. 18.18. The first evaporator uses mechanical vapor recompression (MVR) to remove most of the water. The second evaporator is a steam-heated multiple-effect finishing evaporator that concentrates the product to 65°Brix. The unique feature is that the compressor for the MVR unit is driven by the gas turbine which also provides all the heat required for the finishing evaporator. Fuel is burned in the gas turbine to operate the vapor compressor and at the same time provide heat to the waste-heat boiler to raise steam for the finishing evaporator and pasteurizer. Heat exchangers are used to recover heat from the condensate and hot juice leaving the pasteurizer. Properly designed, the system could be completely energy-independent, generating all the electric power needed for auxiliary motors and controls.

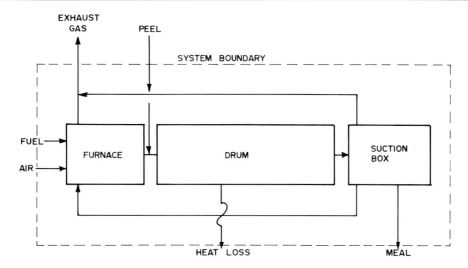

Fig. 18.16. Schematic diagram of citrus peel dryer showing material and energy flow (from Leo, 1982).

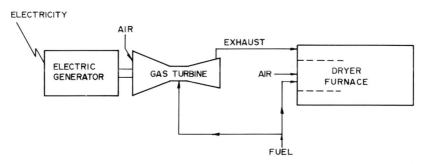

Fig. 18.17. Schematic diagram of proposed gas turbine cogeneration system with citrus peel dryer (from Leo, 1982).

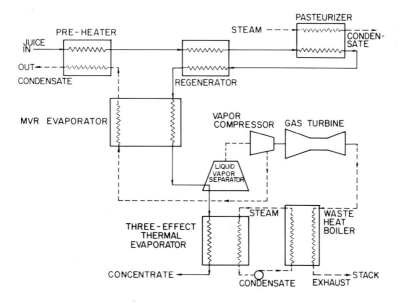

Fig. 18.18. Proposed scheme for use of gas turbine cogeneration system with dual mode citrus juice evaporator (from Leo, 1982). MVR, mechanical vapor recompression.

Chapter 18 references, p. 302.

Further applications for cogeneration in the citrus industry are discussed in a paper by Sickinger (1984). These applications are largely based on the use of smaller scale reciprocating engine systems designed to generate electricity during periods of peak demand to offset costs of high peak demand changes by the public utility (peak shaving). While operating, these engines can be coupled with various heat recovery systems to utilize heat from the engine exhaust and cooling system for various unit operations around the citrus plant.

8. REFERENCES

DPRA, 1974. Energy use statistics for the food and kindred products industry. Rep. PB-237316 to the Federal Energy Administration, Washington, DC. Development Planning and Research Associate, Manhattan, KS, 400 pp.

Leo, M.A., 1982. Energy conservation in citrus processing. Food Technol., 36 (5): 231–244.

Sickinger, D.R., 1984. Economics of peak shaving cogeneration using on-site generating systems in the citrus industry. Trans. 1984 Citrus Engineering Conf., 22 March, American Society of Mechanical Engineering, Lakeland, FL, Vol. 30, pp. 18–27.

Teixeira, A.A., 1979. Energy cogeneration – something for almost nothing. Food. Eng., 51 (12): 72–74.

Teixeira, A.A., 1980. Cogeneration of electricity in food processing plants. Agric. Eng., 61: 26–29.

USDOE, 1980. Industrial cogeneration optimization program. Rep. DOE/CS/05310-1, prepared by Arthur D. Little, Inc., in cooperation with Westinghouse Electric Corp. and Gibbs and Mill Engineering, Inc. U.S. Department of Energy, Washington, DC, 281 pp.

SELECTED READING

Galvin, C., 1983. Pre-packaged cogeneration units now available for small users. Energy User News, 8 (50): 1–10.

Chapter 19

Energy Losses Associated with Food Losses and Wastes

D.R. HELDMAN and R. PAUL SINGH

1. INTRODUCTION

Many components of the food system are known to be highly energy-intensive as indicated by quantities of energy required for specific stages. It is recognized that the efficiency of these energy-intensive stages must be improved in order to increase the overall efficiency of the food system. Another less visible efficiency parameter associated with the food chain is the wastes or losses of product that occur before the final product reaches the consumer. These losses and/or wastes not only represent a monetary loss to the individual handling the product at the point where the loss occurs, but these losses and/or wastes represent a loss of efficiency to the food system when expressed as energy loss. The quantitative extent of this efficiency loss has not been established, but should be a function of the magnitudes of product mass lost and the energy requirements at various stages within the food chain. Until recently, quantitative data on the product losses and the energy requirements were not available.

The overall goal of this investigation was to establish procedures for quantification of energy losses associated with product losses and wastes. Since energy is required at almost every stage within the food chain, the product value at any stage represents some investment of energy as well as other contributors to the 'value added' to the product. It is evident then that the loss of product at any stage in the food chain represents a loss of energy invested and contributes to the energy inefficiencies of the system.

The specific objectives of this chapter are:

(1) To develop and present a mathematical model for describing the relationship between losses and/or wastes in the food chain and the associated inefficiencies in energy use.

(2) To apply the mathematical analysis to specific food commodities using available data on product losses and/or wastes and for energy requirements.

(3) To evaluate the results of the mathematical analysis in terms of identifying locations within the food chain where reduction of product losses and/or wastes and reduction of energy requirements will have major impact on improvement of energy efficiency of the food chain.

2. A MATHEMATICAL MODEL FOR LOSSES IN THE FOOD CHAIN

In order to analyze the energy losses associated with food losses and wastes in the food chain, a mathematical model was developed. The schematic of the

---

Chapter 19 references, p. 311.

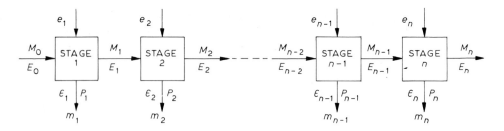

Fig. 19.1. Schematic of model food chain.

NOMENCLATURE

E	total energy entering or leaving a given stage in the food chain
e	energy requirements for a given stage in the food chain per unit product entering
e_c	cumulative energy utilized
ε	total energy loss at a given stage in the food chain
ε_c	cumulative energy loss
M	mass of product entering or leaving a given stage in the food chain
m	total mass loss at a given stage in the food chain
m_c	cumulative mass loss
p	fraction mass loss at each stage in the food chain

food chain with specific attention given to product mass losses as well as energy losses is presented in Fig. 19.1. The 'model food chain' allows for any number of stages with each stage representing a significant step in the delivery of the product from the point of harvest or assembly to the point of consumption. In the model, attention is given to the amount of product mass entering and leaving each stage in the food chain with an incorporation of the fraction loss at each stage. In addition, the model accounts for total energy entering or leaving each stage of the food chain with the primary input being the energy requirement for a given stage per unit of product handled in that stage. Energy entering or leaving a given stage represents the cumulative amount invested in the product for all previous stages minus the amount lost. The energy lost is directly related to the product mass loss in all previous stages.

An analysis of any stage in the food chain would indicate that the total mass loss at the stage would represent the product of mass entering and fraction mass loss at that stage. It would follow that the cumulative mass loss at any point in the food chain would be given by the following (see Nomenclature):

$$m_{cj} = \sum_{n=1}^{j} (p_n M_{n-1}) \tag{1}$$

Expressions for energy loss associated with food losses and wastes are somewhat more difficult to define than those for mass loss. At each stage in the food chain, there is an energy investment to the amount of product mass entering that stage. In addition, there is energy associated with product mass entering the stage based on energy investment at previous stages. The following equation illustrates that the energy loss is obtained by applying the fraction mass loss to the sum of the two sources of energy for a given stage:

$$E_n = p_n[(M_{n-1}e_n) + E_{n-1}] \tag{2}$$

where

$$E_{n-1} = (1 - p_{n-1})[E_{n-2} + (M_{n-2}e_{n-1})]$$

$$M_n = M_{n-1}(1 - p_n)$$

Equation (2) represents the expression needed to quantify the amount of energy invested in the product as it leaves stage n. As indicated, this quantity is directly related to the magnitudes of mass loss at that stage and the energy requirement of the same stage.

The specific expression for cumulative energy loss at a given stage in the food chain becomes:

$$\varepsilon_{cj} = \sum_{n=1}^{j} P_n[(M_{n-1}e_n) + E_{n-1}] \tag{3}$$

Equation (3) accounts for energy invested in the food chain for all stages through the stage being considered. The result should reflect the magnitude of mass losses during all previous stages.

Although equation (3) will provide the quantities of energy lost at any given stage, another important consideration is cumulative amounts of energy used as follows:

$$e_{cj} = \sum_{n=1}^{j} e_n M_{n-1} \tag{4}$$

Equation (4) accounts for the influence of mass loss on energy requirements by incorporating the remaining product fraction at each stage into the computation.

2.1. Application of the mathematical model

The application of the mathematical model depends on the availability of two types of information: (a) fraction mass loss for each stage in the system; and (b) energy requirements for each stage in the system. With these input parameters, the equations in the model will provide cumulative mass losses and energy utilization and the magnitudes of energy loss associated with the mass losses.

In order to apply the mathematical model to the food system, the food chain must be divided into stages. The selection of the stages to be included in the analysis should account for those stages where mass losses and eneryg requirements are significant. Accuracy of output from the model will be directly related to the number of input stages and the accuracy of input for each stage. In a previous application of the model, Heldman (1979) used up to 14 stages to describe the food chain for fresh market potatoes, frozen french fries and potato flakes between harvesting and delivery of product to the consumer at the retail store. In this investigation, the general 14-stage system in Fig. 19.2 has been used for the pototo products as well as fresh market apples, frozen apple slices, canned apple slices and dried apple slices. In most cases, not all 14 stages are utilized and in a few situations, intermediate stages are introduced. The use of the generalized system provides for consistent comparisons of results from analysis of different products and commodities.

The input data for the analysis have been obtained from various sources. The mass loss data for both potatoes and apples are based on values presented by Leite (1979). In situations where only ranges in percentage of loss are available, intermediate and representative values have been selected for use in the analysis. All energy requirement inputs for various potato products have been obtained from Olabode et al. (1977).

The availability of energy requirements for stages associated with apple handling and processing is limited. In order to estimate these requirements, data have been taken from processes for products similar to apples. The first three stages for all apple products are very similar and the energy requirements

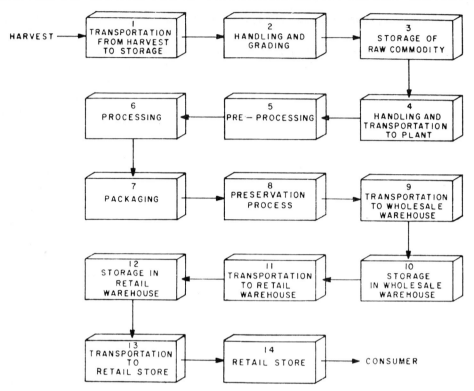

Fig. 19.2. Schematic illustration of general 14-stage food chain.

are assumed to be similar to the same stages for potatoes. Energy requirements for later stages of the fresh market apple system have been estimated based on data from citrus packing (Naughton et al., 1979). The additional energy requirement inputs for canned apples up to the point of distribution have been based on data for canning of peaches (Carroad et al., 1980). The energy requirement data for apples during the final six stages of the food chain have been estimated based on values for similar potato products as presented by Olabode et al. (1977).

3. RESULTS AND DISCUSSION

The mass losses associated with handling, processing and distribution of canned apple slices are illustrated in Fig. 19.3. The results for mass fraction losses at each available stage indicate the locations of more significant mass reductions. The pattern presented is quite similar to results for processed potato products as presented by Heldman (1979). For apple slices, more specific information on pre-processing, peeling, coring, trimming and slicing are available and occur between Stages 5 and 7. There was an absence of data for losses due to can filling separate from the canning preservation process (Stage 8). It is evident that all major reductions in product mass occur before the distribution to wholesale and retail outlets to the consumer.

Similar patterns of mass loss were obtained for fresh market apples, frozen apple slices and dehydrated apple slices. The magnitudes of cumulative mass loss for fresh apples was 32.3% and compared to 38.7% for fresh market potatoes. The cumulative mass loss for frozen apple slices was 51.5% and was significantly less than the 73.7% for frozen french fries Heldman (1979). The 87.6% cumulative mass loss for dehydrated apple slices was only slightly less than the 96.4% mass loss for potato flakes. It must be emphasized that the

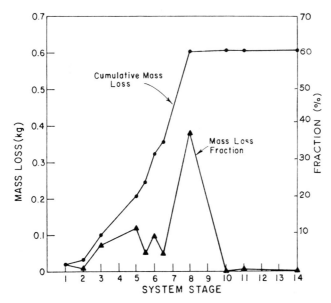

Fig. 19.3. Mass losses for frozen apple slices.

TABLE 19.1

Energy losses for canned apple slices

Stage	Energy required, e(kJ/kg)	Energy leaving, E(kJ)	Total energy loss, ε(kJ)	Cumulative energy loss, ε_c(kJ)	Cumulative energy used, e_c(kJ)	Energy loss (%)
1	700	686	14.0	14.0	700	2
2	140	815	8.2	22.2	837.2	2.7
3	427	1149.1	89.8	112.0	1261.1	8.9
5	4	1014.4	138.3	250.3	1264.7	19.8
5.5	254	1154.8	60.8	311.1	1465.9	21.2
6	17	1050.8	116.8	427.9	1478.7	28.9
6.5	14	1007.3	53.0	480.9	1488.2	32.3
8	2432	1586.4	984.7	1465.6	3052.0	48.0
10	186	1659.4	0.8	1466.4	3125.8	46.9
11	121	1695.4	12.0	1478.4	3173.8	46.6
14	1517	2290.8	2.3	1480.7	3771.5	39.3

magnitudes for dehydrated products includes the removal of significant amounts of water; a reduction that is necessary to achieve the desired final product. A portion of the reduction in mass for frozen and canned products would occur during similar steps for these products. In this investigation, no attempt has been made to separate 'necessary' mass losses since the energy losses associated with the mass losses occur without regard to the fate of the mass removed from the product.

An example of the tabular results associated with computing energy losses are presented for canned apple slices in Table 19.1. The magnitudes of energy requirements in column 1 of Table 19.1 were obtained from various sources discussed in the procedures section of this paper. The values for energy leaving (column 2) each stage were obtained from equation (2) while the total and cumulative loss values were calculated from equation (3). The total energy used after each stage of the system was obtained from equation (4). The percentage energy loss at each stage was calculated using values in columns 4 and 5. Similar tabular results were obtained for fresh market apples, frozen apple slices and dehydrated apple slices.

Chapter 19 references, p. 311.

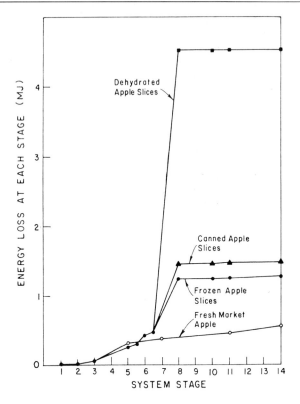

Fig. 19.4. Cumulative energy losses for various apple products.

The magnitudes of cumulative energy loss for the four apple products are compared in Fig. 19.4. The patterns of energy loss for the various products are very similar during the early stages of the food system when mass losses and energy requirements are relatively low. The mathematical model used is sensitive to the stages in the system where mass losses are higher and energy requirements are greater. In addition, the model does establish relative magnitudes of cumulative energy loss that tend to correlate with expected energy intensity associated with delivery of the product.

The magnitudes of cumulative energy losses for apple products are comparable to those for similar potato products reported by Heldman (1979). The value of 554 kJ for fresh market apples is very close to the 534.6 kJ for fresh market potatoes. The cumulative energy loss of 1270.8 kJ for frozen apple slices is slightly lower than the 1645.1 kJ for frozen french fries and the difference may be attributed to the absence of data on energy for packaging used for the apple product. The cumulative energy loss for dehydrated apple slices of 4541.5 kJ is much higher than the 3438 kJ for potato flakes. This difference appears to be most closely associated with the observation that greater mass loss (63.1%) occurs before the dehydration stage in potato flakes as compared to 35.7% mass loss before dehydration of the apple slices. These types of observations emphasize the significant relationship between product mass loss and energy intensity of the food system.

The results in Fig. 19.5 present percentage energy loss for each of the four apple products. The patterns for all products are very similar to the results for cumulative energy loss, but may represent a more equitable way of comparing energy efficiencies of the system. It is evident that the pattern of energy loss associated with mass loss is influenced significantly by those stages where mass loss is greatest and energy requirements are highest.

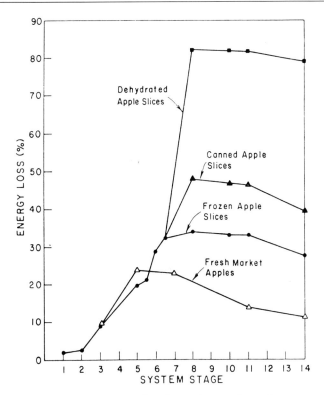

Fig. 19.5. Percent energy loss for various apple products.

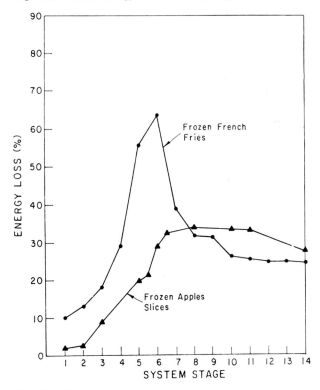

Fig. 19.6. Comparison of energy loss for frozen french fries and frozen apple slices.

A comparison of percentage energy loss associated with frozen apple slices and frozen french fries is presented in Fig. 19.6. The difference in pattern of energy loss is quite evident and deserves further analysis. For frozen french fries, the percentage of energy lost at Stage 6 (processing including plant

---

Chapter 19 references, p. 311.

utilities) is 63.4% while the same value for frozen apple slices is never greater than 33.9%. This dramatic difference appears to be most closely associated with large mass losses during peeling, cutting and blanching of potatoes before and more energy-intensive stages of packaging and freezing. For frozen apple slices, the most significant mass loss and most energy-intensive step is at Stage 8. It is interesting to note that the overall energy loss is 24.3% of the frozen french fries and 27.8% for frozen apple slices indicating considerable similarity in overall energy efficiencies of the two systems. The apparent inefficiencies in the early stages of frozen french fries system would indicate that reductions in mass loss and/or improvements in energy efficiencies during those stages would cause dramatic improvements in the overall efficiency of the total system. The same opportunities for efficiency improvement would not appear to be available in the frozen apple slices system.

Based on the results presented, it is quite evident that a relationship between the product mass loss and those energy losses associated with mass losses does exist. It would appear as though the types of energy losses being discussed are more closely associated with the magnitude of product mass loss than with the intensity of energy utilized at any given stage in the food chain. A quick conclusion would be that a reduction in product mass loss would result in energy conservation. The results presented clearly illustrate that specific stages in the food chain have a definite impact on the overall product mass loss and the associated energy losses. The analysis seems to identify these stages which should receive attention in terms of reducing product losses as well as reducing the energy utilization requirements.

Probably the most evident observation associated with this investigation is that more attention should be given to the locations of an avoidable product loss with respect to the locations at which significant energy inputs are required. The overall efficiency of each food chain investigated would have been improved if some of the avoidable product mass losses had occurred early in the food chain before significant energy investments had been made. The most serious situation is one in which significant energy requirements occur throughout significant portions of the food chain only to reach a point in the food chain where significant product mass loss occurs. Although the examples analyzed do not illustrate the situation directly, there is evidence to support the observation. With these factors in mind, it would seem quite appropriate to reanalyze the chain of events for each food product commodity and attempt to avoid unnecessary losses of product at any stage in the chain beyond the point at which significant energy has been utilized to bring the product to that particular location. It seems evident from the analyses and results presented that significant improvements in the efficient utilization of energy can occur by taking such steps.

4. CONCLUSIONS

A mathematical model can be used to quantify energy losses associated with mass loss in the food chain.

The magnitudes of energy losses associated with product mass loss are a function of fraction mass loss at each stage and magnitudes of energy requirements at each stage.

Percent energy loss at each stage of the food chain appears to be a good indicator of stages needing priority attention to increase system efficiency.

Based on the relationship between energy losses and product mass losses, it must be concluded that processes resulting in significant product loss or wastes should be completed before energy-intensive stages of the food chain occur.

5. REFERENCES

Carroad, P.A., Singh, R.P., Chhinnan, M.S., Jacob, N.L. and Rose, W.W., 1980. Energy use quantification in the canning of clingstone peaches. Presented at 39th Annual Meeting of Institute of Food Technologists, 10–13 June 1979, St. Louis, MO. J. Food Sci., 45: 723–725.

Heldman, D.R., 1979. Estimates of energy losses associated with food wastes and losses. In: D.R. Heldman (Editor), Food Losses and Wastes of the Domestic Food Chain of the United States. NSF Rep. DAR 76-80693.

Leite, E.F., 1979. Total magnitudes of food losses. In: D.R. Heldman (Editor), Food Losses and Wastes of the Domestic Food Chain of the United States. NSF Rep. DAR 76-80693.

Naughon, M., Singh, R.P., Hardt, P. and Rumsey, T.R., 1979. Energy use in citrus packing plants. Trans. ASAE, 22: 188–192.

Olabode, N.A., Standing, C.N. and Chapman, P.A., 1977. Total energy to produce food servings as a function of processing and marketing modes. J. Food Sci., 42(3): 768.

Part V

Economics of Energy Use in Food Processing

Chapter 20

Food Prices and Rising Energy Costs

FLOYD A. LASLEY

1. INTRODUCTION

Modern methods of producing, processing and distributing food depend heavily on energy use. Much of the high productivity of farm labor and land hinges on fuel and energy; even though farmers in the U.S.A. use only about 3% of the Nation's energy in the production process, including that invested in agricultural chemicals and other inputs, about four times this amount is used to assemble, process, distribute and prepare food for consumers.

Increases in energy prices will affect food prices in four ways: (1) each unit of fuel used costs more; (2) constraints upon the availability of energy may lead to decreased food production; (3) constraints upon certain types of fuels could lead to use of higher cost fuels; (4) limited availability and rising prices could lead to the substitution of other inputs (such as labor) for energy.

Each of these adjustments could cause a rise in the production and marketing costs of a unit of food. Rising real costs will be reflected in higher real prices for products, but the pass-through of cost increases in the form of higher nominal prices is not automatic. If the economic system accommodates these cost increases, they will be passed through the production-marketing system and food prices will increase. However, prices of different foods will not rise uniformly in degree or timing, even assuming constant food demand and output mix. Real prices will be bid up for those products requiring relatively more energy – or energy from a higher priced alternative. This study does not measure impacts caused by the fact that different activities consume varying proportions of fuel types. Changing cost-returns relationships affect the ability to attract and maintain productive resources in the various food sectors. This may also contribute to increasing price volatility.

This study finds that the commonly used methods of measuring the effect of fuel costs on food prices may understate the impact on retail prices if fuel prices were to double. Instead of measuring fuel costs as a percentage of cash sales or expenses, this study suggests that energy costs as a percentage of the value added by production or manufacture and as a percentage of labor and management earnings may be better measurements.

2. FUELS IN PRODUCTION AND MARKETING

Current food production and marketing technology were developed largely during the era of low-priced energy. While essential for current high-technology processes, energy has represented only a small part of the total cost of producing, processing and distributing food. Labor, land, and equipment each are

---

Chapter 20 references, p. 325.

more costly, and have limited food production and marketing more than has energy.

Historically, the price of energy did not heavily influence the output of most food processing industries; low-priced energy enhanced productivity and provided savings in total unit costs. Even during fuel shortages, food processing and distribution have received high-priority fuel allocations. Barring an extreme crisis, these industries process and market the quantity of food available, although there may be some adjustment of product mix, and both inputs and methods may be selected primarily to minimize costs.

Estimates based on energy cost at a particular sector (farm, processing, wholesaling, or retailing) compared with the sales or shipments by that sector tend to understate energy's impact on prices. Energy is used in all stages, and meaningful estimates must consider how energy contributes to cost at each level. Increases in cost are cumulative as the product moves through the production-marketing system.

The following comparisons assume that fuel will be available for producing and marketing foodstuffs, that output will not be changed, and that physical inputs will be used in about the same proportions as in the immediate past in each level of the system. It is also assumed that price increases can be passed on to the consumer. These simplifying assumptions do not deny that adjustments would be expected in all areas, but they illustrate the pressures for food price adjustments resulting from increasing energy prices. Questions regarding management decisions alter output, product mix and input combinations are not addressed in these comparisons.

3. MEASURING FARMERS' FUEL COSTS

Farmers, for whom energy is a critical input, will face higher production costs as fuel prices rise. How one expects farmers to adjust to higher fuel prices will be influenced by how the impact of fuel price increases is measured. The importance of energy costs to production costs for six types of farms is illustrated by selected cost and return data (Table 20.1). While considerable variation exists between individual farms in a given community and from State to State, these data provide insight into the anticipated impacts on commodities as energy prices rise.

Dairy and broiler farm expenditures for energy in 1978 were about 5% of total cash sales, while egg and beef producers spent only one-half this amount (Table 20.1). This measure, perhaps the one most commonly applied, could lead one to conclude that doubling energy prices would not have much effect on either farmers or food prices. Fuel costs as a percentage of cash farm expenses is another frequently used measure at the producer level. As expected with this comparison, fuel costs are slightly greater than when measured as a proportion of cash receipts (Table 20.1). Both of these measures, although frequently used, understate the significance of fuel costs and their impact on returns to farmers.

Comparing fuel costs with cash balances and labor and management earnings reveals that uncompensated rising fuel costs would have considerably more impact on net returns than on total costs. Although not strictly the same as 'value added by manufacture', cash balance, the difference between cash sales of farm products and cash farm expenses, is used here to represent 'value added' by farm production. Fuel costs in 1978 were equal to 44% of the cash balance for beef producers. Without compensating adjustment, doubling fuel costs would reduce cash available for other purposes by 44% of the cash balance. Milk and pork producers would see their cash balances reduced about 20% by a doubling of fuel costs. The proportion is about 17% for broiler producers, 13% for egg producers, and 10% for grain farmers.

TABLE 20.1

Relationship of fuel and energy costs to sales and returns for six types of farms, average per farm

Item	Type of farm					
	Dairy	Beef[a]	Hog	Egg[b]	Broiler[c]	Grain
Number of farms	340	189	678	–	–	2002
Cash sales of product (US$)	130577	313412	207664	259560	92736	150704
Cash expenses (US$)	101204	295930	166337	208260	66624	90991
Cash balance (value added)[d] (US$)	29373	17482	41327	51300	26112	59713
Labor and management earnings (US$)	22642	13553	31456	16980	15456	17217
Purchased fuel and energy[e] (US$)						
1971	2400	2746	1899	–	–	2616
1978	6509	7733	8643	6600	4512	6255
Purchased fuel and energy as a percentage of:						
Cash sales						
1971	4.8	1.9	2.5	–	–	3.8
1978	5.0	2.5	4.2	2.5	4.9	4.2
Cash expenses						
1971	6.4	2.2	3.3	–	–	6.1
1978	6.4	2.6	5.2	3.2	6.8	6.9
Cash balance (value added)						
1971	18.6	13.9	11.7	–	–	10.5
1978	22.2	44.2	20.9	12.9	17.3	10.5
Labor and management earnings						
1971	39.4	27.4	23.5	–	–	18.6
1978	28.7	57.1	27.5	38.9	29.2	36.3

–, Not available.

[a]Beef farms include cow–calf operations, but are heavily weighted by farms feeding out beef (not commercial feedlots).

[b]Includes total production estimates for 30000 hen egg production units.

[c]Includes total production estimates for 96000 broilers per year production units. Comparable results would be expected from larger units.

[d]Cash balance is shown in Illinois farm records as the difference between cash sales of product and cash expenses. This difference is later used as a proxy for value added by farming.

[e]Purchased fuel and energy estimated by adjusting farm record summaries to aggregate fuel costs including gasoline, oil, electricity, natural and propane gas, fuel oils, diesel, fuel portion of hired machine work, and fuel portion of hired transport.

Source: Univ. Ill., 1971, 1978 for dairy, beef, hogs and grain farms. Unpublished data and budget estimates compiled by National Economics Division and Economic Research Service U.S. Department of Commerce for egg and broiler producers.

Note: Data are for 1978 unless otherwise indicated.

4. IMPACT OF FUEL PRICE INCREASES ON FARM COSTS

The severity of the impacts caused by a doubling of fuel costs can best be seen by looking at the potential effect on labor and management earnings. Unless product prices increased, doubling fuel costs at the producer level would cut earnings by more than half for beef producers, by more than one-third for egg and grain producers, and by more than one-quarter for broiler, milk and pork producers. Such changes in the relative well-being of these various producers are likely to result in differential changes in production and product prices. If these producers were near equilibrium positions in 1978, then beef producers would be more severely affected by rising fuel costs than pork producers.

Chapter 20 references, p. 325.

TABLE 20.2

Costs of fuel and energy purchased by food industries

SIC code and industry grouping	Cost (US$) of fuel purchased per establishment			Cost (US$) of fuel purchased per production worker			Cost (US$) of fuel purchased per dollar value of shipments			Cost (US$) of fuel purchased per dollar of value added by manufacturer		
	1967	1972	1977	1967	1972	1977	1967	1972	1977	1967	1972	1977
All manufactures	24 721	32 528	92 740	551	771	2438	1.38	1.38	2.46	2.94	2.95	5.70
20 Food and kindred	20 346	31 401	95 206	590	815	2368	0.79	0.77	1.32	2.48	2.48	4.53
201 Meat	18 519	29 344	71 217	366	520	1271	0.42	0.41	0.70	2.56	2.62	4.32
2011 Meatpacking	21 023	33 064	66 217	433	663	1472	0.36	0.36	0.55	2.55	2.76	4.30
2015 Poultry	21 352	38 804	134 391	232	302	920	0.61	0.66	1.22	3.06	2.83	5.63
2016 Poultry dressing	–	–	158 296	–	–	909	–	–	1.23	–	–	5.71
2017 Poultry and egg	–	–	64 706	–	–	1010	–	–	1.16	–	–	5.16
202 Dairy	18 859	26 841	77 647	1088	1325	3404	0.91	0.76	0.80	3.37	3.04	5.16
2021 Butter	19 259	35 498	57 971	1625	2828	4706	1.08	1.02	0.89	9.19	9.96	10.73
2022 Cheese	11 988	19 839	75 095	741	840	2676	0.72	0.54	0.97	5.43	3.51	6.26
2026 Fluid	19 104	26 047	66 996	1099	1360	3159	0.85	0.70	0.94	2.83	2.56	4.06
203 Preserved fruits and vegetables	24 178	46 852	154 435	376	601	1849	0.92	1.04	1.81	2.38	2.65	4.77
204 Grain milling	27 358	37 565	121 558	1125	1474	4665	0.88	0.95	1.66	3.04	3.13	5.58
205 Bakery	12 073	18 277	47 755	332	466	1231	0.82	0.84	1.32	1.52	1.46	2.29
206 Sugar and confections	42 194	71 177	238 898	641	1024	3423	1.20	1.34	2.64	3.16	3.60	6.90
207 Fats and oils	57 229	97 445	314 039	1833	2863	9251	1.12	1.21	1.88	6.20	6.49	14.29
208 Beverages	15 928	28 918	93 331	614	981	2914	0.77	0.76	1.24	1.46	1.57	2.93
209 Miscellaneous	11 822	12 473	40 186	655	525	1602	0.85	0.62	1.04	2.04	1.52	3.17

–, not available.
Source: USDC, 1967, 1967, 1972, 1977.

A similar comparison for 1971 showed that fuel costs were equal to about 25% of labor and management earnings for both beef and hogs, but nearly 40% for dairy (Table 20.1). This emphasizes the fact that the impact of rising fuel prices on producers of farm products will be influenced by the current stage of existing price cycles for those products. It also suggest that rising fuel prices may add further instability to producer earnings, thereby resulting in greater volatility in commodity price cycles and quantities produced. At any rate, one should expect different price and producer response to rapidly rising fuel costs for various commodities.

Cash expenses grow in significance as farmers purchase increasing proportions of inputs from off-farm sources. In 1978, milk, pork and egg producers spent about four-fifths of each dollar received for cash expenses. Beef producers spent the highest portion, 94% of each sales dollar, while grain farmers, at 60%, spent the lowest. Thus, a change in the price of any input becomes critical for farmers' cash balance, labor and management earnings, and living standards. Although the cost of fuel is a relatively small proportion of total farm sales, the impact of rising fuel prices on net earnings and living standards will influence producers' decisions and affect the price of farm products.

High fuel prices would also influence costs of production for farmers by increasing the costs of purchased inputs other than fuel. The fuel costs for all manufacturers, as reported by the *Census of Manufactures* (USDC, 1967–1977), provided a suitable approximation of the fuel costs of purchased inputs. The cost and impact on these inputs was not differentiated. The average fuel cost for all industries in 1977 was 2.46% of the value of shipments, up from 1.38% in 1967 and 1971. This 2.46% was used as the fuel cost of inputs purchased by farmers, except for beef and pork costs, which were adjusted to account for the purchase of farm-produced feeder livestock. Thus, rising fuel prices were assumed to increase the prices of inputs purchased by farmers by 2.46% of the purchase price.

5. FUEL PRICES AND THE FOOD INDUSTRIES

Farm products tend to be bulky per unit of value, but they require far less processing than the average manufactured product. (The value of shipments by manufacturers is considered comparable to cash sales by farmers, and value added by manufacture as comparable to the difference between farmers' cash sales and cash expenses.) Value added by manufacture averaged 43% of the value of shipments for all industries in 1977 (Table 20.2). Food and kindred manufacturing added an average 29%, with the fats and oils, meatpacking and dairy products industries adding 13, 16 and 22%, respectively. Bakery products were highest, with 58% of the value of their shipments added by manufacturing. The meatpacking (at 0.5%) and dairy products (at 0.8%) industries purchased less energy per dollar value of shipment than any of the other major (3-digit Standard Industrial Classification, SIC) food industries. Primarily as a result of rising dairy product prices and energy-conserving adjustments by the dairy industry, dairy product manufacturers spent less for fuel per dollar of sales in 1977 than in 1967. The dairy products industry was the only major food industry to experience such a decline. The sugar and confections industry was the only 3-digit food industry spending more than 2% of sales to purchase fuel and energy.

Fuel cost per dollar of value added by manufacture at each stage provides a more useful measure of fuel cost's importance than does fuel cost per dollar value of shipments. The average fuel cost per dollar of value added by all manufacturers was 5.7 cents in 1977, up from about 2.9 cents in 1967 and 1972

Chapter 20 references, p. 325.

(Table 20.2). The ratio for food and kindred products was somewhat lower, with a value of 4.5 cents in 1977 and 2.5 cents in 1967 and 1972. Fats and oils (SIC 207) and sugar and confections (SIC 206) both required relatively large expenditures for fuel per dollar of value added, with grain milling and dairy products about average for all manufactures. Meat products' (SIC 201) fuel cost per dollar of value added ran at about the average for all food products (SIC 20).

Smaller groupings of industries (4-digit SIC codes) present more classification and allocation problems. Although assigning costs at various levels may not be accurate due to these problems, some of the differences among these subindustries appear to be significant. In 1977, the butter industry (2021) spent more than 10 cents for fuel for each dollar of value added by manufacture. Fluid milk processors spent only 4 cents and cheese manufacturers just over 6 cents in this category. Rising fuel prices would thus tend to be more of a problem for butter manufacturing than for fluid milk processing. Poultry plants spent 5.6 cents, while meatpackers spent only 4.3 cents. In 1972, poultry plants spent only 0.2 cent more than meatpackers for fuel per dollar of value added. Poultry plants spent nearly twice as much per establishment in 1977 as meatpackers – $134 000 compared with $71 000.

Rising fuel prices would increase costs for each food industry. The resulting changes in costs and returns would affect their relative competitive positions. The possibility of passing these increased costs on to the consumer through higher product prices also varies greatly, and creates further pressures on industry structure.

6. FUEL COSTS' INFLUENCE ON RETAIL PRICES

Transportation, wholesaling and retailing functions also require energy. Breaking down costs by product and function becomes increasingly difficult at this point because of the complexity of joint costs involved. This study differentiates the energy used at four stages, from production through distribution. This differentiation, although limited in scope, illustrates how marketing and pricing practices respond to and interact with increased costs at different stages of production and marketing.

Costs of processing, wholesaling and retailing increase with higher wage rates and prices of energy and other inputs. Retail food prices reflect changes in costs at all stages of production or marketing. General inflationary pressures influence these costs, but prices for each product or level are also subject to specific supply or demand pressures for individual foods which can cause costs and prices of food products to change at different rates (Table 20.3). Although food product prices at wholesale tend to move up or down with farm level prices, operating costs for marketing firms have moved persistently upwards and have been a major factor in rising food prices.

The marketing bill for U.S. farm foods was $123 500 million in 1977, while the farm value of these foods was $56 500 million. As both of these values have increased, so has the amount consumers have paid for farm-produced foods (Tables 20.3 and 20.4). Although production, marketing, and consumer costs tend to increase together, farm value has not risen as steadily as the marketing bill and consumer expenditures. A comparison of year-to-year and 3-year changes illustrates the greater volatility of farm prices (Table 20.4). The cost of those functions closer to the retail level tends to be less affected by farm level prices than by operating expenses. However, both higher farm level prices and higher marketing costs are reflected in the retail price.

Detailed information on cost components indicates that the combined wholesale and retail functions accounted for 10–52% of the retail prices for 16

TABLE 20.3

Prices and costs (US¢) for selected foods, energy, and food production workers' earnings

Item	Year		
	1967	1972	1977
Milk, half gallon retail	58.6	59.8	83.9
Net farm value[a]	25.4	29.4	45.8
Butter, pound retail	83.1	87.1	133.1
Net farm value[a]	59.8	63.8	91.5
Beef, choice pound retail	82.6	113.8	138.3
Net farm value[a]	53.0	72.5	79.9
Pork, pound retail	67.2	83.2	125.4
Net farm value[a]	34.8	47.9	73.4
Frying chicken, pound retail	38.1	41.4	60.1
Net farm value[a]	18.6	20.1	33.0
Eggs, grade A large, dozen retail	49.2	52.4	82.3
Net farm value[a]	29.0	29.9	53.8
Bread, white, pound retail	22.2	24.7	35.5
Net farm value[a]	2.8	2.8	4.5
Purchased energy[b] (US$ per 10^6 Btu)	0.67	0.80	2.58
Hourly earnings (US$) of production workers in food manufacturing, wholesale and retail trade	2.56	3.49	5.20
U.S. farm foods (10^9 US$)			
Consumer expenditures	90.2	122.2	192.3
Farm value[a]	28.8	39.8	58.0
Marketing bill	61.4	82.4	134.3
Market basket (Index 1967 = 100)			
Farm foods, retail	100.0	121.3	179.2
Farm value[a]	100.0	125.1	178.3
Farm-retail spread	100.0	119.1	179.7

$\frac{1}{2}$ gal (US) $\approx$ 2.28 l.

lb, pound (avdp) $\approx$ 0.4536 kg.

10^6 Btu $\approx$ 1.055 × 10^9 J = 1.055 GJ.

[a]Net farm value for farm equivalent of retail unit.

[b]Energy price of 80 cents as reported for 1971. There was a 4-cent price increase in 1972 to 84 cents.

Source: USDA, 1974–1980; USDC, 1967–1977[b].

selected foods in 1977, with a simple average of 30% for these functions (USDA, 1974–1980). This combined wholesale–retail margin was 23.3% for dairy products, 29.0% for meat, 23.4% for poultry, and 46.7% for grain mill products (bread was used to represent grain mill products at this stage).

The dollar spent at retail by the consumer would be divided quite differently among the various production–marketing levels for the four food groups (dairy, meat, poultry and grain mill products). The consumer therefore might expect a variation in price changes among food products resulting from a given rise in fuel prices. These differences are approximated by starting with a $1 retail value for each of the four food groups and working backwards through processing and farm production to the purchased farm inputs, showing the value of shipments, value added, cost of inputs, and the fuel cost at each stage (Table 20.5). Purchased inputs for each stage are assumed to be the corresponding sales of that product from the preceding stage. Further refinements could

Chapter 20 references, p. 325.

TABLE 20.4

Farm value, marketing bill, and consumer expenditures for U.S. farm foods

Year	Farm value (10^9 US\$)	Marketing bill (10^9 US\$)	Consumer expenditures (10^9 US\$)	Change from previous year (%)			Change from 3 years earlier (%)		
				Farm value	Marketing bill	Consumer expenditures	Farm value	Marketing bill	Consumer expenditures
1967	28.8	61.4	90.2	–	–	–	–	–	–
1968	30.4	63.6	94.0	5.6	3.6	4.2	–	–	–
1969	33.4	64.1	97.8	9.9	0.8	4.0	–	–	–
1970	34.8	71.2	106.0	4.2	11.1	8.4	20.8	16.0	17.5
1971	35.3	75.5	110.8	1.4	6.0	4.5	16.1	18.7	17.9
1972	39.8	82.4	122.2	12.7	9.1	10.3	19.2	28.5	24.9
1973	51.7	87.1	138.8	29.9	5.7	13.6	48.6	22.3	30.9
1974	56.4	98.2	154.6	9.0	12.7	11.4	59.8	30.0	39.5
1975	55.6	111.3	169.0	-1.4	13.3	9.3	39.7	35.1	38.3
1976	58.3	125.4	183.7	4.9	12.7	8.7	12.8	44.0	32.3
1977	58.0	134.3	192.3	-0.5	7.1	4.7	2.8	36.8	24.4
1978	69.7	146.0	215.7	20.2	8.7	12.2	25.4	31.2	27.6
1979	80.6	164.5	245.1	15.6	12.7	13.6	38.2	31.2	33.4
1980[a]	86.0	183.0	269.0	6.7	11.2	9.8	48.3	36.3	39.9

–, Not applicable.
[a]Preliminary.

TABLE 20.5

Production and marketing energy costs (¢) per dollar of retail sales of dairy, meat, poultry, and grain mill products, 1977

Food group	Function or stage of production			
	Wholesale and retail[a]	Processing and distribution[b]	Farm production and shipping[c]	Purchased farm inputs
	Cents			
Dairy products:				
Total sales	100.0	76.7	60.1	46.6
Cost of inputs	76.7	60.1	46.6	26.5
Value added	23.3	16.6	13.5	20.1
Fuel cost	3.0	0.6	3.0	1.1
Cumulative fuel[d]	7.7	4.7	4.1	1.1
Cumulative fuel as a proportion (%) of sales	7.7	6.1	6.8	2.5[f]
Meat products:				
Total sales	100.0	71.0	59.5	51.2
Cost of inputs	71.0	59.5	51.2[e]	29.1
Value added	29.0	11.5	8.3	22.1
Fuel cost	3.0	0.5	1.8	1.3
Cumulative fuel[d]	6.6	3.6	3.1	1.3
Cumulative fuel as a proportion (%) of sales	6.6	5.1	5.2	2.5[f]
Poultry products:				
Total sales	100.0	76.6	60.1	46.9
Cost of inputs	76.6	60.1	46.9	26.7
Value added	23.4	16.5	13.2	20.2
Fuel cost	3.0	0.9	1.9	1.2
Cumulative fuel[d]	7.0	4.0	3.1	1.2
Cumulative fluel as a proportion (%) of sales	7.0	5.2	5.2	2.5[f]
Grain mill products:				
Total sales	100.0	53.3	37.5	22.7
Cost of inputs	53.3	37.5	22.7	12.9
Value added	46.7	15.8	14.8	9.8
Fuel cost	0.5	0.9	1.6	0.6
Cumulative fuel[d]	3.6	3.1	2.2	0.6
Cumulative fuel as a proportion (%) of sales	3.6	5.8	5.9	2.5[f]

[a]Current estimated fuel costs for food retailing are 1.1% of sales. Estimates for wholesaling plus fuel portion of transportation for wholesaling and retailing are allocated to product groupings.
[b]Compiled from USDG, 1977.
[c]Farm production costs were calculated from after Univ. Ill., 1978, and unpublished data from Economic Research Service, U.S. Department of Agriculture.
[d]Cumulative fuel is the sum of fuel costs, up to and including, each stage of production and marketing.
[e]Adjusted to reflect farm production of purchased feed livestock.
[f]Average for all manufactures (2.46% of sales or 5.70% of value added).

be made, but this breakdown provides a meaningful approximation of cost–sales relationships.

This technique enables one to trace through the production–marketing system and determine the proportion of cost each phase contributes to the production of the final product for which the consumer pays $1 at retail. It is

TABLE 20.6

Possible impacts of increased energy costs (¢) on the price of selected food products

Item	Purchased farm inputs		Farm production and shipping		Processing and distribution		Whole sale and retail	
	A	B	A	B	A	B	A	B
	Cents							
Dairy products:								
Sales or shipments	47.7	48.2	64.2	66.0	81.4	85.0	107.7	114.7
Cost of inputs	27.6	27.6	50.7	51.2	64.8	66.6	84.4	88.0
Value added	20.1	20.6	13.5	14.8	16.6	18.4	23.3	26.7
Fuel cost	2.2	2.2	6.0	1.2	1.2	6.0	6.0	
Cumulative fuel cost as a proportion (%) of sales	4.6	4.6	12.8	12.4	11.5	11.1	14.3	13.4
Meat products:								
Sales or shipments	52.5	53.5	62.6	64.3	74.6	77.3	106.6	113.1
Cost of inputs	30.4	30.4	54.3	55.3	63.1	64.8	77.6	80.3
Value added	22.1	23.1	8.3	9.0	11.5	12.5	29.0	32.8
Fuel cost	2.6	2.6	3.6	3.6	1.0	1.0	6.0	6.0
Cumulative fuel cost as a proportion (%) of sales	5.0	4.9	9.9	9.6	9.7	9.3	12.4	11.7
Poultry products:								
Sales or shipments	48.1	49.0	63.2	65.2	80.6	84.2	107.0	113.8
Cost of inputs	27.9	27.9	50.0	50.9	64.1	66.1	83.6	87.2
Value added	20.2	21.1	13.2	14.3	16.5	18.1	23.4	26.6
Fuel costs	2.4	2.4	3.8	3.8	1.8	1.8	6.0	6.0
Cumulative fuel cost as a proportion (%) of sales	5.0	4.9	9.8	9.5	9.9	9.5	13.1	12.3
Grain mill products:								
Sales or shipments	23.3	23.8	39.7	42.0	56.4	60.9	103.6	115.2
Cost of inputs	13.5	13.5	24.9	25.4	40.6	42.9	56.9	61.4
Value added	9.8	10.3	14.8	16.6	15.8	18.0	46.7	53.8
Fuel cost	1.2	1.2	3.2	3.2	1.8	1.8	1.0	1.0
Cumulative fuel cost as a proportion (%) of sales	5.2	5.0	11.1	10.5	110.0	10.2	7.0	6.2

[a]The estimates deal only with the impact of doubling fuel and energy prices. Alternative A passes the increased cost through the system, while alternative B adds in the increased cost of fuel and maintains the 1977 percentage relationship between cost of inputs and sales. Computations based upon Table 20.5. Sales at retail compare with $1 of retail sales in Table 20.5, the difference shown in the last two columns representing the price increase for each alternative.

then a simple matter to reverse the process, starting with the value of purchased inputs used by farmers to produce that quantity of the commodity (as defined in Table 20.5), and moving forward through the production–marketing complex, observing the sequential impact of a price change.

Assuming no significant change in production processes or in the quantities of fuel used, the expected impact on the price of each food group is fuel prices doubled is illustrated in Table 20.6. This breakdown, using the value that each sector adds to the product (as shown in Table 20.5), starts with the inputs purchased by farmers and works forward through the production–marketing system. If the 1977 cost of fuel is doubled, then the cost of purchased inputs is increased by that amount. This same increase in cost is then assumed to be passed on to the next stage in the system, thus having a cumulative effect on the cost of inputs at each successive stage. Following this procedure, alternative A in Table 20.6 shows that doubling fuel costs would lead to a 7.7% increase in the retail price of dairy products, a 6.6% increase in meat products, 7% for poultry and only 3.6% for grain mill products.

A more likely series of effects is represented by alternative B. Due to mark-up practices and cost changes associated with inventory values, retail prices would probably increase more than the absolute amount of the added fuel cost. If the increased costs were added to the 1977 cost, and existing cost–price relationships (percentage margins) were maintained, then price increases at retail would be greater than the cumulative increase in fuel costs.

Both alternatives A and B represent possible retail prices for the same product which cost consumers $1 in 1977. The prices shown in the last two columns represent possible absolute and percentage increases, which are the differences between the retail prices in Table 20.6 and the 1977 retail sales prices of $1.

The cumulative absolute increase in fuel costs at all stages of production and marketing would be twice as much for poultry products (7.0%) as for grain mill products (3.6%). However, adjusting these increases at each stage by the existing percentage marketing margin would result in a greater price increase for grain mill products (15.2%) than for poultry (13.8%). Surprisingly, the differences in price changes among commodities would not be quite as great under alternative B as they would be if absolute cost increases were simply passed on through the system.

These comparisons emphasize that the price impact of changes in energy prices will vary among foods, depending both on the cost of fuel used and the pricing patterns followed. Differences in pricing practices may outweigh differences in absolute cost increases. This may be especially noticeable for items which are not major production or marketing costs.

This study suggests that the commonly used methods of measuring fuel costs, a percentage of cash sales or expenses, may understate the impact expected on retail prices if the price of fuels and energy were to double. These methods tend to err on the low side for two reasons. First, the practice that considers the cost of fuel used at a given level (production or manufacturing) as a percentage of sales rather than as a proportion of value added at each stage minimizes the significance of the change in cost as a product moves through the system. Secondly, forecasts frequently consider energy cost as an absolute amount to be added to the retail price and neglect to acknowledge possible differences in mark-up practices (percentage mark-ups) employed by marketing firms at all stages of the food system. Considering their interaction, these two factors could result in significantly greater price changes at the retail level. The differences may be sufficient to lead suppliers and customers to alter past response patterns and rates, thereby bringing about additional changes in price and structural relationships of various food industries.

7. REFERENCES AND LITERATURE CONSULTED

Lasley, F.A., 1974. Fuel and the cost of food. J. Northeast. Agric. Econ. Counc., 3(2): 46–55.

Univ. Ill., 1967–1978. *Summary of Illinois Farm Business Records.* Coop. Ext. Serv. Circ., University of Illinois, various issues.

Univ. Minn., 1967–1978. *Vocational Agriculture Farm Analysis Annual Report.* Minnesota Department of Education and Agricultural Education Department, University of Minnesota, various issues.

Univ. Mo., 1981. Farm Manage. Newsl. FM81-1, Missouri Cooperative Extension Service, University of Missouri.

Univ. Wis., 1967–1978. *Wisconsin Farm Business Summary.* Cooperative Extension Service, University of Wisconsin, various issues.

USDA, 1974–1980. *Developments in Farm to Retail Price Spreads for Food Products*. Economic Research Service, U.S. Department of Agriculture, Washington, DC, annual issues.

USDC, 1967–1977a. Census of manufactures. General summary. Bureau of Census, U.S. Department of Commerce, Washington, DC, various issues.

USDC, 1967–1977b. Census of manufactures. Fuels and electric energy consumed. Special Report Series, Bureau of Census, U.S. Department of Commerce, Washington, DC, various issues.

Chapter 21

Food Industry and Rising Fuel Costs

MIKAEL TOGEBY, ERIK MOSEKILDE, KIM PAAMAND and EJVIND PEDERSEN

1. INTRODUCTION

Among members of the International Energy Agency (IEA), Denmark appears to have been the most successful in reducing its total energy demand in response to the rising fuel costs. Since 1972, Denmark's net energy consumption has decreased by about 13% while at the same time the gross national product has increased by approximately 17% in fixed prices. The energy efficiency for the country as a whole may thus be said to have increased by 25% over the last decade.

Private households have contributed significantly to the reduced energy consumption by lowering indoor temperatures, sealing windows and doors, replacing single-glazed windows with double-glazed ones, and insulating ceilings and hollow double-brick walls. To a certain extent, refrigerators, freezers, washing machines, etc., have been replaced by more energy-efficient units to curtail the growth in electricity consumption. Likewise, a significant fraction of the private cars have been renewed, and together with less and more careful driving, enforcement of general speed limits, and better roads, this has led to a stagnation in gasoline consumption.

Industry has also reduced its energy consumption. According to information from the Danish Department of Energy, process energy consumption (excluding electricity) has fallen by 30% during the period 1979–1982. Although part of this reduction may be associated with internal shifts between the various industrial sectors, i.e., with a relative reduction of the output from some of the most energy-intensive sectors, significant energy savings have also been achieved in many individual branches. Slaughterhouses and meat processing factories, for instance, have reduced their gross energy consumption (including electricity) per unit output by more than 40% since 1972, and similar numbers hold for branches such as Manufacture of dairy products and Manufacture of beverages. As a whole the food industry has reduced its energy intensity by about 18% in the period 1970–1980

Purpose of this chapter is: (a) to analyse basic statistical data on energy consumption, production and energy intensity for the major branches of the Danish food industry; (b) through a series of case studies to show how significant energy savings have been achieved during the last decade; (c) through technical–economic analyses to examine the magnitude of energy savings which can be achieved in the future; and by means of a model to project the energy consumption in the food industry with 'official' assumptions about the development in fuel prices and in general economic conditions.

In addition, we present the results of interviews with 28 major energy-consuming companies to clarify among other things the food industry's own valuation of its potential for energy conservation.

Chapter 21 references, p. 353.

Our work on the Danish Production Sector Model (DEMO-PSM) aims at illuminating particularly the long-term response in the food industry to rising fuel costs. The model is adjusted to fit historical data from 1950 to 1980, but the projections of future energy requirements are predominantly based upon technical–economic investigations of the potential for energy conservation in the various sectors. With its 'vintage' approach, the model basically addresses the questions: (a) how long will it take for the industry to renew its production capital and achieve an energy efficiency corresponding to today's fuel prices; (b) how much better can this energy efficiency be expected to be; and (c) how much can be done in the meantime to reduce the energy consumption through retrofitting the existing capital?

Our technical–economic investigations of the potential for energy conservation involve thermodynamic analyses, studies of alternative production methods, comparisons of specific energy consumptions between similar companies, and interviews with industrial energy managers. In almost all cases, a production system constructed in accordance with 1984 fuel prices and today's technology will have a considerably smaller energy consumption per unit output than a more conventional system. However, boilers, cooling machines, ovens, etc., are used for many years, sometimes almost for half a century. On top of this, the investment in new production capital has been unusually small during the last decade. Most of the energy consumption in the Danish food industry is therefore still associated with capital installed in a period when the relative price of energy was one-fifth of its 1984 value. If the fuel prices remain high, one must expect a considerable reduction in the average industrial energy intensity as the present production system is renewed. The same will be the case if falling fuel prices are contracted by increased taxation of energy consumption.

2. STATISTICAL DATA

Denmark is one of the countries which has been most successful in reducing its energy consumption. At the same time, Denmark has a very good statistical service, and its food industry has international recognition. For these reasons, we believe that it can be of general interest both to show the trends in the statistical data and to underline the considerable uncertainties with which such data are associated.

Production of bread, cereals, sugar, butter, cheese, margarine, beer, spirits, animal feed, etc., and preparation of meat, vegetables, fish and other food products at present account for about 25% of the total industrial energy consumption in Denmark. About one-fifth of the gross disposable income is spent on food, beverages and tobacco, and, together with the fact that two-thirds of Danish food production is exported, this makes the food industry a very important factor in Denmark's economy. Meat and milk products constitute 25% of the export to other OECD-countries, and more than 30% of the total Danish export relates to the food industry.

In the last decade, the food industry has experienced a slightly higher rate of growth than the rest of the economy, indicating that food consumption is relatively unaffected by the general economic recession. Due to advances in productivity, employment in the food sector has been slowly decreasing since it peaked in 1966 at about 106 000 people. According to current theories of technological innovation and long-term economic growth (Mensch, 1979; Van Duijn, 1983; Sterman, 1985), a new and lasting economic upswing cannot be expected until the mid- or late 1990's. The upswing has to wait for a significant fraction of the present production capital to depreciate, and for basic new

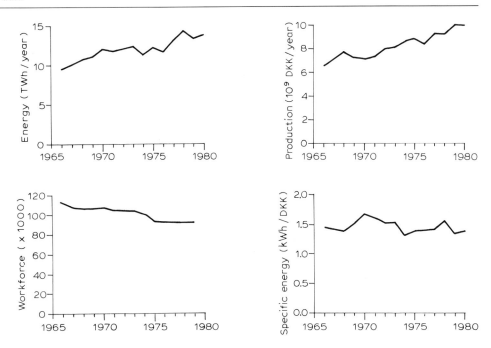

Fig. 21.1. Statistical data for the gross energy consumption, production, workforce, and specific energy consumption for the aggregated food industry. The workforce varies around 100 000 people, the specific energy consumption is about 1.5 kWh/DKK.
DKK, Danish Crown: 1 1975-DKK equals approximately 0.25 1984-US$.

industries to grow up and acquire sufficient economic weight to create jobs for those laid-off by the old industries. When such an upswing sets in, the technologies of the 1950's and 60's will be completely outdated, and basically new production methods will be adopted. Food production in general is expected to remain a low growth area, although the newly developed biotechiques promise a rapid expansion of particular branches of the sector. Altogether, we expect the food industry to have a more smooth development than the economy as a whole.

Figure 21.1 shows historical data for the development in gross energy consumption, gross factor product, labor force and specific energy consumption for the aggregated Danish food industry. The gross factor product is taken here as a measure of sector production. It is obtained as the sector output minus raw material input, both in fixed prices. The specific energy consumption is defined as the *gross* energy consumption per unit factor product, i.e., central conversion losses associated with the production of electricity have been included. It should also be mentioned that the present data, which originate in the National Accounts Statistics, include all production units in the sector. In contrast, the Industrial Statistics only include companies with more than 20 employees. With the industrial structure of Denmark, the difference between these two sets of statistics can be quite significant.

The aggregated data for the food sector show a smoothly growing production and a slowly falling labor force. The gross energy consumption shows a dip immediately after the first oil crisis in 1973, and a partial 'recovery' 3–4 years later as workers, engineers, etc., forget the shock associated with the sudden increase in fuel prices. A new dip then follows after the second oil crisis in 1979. This development illustrates particularly the short-term response to the rising oil prices. In addition, there is a medium-term response which is associated with retrofitting of existing capital, and a long-term response associated with total renewal of the production capital.

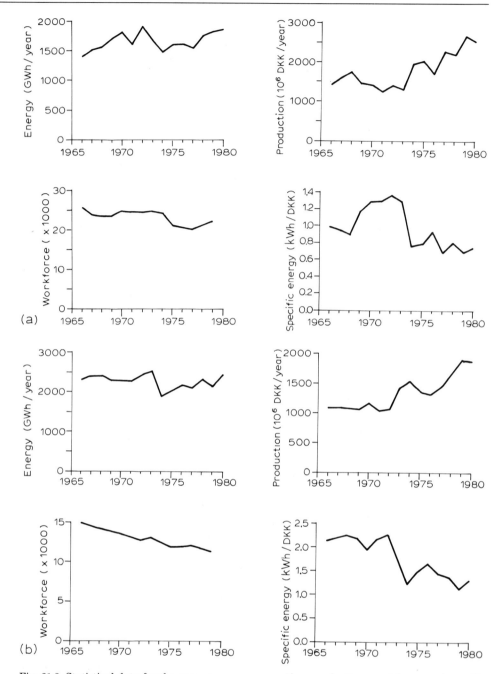

Fig. 21.2. Statistical data for the gross energy consumption, production, workforce, and specific energy consumption.
(a) Slaughtering and meat processing.
(b) Manufacture of dairy products.
(c) Food manufacturing excluding meat and milk products.
(d) Manufacture of beverages.

With an average value of about 1.5 kWh/1975-DKK (approximately 20 MJ/1984-US$), the specific energy consumption shows a slight downward trend throughout the 1970's. Based upon available data for the industry's expenditures on fuel and power and the respective prices for these types of energy, it appears that the *net* energy consumption per unit factor product has decreased from about 1.75 kWh/1975-DKK in 1950 to 1.17 kWh/1975-DKK in 1980, or approximately by 1.3% per year.

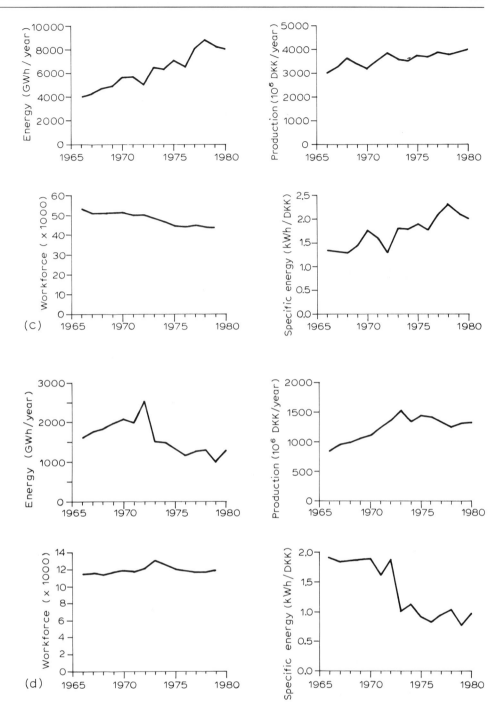

The decrease in energy consumption per unit factor product must be considered to be the combined result of: a general technological development which has introduced more and more efficient production methods; deliberate energy conserving measures; and shifts within the industry between branches of different energy intensity. To illuminate particularly the last of these points, we have considered the development in each of the five main branches in the sector: Slaughtering and meat processing, Manufacture of dairy products, Food manufacturing excluding meat and milk products, Manufacture of beverages, and Tobacco manufacturing. Table 21.1 gives the respective values for the average rates of economic growth during the period 1968–1979. Data for the gross factor product and the specific energy consumption (both in 1980) are

Chapter 21 references, p. 353.

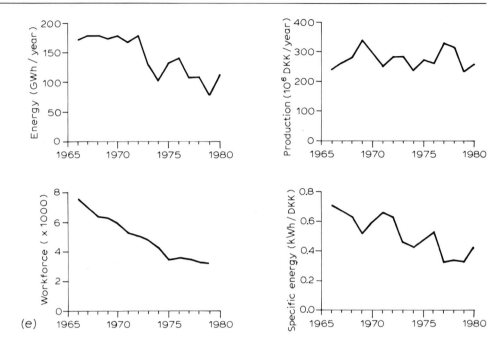

(e) Statistical data for the gross energy consumption, production, workforce, and specific energy consumption in the tobacco manufacturing.

TABLE 21.1

Overview of the five main branches in the food industry

	Gross factor product 1980 (10^6 1975-DKK)	Specific energy consumption (kWh/DKK)	Average growth rate (%/year)
Slaughtering and meat processing	2600	0.74	4.2
Manufacture of dairy products	1880	1.31	5.3
Other food manufacturing	4000	2.01	0.9
Manufacture of beverages	1330	0.97	2.3
Tobacco manufacturing	260	0.43	− 1.2

also presented. Figure 21.2 illustrates the development for each of the five branches in more detail.

We observe that most of the branches have reduced their specific energy consumption significantly after the first oil crisis in 1973. For Manufacturing of dairy products, for instance, the specific energy consumption has fallen from about 2.2 kWh/1975-DKK in 1972 to 1.3 kWh/1975-DKK in 1980. In several cases, even the gross energy consumption has decreased between 1972 and 1980. An exception to this development is Food manufacturing excluding meat and milk products for which the specific energy consumption has continued to increase. This branch includes fruit and vegetable processing industries which relative to their gross factor products have experienced a considerable increase in energy consumption (more than a factor of 3). Food manufacturing excluding meat and milk products also includes the growing and relatively energy-intensive animal feeds industries.

To obtain a more detailed understanding, we have tried to analyse data on the level of individual types of industries. For the food industry, the National Accounts Statistics operate with 21 such sub-branches. However, in spite of the

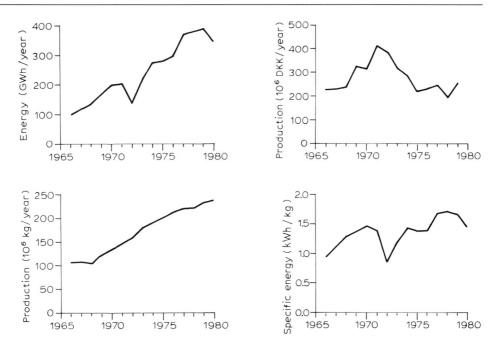

Fig. 21.3. Statistical data for the gross energy consumption, production (upper right measured as gross factor income and lower left in physical units) and specific energy consumption in the fruit and vegetable preparing industries. In this figure the specific energy consumption is based on the physical production volume. The energy consumption shows an unexplainable dip in 1972.

care with which the statistical data have been collected and checked, at this level they often show unrealistic variations, Fig. 21.3 gives an example of this. For fruit and vegetable preparation industries, the energy consumption in 1972 as obtained from the official statistics shows an unexplainable 30% dip relative to the consumptions in 1971 and 1973, and this dip is reproduced in the variation of the specific energy consumption.[1] Figure 21.2d shows that the specific energy consumption for breweries and other beverage manufacturing industries should have fallen by almost 50% from 1972 to 1973. Confronted with these curves, energy managers from major Danish breweries have expressed their strong disbelief. They do not know of any event or measure which could explain such a development. Figure 21.3 also illustrates the difficulties encountered when trying to use the gross factor product as measure of production volume. The top right curve gives the development of the gross factor income in fixed prices, while the lower left curve gives the development in physical production volume, i.e., in kg. The two curves show a very different variation, and in fact only the development in energy consumption per kg produced makes sense. Unfortunately a similar physical measure of the production volume cannot be defined on a more aggregate level.

We conclude that even with the quality of energy data available in Denmark, a forecast or an analysis based solely upon official time series can give quite misleading results. The data of the National Accounts Statistics are constructed on information from individual companies. Even if this information were always accurate, the raw data are aggregated, adjusted and renormalized in various ways, and these procedures involve several uncertain assumptions. Many companies, of course, produce their own time series for the relevant data, and we have therefore collected examples thereof, so as to obtain a better understanding of the factors which influence the development in specific energy consumption.

---

[1] Note added in proof, p. 354.

Chapter 21 references, p. 353.

Due to the time lags involved, aggregate statistical data do not yet provide information on the true long-term response to the fuel price increases in the 1970's. To assess this response, which is associated with a renewal of the industry's production capital, we have investigated the age structure of the present production capital, compared energy efficiencies between today's average production capital and the most modern units, analysed alternative production methods, and performed thermodynamic studies of limiting energy efficiencies. Kraemer et al. (1983) give the results of a similar analysis for the building materials industry. As discussed in Section 3, we have also interviewed industrial energy managers to learn their valuation of the potential for energy conservation.

3. INTERVIEWS WITH INDUSTRIAL ENERGY MANAGERS

With the purpose, primarily, of illuminating the industry's potential for supplying surplus (or waste) heat for residential heating, The Danish Boiler Owners' Association has carried out about 160 interviews with energy managers from major energy-consuming companies. Twenty-eight of the first 60 of these interviews relate to the food industry, and some of these results are reported below.

First, however, it may be of interest to note that district heating plays a very significant role in Denmark. At present about 40% of the total residential heating requirements are met in this way, and the percentage is planned to increase to about 50% within the next 10–20 years. One-third of the district heating is at present provided as waste heat from central power stations, and this fraction is expected to increase to about two-thirds.

On a national basis, only a very limited fraction of the residential heating requirements are met with industrial surplus heat. For certain towns, however, this type of heat supply is predominant. A fertilizer factory, for instance, delivers about 1200 TJ/year from its sulfuric acid production, and a steel-works delivers about 100 TJ/year from its cooling water. Altogether almost 30 projects of this type have been realized, although those mentioned above are the largest.

In the interviews, each company was asked to provide information about:

(1) Its annual use of fuel and electricity. In general only companies with an energy consumption of more than 40 TJ/year were visited.

(2) The development of the production and energy consumption over the last few years, and the potential for substitution between various types of energy.

(3) The types of energy conserving measures instituted since 1973, the results thereof, and the potential for further reductions in the specific energy consumption.

(4) The amounts of surplus heat available at different temperatures considering flue gas, exhaust steam, and ventilation air from drying chambers, as well as cooling and waste water.

(5) The age distribution of the production machinery, plans for expansion, and the potential energy efficiency of a completely new production line.

Each interview usually took 2–3 h and often included a tour of the production site. Not all companies gave complete answers to all the questions. Particularly questions about the future development in production volume were often left unanswered, partly because of the uncertainty which characterizes our present economic situation, and partly because it was not the business of the energy manager. In this connection it should be noted that the term 'energy manager' covers everything from chief production engineer to boilerman, depending on the size and the type of company.

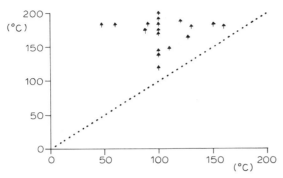

Fig. 21.4. Boiler temperature vs. highest process temperature for 19 companies in the food industry.

Including already established projects, but *excluding* cities and towns which are, or according to official plans will be, supplied with waste heat from central power stations, the Danish industry can deliver about 3.5 PJ/year at temperatures directly applicable in district heating systems (i.e., above 55°C). This corresponds to about 2% of the total industrial energy consumption. With the use of heat pumps, additional 6.5 PJ/year can become available. Most of this last contribution occurs at relatively high temperatures, so that the COP-factors for the heat pumps will be 4 or better. In many cases, the usage times for the heat pumps will be relatively short (1000–2000 h/year). Nevertheless, preliminary estimates show that at least half of the possible projects are economically feasible at present fuel prices.

Of the 28 companies interviewed in the food industry, five were slaughter houses and meat processing factories, six were bread and biscuit factories, and four were breweries. Except for three firms with gas ovens, all of the companies had steam systems, even though the highest process temperatures in many cases were at, or below, 100°C. Figure 21.4 shows the relationship between the highest process temperature and the boiler temperature for the 19 companies which provided both pieces of information. In some cases, steam at 180°C is produced to provide heat at 50°C. Under these conditions, one would expect other solutions to be considerably more efficient. For slaughter houses, for instance, hot water for scalding and cleaning can be produced with heat reclaimed from freezing machines and singe ovens. According to our estimates, the steam system can actually be avoided altogether. In other cases, hot-water systems will be appropriate because they have lower transmission and re-evaporation losses.

Figure 21.5 shows the age distribution of boilers for the 17 companies which provided information about the year of installation. This figure also shows the relationship between boiler efficiency and year of installation for the six companies which provided both of these numbers. Most boilers in the food industry are low pressure, oil-fired units installed after World War II. One can also find Cornish, built-in units and other types of boilers from the 1930's, and it has been customary that particularly breweries and sugar factories produced their own electricity by cogeneration. The upper curve indicates a significant increase in boiler efficiency over the last 30 years.

During the interview, the companies were also asked to give information about energy conserving measures that they had instituted since the first oil crisis, as well as about measures under present consideration. Figure 21.6 shows the distribution of answers over different types of measures with the cross-hatched parts of the columns indicating the number of companies in which a particular measure had already been made. The remaining parts of the columns indicate the number of companies where the measure was under consideration. Only provisions which require investments outside the range of usual operational costs are included.

Chapter 21 references, p. 353.

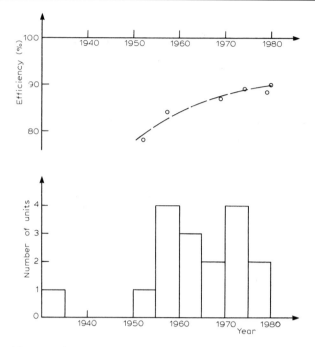

Fig. 21.5. Age distribution of boilers in 17 companies from the food industry. Also shown is the relationship between boiler efficiency and year of installation. Several of the boilers installed since 1973 have replaced units with efficiencies as low as 60–65%.

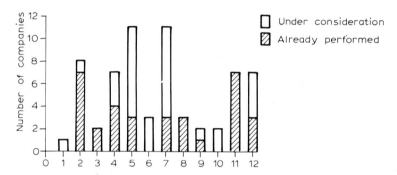

Fig. 21.6. Distribution of energy conserving measures (performed, or under consideration) over twelve different categories: (1) cogeneration of steam and electricity, (2) insulation of buildings, (3) insulation of hot process equipment, (4) renewal of boilers, (5) re-use of process heat, (6) installation of economizers, (7) reclamation of heat from cooling machines, (8) reclamation of heat from air-compressors, (9) other forms of heat recovery, (10) installation of heat pumps, (11) adjustment of production processes, and (12) renewal of machinery and process equipment.

We concluded from this investigation that the food industry is continuing the second phase of its adjustment to the increased fuel prices: the improvement of the existing production capital through energy conserving investments.

In the following sections we shall analyse the development in energy consumption per unit volume of production for selected companies in more detail, and we shall also discuss the potential for further energy conservation in particular processes such as blanching.

4. PRESERVED-FOOD FACTORY

As our first example we shall consider the energy consumption for a preserved-food factory. This plant produces frozen and canned vegetables

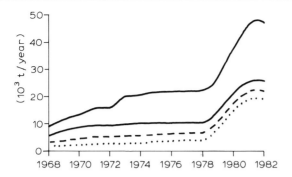

Fig. 21.7. Development in production volumes for the considered preserved food factory. From the bottom up, the various products are: frozen vegetables, marmalade, canned products and wine.

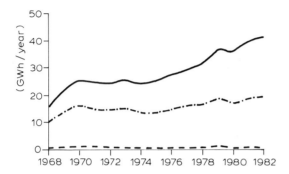

Fig. 21.8. Development in the components of gross energy consumption for the considered preserved food factory. From the bottom up, gas oil, fuel oil and electricity.

(peas, carrots, red cabbage, broccoli and spinach), various fruit products such as marmalade and stewed fruit, and wine. There is also a small production of aromatic agents. Figure 21.7 illustrates the volumes of production for each of these commodities since 1968. The production mix has shifted somewhat over the years. In particular the production of wine increased significantly both in 1973 and in 1980, while the production of frozen vegetables multiplied by almost a factor of 4 between 1978 and 1980 when an export of frozen peas to Italy was initiated. Changing tax rules in connection with Denmark's association with the European Common Market in 1973 partly explain the enhanced wine production. In total, the production has increased by a factor of 4.7 since 1968, and the yearly output is now 22 million litres of wine, 19 000 t of frozen vegetables, and 7000 t of other fruit and vegetables products.

The rising production volume has led to a steadily increasing gross energy consumption. This is shown in Fig. 21.8. Blanching and freezing of vegetables are the two most energy-intensive processes, and with frozen products playing a more significant role, electricity covers a growing fraction of the total energy consumption. Other major energy-consuming processes are pasteurizing of wine, retorting of cans, steam peeling of carrots and cleaning of returnable bottles.

The energy consumption per unit of output depends upon: (a) changes in the plant's product mix, for instance towards a larger fraction of products which require electricity for freezing; (b) changes in the utilization of the existing equipment so as to reduce for instance the significance of fixed (production-independent) contributions to the total energy consumption; and (c) energy conserving measures and changes in technology.

It is not possible to distribute the plant's energy consumption in detail over the various products. As a rule of thumb, however, wine production per unit

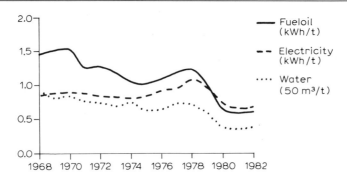

Fig. 21.9. Development in the consumption of fuel oil, electricity and water per t of preserved food products for the considered preserved food plant.

weight requires about one quarter of the energy needed for the other products. When calculating the energy consumption per unit of output we have therefore equated 4 l of wine with 1 kg of the company's other products.

With this attempt to correct for shifts in product mix between wine and other products, Fig. 21.9 shows the consumption of oil, electricity and water per t of output over the last 14 years. Since 1968, the use of oil has decreased from about 150 to 60 l/t, while at the same time electricity consumption has fallen from 280 to 220 kWh/t, and water consumption from 47 to 20 m³/t.

It is an interesting feature that the consumptions of fuel oil and of water have changed almost in parallel. We believe that this is a rather general result which illustrates the significance of adopting a broader view on the energy conservation possibilities. Many food processing factories handle extraordinary amounts of water, and to the extent that the use of water can be cut down, the energy required to heat, evaporate, cool and pump this water will also be reduced.

In 1975, the factory introduced returnable wine bottles, and the requirements for bottle washing led to increases in both water and oil consumption per unit output between 1975 and 1979. In 1978 the steam consumption for pea blanching was measured to be 240 kWh/t. Three years later, after the installation of a new blancher in 1980, the steam consumption had fallen to 96 kWh/t, or about 40% of its 1978 value. Equating 4 l of wine with 1 kg of the plant's other products, 60% of the total production in 1980 passed the blanching process. Installation of the new blancher has thus reduced the aggregate oil consumption per unit output by $0.6(240 - 96)$ kWh/t ≈ 86 kWh/t.

In 1978, the factory installed a new pasteurizer. It appears, that this has given an energy conservation of 30% or approximately 260 kWh/t, and pasteurizing hereafter requires about 600 kWh/t. At the time of installation, 20% of the aggregate production was pasteurized, and the replacement thus caused a 0.20×260 kWh/t $= 52$ kWh/t reduction in specific energy consumption. In 1982, the fraction of products being pasteurized had fallen to 9%, causing a further reduction in specific energy consumption of $(0.20 - 0.09) \times 600$ kWh/t ≈ 66 kWh/t.

In 1979, new boilers were installed. The year before the thermal efficiency of the old boilers had been measured to be 87, 82 and 78%, respectively. The new boilers have efficiencies in the range 90–92%, and replacement of boilers has thus caused a reduction in oil consumption per unit output of about 8% or 120 kWh/t. In spite of increasing production, the heated buildings area (mainly the administration building) has not been expanded. Distributing the energy consumption for space heating over a larger production volume explains a reduction in specific oil consumption by 50 kWh/t between 1978 and 1982.

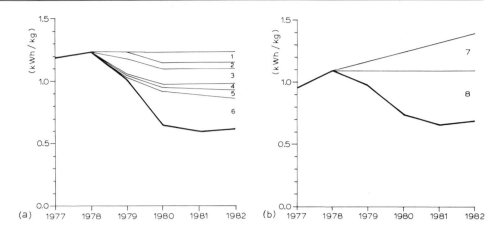

Fig. 21.10. Reductions in oil and electricity consumption per unit output for a conserved food factory as explained in terms of their various causes.
(a) For the specific oil consumption: (1) a new blancher, (2) a new pasteurizer, (3) new boilers, (4) a reduction in the relative significance of pasteurizing, (5) a distribution of space heating requirements over a larger production, (6) other causes, including effects of an improved usage of the production equipment.
(b) For the specific consumption of electricity: (7) an increase due to a larger fraction of frozen products is masked by the distribution of electricity for lighting over a larger production, (8) other causes, including effects of an improved usage of freezers, etc.

In Fig. 21.10a we have sketched the estimated significance of these various changes in comparison with the actual changes in specific oil consumption from 1978 to 1982. It appears that we have accounted for about two-thirds of the observed fall in oil consumption per unit output, and that a fall of approximately 200 kWh/t remains to be explained. We assume that this fall is due to the reduced significance of various idle losses as the factory's production has increased. Measurements performed by the company have indicated, for instance, that oil consumption for blanching can be expressed approximately as

$$E = a + bP$$

where $a = 160$ kW and $b = 75$ kWh/t are constants which characterize the existing equipment, and P is the rate of production in t/h. Increasing P from 3 to 7 t/h thus reduces the specific energy consumption in the process from 128 to about 98 kWh/t – a reduction of 25%.

Figure 21.10b attempts to analyse the specific consumption of electricity in a similar manner. Taken alone, the shift towards producing a larger fraction of frozen vegetables should have increased the aggregate electricity consumption per unit output by approximately 300 kWh/t between 1978 and 1982. Instead, the consumption has decreased by about 400 kWh/t. Distributing the electricity consumption for lighting, etc., over a larger production volume explains a fall of about 300 kWh/t, and a fall of 400 kWh/t thus remains to be explained. Part of it can be ascribed to a reduction in the requirements for pumping and other forms of mechanical work by virtue of the reduced specific water consumption, but the majority must presumably be ascribed to improved utilization of freezers, etc., as a consequence of the increase in annual production.

To conclude this discussion of preserved-food factories: we have shown how the significant decrease in gross energy consumption per unit output can be decomposed into a number of effects including an improved energy utilization as a result of increasing production, replacement of production equipment such as boilers, blanchers and pasteurizers with more energy-efficient units, and changes in product mix and production processes.

Chapter 21 references, p. 353.

Additional possibilities for energy conservation are associated with a replacement of the present (5 years old) screw conveyor blancher with a newly developed integrated blancher/cooler (see Section 6). Such a replacement would reduce the energy consumption in the blanching process from 96 to 46 kWh/t. Blancher and freezer could also be integrated, so that heat from the condensor of the freezing machines was used to preheat water for blanching. Exhaust vapor from the carrot steam peeler is at present let into the open air. Heat recovery from this vapor or re-introduction of mechanical peeling could reduce the energy consumption in the peeling process, etc.

5. OTHER COMPANIES IN THE FOOD INDUSTRY

The allotted space does not allow us to review the developments in other companies in similar detail. We would like, however, to use this section to illustrate additional aspects of the way in which the food industry has responded to rising fuel costs.

5.1. Brewery

We are considering a relatively old brewery with an annual production of beer of about 900 000 hl. During the last 10–15 years, the company has experienced a considerable success in connection with the introduction of new types of beverage products, and as a result part of the production system has been renewed. In particular the mineral water factory and the bottling station are new, while on the other hand the brewing kettle is quite old. Also the central boilers and the heat distribution system, which is based on pressurized hot water, have recently been modernized.

In 1980 the company performed an analysis of its energy flows in order to find possibilities for reducing the energy consumption. Some of the main results of this analysis are presented in Table 21.2. Electricity consumption is measured here as net energy, i.e., distribution and central conversion losses are not included. Of the heat produced, 38% went to the brewing kettle, about 40% was used to heat process water (for cleaning of returnable bottles, beerboxes, etc.), and 18% was used for space heating. Estimates of heat losses from the buildings showed that 70–80% was due to ventilation. A dominant fraction of the electricity went to pumps and to cooling and air compressors.

TABLE 21.2

Components of energy consumption in a brewery

	Heat (%)	Electricity (%)
Brewing house	50	18.2
Bottling station	32	18.7
Space heating	18	
Cooling machines		24.5
Boiler central		5.5
Ventilation		5.6
Lighting		18.4
Pressurized air, CO_2-system, etc.		19.1
1980 total (TJ)	154	37

In 1981, two-speed motors were installed on the main pumps, the evaporation temperature on the cooling machines was increased by 2°C, and a system for recovering heat from waste water was built. With a total investment of DKK-1.5 million (approximately US$150 000) and a repayment time of 1.5–2 years, this lead to 9 and 6% reductions in the consumption of heat and electricity, respectively. In 1982 the boilers were modernized with the introduction of oxygen control on the burners and of frequency converters on the combustion air blowers. However, the energy conserving results were masked by the simultaneous introduction of a new type of light beer which requires relatively more energy.

With a traditional brewing kettle, as used in this plant, wort is boiled for 1.5–2 h at atmospheric pressure. During this period about 8% of the water evaporates, and the vapor produced is let out into the open air. It is relatively simple to mount a heat exchanger to recover the evaporation heat and use it for space heating, for instance, or to heat process water. In the present case, this solution has not been found to be practicable, as the heat distribution system operates with water at temperatures above 100°C. Neither has it been possible, at least so far, to arrange for surplus heat to be sold to external customers.

To avoid foaming, the conventional wort kettle usually operates with a significant through-flow of air. Besides the additional energy losses associated with heating the fresh air, this reduces the dew point of the vapor produced, and as a consequence heat recovery seldom produces water at temperatures higher than 80°C.

Alternatives to classic open boiling are low and high pressure wort boiling. Huppmann (1981), for instance, offers a low pressure system in which the boiling takes place at 110°C in a pressurized kettle connected to a preheater and a vapor heat-recovery unit. The higher boiling temperature speeds up the chemical reactions, and as a consequence the holding time in the kettle can be reduced to 30–40 min. During this period there is a primary evaporation of about 1.2%. The pressure is thereafter released, and during a 15 min boiling at 100°C, a secondary evaporation of about 1.8% takes place. The total evaporation thus amounts to about 3%. Without infiltration of air, the vapor dew point is raised, and recovery of evaporation heat can usually occur at temperatures above 90°C. The brewery estimates that its net energy consumption for wort boiling could be reduced by 40% if such a system was installed.

On the other hand, Alfa Laval offers a compact, continuous high temperature wort boiling system which promises to cut steam consumption to about one-third as compared to the traditional kettle. This is obtained through efficient recycling of heat. The wort is preheated to 115°C in a two-stage regenerative heat exchanger and thereafter heated to 140°C with primary steam. The wort then circulates in a tubular holding cell for approximately 5 min before it passes through a two-stage pressure-release system in which boil-off takes place at 120 and 100°C, respectively. This vapor is recycled and used to preheat the incoming wort. With such a system, this brewery could reduce its energy consumption in the wort boiling process from 8.4 to 3.7 kWh/hl.

The three types of wort boiling systems: the open kettle, the low-pressure kettle, and the integrated high-temperature system, are rather different with respect to parameters such as boil-off, primary energy requirements, internal and external heat recovery, and temperatures of externally recovered heat. To provide basis for a comparison, Table 21.3 gives the total boil-off and the typical primary energy supply per hl for each of the three systems. We have also specified average energy and exergy losses for the systems both with heat recovery in 4 months per year and with heat recovery in 12 months per year. The first option is of interest if the recovered heat is used for space heating.

TABLE 21.3

Comparison between three wort boiling systems

Boil-off		Primary energy supply (kWh/hl)	Energy losses with heat recovery (kWh/hl)		Exergy losses with heat recovery (kWh/hl)	
	(%)		4 m/year	12 m/year	4 m/year	12 m/year
(1)	8	8.4	4.0	1.5	2.9	2.8
(2)	3	5.7	1.4	0.2	1.7	1.5
(3)	8	3.7	0.5	0.5	1.2	1.2

(1) open kettle
(2) low-pressure kettle
(3) continuous, high-temperature system.

The specific exergy losses can be considered a thermodynamic measure of the efficiency of the systems. With exergy losses less than half of those for the open kettle, the continuous high temperature system is clearly the most efficient.

Besides, with a new kettle, a modern brewery would also be equipped with provisions for heat recovery from the ventilation air. Remaining needs for space heating could thereafter, to a large extent, be met by heat pumps installed in conjunction with the cooling machines.

The above discussion exemplifies the very significant energy conservation possibilities in a conventional brewery. It also shows, that these possibilities are largely associated with a renewal of plant equipment and a change of production methods. This is clearly a very slow process. Kettles, boilers and heat distribution systems have very long life times and brewing methods do not change rapidly, even if increasing fuel costs should indicate the adoption of new techniques. The risks involved, if the taste of the beer should change in a direction not appreciated by the customers, are considered to be too large. In the long run, however, change in technology is almost certain to cause a very significant reduction in specific energy consumption.

5.2. Fish meal factory

Fish meal is used as an animal feed. It is produced from fishes which, because of their size, or for other reasons, are unsuitable for human consumption. Associated with the production of meal is a production of fish oil which can be used for instance for margarine. Figure 21.11 shows the product flow in a fish meal factory. Major processes involved in the separation of meal, oil and water are boiling, screw-pressing, decanting, centrifuging, evaporation and drying.

A satisfactory product quality in terms of a good nutrient value depends upon specific process conditions. The drying temperature should not be too high, for instance. Where direct firing is applied, fresh air is therefore often mixed into the drying air. Similarly, to prevent protein decomposition, the screw-pressing must be stopped at a rather early stage, and more energy requiring thermal processes used for further dewatering of the press cake. It is important that such process requirements are observed when energy conserving measures are suggested. On the other hand, the dramatic changes in fuel costs which have taken place since 1972 will slowly open the way for a change in traditions and for the introduction of completely new process combinations.

For the fish meal factory under consideration energy costs at present amount to about 40% of the total production costs excluding costs of raw fish. Fuel and electricity account for about 80 and 20%, respectively, of total energy

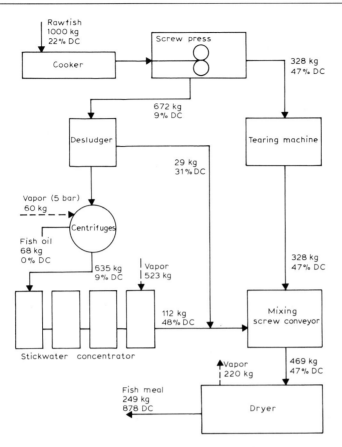

Fig. 21.11. Product flow in a fish meal factory. DC, dry matter content.

costs. Distributed over the main processes the fuel consumption per mass of fish produced is:

	(kWh/t)
Boiling	134
Evaporation	167
Drying	279
Other processes	33
Total	614

There are two major sources of surplus heat in the factory: the vacuum steam exiting from the evaporator, and the exhaust air from the drying oven. The vacuum steam has a temperature of 40–60°C. It has been attempted to raise the temperature level in the evaporator to obtain an exit steam pressure of 2–3 bar. This would allow the steam to be applied for boiling raw fish. Technically, this approach was quite feasible. However, when a production is started up, the boiler has to be in operation several hours before steam from the evaporator is available. This experiment in energy cascading was therefore given up by the factory. As it turned out, the elevated evaporation temperatures also caused a reduction in the nutrient value of the product.

The use of vacuum steam for preheating raw fish in periods where the steam is available is still being considered. This is expected to cut energy consumption in the boiling process from 134 to about 70 kWh per t of fish.

Chapter 21 references, p. 353.

With respect to the exhaust air from the drying oven the problem is that although the temperature is 100°C or more, the dew point is only about 87°C. To raise the dew point and increase the applicability of the heat for boiling or preheating of raw fish, inlets of false air must be reduced. It is also possible that the heat in the exhaust air from the oven could be used to drive the evaporator. A customary evaporator operates between 165°C in the first stage and 40–50°C in the last stage. If a flash evaporator is used, the temperature fall per stage can be reduced to 13–15°C, and a three-stage system can thus be operated between the exhaust air temperature of 80–90°C from the drying process and a vacuum steam temperature of 40–50°C.

Together with the energy conservation obtained through improved boiler efficiency, insulation of steam tubes, insertion of steam recompressors, recirculation of clean condensate, and operational optimization of the decanter, it is estimated that heat recovery from the drying oven can reduce the company's specific fuel consumption from 614 to less than 380 kWh/t. As an alternative to an internal use of recovered heat, the company has also considered supplying district heat to a nearby town. This would require installation of heat exchangers and a transmission line, but the evaporator would not have to be renewed. The company has also considered cogeneration of electricity and steam.

The conclusion of this discussion is that even with such a 'simple' product as fish meal there are so many combinations of processes and techniques to consider, that it is difficult for the individual relatively small company to evaluate all of them and actually to optimize its energy consumption. Instead, the company often chooses to wait for other companies to report their results with new techniques. This is a kind of stalemat in technology which can cause a considerable delay in the response of the food industry to rising fuel costs.

6. BLANCHING

To illuminate the potential for energy conservation in the food industry further, we have investigated a number of unit operations such as (pea) blanching, (wort) boiling, (fish meal) drying, and evaporation. Here, we shall consider the main results of an analysis of pea blanching with a newly developed integrated blancher/cooler (Cabinplant, 1981).

Blanching is often one of the single most energy-consuming processes in the preparation of frozen and canned vegetables. Carrots, peas, broccoli, cauliflower, green beans and spinach are usually treated by this process, i.e., they are heated in steam or water for a few minutes and thereafter rapidly cooled. Peas, for instance, are blanched for 2–5 min at temperatures of the order of 90°C.

The purpose of the operation, and the process temperature and holding period may vary somewhat with the product as well as with the subsequent conservation treatment (freezing or retorting). For peas to be frozen, the purposes are typically: (a) To destroy enzymes which could cause unwanted changes in the colour, taste or vitamin content of the final product; (b) To reduce or adjust preparation times in the private households, and to avoid development of bitter agents when the peas are heated for serving; (c) To remove air contained in the plant material and thereby reduce the significance of oxidation processes during cold storage; and (d) To improve the microbiotic condition of the product.

Blanching causes a wash out of sugar and nutrients, vitamin losses, and changes of product consistency. If the process is performed at higher temperatures or for longer periods than necessary, these effects can deteriorate the quality of the product.

Chhinnan et al. (1980) have performed a detailed analysis of energy utilization in spinach processing. According to their account, the typical blanching process requires a specific energy consumption of 1.48 MJ per kg of spinach. As a basis for suggesting energy conserving modifications, Rumsey et al. (1981) have measured the specific energy consumption for a tubular water blancher and compared it with that of a water blancher with a screw-conveyor. The former was found to require 0.54 MJ per kg of spinach and the latter 0.91 MJ/kg, indicating the significance of complete steam condensation (for more details see Chapter 13).

In order to identify design characteristics of particular significance for the energy consumption, Scott et al. (1981) have monitored several steam blanchers. A steam blancher without end seals was found to have a specific energy consumption of 2.12 MJ per kg of product. With water curtains to reduce the leak of live steam through the blancher ends, the specific energy consumption was reduced to 1.56 MJ per kg of product, while the specific energy consumption for a steam blancher with hydrostatic water seals was measured to be 0.95 MJ/kg. In the first and third cases, spinach was treated, and the blanching temperatures were 71 and 65°C, respectively. In the second case, the product was green beans with a blanching temperature of 78°C.

The specific energy consumptions were (rather arbitrarily) compared with the heat required to raise the product temperature by $\Delta T = 72°C$ (Bomben, 1977), and in this way a set of thermal energy efficiencies was defined. These efficiencies ranged from 13% with no end seals to 27% with hydrostatic water seals. It should be borne in mind, however, that thermodynamics allow the process to be performed with thermal efficiencies well beyond 100% if heat recovered from the cooling stage is recycled and used to preheat the product. Significant as the thermal efficiency measure may be as a bench mark for practical improvements, from a thermodynamic point of view it has little meaning.

To improve conventional water blanchers one can replace the direct steam injection with indirect heating. With the former construction a significant fraction of the injected steam usually escapes from the blanching water without condensing. With an intermediate heat exchanger, however, the loss of steam can be reduced significantly, and the condensate can be returned to the boiler. In this way one can obtain thermal efficiencies of the order of 70–90%.

An energetically better solution, however, is the recently developed integrated blancher/cooler (Cabinplant, 1981). In this system, water and products pass in multiple stages counterflow arrangements both in the heating and in the cooling zones of the blancher, and heat recovered from the cooling zone is used to heat incoming products. The thermal efficiency of this system has been measured to be 170%. At the same time, the system gives: a reduction of the consumption of fresh water by a factor of 15–20 as compared with conventional systems; a significant reduction in washed out nutrients as measured by the chemical oxygen demand of the waste water; and an improvement of the indoor environment because of a reduced noise level and virtually no steam leak out.

Compared with the typical steam blancher analysed by Chhinnan et al. (1980), the integrated system gives a reduction in specific energy consumption by a factor of 8.5. To this we must add the significant advantages of a lower environmental impact due to the reduced amount of waste water. The more gradual heating and cooling, required to reduce the energy consumption, presumably causes certain changes in the taste and consistency of the product.

The concepts of entropy production and exergy losses are the appropriate tools for evaluating the thermodynamic efficiency of a blancher. Exergy is a measure of the thermodynamic value of energy, i.e., of its potential for producing mechanical work. The finite time available for the blanching process

Chapter 21 references, p. 353.

imposes a lower limit on the required temperature gradients to drive the heat from the surface to the center of the product. Heat flow in finite temperature gradients is an irreversible process which causes entropy production. The physical dimensions of the product, its heat capacity and thermal conductivity, the surface heat transfer coefficient, and the available process time together thus define a minimum exergy loss attainable in the process. This loss of exergy again determines the minimal fuel requirements in the process.

The total loss of exergy in a blanching process (ΔEx_{tot}) can be divided into losses associated with heat flows into and through the product (ΔEx_{prod}), and losses associated with other irreversible processes (ΔEx_{aux}) in the blancher, i.e., mixing of water of different temperatures, temperature losses in heat exchangers, and heat losses to the surroundings. As discussed above we can define a minimum exergy loss (ΔEx_{min}) which depends upon the rate at which the process takes place. As a measure of this rate we shall use the heating time, i.e., the time allowed for the temperature in the center of the product to rise to the blanching temperature. Using pea blanching as an example we shall take the initial product temperature to be 18°C, and the blanching temperature to be 89°C.

ΔEx_{min} is the minimal exergy loss which can be obtained with any process with the specified heating time. An approximation to a process with minimal exergy losses could be a water blanching where the water is maintained at a constant over-temperature relative to the pea surface, provided this over-temperature is adjusted to give the allowed heating time.

We have simulated pea blanching by means of a mathematical model in which the individual pea is described as a sphere with six concentric shells. The loss of exergy by transfer of heat from one temperature T_1 to a lower temperature T_2 is calculated as:

$$\Delta Ex = \Delta S T_0 = \Delta Q(1/T_2 - 1/T_1)T_0$$

where ΔS is the corresponding entropy production, ΔQ is the transferred heat, and T_0 is a reference temperature. We have assumed that $T_0 = 283$ K ($= 10$°C). The total contribution to ΔEx_{prod} in the blanching process is hereinafter given by the above expression for ΔEx summed over the six shells, and integrated over the course of the process.

The simulation model is constructed so that arbitrary process routes can be defined, and the temperature profile as well as the flows of energy and exergy are continuously calculated. Figure 21.12 shows the developments in the temperatures (left) and in the rates of entropy production (right) for four different blanching processes:

(1) Blanching in an integrated blancher/cooler with six stages heating and cooling. The full line in the left picture gives the water temperature, and the six broken curves show the temperature in each of the six pea shells. The heating time is 131 s, and the exergy losses due to heat transfer into and conduction through the peas are 3.5 kWh/t for the process as whole.

(2) An ideal process with a similar heating time and a constant temperature difference between water and pea surface during the heating and cooling processes of $+2.8$°C$/-2.8$°C. The integrated exergy losses are here 1.7 kWh per ton of peas.

(3) Blanching in a conventional screw conveyor blancher. The heating time is 57 s, and the integrated exergy losses 12.4 kWh/t.

(4) An ideal process with a similar heating time to (3), but with a constant temperature difference between water and pea surface. This temperature difference must now be 10°C. The exergy losses for the process as a whole amount to 6.5 kWh/t.

To provide a comparison between the conventional screw conveyor blancher and the integrated blancher/cooler, Table 21.4 gives an overview of the results

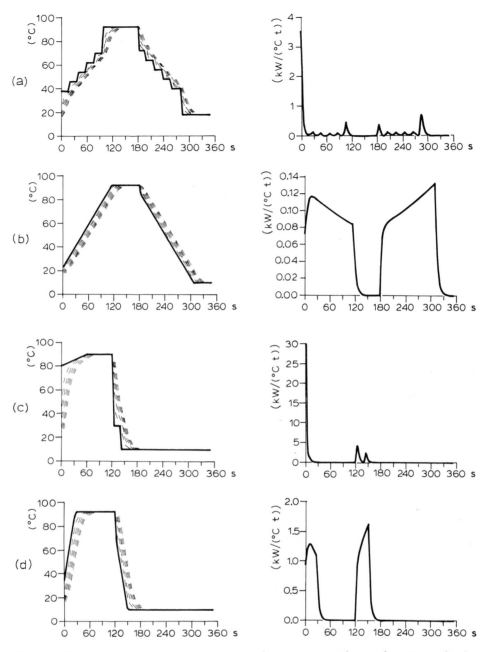

Fig. 21.12. Simulation results for the developments of temperatures and rates of entropy production for four blanching processes: (a) and (c) represent real processes in an integrated blancher/cooler and a conventional screw-conveyor blancher, respectively; (b) and (d) are ideal processes with similar heating times to (a) and (c).

obtained. The integrated system is seen to have total exergy losses which are less than half of the exergy losses for the screw-conveyor blancher. This improvement has been obtained through a reduction of the exergy losses associated with heat conduction in the peas from 12 to 4 kWh/t, while the remaining exergy losses only have been cut from 8 to 5 kWh/t.

Figure 21.13 shows the variation of ΔEx_{min} as a function of the heating time. An average pea diameter of 6 mm has been assumed. In addition we have indicated $\Delta Ex_{\mathrm{prod}}$ for the two considered blanchers. This figure clearly illustrates the thermodynamic significance of using a relatively long heating time, i.e., for peas more than 90 s.

Chapter 21 references, p. 353.

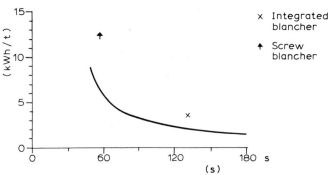

Fig. 21.13. Variation of the minimal exergy losses in a pea blanching process with heating time. Also shown are the actual exergy losses associated with heat transfer to and through the peas for two different water blanchers.

TABLE 21.4

Comparison of exergy losses (kWh/t) for a screw-conveyor blancher and an integrated blancher/cooler

	Screw-conveyor	Integrated
ΔEx_{min}	7	2
ΔEx_{prod}	12	4
ΔEx_{aux}	8	5
ΔEx_{tot}	20	9
Heating time (s)	60	130

ΔEx_{min} denotes the thermodynamic minimal exergy losses for the applied heating times; ΔEx_{prod} is the actual exergy losses associated with heat conduction into and through the product, ΔEx_{aux} measures the additional exergy losses in the machine, and $\Delta Ex_{tot} = \Delta Ex_{prod} + \Delta Ex_{aux}$.

Let us hereafter consider how the total exergy losses ΔEx_{tot} for the integrated blancher/cooler could be further reduced. At present it is not clear if additional energy conserving measures are economically feasible, but our suggestions will illustrate how the exergy analysis can be used to point out irreversibilities and loss-giving processes.

ΔEx_{prod} can be reduced further by increasing the number of stages in the heating and cooling zones of the blancher. This would also reduce the exergy losses (presently estimated to be 0.2 kWh/t) associated with mixing of water at different temperatures. Exergy losses in the heat exchanger between cooling and preheating zones (presently at 0.9 kWh/t) can be reduced by using a larger heat exchanger. Finally the exergy losses due to heat losses to the surroundings (1.4 kWh/t) can be reduced through an improved thermal insulation of the blancher/cooler. It is interesting to note, that the cooling zone must also be insulated.

7. FORECASTING SECTORIAL ENERGY DEMAND

The basic structure of the Danish Production Sector Model (DEMO-PSM) has been outlined elsewhere (Mosekilde et al., 1983), and we have also discussed (Kraemer et al., 1983) how information derived from thermodynamic investigations, comparisons between similar companies, interviews with industrial energy managers, etc., are combined into a useful dynamic description. Here, we shall only give an overview of some of the basic features of the model and thereafter discuss how the model is applied to forecast the energy requirements of the Danish food industry.

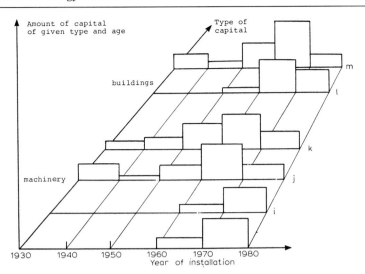

Fig. 21.14. Disaggregation of production capital after type and year of installation. The letters i, j, k, l and m represent transport means, gas ovens, cooling machines, boilers, cold storage area, and production area, respectively.

Besides its engineering approach, our model is also characterized by its vintage structure. DEMO-PSM divides the sectorial energy demand into a number of relatively homogeneous end-use categories, each of which is associated with a corresponding component of the sector's production capital. Energy consumption for space heating, for instance, is related to the building area which is disaggregated by type and by time of construction to account for differences in indoor temperatures and insulation levels. Process energy consumption is related to the production volume, but it is also assumed to depend upon the applied technology. The machine capital is therefore divided into age groups, and depending upon the time of acquisition, the energy prices at that time, and the amount of retrofitting performed, the model ascribes characteristic values of the process energy consumption per unit factor product to each of these groups.

Figure 21.14 illustrates how the production capital can be disaggregated after age and type. Different kinds of capital can be transport means, gas ovens, cooling machines, boilers, cold storage area, production area, etc., assuming that the capital components are measured in principle in physical units. In practice, such a detailed description of the production capital in the food industry has not been possible, partly because statistical data on the size and age distribution of the sector's capital components are scattered and incomplete.

At present, the model therefore only operates with two types of capital: machinery capital and building capital, and data for these capital components are constructed from relatively aggregate investment series. Likewise, the age distribution is in only three categories: old capital installed before 1950 (the year in which our model was initiated), new capital installed between 1950 and 1980, and future capital installed after 1980. The important point to notice is that only as the production capital is gradually replaced to achieve an energy efficiency corresponding to today's oil prices, will the full response of the increased fuel prices show up. The food industry has a rather slow capital renewal rate, both because the general rate of growth is moderate, because the technological development is moderate, and because the physical capital life times are long. All of these factors tend to give the food industry a relatively slow response to changing fuel prices. It is also significant, of course, that the energy costs only constitute a very small fraction (about 2%) of the total production costs in this industry.

Chapter 21 references, p. 353.

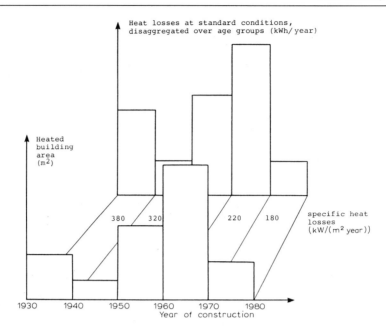

Fig. 21.15. Conversion of age-distributed capital into energy consumption, here considered using heating of factory buildings as an example.

Figure 21.15 illustrates the way in which a component of the energy consumption is obtained from the age distribution of the corresponding capital component. Here we consider the heat losses through the walls, roofs, and floors of factory buildings. For each age group of building area, the model operates with a specific heat loss, i.e., the yearly heat losses to the surroundings per m² of building area at a constant indoor temperature of 22°C (72°F) and a standard outdoor temperature variation through the year. Starting with 380 kWh/m² per year for factory buildings constructed before 1940, the specific heat losses are typically reduced as the buildings become more and more up-to-date, to reach a level of about 180 kWh/m² per year for a modern factory. The total heat losses are obtained by summing the product of the specific heat losses and the building area over the individual age groups.

The specific heat losses directly measure the insulation standard of the buildings. In the model, corrections are made for changes in average indoor temperatures, for heat contribution from production processes, for application of process waste heat for space heating, etc. The model also allows for capital retrofitting. For each age group of factory buildings, a characteristic relation is defined between the investment in energy conservation, and the resulting reduction in specific heat losses. Arranged according to profitability, the energy conservation measures considered for an old factory building are: tightening of windows and doors, insulation of ceilings, floors, and hollow double-brick walls, introduction of double-glazed windows, additional insulation of lightly insulated ceilings, and insulation of solid brick walls. It is assumed that the industry actually institutes those measures that have a repayment time below a certain maximum value (usually 3 years).

When applied to simulate an industrial production sector, our model is initiated in 1950 and adjusted to reproduce the historical development in workforce, machine and building capitals, and energy consumption until 1980. Based upon various assumptions about the general economic development and the development in fuel prices, the model hereafter projects the development in the above sector variables until the year 2010.

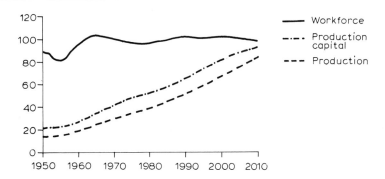

Fig. 21.16. Simulation results for the developments in production, workforce, and total production capital for the food industry with expected economic growth. The scales are such that 100 = 100 000 people for the workforce, $100 = 25 \times 10^9$ DKK/year for the gross factor product, and $100 = 50 \times 10^9$ DKK for the production capital.

In the present study we have combined an expected economic growth scenario with an expected fuel price development. Generally speaking, these scenarios agree with the corresponding fuel price and economic growth alternatives considered in the official energy plan (Energiplan 81, Department of Energy, Denmark, 1981).

The fuel prices are assumed to remain relatively constant until in 1985–1986 the economic activity in the oil importing countries has recovered sufficiently from the shock of the 1979 oil price increase. The rising demand for energy is then expected to cause a new fuel price increase by about 30%, and the fuel prices thereafter are taken to increase rather slowly for the rest of the simulation period. The model has also been run with a variety of other fuel price scenarios such as for instance slightly falling fuel prices and more drastically increased fuel prices.[2] It is important to realize, however, that independent of possible future price changes the significant fuel price increases which have already occurred will continue to influence the development in sectorial energy demand for many years to come.

In the expected growth scenario, the country's general economic development is taken to reassume its 'historical' growth rate of 3.5–4.0% per year after a few years of recovery from the 1979 oil price increase. Towards the end of the century, the increase in the gross national product is assumed to slow down, partly because of a slower expansion of the workforce.

Figures 21.16–21.18 show some of the obtained simulation results for the food industry. In Fig. 21.16, we have plotted the development in production volume, workforce, machinery capital and total production capital. We have determined the developments in workforce and capital from a generalized Cobb-Douglas function (Mosekilde et al., 1983), in which the rate of technological development is considered as a function of capital renewal rate. To account for medium-term variations in the workforce, we have also added a correction term which gives a larger workforce in periods with higher than usual capital renewal rates, and vice-versa.

Figure 21.17 shows the development in the three components of the machinery capital: old capital installed before 1950, new capital installed between 1950 and 1980, and future capital installed after 1980. With exponential depreciation and with an average life time for machinery capital of 16 years, in the year 2010, 8% of the machinery capital will still be from the period before 1980. The model assumes that future machinery capital will be about 30% more energy efficient than the average present capital.

---

[2]Note added in proof, p. 354.

Chapter 21 references, p. 353.

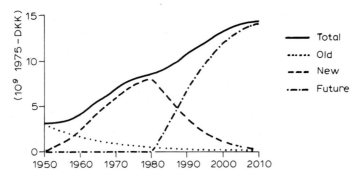

Fig. 21.17. Simulations results for the developments in the three components of machinery capital for the food industry with expected economic growth.

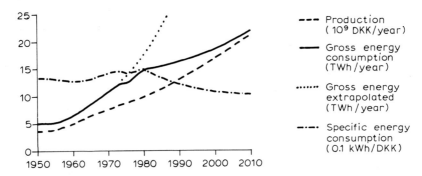

Fig. 21.18. Simulation results for the developments in total production and gross energy consumption for the food industry with expected economic growth. Also shown is the development in specific energy consumption.

Figure 21.18 shows our simulation results, for the development in the food industry's production volume, total energy consumption, and energy intensity. For comparison we have also plotted an exponential extrapolation of the growth in energy consumption characterizing the food industry before 1973.

8. CONCLUSION

In this chapter, we have discussed the response of the food industry to rising fuel prices in terms of recent statistical data, interviews with industrial energy managers, reports on the response of particular companies, comparisons of energy requirements for different production methods, and an analysis of the thermodynamic efficiency of a particular process. The purpose has been to illustrate the range of information required to appreciate the future demand for energy in the food industry. A forecast of sectorial energy requirements should be based upon a detailed understanding of the potential for energy conservation in the various processes and branches, of the time delays involved in capital renewal, and of the shift in dominance between the branches.

Our projections show that even if the general economic development is supposed to reassume its historical trend, the influence of the fuel price increases during the 1970's will continue to influence the energy intensity in the food industry for the rest of the century. As a result, the sector's gross energy consumption is expected to increase only by 60% from now till the year 2010. This should be compared with an increase in production volume by 110%.

In reality we do not expect the economic development to reassume its historical growth rate as quickly as the above simulation presumes. The economic development in this simulation was taken to be in accordance with 'official' expectations by the Danish Department of Energy. Rather, we expect the relative slow growth rate that the industrialized countries have known for the last decade to continue for another 10–15 years. The reasons for this are:

(1) During the rapid growth period of the 1960's, the industrialized countries have over-expanded their production systems and infrastructure. Capital production must therefore remain below the level required for replacements until the excess capital has been depreciated, and room for a new expansion created. The reduced investments lead to contraction in the capital sector, and consequently also to stagnating employment, real wages, aggregate demand, and GNP.

(2) The present technologies are approaching full exploitation. The old leading industries have saturated, and the next lasting upswing must await for basic new technologies to be introduced and new industries to grow from virtually nothing to a macro-economically significant level, i.e., to a level where they can create employment for the workers laid-off by the old industries.

(3) Many countries have built up an enormous debt, which for many years to come will threaten the stability of the international monetary system.

A new upswing cannot be expected to take off, until these structural problems have been solved. Due to the long lifetimes of capital, and due to the significant delays in the build up of new industries, this may take a decade or two. To appreciate the long-term requirements for energy in the food industry correctly, the energy intensity of possible future leading branches should be considered in more detail, and an estimate should be made of the time at which these branches (or industries) will reach significant economic weight. This is a problem that we are presently engaged on.

9. ACKNOWLEDGMENTS

Thanks are due to Ellen Pløger, The Statistical Bureau of Denmark for providing data from the energy balances of the National Accounts Statistics, and for discussing the basic assumptions underlying the construction of these balances.

The authors thank a number of companies in the Danish food industry for making their data on production, energy consumption and energy conservation possibilities available to us.

The study was performed with support from the Danish Department of Energy.

10. REFERENCES

Bomben, J.L., 1977. Effluent generation, energy use and cost of blanching. J. Food Proc. Eng., 1: 329–341.

Cabinplant, Inc., 1981. Roesbjergvej 9, DK-5683 Haarby, Denmark.

Chhinnan, M.S., Singh, R.P., Pedersen, L.D., Carroad, P.A., Rose, W.W. and Jacob, N.L., 1980. Analysis of energy utilization in spinach processing. Trans. ASAE 23: 503–507.

Huppman, Inc., 1981. Maschinen Fabrik, Schwarzacher Strasse 51, 8710 Kitzinger, Germany.

Kraemer, F., Mosekilde, E. and Meyer, N.I., 1983. A dynamic model of energy conservation in the building materials industry. Proc. Risø Int. Conf. Use of Simulation Models in Energy Planning, 9–11 May, Roskilde, Denmark.

Mensch, G., 1979. Stalemate in Technology, Ballinger, London.

Mosekilde, E., Paamand, K. and Meyer, N.I., 1983. Dynamic simulation of industrial energy requirements. In: A.S. Kydes (Editor), IMACS Trans. Scientific Computation. Vol. 4, Energy Modeling and Simulation. North-Holland, Amsterdam, p. 235–249.

Rumsey, T.R., Scott, E.P. and Carroad, P.A., 1981. Energy consumption in water blanching. J. Food Sci., 47: 295–298.

Scott, E.P., Carroad, P.A., Rumsey, T.R., Horn, J., Buhlert, J. and Rose, W.W., 1981. Energy consumption in steam blanchers. J. Food Process Eng., 5: 77–89.

Sterman, J., 1985. An integrated theory of the economic long wave. Futures, April: 104–130.

Van Duijn, J.J., 1983. The Long Wave in Economic Life. George Allen and Unwin, Boston, MA, 239 pp.

NOTES ADDED IN PROOF

[1] In response to the doubts we have expressed about the accuracy of the official data, The Statistical Bureau of Denmark has reassessed their sectorial energy consumption data for 1972. For this year, the energy consumption and the specific energy consumption should hereafter be corrected as follows:

Fig. 21.1	Aggregated food industry	+3%
Fig. 21.2a	Slaughtering and meat processing	−6%
Fig. 21.2b	Manufacture of dairy products	+1%
Fig. 21.2c	Other food manufacturing	+16%
Fig. 21.2d	Manufacture of beverages	−15%
Fig. 21.2e	Tobacco manufacture	−1%
Fig. 21.3	Fruit and vegetable industry	+44%

[2] The above simulation results were based on official projections for fuel prices and gross domestic product established by the Danish Department of Energy in 1981. In view of the dramatic changes in crude oil prices and US$-exchange rates which have occurred since the summer of 1985, we have performed a number of reruns with the model. Assuming the fuel prices to remain constant at their 1980 values throughout the simulation period, for the specific energy consumption of the aggregated food industry we find the results specified in the third colume of the following table:

Specific energy consumption (kWh/1975-DKK)

Year	Standard	1980-price level	1978-price level
1980	1.51	1.51	1.51
1990	1.23	1.28	1.33
2000	1.08	1.19	1.29
2010	1.04	1.21	1.32

The second column gives the results obtained with the 'official' fuel price scenario. The fourth column gives the results obtained under the assumption that the fuel prices fall to their 1978 values and remain at this level till 2010. The Danish Government is presently (February 1986) considering to counteract the falling oil prices by increased taxation of energy consumption.

List of Contributors

Bengt HALLSTRÖM, Chapter 15. Born in 1924, he graduated at the Chalmers Technical University in Gothenburg 1949, tekn lic 1962. He worked until 1968 with the Alfa-Laval Company in process and equipment development. Appointed professor in Chemical Engineering at Lund University 1968 and in Food Engineering 1971.

D.R. HELDMAN, Chapter 19. Born in 1938, he received his B.S. (Dairy Technology) in 1960 and M.S. (Dairy Engineering) in 1962 at the Ohio State University. Received Ph.D. (Agricultural Engineering) from Michigan State University in 1965. He joined faculty at Michigan State in 1965 to conduct research and teaching in the area of food engineering with joint appointment in Agricultural Engineering with Food Science and Human Nutrition. He remained on faculty at MSU until 1984. His sabbatical leaves were at University of California, Davis, in 1970 and 1980, and he participated in Academic Administration Internship in 1974–1975 at Ohio State University. He served as Chairman of the Agricultural Engineering Department at MSU from 1975 to 1979. His current position is Vice President for Process Research and Development in Campbell Institute for Research and Technology at Campbell Soup Company.

Gerald D. KNUTSON, Chapter 6. Born in 1948, he studied at the University of California at Davis, where he received his B.S. in Agricultural Engineering (1972). He continued his education at the University of Hawaii where he received his M.S. degree in 1974. Since 1974 he has been a Development Engineer for the University of California Cooperative Extension. Most of his work has dealt with energy conservation and energy from renewable resources.

Floyd A. LASLEY, Chapter 20. Born in 1925, he studied at the University of Missouri, Columbia, MO, where he received his B.S. (1948), M.Ed. (1957) and Ph.D. (1962), and was Assistant Professor in the Agricultural Economics Department. Agricultural Economist, Economic Research Service, U.S. Department of Agriculture 1962–85; served 8 years as Dairy Group Leader and 6 years as Poultry Group Leader. Lecturer (part-time) University of Maryland 1967–85. Now retired and serving as an Economic Consultant.

D.B. LUND, Chapter 17. Born in 1941, he graduated B.S. University of Wisconsin–Madison in 1963, M.S. UW–Madison in 1965 and Ph.D. UW–Madison in 1968. Assistant Professor at UW–Madison Department of Food Science (1968–1972), Associate Professor UW–Madison (1972–1977), Professor UW–Madison (1977–present), Chairman Department of Food Science UW–Madison (1984–present). He has been an invited participant at many international meetings on Food Science and Food Engineering with international experience primarily in Indonesia and The Netherlands. He is the author of over 130 research and review publications.

Einar MATTHIASSON, Ph.D., Chapter 14. Born in 1950. Studied at Lund University where he got his M.Sc. in food engineering as well as Ph.D. degree.

E.J. MILLER, Chapter 8. Born in 1954, he studied mechanical engineering at Canterbury University, Christchurch, New Zealand; graduated B.E. (hons) in 1976. From 1976 to 1985 employed as a Research Officer in the Engineering Services Sector Dairy Research Institute. Moved to Northland Co-operative Dairy Co. Ltd. in 1985 to take up the position of Senior Production Engineer.

E. MOSEKILDE, Chapter 21. M.Sc. in electrical engineering 1966, Ph.D. in solid state physics Technical University of Denmark 1968, Dr.Sc. in experimental and theoretical physics University of Copenhagen 1977. Associate Professor of modern physics, Technical University of Denmark, author of 90 scientific papers. Vice president of The System Dynamics Society and managing editor of The System Dynamics Review.

K. PAAMAND, Chapter 21. M.Sc. in mechanical engineering from the Technical University of Denmark, 1982. Engaged with industrial energy conservation under a grant from the Danish Department of Energy, 1982–84. Presently serving as a volunteer in Zimbabwe.

E. PEDERSEN, Chapter 21. Born 1949, he graduated from the Technical University of Denmark as a mechanical engineer in 1974. Process development at Rockwool International 1976–80, energy–economics and industrial energy analysis at The Danish Boiler Owners Association 1980–84, director for process development at Rockwool International 1985.

K. Porsdal POULSEN, Chapter 9. Born in 1937. M.Sc. in chemical engineering 1961, H.D. 1970. 10 years occupation in food industry. Since 1971 employed at the Technical University of Denmark in Lyngby, Denmark. A large number of publications about freezing of foods, shelf life of frozen foods and economy of storing frozen foods. Member of International Institute of Refrigeration, commission C2. Member of different working groups related to frozen and chilled foods. Worked with frozen and chilled food in relation to developing countries.

M.A. RAO, B.S., M.S., Ph.D., Chapter 2. Born in 1937, he studied Chemical Engineering at Osmania University (India), University of Cincinnati and The Ohio State University. After a stint in industry (1969–1971) he was a Professor of Food Engineering (1971–1973), University of Campinas, Brazil. Since 1973 he has been at Cornell University, New York State Agricultural Experiment Station, Geneva, NY, as Assistant Professor (1973–1978), Associate Professor (1978–1986), and now as Professor. He is the co-editor of the book *Engineering Properties of Foods*, Marcel Dekker, New York, 1986, and is a member of the editorial board of the *Journal of Texture Studies*.

Enrique ROTSTEIN, Ph.D., D.I.C., I.Q., Chapter 4. Born in 1934, he obtained his first degree at Universidad Nacional del Sur (UNS), Argentina and his D.I.C. and Ph.D. at Imperial College (London University). Head of PLAPIQUI (Planta Piloto at Ingeniería Química, UNS (1963–1975), he has been Hill Visiting Professor at the University of Minnesota and is Principal Researcher at PLAPIQUI. He has published a number of papers in leading journals and three books, mainly on the applications of thermodynamics and transport phenomena. He is member of the advisory board of the Argentinian National Research Council.

T.R. RUMSEY, Ph.D., P.E., Chapters 11 and 13. Born in 1943, he studied at the University of California at Davis, where he received his Ph.D. in Engineering in 1974. He served as an engineering officer in the U.S. Air Force Systems Command (1967–1971). From 1974 to 1977 he was a research mechanical engineer in a food engineering group at the Western Regional Research Center, U.S. Department of Agriculture. He is currently an Associate Professor in the Agricultural Engineering Department at the University of California, Davis.

Steven A. SARGENT, Ph.D., Chapter 16. Born in 1954, he graduated from Michigan State University with B.S. (1976) and M.S. (1979) in Horticulture, and in 1984 a Ph.D. in Agricultural Engineering Technology. He is currently Assistant Professor in the Department of Horticulture, Michigan State University, with research interests in the areas of postharvest handling and storage of perishable crops and international agricultural development.

R. Paul SINGH, Ph.D., Editor, Chapters 1, 3, 7, 10, 19. Born in 1949, he studied at the Punjab Agricultural University, India, where he received his B.Sc. in Agricultural Engineering (1970). He continued his graduate studies in the United States and received M.S. in Agricultural Engineering from University of Wisconsin at Madison (1972) and Ph.D. in Agricultural Engineering from Michigan State University (1974). He joined the University of California at Davis as Assistant Professor in 1975, and was promoted to full professor in 1983. His appointment involves research and teaching in the general area of food engineering. He has written two textbooks in food engineering and authored over 90 technical papers.

Christina SKJÖLDEBRAND, Ph.D., Chapter 14. Born in 1945. Studied at Lund University where she got her M.Sc. as well as Ph.D. degree. She was Associate Professor at Lund University and a scientific advisor for Ph.D. students in the field of 'Heat and mass transfer in solid foodstuffs'. Since 1985 a group leader at SIK in process engineering.

James F. STEFFE, Ph.D., P.E., Chapter 16. Born in 1950, he received a B.A. (Religion; 1972) degree from Albion College, Albion, MI. B.S. (1975) and M.S. (1976) degrees in the field of agricultural engineering were obtained from Michigan State University, East Lansing. He studied food engineering at the University of California, Davis and received a Ph.D. degree from that institution in 1979. After leaving Davis, he went to Michigan State University where he served as an Assistant Professor from 1979 to 1984, and is currently employed as an Associate Professor of Food Engineering.

Arthur A. TEIXEIRA, Ph.D., P.E., Chapter 18. Born in 1944, he studied at the University of Massachusetts in Amherst, where he received his B.S. (1966) and M.S. (1968) in Mechanical and Aerospace Engineering, and Ph.D. (1971) in Food and Agricultural Engineering. Research Manager at Ross Laboratories Division of Abbott Laboratories in Columbus, OH (1971–1977), where he received the company's Presidential Award for outstanding research in energy-saving technology (1975). Senior consultant in Food and Agribusiness at Arthur D. Little, Inc., in Cambridge, MA (1977–1982), prior to joining the University of Florida as Associate Professor of Food Engineering. Registered professional engineer in the State of Florida and the Commonwealth of Massachusetts, and executive officer in the Food Engineering Divisions of both the American Society of Agricultural Engineers and the Institute of Food Technologists; along with membership in engineering (Tau Beta Pi) and research (Sigma Xi) honor societies.

M. TOGEBY, Chapter 21. Graduated from the Technical University of Denmark as a mechanical engineer 1983. Currently a Ph.D. student at Physics Laboratory III, specializing in irreversible thermodynamics and industrial energy analysis.

A. Christian TRÄGÅRD, Chapters 5 and 12. Born in 1944, he graduated M.Sc. chemical engineering at Lund University in 1979 and the doctor's degree in Food Engineering also at Lund University in 1978. Since 1985 Senior Lecturer. Apart from activities in relation to thermodynamics and energy use in food processing, major work is done in fluid dynamics as applied to food processing.

List of SI Units and Conversion Factors to SI

Compiled by

VICTOR H.A.M. OOSTERBAAN

Agricultural Sciences Department, Elsevier Science Publishers B.V., P.O. Box 330, 1000 AH Amsterdam (The Netherlands)

SI base units

metre (U.S.A.: meter)	m
kilogram(me)	kg
second	s
ampere	A
kelvin	K
mole	mol
candela	cd

SI supplementary units with dimension 1

| radian | rad |
| steradian | sr |

SI derived units with special names

hertz	Hz	$= s^{-1}$
newton	N	$= kg\ m\ s^{-2}$
pascal	Pa	$= N\ m^{-2}$
joule	J	$= N\ m$
watt	W	$= J\ s^{-1}$
coulomb	C	$= A\ s$
volt	V	$= W\ A^{-1}$
farad	F	$= C\ V^{-1}$
ohm	Ω	$= V\ A^{-1}$
siemens	S	$= A\ V^{-1}$
weber	Wb	$= V\ s$
tesla	T	$= Wb\ m^{-2}$
henry	H	$= Wb\ A^{-1}$
lumen	lm	$= cd\ sr$
lux	lx	$= lm\ m^{-2}$
becquerel	Bq	$= s^{-1}$
gray	Gy	$= J\ kg^{-1}$
sievert	Sv	$= J\ kg^{-1}$

SI prefixes

				U.S.A.	Outside U.S.A.
atto	a	10^{-18}			
femto	f	10^{-15}			
pico	p	10^{-12}			
nano	n	10^{-9}			
micro	μ	10^{-6}			
milli	m	10^{-3}			
centi *	c	10^{-2}			
deci *	d	10^{-1}			
deca *	da	10			
hecto *	h	10^{2}			
kilo	k	10^{3}			
mega	M	10^{6}		billion	milliard **
giga	G	10^{9}		trillion	billion
tera	T	10^{12}		quadrillion	thousand billion
peta	P	10^{15}		quintillion	trillion
exa	E	10^{18}			

* Strictly, these should not be used.
** In the U.K., nowadays the US convention is followed.

IMPORTANT ANGLO-SAXON UNITS

inch (1/36 yd)	in	= 25.4	mm
foot (1/3 yd)	ft	= 0.3048	m
yard	yd	= 0.9144	m (def)
mile (1760 yd)		1.609	km
square inch, sq in	in^2	6.45	cm^2
square foot, sq ft	ft^2	9.29	dm^2
square yard, sq yd	yd^2	0.836	m^2
acre (4840 yd^2)		4047	m^2
square mile (640 acre)		2.59	km^2
cubic inch, cu in	in^3	16.387	cm^3
cubic foot, cu ft	ft^3	28.32	dm^3
cubic yard, cu yd	yd^3	0.765	m^3
U.K.			
fluid ounce (1/160 gal)	fl oz (UK)	28.41	cm^3
pint (1/8 gal)	pt (UK)	0.568	dm^3
gallon	gal (UK)	4.54609	dm^3
bushel (8 gal)	bushel (UK)	36.3687	dm^3
U.S.A.			
Liquid measure			
fluid ounce (1/128 gal)	fl oz (US)	29.57	cm^3
liquid pint (1/8 gal)	liq pt (US)	0.473	dm^3
gallon (231 in^3)	gal (US)	3.78541	dm^3
Dry measure			
dry pint (1/64 bu)	dry pt (US)	0.551	dm^3
bushel (2150.42 in^3)	bu (US)	35.2391	dm^3
AVOIRDUPOIS (avdp)			
ounce (1/16 lb)	oz	28.35	g
pound	lb	0.4536	kg
U.K.			
(long) hundredweight (112 lb)	cwt	50.80	kg
(long) ton (2240 lb)	ton	1016	kg
U.S.A.			
short hundredweight (100 lb)	sh cwt	45.36	kg
short ton (2000 lb)	sh tn	907	kg
(metric) tonne	t	= 1000 kg	
megagram	Mg	= 1000 kg	

t, recognized by BIPM, International Bureau of Weights and Measures.
Mg, recommended by ASTM, American Society for Testing and Materials.

UNITS SPECIFIC TO ENERGY AND POWER

Work, and (specific) energy and heat

J	joule (SI derived unit) $= 1$ N m $= 1$ W s
kW h	kilowatt-hour $= 3.6 \times 10^6$ J $= 3.6$ MJ
erg	$= 1$ dyn cm $= 1$ g cm^2 s$^{-2} = 10^{-7}$ J
hp h	metric horsepower-hour ≈ 2.65 MJ
	(British) horsepower-hour ≈ 2.68 MJ
cal	cal$_{IT}$ = cal$_{IT1956}$, calorie (International Table) $= 4.1868$ J (def)
	cal$_{th}$, thermochemical calorie $= 4.184$ J (def)
	cal$_{15}$, calorie at $15°$C ≈ 4.1855 J
th	thermie $= 1000$ kcal$_{15} \approx 4.1855 \times 10^6$ J ≈ 4.2 MJ
CHU	centigrade heat unit ≈ 1.899 kJ
	CHU lb$^{-1} = 1$ kcal kg$^{-1} = 4.1868$ kJ kg^{-1}
CTU	centigrade thermal unit ≈ 1.898 kJ
	CTU lb$^{-1} = 1$ kcal$_{15}$ kg$^{-1} \approx 4.1855$ kJ kg^{-1}
Btu	British thermal unit ≈ 1055.06 J ≈ 1.055 kJ
	Btu lb^{-1} $°$F$^{-1} = 1$ kcal kg^{-1} $°$C$^{-1} = 4.1868$ kJ kg^{-1} K^{-1} (def)
	Btu lb$^{-1} = 2.326$ kJ kg^{-1}
thm	therm $= 10^5$ Btu $\approx 0.1055 \times 10^9$ J ≈ 0.1 GJ
QUAD	quadrillion Btu $= 10^{15}$ Btu $\approx 1.055 \times 10^{18}$ J ≈ 1 EJ

Power and heat flux

W	watt (SI derived unit) $= 1$ J s^{-1}
hp	metric horsepower $= 75$ kgf m s$^{-1} \approx 735.5$ W
	(British) horsepower $= 550$ lbf ft s$^{-1} \approx 745.7$ W
kcal h^{-1}	$= 1.163$ W
	kcal min$^{-1} = 69.78$ W
	kcal cm^{-2} min$^{-1} = 697.8$ kW m^{-2}
Btu h^{-1}	≈ 0.2931 W
	Btu h^{-1} ft$^{-2} \approx 3.155$ W m^{-2}
	Btu h^{-1} ft^{-2} $°$F$^{-1} \approx 5.678$ W m^{-2} K^{-1}
	Btu in h^{-1} ft^{-2} $°$F$^{-1} \approx 0.1442$ W m^{-1} K^{-1}

Energy sources

barrel	barrel for petroleum, etc. $= 42$ gal (US) ≈ 158.987 dm^3
	BPD, barrel per day ≈ 1.840 cm^3 s^{-1} ($\hat{=} 50$ t/year)
BOE	barrel oil equivalent $= 6$ million Btu $\approx 6.3 \times 10^9$ J ≈ 6 GJ
TCE	ton coal equivalent $= 7$ million kcal $\approx 31.6 \times 10^9$ J ≈ 32 GJ
TOE	ton oil equivalent $= 10$ million kcal $\approx 42.2 \times 10^9$ J ≈ 42 GJ

GROSS LIST OF UNITS

Å   ångström $= 10^{-10}$ m

a   are $= 10^2$ m^2

       ca $= 0.01$ a $= 1$ m^2

       ha $= 100$ a $= 10^4$ m^2

       ha mm $= 10$ m^3

       ha mm day$^{-1} \approx 0.1157$ dm^3 s^{-1}

acre $= 4$ rood $= 4840$ yd$^2 \approx 0.404686$ ha ≈ 4047 m^2

       acre in, acre-inch ≈ 102.8 m^3

       acre ft, acre-foot ≈ 1233.5 m^3

       acre ft day$^{-1} \approx 123.35$ ha mm day$^{-1} \approx 14.28$ dm^3 s^{-1}

       acre lb$^{-1} \approx 8922$ m^2 kg^{-1}

amu   atomic mass unit (*see* u)

asb   apostilb $= 1/\pi$ cd m$^{-2} \approx 0.318$ cd m^{-2} (*see also* sb)

at   technical atmosphere $= 1$ kgf cm$^{-2} = 0.980665 \times 10^5$ Pa

atm   (normal) atmosphere $= 760$ mmHg $= 1013.25$ mbar

       $= 1.01325 \times 10^5$ Pa (def)

°B   degree Brix $= \%$ sucrose (w/w)

bar $= 10^5$ Pa

barye $= 1$ dyn cm$^{-2} = 0.1$ Pa

bbl   standard barrel for fruit, vegetables and dry commodities (U.S.A.)

       $= 7056$ in$^3 \approx 115.627$ dm^3

       cranberry barrel (U.S.A.)

       $= 5826$ in$^3 \approx 95.5$ dm^3

       barrel for fermented beverage (U.S.A.)

       $= 31$ gal (US) $= 7161$ in$^3 \approx 117.3$ dm^3

       liq barrel $= 36$ gal (UK) ≈ 163.6 dm^3

       liq bbl $= 31\frac{1}{2}$ gal (US) ≈ 119.2 dm^3

       mass barrel $= 160$ lb ≈ 72.6 kg

Bd   baud $=$ pulses or bits s^{-1}

bd ft   board foot (*see* fbm)

Btr   British ton of refrigeration (*see* ton)

bu   bushel

       (Imperial) bushel (UK) $= 8$ gal (UK) ≈ 36.3687 dm^3

       (Winchester) bu (US) $= 2150.42$ in$^3 \approx 35.2391$ dm^3

       liq bu (US) $= 8$ gal (US) ≈ 30.28 dm^3

       international bushel for grains $= 60$ lb ≈ 27.2155 kg

       60-lb bushel of wheat, white potatoes, soybeans ≈ 27.2155 kg (U.S.A.)

       56-lb bushel of corn, rye, sorghum grain, flaxseed ≈ 25.40 kg (U.S.A.)

       48-lb bushel of barley, buckweed, apples ≈ 21.77 kg (U.S.A.)

       32-lb bushel of oats ≈ 14.51 kg (U.S.A.)

       38-lb bushel of oats ≈ 17.24 kg (U.S.A.)

°C   degree Celsius

       x °C $\triangleq (x + 273.15)$ K (def)

ca   centiare (*see* a)

Cal   food calorie $= 1$ kcal$_{15} \approx 4.1855$ kJ

caliber $= 0.01$ in $= 0.254$ mm

cc   cm$^3 = 10^{-6}$ m^3

cd   (timber) cord $= 128$ ft$^3 \approx 3.625$ dm^3

       cd acre$^{-1} \approx 8.96$ m^3 ha$^{-1} = 0.896$ dm^3 m^{-2}

ch   (Gunter's or surveyor's) chain = 4 rod = 22 yd = 20.1168 m
$ch^2 = 16$ $rod^2 = 484$ $yd^2 \approx 405$ m^2
Ramsden's or engineer's chain = 100 ft = 30.48 m

chaldron   = 36 bushel (UK) ≈ 1.309 m^3

Ci   curie = 37×10^9 disintegrations $s^{-1} = 37 \times 10^9$ Bq (def)

cP   centipoise (*see* P)

cSt   centistokes (*see* St)

ctl   cental = 1 sh cwt = 100 lb ≈ 45.36 kg

cusec   cubic foot per second = 1 ft^3 $s^{-1} \approx 28.32$ dm^3 s^{-1}
cusec h ≈ 0.992 acre in ≈ 102 m^3
cusec day ≈ 1.983 acre ft ≈ 2446 m^3
cusec $mile^{-2} \approx 0.109$ dm^3 s^{-1} ha^{-1} (0.945 mm/day)
cusec $acre^{-1} \approx 70$ dm^3 s^{-1} ha^{-1} (604 mm/day)

cwt   hundredweight
(long or gross) hundredweight = 112 lb ≈ 50.80 kg
cwt $acre^{-1} \approx 125.5$ kg $ha^{-1} \approx 12.6$ g m^{-2}
sh cwt, short or nett hundredweight = 100 lb ≈ 45.36 kg
sh cwt $acre^{-1} \approx 112.1$ kg $ha^{-1} \approx 11.2$ g m^{-2}

dalton   = 1 amu ($^{16}O = 16$) ≈ 0.99968218 u $\approx 1.660038 \times 20^{-27}$ kg (*see* u)

dr   dram (avdp) = 1/256 lb ≈ 1.772 g
drachm (UK) = dram (US) = 60 gr ≈ 3.888 g
   dr apoth, (apothecaries') drachm (UK)
   dr ap, apothecaries' dram (US)
fl dr (UK), fluid drachm = 1/8 fl oz (UK) = 1/1280 gal (UK) ≈ 3.552 cm^3
fl dr (US), fluid dram = 1/8 fl oz (US) = 1/1024 gal (US) ≈ 3.697 cm^3

duty x = $1/x$ cusec

dwt   pennyweight = 24 gr ≈ 1.555 g

dyn   dyne = 1 g cm $s^{-2} = 10^{-5}$ N

eV   electron-volt $\approx 1.60219 \times 10^{-19}$ J

°F   degree Fahrenheit
x °F $\hat{=} (5/9)(x - 32)$°C = $(5/9)(x + 459.67)$ K (def)

fath   fathom = 2 yd = 1.8288 m

fbm   foot board measure = (timber) board foot = 1 ft^2 in ≈ 2.360 dm^3
fbm $acre^{-1} \approx 5.83$ dm^3 $ha^{-1} = 0.583$ cm^3 m^{-2}

fc   foot-candle = 1 lm $ft^{-2} \approx 10.764$ lx

fg   frigorie = -1 kcal = -4.1868 kJ

fL   foot-lambert = $1/\pi$ cd $ft^{-2} \approx 3.426$ cd m^{-2}

ft   foot = 1/3 yd = 0.3048 m
$ft^2 \approx 9.29$ dm^2
$ft^3 \approx 28.32$ dm^3
ft^3 $day^{-1} \approx 0.328$ cm^3 s^{-1}
ft pdl $\approx 42.14 \times 10^{-3}$ J
ft lbf ≈ 1.356 J

ftH_2O = 0.3048 $mH_2O \approx 2.99$ kPa

furlong   = 1/8 mile = 220 yd ≈ 201 m

g   gram(me)
g $cm^{-3} = 1000$ kg m^{-3}
mg dm^{-2} $h^{-1} \approx 27.8 \times 10^{-6}$ g m^{-2} s^{-1}
kg $ha^{-1} = 0.1$ g m^{-2}

gal   gallon
gal (UK) $\approx$ 4.54609 dm^3
gal (US) = 231 in^3 $\approx$ 3.78541 dm^3
gal (US) acre^{-1} $\approx$ 9.354 dm^3 ha^{-1} $\approx$ 0.935 × 10^{-6} m^3 m^{-2}
gal (US) min^{-1} $\approx$ 63.1 cm^3 s^{-1}
ale or beer gallon = 282 in^3 $\approx$ 4.6222 dm^3
dry gallon (US) = 1/8 bu (US) $\approx$ 4.405 dm^3

gi   gill
gi (UK) = 5 fl oz (UK) = 1/32 gal (UK) $\approx$ 0.1421 dm^3
gi (US) = 4 fl oz (US) = 1/32 gal (US) $\approx$ 0.1183 dm^3

gr   grain = 1/7000 lb = 64.79891 mg

h   hour = 3600 s
ha   hectare (*see* a)
hand   = 4 in = 0.1016 m (U.S.A.)
hhd   hogshead = 63 gal (US) $\approx$ 0.2385 m^3
hl   hectoliter (U.S.A.) or hectolitre (*see* L or l)

in   inch = 1/36 yd = 25.4 mm
in^2 = 6.4516 cm^2
in^3 $\approx$ 16.387 cm^3
in day^{-1} $\approx$ 0.294 × 10^{-3} mm s^{-1}

inHg   = 25.4 mmHg $\approx$ 3.386 kPa
inH$_2$O   = 25.4 mmH$_2$O $\approx$ 249.1 Pa
iron   = 1/48 in $\approx$ 0.529 mm (U.K.)

kat   katal = 1 mol s^{-1}
kayser   = 100/m = 10^2 m^{-1}
kgf   kilogramforce = 9.80665 kg m s^{-2} = 9.80665 N (def)
knot   n mile h^{-1} $\approx$ 0.514 m s^{-1}

L or l   liter (U.S.A.) or litre = 1000 cm^3 = 1 dm^3 = 10^{-3} m^3
ml = 10^{-3} l = 10^{-6} m^3
hl = 100 l = 0.1 m^3
l s^{-1} ha^{-1} = 10^{-7} m s^{-1} (8.64 mm/day)

L or La   lambert = 1/π cd cm^{-2} $\approx$ 3183 cd m^{-2}

lb   pound (avdp) = 0.45359237 kg (def)
lb ft^2 $\approx$ 42.14 g m^2
lb bu^{-1} (US) $\approx$ 12.87 kg m^{-3}
lb ft^{-3} $\approx$ 16.02 kg m^{-3}
lb in^{-3} $\approx$ 27 680 kg m^{-3}
lb acre^{-1} $\approx$ 1.1208 kg ha^{-1} $\approx$ 0.112 g m^{-2}
troy pound = 5760 gr $\approx$ 373 g
     lb tr, troy pound (UK)
     lb t, troy pound (US)

lbf   poundforce = 1 lb × 9.80665 N/kg $\approx$ 4.448 N
lbf ft $\approx$ 1.356 N m
psf, poundforce per square foot = 1 lbf ft^{-2} $\approx$ 47.88 Pa
psi, poundforce per square inch = 1 lbf in^{-2} $\approx$ 6.895 kPa

league   = 3 mile
(statute) league $\approx$ 4.828 km
(international) nautical league = 5.556 km
nautical league (UK) $\approx$ 5.560 km

li   link = 1/100 ch $\approx$ 201 mm
Ly   langley = 1 cal cm^{-2} = 41.868 kJ m^{-2}

M   thousand $= 10^3$

m   meter (U.S.A.) or metre

          mm day^{-1} $\approx 11.6 \times 10^{-9}$ m s^{-1}

          mm h^{-1} $\approx 278 \times 10^{-9}$ m s^{-1}

          mm^2 g^{-1} $= 10^{-3}$ m^2 kg^{-1}

          cm^2 g^{-1} $= 0.1$ m^2 kg^{-1}

mb   mbar $= 100$ Pa

MHA   million hectare $= 10^6$ ha $= 10^{10}$ m^2 $= 10^4$ km^2

mho $= 1$ S

          mmho cm^{-1} $= 0.1$ S m^{-1}

mile   (statute) mile $= 1760$ yd $= 1.609344$ km

          mile^2 $= 640$ acre ≈ 2.59 km^2

          mile^2 in $\approx 65\,786$ m^3

          mile^2 in year^{-1} ≈ 18.024 ha mm day^{-1} ≈ 2.086 dm^3 s^{-1}

          MPH, mile per hour $= 1$ mile h^{-1} ≈ 0.447 m s^{-1}

          n mile, (international) nautical mile $= 1.852$ km (def)

          n mile h^{-1} (*see* knot)

          n mile (UK) $= 6080$ ft ≈ 1.853 km

          telegraph nautical mile $= 6087$ ft ≈ 1.855 km

min   minute $= 60$ s

min   minim

          min (UK) $= 1/480$ fl oz (UK) $= 1/76800$ gal (UK) ≈ 59.2 mm^3

          min (US) $= 1/480$ fl oz (US) $= 1/61440$ gal (US) ≈ 61.6 mm^3

ml   milliliter (U.S.A.) or milliliter (*see* L or l)

MM   million $= 10^6$

mmHg $= 133.322$ Pa

mmH$_2$O $= 9.80665$ Pa

MMT   million metric tonne $= 10^6$ t $= 10^9$ kg

mol   mole

          μmol H$_2$O ≈ 180 mg H$_2$O

n mile (*see* mile)

nt   nit $= 1$ cd m^{-2}

oz   ounce (avdp) $= 1/16$ lb ≈ 28.35 g

          oz gal^{-1} (UK) ≈ 6.236 kg m^{-3}

          oz gal^{-1} (US) ≈ 7.489 kg m^{-3}

          apothecaries' ounce $= 1$ troy ounce $= 480$ gr ≈ 31.10 g

            oz apoth, apothecaries' ounce (UK)

            oz ap, apothecaries' ounce (US)

            oz tr, troy ounce (UK)

            oz t, troy ounce (US)

          fl oz (UK), fluid ounce (UK) $= 1/160$ gal (UK) ≈ 28.41 cm^3

          fl oz (US), fluid ounce (US) $= 1/128$ gal (US) ≈ 29.57 cm^3

P   poise $= 1$ dyn s cm^{-2} $= 0.1$ Pa s

          cP $= 0.01$ P $= 10^{-3}$ Pa s

pdl   poundal $= 1$ lb ft s^{-2} ≈ 0.1382 N (def)

          pdl ft $\approx 42.14 \times 10^{-3}$ N m

          pdl ft^{-2} ≈ 1.488 Pa

ph   phot $= 1$ lm cm^{-2} $= 10^4$ lx

pk	peck
	pk (UK) = 2 gal (UK) $\approx$ 9.092 dm^3
	pk (US) = 1/4 bu (US) $\approx$ 8.810 dm^3
Pl	poiseuille = 1 Pa s
ppb	parts per billion
	Outside U.S.A.: 10^{-12}
	U.S.A. and nowadays in the U.K.: 10^{-9}
pphm	parts per hundred million = 10^{-8}
ppm	parts per million = 10^{-6}
ppt	parts per thousand = 10^{-3}
psf	poundforce per square foot (*see* lbf)
psi	poundforce per square inch (*see* lbf)
pt	pint
	pt (UK) = 20 fl oz (UK) = 1/8 gal (UK) $\approx$ 0.568 dm^3
	liq pt (US) = 16 fl oz (US) = 1/8 gal (US) $\approx$ 0.473 dm^3
	dry pt (US) = 1/64 bu (US) $\approx$ 0.551 dm^3
q	metric quintal = 100 kg
	q ha^{-1} = 10 g m^{-2}
qr	quarter
	= 1/4 cwt = 28 lb $\approx$ 12.70 kg
	= 64 gal (UK) $\approx$ 0.291 m^3
qt	quart
	qt (UK) = 40 fl oz (UK) = 1/4 gal (UK) $\approx$ 1.136 dm^3
	liq qt (US) = 32 fl oz (US) = 1/4 gal (US) $\approx$ 0.946 dm^3
	dry qt (US) = 1/32 bu (US) $\approx$ 1.101 dm^3
°R	degree Rankine
	$x°R = (5/9)x$ K $\approx$ 0.5556 K
°R	degree Réaumur
	$x°R \triangleq 1.25°C \triangleq (1.25x + 273.15)$ K
R	röntgen = 0.258 $\times$ 10^{-3} C kg^{-1} (def)
rad	radiation absorbed dose = 10^{-2} J kg^{-1} = 10^{-2} Gy
Rd	rutherford = 10^6 Bq
rem	rad-equivalent, man = 10^{-2} J kg^{-1} = 10^{-2} Sv
rod	= 1/4 ch = $5\frac{1}{2}$ yd = 5.0292 m
	rod^2 = 1/16 ch^2 = 30.25 yd^2 $\approx$ 25.3 m^2
rood	= 40 rod^2 = 1210 yd^2 $\approx$ 1012 m^2
rpm	revolutions per minute = 2π rad min^{-1} $\approx$ 0.1047 rad s^{-1}
rps	revolutions per second = 2π rad s^{-1} $\approx$ 6.283 rad s^{-1}
rt	register ton (see ton)
S	siemens
	S cm^{-1} = 10^2 S m^{-1}
	dS m^{-1} = 10^{-2} S m^{-1}

s   (apothecaries') scruple = 20 gr ≈ 1.296 g
sb   stilb = 1 cd cm^{-2} = 10^4 cd m^{-2} (*see also* asb)
section   = mile^2 ≈ 2.59 km^2
span   = 9 in = 0.2286 m
sr   steradian (SI supplementary unit with dimension 1)
St   stokes = 1 cm^2 s^{-1} = 100 mm^2 s^{-1}
             cSt = 0.01 St = 1 mm^2 s^{-1}
stone   = 14 lb ≈ 6.350 kg

t   (metric) tonne = 1000 kg
             t ha^{-1} = 0.1 kg m^{-2}
ton   (long or gross) ton = 2240 lb ≈ 1016 kg
             ton acre^{-1} ≈ 2511 kg ha^{-1} ≈ 251 g m^{-2}
             sh tn, short or nett ton = 2000 lb ≈ 907 kg
             sh tn acre^{-1} ≈ 2242 kg ha^{-1} ≈ 224 g m^{-2}
             rt, register ton ≈ 2.83 m^3
             tr, (standard) (commercial) ton of refrigeration = 12 000 Btu h^{-1} ≈ 3.517 kW
             Btr, British ton of refrigeration = 332 000 Btu day^{-1} ≈ 3.932 kW
Torr   = 1/760 atm ≈ 133.3 Pa
township   = 36 mile^2 ≈ 93.24 km^2

u   amu (^{12}C = 12), atomic mass unit ≈ 1.66057 × 10^{-27} kg

yd   yard = 0.9144 m (def)
             yd^2 ≈ 0.836 m^2

γ   gamma = 1 μg = 10^{-9} kg
λ   lambda = 1 μl = 10^{-9} m^3
μ   micron = 1 μm = 10^{-6} m
             mμ, millimicron = 10^{-3} μm ≈ 10^{-9} m
σ   sigma = 1 μs = 10^{-6} s

g   gon, decimal angle degree = π/200 rad ≈ 15.71 × 10^{-3} rad
°   degree
             angle degree = π/180 rad ≈ 17.45 × 10^{-3} rad
             (*see also* °C, °F and °R)
′   angle minute = (1/60)° ≈ 0.291 × 10^{-3} rad
′   foot (*see* ft)
″   angle second = (1/60)′ = (1/360)° ≈ 4.848 × 10^{-6} rad
″   inch (*see* in)

Subject Index